Looking Out, Looking In

Special Edition

Ronald B. Adler | Russell F. Proctor II

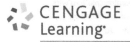

Australia • Brazil • Japan • Korea • Mexico • Singapore • Spain • United Kingdom • United States

Looking Out, Looking In, Special Edition
Ronald B. Adler | Russell F. Proctor II

Looking Out, Looking In, 15th Edition

For product information and technology assistance, contact us at
Cengage Learning Customer & Sales Support, 1-800-354-9706

For permission to use material from this text or product,
submit all requests online at **cengage.com/permissions**
Further permissions questions can be emailed to
permissionrequest@cengage.com

This book contains select works from existing Cengage Learning resources and was produced by Cengage Learning Custom Solutions for collegiate use. As such, those adopting and/or contributing to this work are responsible for editorial content accuracy, continuity and completeness.

Compilation © 2016 Cengage Learning

ISBN: 978-1-337-03321-3

Cengage Learning
20 Channel Center Street
Boston, MA 02210
USA

Cengage Learning is a leading provider of customized learning solutions with office locations around the globe, including Singapore, the United Kingdom, Australia, Mexico, Brazil, and Japan. Locate your local office at: **www.international.cengage.com/region.**

Cengage Learning products are represented in Canada by Nelson Education, Ltd.

For your lifelong learning solutions, visit **www.cengage.com/custom.**

Visit our corporate website at **www.cengage.com.**

A Note to Our Students

The Department of English and Communication here at Terra State Community College is pleased to be able to offer you, the students in our Interpersonal Communication course, this customized version of Ronald Adler's renowned text *Looking Out, Looking In*. Our faculty carefully reviewed the book and selected the material that best fits our curriculum. This effort has produced a more focused text and one that comes to you at significantly reduced cost. We hope that you find this text as accessible and helpful as we intend it to be.

This text is the only required material for SPE 2200, Interpersonal Communication. The course description and outcome goals follow:

Course Description:

Interpersonal Communication concerns the study and practice of how communication affects relationships in everyday situations, with a special emphasis on workplace relationships, ranging from employee/employer, employee/employee, health care provider/patient and business person/client. Through role playing, small group, and individual presentations, this course provides students with practical skills necessary to analyze and solve communication problems. It emphasizes interpersonal verbal and non-verbal behaviors and includes practice in the articulation of ideas and feelings. Emphasis is also placed on listening and response techniques, as well as on role relationships.

Learning Outcomes:

General Education

- Communicate effectively
- Describe how cultural differences can affect interpersonal communication and how these differences can affect work in a global and diverse society

Course:

- Identify components and goals of the communication process and employ strategies to improve interpersonal communication,
- Identify how the assessment and development of self affects communication,
- Explain the interpersonal communication perception process and employ strategies to improve perception,

- Describe the functions of verbal and non verbal communication in interpersonal relationships and formulate a strategy for improving interpretation of verbal and nonverbal messages,
- Identify the elements of the listening process and employ skills for listening improvement,
- Identify stages of and strategies for effective conflict resolution
- Define confirmation and disconfirmation

On behalf of the entire English and Communication Program, I would like to thank the team at Cengage Publishing that made this handbook possible, with special thanks to Ms. Lauren Grubb and Ms. Carrie Fremder. We also would like to thank you, our students, and we wish you the best of success in this course and in all of your courses here at Terra State Community College and throughout your college education as well.

Sincerely,

Professor Steven R. Mohr
Lead Faculty in English and Communication
Terra State Community College

Brief Contents

MindTap START…
Explore this chapter's topics online.

A FIRST LOOK AT INTERPERSONAL COMMUNICATION

AFTER STUDYING THE TOPICS IN THIS CHAPTER, YOU SHOULD BE ABLE TO:

1. Assess the needs (physical, identity, social, and practical) that communicators are attempting to satisfy in a given situation or relationship.

2. Apply the transactional communication model to a specific situation.

3. Describe how the communication principles and misconceptions identified in this chapter are evident in a specific situation.

4. Describe the degree to which communication (in a specific instance or a relationship) is qualitatively impersonal or interpersonal, and describe the consequences of this level of interaction.

5. Diagnose the effectiveness of various communication channels in a specific situation.

6. Determine the level of communication competence in a specific instance or a relationship.

*P*erhaps you played this game when you were younger. The group chooses a victim—either as punishment for committing a real or imagined offense or just for "fun." Then for a period of time, that victim is given the silent treatment. No one speaks to him or her, and no one responds to anything the victim says or does.

If you were the subject of this silent treatment, you probably experienced a range of emotions. At first you might have felt—or at least acted—indifferent. But after a while, the strain of being treated as a nonperson probably began to grow. If the game went on long enough, it's likely you found yourself either retreating into a state of depression or lashing out with hostility—partly to show your anger and partly to get a response from the others.

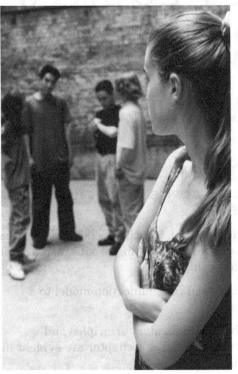

Vicky Kasala/Getty Images

Adults, as well as children, have used the silent treatment in virtually every society throughout history as a powerful tool to express displeasure and for social control.[1] We all know intuitively that communication—the company of others—is one of the most basic human needs, and that lack of contact is among the cruelest punishments a person can suffer. In fact, workplace studies show that employees would rather get negative attention from bosses and coworkers than receive no attention at all. It hurts to be picked on, but it's worse to be ostracized.[2]

Besides being emotionally painful, being deprived of companionship is so serious that it can affect life itself. Frederick II, emperor of Germany in the 13th century, may have been the first person to prove the point systematically. A medieval historian described one of his significant, if inhumane, experiments:

> He bade foster mothers and nurses to suckle the children, to bathe and wash them, but in no way to prattle with them, for he wanted to learn whether they would speak the Hebrew language, which was the oldest, or Greek, or Latin, or Arabic, or perhaps the language of their parents, of whom they had been born. But he labored in vain because all the children died. For they could not live without the petting and joyful faces and loving words of their foster mothers.[3]

Fortunately, contemporary researchers have found less barbaric ways to illustrate the importance of communication. In one study of isolation, subjects were paid to remain alone in a locked room. Of the five subjects, one lasted for eight days. Three held out for two days, one commenting, "Never again." The fifth subject lasted only two hours.[4]

The need for contact and companionship is just as strong outside the laboratory, as individuals who have led solitary lives by choice or necessity have discovered. W. Carl Jackson, an adventurer who sailed across the Atlantic Ocean alone in fifty-one days, summarized the feelings common to most loners:

> I found the loneliness of the second month almost excruciating. I always thought of myself as self-sufficient, but I found life without people had no meaning. I had a definite need for somebody to talk to, someone real, alive, and breathing.[5]

WHY WE COMMUNICATE

You might object to stories like this, claiming that solitude would be a welcome relief from the irritations of everyday life. It's true that all of us need solitude, often more than we get, but each of us has a point beyond which we do not want to be alone. Beyond this point, solitude changes from a pleasurable to a painful condition. In other words, we all need relationships. We all need to communicate.

Physical Needs

Communication is so important that its presence or absence affects physical health. In extreme cases, communication can even become a matter of life or death. When he was a Navy pilot, U.S. Senator John McCain was shot down over North Vietnam and held as a prisoner of war for six years, often in solitary confinement. He and his fellow POWs set up clandestine codes in which they sent messages by tapping on walls to laboriously spell out words. McCain describes the importance of keeping contact and the risks that inmates would take to maintain contact with one another:

> The punishment for communicating could be severe, and a few POWs, having been caught and beaten for their efforts, had their spirits broken as their bodies were battered. Terrified of a return trip to the punishment room, they would lie still in their cells when their comrades tried to tap them up on the wall. Very few would remain uncommunicative for long. To suffer all this alone was less tolerable than torture. Withdrawing in silence from the fellowship of other Americans... was to us the approach of death.[6]

Other prisoners have also described the punishing effects of social isolation. Reflecting on his seven years as a hostage in Lebanon, former news correspondent Terry Anderson said flatly, "I would rather have had the worst companion than no companion at all."[7]

The link between communication and physical well-being isn't restricted to prisoners. Medical researchers have identified a wide range of health threats that can result from a lack of close relationships. For instance:

- A meta-analysis of nearly 150 studies and over 300,000 participants found that socially connected people—those with strong networks of family and friends—live an average of 3.7 years longer than those who are socially isolated.[8]

- A lack of social relationships jeopardizes coronary health to a degree that rivals cigarette smoking, high blood pressure, blood lipids, obesity, and lack of physical activity.[9]

- Socially isolated people are four times more susceptible to the common cold than are those who have active social networks.[10]

- Divorced, separated, and widowed people are five to ten times more likely to need mental hospitalization than their married counterparts. Happily married people also have lower incidences of pneumonia, surgery, and cancer than do single people.[11] (It's important to note that the quality of the relationship is more important than the institution of marriage in these studies.)

By contrast, a life that includes positive relationships created through communication leads to better health. As little as ten minutes per day of socializing improves memory and boosts intellectual function.[12] Conversation with others reduces feelings of loneliness and its accompanying maladies.[13] Stress hormones decline the more often people hear expressions of affection from loved ones.[14]

Research like this demonstrates the importance of having satisfying personal relationships. Not everyone needs the same amount of contact, and the quality of communication is almost certainly as significant as the quantity. The key point is that personal communication is essential for our well-being.

Identity Needs

Communication does more than enable us to survive. It is the way—indeed, the only way—we learn who we are. As Chapter 3 explains, our sense of identity comes from the way we interact with other people. Are we smart or stupid, attractive or plain, skillful or inept? The answers to these questions don't come from looking in the mirror. We decide who we are based on how others react to us.

Deprived of communication with others, we would have no sense of ourselves. A dramatic example is the "Wild Boy of Aveyron," who spent his early childhood without any apparent human contact. The boy was discovered in January 1800 digging for vegetables in a French village garden. He showed no behaviors that one would expect in a social human. The boy could not speak but rather uttered only weird cries. More significant than this lack of social skills was his lack of any identity as a human being. As one author put it, "The boy had no human sense of being in the world. He had no sense of himself as a person related to other persons."[15] Only with the influence of a loving "mother" did the boy begin to behave—and, we can imagine, think of himself—as a human.

Like the boy of Aveyron, each of us enters the world with little or no sense of identity. We gain an idea of who we are from the way others define us. As Chapter 3 explains, the messages we receive in early childhood are the strongest, but the influence of others continues throughout life.

Social Needs

Besides helping to define who we are, communication provides a vital link with others. Researchers and theorists have identified a whole range of social needs that we satisfy by communicating. These include pleasure, affection, companionship, escape, relaxation, and control.[16]

Research suggests a strong link between effective interpersonal communication and happiness. In one study of more than 200 college students, the happiest 10 percent described themselves as having a rich social life. (The very happy people were no different from their classmates in any other measurable way such as amount of sleep, exercise, TV watching, religious activity, or alcohol consumption.)[17] In another study, women reported that "socializing" contributed more to a satisfying life than virtually any other activity, including relaxing, shopping, eating, exercise, TV, or prayer.[18] Married couples who are effective communicators report happier relationships than less skillful husbands and wives—a finding that has been supported across cultures.[19]

Despite knowing that communication is vital to social satisfaction, a variety of evidence suggests that many people aren't very successful at managing their interpersonal relationships. For example, one study revealed that a quarter of the more than 4,000 adults surveyed knew more about their dogs than they did about their neighbors' backgrounds.[20] Research also suggests that the number of friendships is in decline. One widely recognized survey reported that, in 1985, Americans had an average of 2.94 close friends. Twenty years later, that number had dropped to 2.08.[21] It's worth noting that educated Americans reported having larger and more diverse networks. In other words, a higher education can enhance your relational life as well as your intellect.

Because connections with others are so vital, some theorists maintain that positive relationships may be the single most important source of life satisfaction and emotional well-being in every culture.[22] If you pause now and make a mental list of your own relationships, you'll probably see that, no matter how successfully you interact with friends, at home, at school, and at work, there is plenty of room for improvement in your everyday life. The information that follows will help you improve the way you communicate with the people who matter most to you.

⋀ In his TV show *Louie*, comedian Louie CK is a relational pessimist who is chronically unlucky in love. Nonetheless he keeps trying because life without companionship is too lonesome to bear. How well does your communication fulfill your needs for connection? How can you use the information in this book to help you meet your social needs?

Practical Goals

Besides satisfying social needs and shaping our identity, communication is the most widely used approach to satisfying what communication scholars call **instrumental goals**: getting others to behave in ways we want. Some instrumental goals are quite basic: Communication is the tool that lets you tell the hair stylist to take just a little off the sides, lets you negotiate household duties, and lets you convince the plumber that the broken pipe needs attention *now*!

Other instrumental goals are more important. Career success is the prime example. As the On the Job box in this section shows, communication skills are essential in virtually every career. They can even make the difference between life and death. The Los Angeles Police Department cited "bad communication" among the most common reasons for errors in shooting by its officers.[23] The ability to communicate effectively is just as essential for doctors, nurses, and other medical practitioners.[24] Researchers discovered that "poor communication" was the root of more than 60 percent of reported medical errors—including death, serious physical injury, and psychological trauma.[25] Research published in the *Journal of the American Medical Association* and elsewhere revealed a significant difference between the communication skills of physicians who had no malpractice claims against them and those with previous claims.[26]

On The JOB

Communication and Career Success

No matter what the field, research confirms what experienced workers already know—that communication skills are crucial in finding and succeeding in a job. Communication skills often make the difference between being hired and being rejected. In one widely followed annual survey, employers list the skills and qualities for their ideal candidate. Communication skills always top the list, ahead of technical skills, initiative, analytical ability, and computer skills.[a]

In another survey, managers across the country rated the abilities to speak and listen effectively as the two most important factors in helping college graduates find jobs in a competitive workplace—more important than technical competence, work experience, and specific degree earned.[b] When 170 well-known business and industrial firms were asked to list the most common reasons for *not* offering jobs to applicants, the most frequent replies were "inability to communicate" and "poor communication skills."[c]

Once you have been hired, the need for communication skills is important in virtually every career.[d] Engineers spend the bulk of their working lives speaking and listening, mostly in one-to-one and small-group settings.[e] Accountants and the firms that hire them consistently cite effective communication as essential for career success.[f] One executive at computer giant Sun Microsystems made the point forcefully: "If there's one skill that's required for success in this industry, it's communication skills."[g] Writing in *The Scientist*, a commentator echoed this sentiment: "If I give any advice, it is that you can never do enough training around your overall communication skills."[h]

Psychologist Abraham Maslow suggested that the physical, identity, social, and practical needs we have been discussing fall into five hierarchical categories, each of which must be satisfied before we concern ourselves with the less fundamental needs.[27] The most basic of these needs are *physical:* sufficient air, water, food, and rest, and the ability to reproduce as a species. The second of Maslow's needs is *safety:* protection from threats to our well-being. Beyond physical and safety needs are the *social needs* we have mentioned already. Beyond these, Maslow suggests, each of us has *self-esteem* needs: the desire to believe that we are worthwhile, valuable people. The final category of needs described by Maslow is *self-actualization:* the desire to develop our potential to the maximum, to become the best person we can be. As you read on, think about the ways in which communication is often necessary to satisfy each level of need.

THE PROCESS OF COMMUNICATION

We have been talking about *communication* as though the meaning of this word were perfectly clear. Communication scholars have argued for years about communication definitions. Despite their many disagreements, most would agree that, at its essence, communication is about using messages to generate meanings.[28] Notice how this basic definition holds true across a variety of contexts—public speaking, small groups, mass media, etc. Before going further, we need to explain systematically what happens when people exchange messages and create meanings in interpersonal communication. Doing so will introduce you to a common working vocabulary and, at the same time, preview some of the topics that are covered in later chapters.

A Linear View

In the early days of studying communication as a social science, researchers created models to illustrate the communication process. Their first attempts resulted in a **linear communication model**, which depicts communication as something a sender "does to" a receiver. According to the linear model in Figure 1.1,

A **sender** (the person creating the message)

encodes (puts thoughts into symbols and gestures) a

message (the information being transmitted), sending it through a

channel (the medium through which the message passes) to a

receiver (the person attending to the message) who

decodes (makes sense of the message), while contending with

noise (distractions that disrupt transmission).

Notice how the appearance of and vocabulary in Figure 1.1 are similar to how radio and television broadcasting operate. This isn't a coincidence: The scientists who created it were primarily interested in early electronic media. The widespread use of this model has affected the way we think and talk about communication. There is a linear, machine-like quality to familiar phrases, such as "We're having a communication breakdown" and "I don't think my message is getting through." While this is sometimes the case in mediated forms of communication, these familiar phrases (and the thinking they represent) obscure some important features of human communication. Does interpersonal communication really "break down," or are people still exchanging information even when they're not talking to each other? Is it possible to "get a message through" to someone loudly and clearly, but still not get the desired reaction? Here are some other questions to consider about the shortcomings of the linear model:

- When you're having a face-to-face conversation with a friend, is there only one sender and one receiver, or do both of you send and receive messages simultaneously?

◄ **FIGURE 1.1**
Linear Communication Model

© Cengage Learning

- Do you purposely encode every message you send, or do you engage in some behaviors unconsciously that still communicate messages to others?

- Even when you send a message electronically (e.g., through texting or email), is the message's meaning affected by larger factors such as culture, environment, and relational history?

These and other questions have led scholars to create models that better represent interpersonal communication. We will look at one of these models now.

A Transactional View

A **transactional communication model** (Figure 1.2) updates and expands the linear model to better capture communication as a uniquely human process. Some concepts and terms from the linear model are retained in the transactional model, whereas others are enhanced, added, or eliminated.

The transactional model uses the word *communicator* instead of *sender* and *receiver*. This term reflects the fact that people typically send and receive messages simultaneously and not in a unidirectional or back-and-forth manner, as suggested by the linear model. Consider, for example, what might happen when you and a housemate negotiate how to handle household chores. As soon as you begin to hear (receive) the words sent by your housemate, "I want to talk about cleaning the kitchen…," you grimace and clench your jaw (sending a nonverbal message of your own while receiving the verbal one). This reaction leads your housemate to interrupt defensively, sending a new message: "Now wait a minute…."

A transactional model also shows that communicators often occupy different **environments**—fields of experience that affect how they understand others' behavior. In communication terminology, *environment* refers not only to a physical location but also to the personal experiences and cultural background that participants bring to a conversation.

Consider just some of the factors that might contribute to different environments:

- Person A might belong to one ethnic group, and person B to another.

- Person A might be rich, and B poor.

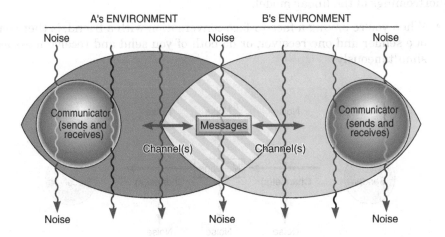

FIGURE 1.2 >
Transactional
Communication Model
© Cengage Learning

- Person A might be rushed, and B have nowhere to go.

- Person A might have lived a long, eventful life, and B might be young and inexperienced.

- Person A might be passionately concerned with the subject, and B indifferent to it.

Notice how the model in Figure 1.2 shows that the environments of persons A and B overlap. This area represents the background that the communicators have in common. As the shared environment becomes smaller, communication usually becomes more challenging. Consider a few examples in which different perspectives can make understanding difficult:

- Bosses who have trouble understanding the perspectives of their employees will be less effective managers, and workers who do not appreciate the challenges of being a boss are more likely to be uncooperative (and probably less suitable for advancement).

- Parents who have trouble recalling their youth are likely to clash with their children, who have never known and may not appreciate the responsibility that comes with parenting.

- Members of a dominant culture who have never experienced how it feels to be marginalized may not appreciate the concerns of people from minority co-cultures, whose own perspectives make it hard to understand the cultural blindness of the majority.

Communication channels retain a significant role in the transactional model, as they did in the linear model. Although it's tempting to see channels simply as neutral conduits for delivering a message, a closer look reveals the important role they play.[29] For instance, should you say "I love you" in person? Over the phone? In a text message? By renting space on a billboard? By sending flowers and a card? Via email? In a voicemail? On a Facebook wall? Mediated channels have become so important that Chapter 2 is devoted to explaining the role they play in interpersonal relationships.

The transactional model also retains the concept of noise but with a broader focus. In the linear model, the focus is on noise in the channel—what is known as *external noise*. For instance, loud music or too much cigarette smoke in a crowded room might make it difficult for you to pay attention to another person. The transactional model shows that noise also resides *within* communicators. This includes *physiological noise*, which involves biological factors that interfere with accurate reception: illness, fatigue, hearing loss, and so on. Communicators can also encounter *psychological noise*: forces within that interfere with the ability to understand a message accurately. For instance, a student might become so upset upon learning that she failed a test that she would be unable (perhaps *unwilling* is a better word) to understand clearly where she went wrong. Psychological noise is such an important communication problem that we have devoted much of Chapter 11 to investigating its most common cause, defensiveness.

For all the insights they offer, models can't capture some important features of interpersonal communication. A model is a "snapshot," while communication more closely resembles a "motion picture." In real life it's difficult to isolate a single discrete "act" of communication from the events that precede and follow it.[30] Consider the "Zits" cartoon seen here. If you read only the final frame, it appears that Jeremy is the victim of his mother's nagging. If you then read the first three frames, you might conclude that if Jeremy were more responsive to his mother, she might not need to be so persistent. And if you watched the two of them interact over the days and weeks preceding the incident in this cartoon, you would have a larger (but still incomplete) picture of the relational history that contributed to this event. In other words, the communication pattern that Jeremy and his mother have created together contributes to the quality of their relationship.

This leads to another important point: Transactional communication isn't something that we do *to* others; rather, it is an activity that we do *with* them. In this sense, interpersonal communication is rather like dancing—at least the kind of dancing we do with partners. Like dancing, communication depends on the involvement of a partner. And like good dancing, successful communication doesn't depend only on the person who takes the lead. A great dancer who forgets to consider and adapt to the skill level of his or her partner can make both people look bad. In communication and dancing, even having two talented partners doesn't guarantee success. When two skilled dancers perform without coordinating their movements, the results feel bad to the dancers and look foolish to an audience. Finally, relational communication—like dancing—is a unique creation that arises out of the way in which the partners interact. The way you dance probably varies from one partner to another. Likewise, the way you communicate almost certainly varies from one partner to another.

Now we can summarize the definition of interpersonal communication that we have been developing. **Interpersonal communication** is a transactional process involving participants who occupy different but overlapping environments and create meaning and relationships through the exchange of messages, many of which are affected by external, physiological, and psychological noise. Whether or not you memorize this definition is a matter

▼ The movie *Boyhood* chronicles the life of Mason (Ellar Coltrane) from early childhood until he enters college. Shot over a 12-year period with actors who aged with the story, the film illustrates the irreversible, unrepeatable, and transactional nature of interpersonal communication. How have events from your upbringing affected the way you communicate today?

for you and your instructor to decide. In any case, notice how it reflects a more sophisticated view of the process than you might have had before reading this far. With this definition in mind, let's look at how interpersonal communication differs from less personal kinds of interaction.

Interpersonal and Impersonal Communication

Scholars have characterized interpersonal communication in a number of ways.[31] The most obvious definition focuses on the number of people involved. A *quantitative* definition of interpersonal communication includes any interaction between two people, usually face to face. Social scientists call two interacting people a **dyad,** and they often use the adjective *dyadic* to describe this type of communication. So, in a quantitative sense, the terms *dyadic communication* and *interpersonal communication* can be used interchangeably. Using a quantitative definition, a salesclerk and customer or a police officer ticketing a speeding driver would be examples of interpersonal acts, whereas a teacher and class or a performer and audience would not.

You can probably see the problems with a quantitative definition of interpersonal communication. For example, consider a routine transaction between a salesclerk and customer, or the rushed exchange when you ask a stranger on the street for directions. Communication of this sort hardly seems interpersonal—or personal in any sense of the word. In fact, after transactions like this, we commonly remark, "I might as well have been talking to a machine."

The impersonal nature of some two-person exchanges and the personal nature of others have led some scholars to argue that *quality*, not quantity, is what distinguishes interpersonal communication.[32] Taking a *qualitative* approach, interpersonal communication occurs when people treat one another as unique individuals, regardless of the context in which the interaction occurs or the number of people involved. When quality of interaction is the criterion, the opposite of interpersonal communication is **impersonal communication,** not group, public, or mass communication.

Several features distinguish qualitatively interpersonal communication from less-personal communication.[33] The first feature is *uniqueness*. Communication in impersonal exchanges is determined by social *rules* (e.g., laugh politely at others' jokes, don't dominate a conversation) and by social *roles* (e.g., the customer is always right, be especially polite to senior citizens). Qualitatively interpersonal relationships are characterized by the development of unique rules and roles. For example, in one relationship you might exchange good-natured insults, whereas in another you are careful never to offend your partner. Likewise, you might handle conflicts with one friend or family member by expressing disagreements as soon as they arise, whereas the unwritten rule in another relationship is to withhold resentments until they build up and then clear the air periodically. Communication scholars use the term *relational culture* to describe people in close relationships who create their own unique ways of interacting.[34]

A second feature of qualitatively interpersonal relationships is *irreplaceability*. Because interpersonal relationships are unique, they have no substitute. This explains why we usually feel so sad when a close friendship or love affair

ETHICAL *Challenge*

Martin Buber's I and Thou

Martin Buber is arguably the most influential advocate of qualitatively interpersonal communication, as defined in this section. His book *Ich und Du* (*I and Thou*) is a worldwide classic, selling millions of copies since its publication in 1922.[a]

Buber states that "I-It" and "I-Thou" represent two ways in which humans can relate to one another. "I-It" relationships are stable, predictable, detached. In an "I-It" mode we deal with people because they can do things for us: pump gas, laugh at our jokes, buy products we are selling, provide information or amusement. "I-It" is also the approach of science, which attempts to understand what makes people tick in order to explain, predict, and control their behavior. Buber would have regarded advertisers as operating in an "I-It" mode, crafting messages that lead people to buy their products or services. "I-It" relationships exist in personal relationships as well as impersonal ones: On an everyday basis, parents and children, bosses and employees, service providers and customers—even lovers—deal with one another as objects ("I wish she would leave me alone." "Can you pick me up after work?" "How can I get him/her to love me?").

In profound contrast to "I-It" relationships, Buber described an "I-Thou" way of interacting. "I-Thou" relationships are utterly unique. Because no two teachers or students, parents or children, husbands or wives, bosses or employees are alike, we encounter each person as an individual and not as a member of some category. An "I-Thou" posture goes further: Not only are people different from one another, but they change from moment to moment. An "I-Thou" relationship arises out of how we are now, not how we might have been yesterday or even a moment ago. In an "I-Thou" relationship, persuasion and control are out of the question: We certainly may explain our point of view, but ultimately we respect the fact that others are free to act.

Buber acknowledges that it is impossible to create and sustain pure "I-Thou" relationships. But without this qualitatively interpersonal level of contact, our lives are impoverished. To paraphrase Buber, without "I-It" we cannot exist, but if we live only with "I-It," we are not fully human.

MindTap APPLY... the ethical principle(s) introduced here by answering the following questions, either here or online.

Think of your most important relationships:

1. To what degree can they be described as "I-Thou" or "I-It"?

2. How satisfied are you with this level of relating?

3. What obligation do you have to treat others in an "I-Thou" manner?

Based on your answers to these questions, how might you change your style of communication?

---

cools down. We know that no matter how many other relationships fill our lives, none of them will ever be quite like the one that just ended.

Interdependence is a third feature of qualitatively interpersonal relationships. At the most basic level, the fate of the partners is connected. You might be able to brush off the anger, affection, excitement, or depression of someone you're not involved with personally, but in an interpersonal relationship the other's life affects you. Sometimes interdependence is a pleasure, and at other times it is a burden. In either case, it is a fact of life in qualitatively interpersonal relationships. Interdependence goes beyond the level of joined fates. In interpersonal relationships, our very identity depends on the nature of our interaction with others. As psychologist Kenneth Gergen puts it: "One cannot be 'attractive' without others who are attracted, a 'leader' without others willing to follow, or a 'loving person' without others to affirm with appreciation."[35]

A fourth feature of interpersonal relationships is often (though not always) the amount of *disclosure* of personal information. In impersonal relationships we don't reveal much about ourselves, but in interpersonal relationships we feel more comfortable sharing our thoughts and feelings. This doesn't mean that all interpersonal relationships are warm and caring, or that all self-disclosure is positive. It's possible to reveal negative, personal information: "I'm really angry with you." The point is, we tend to reserve these kinds of disclosures—both positive and negative—for our more personal relationships.

A fifth feature of interpersonal communication is *intrinsic rewards*. In impersonal communication, we seek payoffs that have little to do with the people involved. You listen to instructors in class or talk to potential buyers of your used car in order to reach goals that usually have little to do with developing personal relationships. By contrast, you spend time in qualitatively interpersonal relationships with friends, lovers, and others because you find the time personally rewarding. It often doesn't matter *what* you talk about: The relationship itself is what's important.

Because relationships that are unique, irreplaceable, interdependent, disclosing, and intrinsically rewarding are rare, qualitatively interpersonal communication is relatively scarce. We chat pleasantly with shopkeepers or fellow passengers on the bus or plane; we discuss the weather or current events with most classmates and neighbors; we enjoy bantering with online acquaintances on social networking websites. However, considering the number of people with whom we communicate, personal relationships are by far in the minority.

Most relationships aren't *either* interpersonal *or* impersonal. Rather, they fall somewhere on a continuum between these two extremes. Your own

PAUSE *and* REFLECT

How Personal Are Your Facebook Relationships?

MindTap° REFLECT... on your own communication by answering the following questions, either here or online.

If you're a Facebook user, scroll through your list of friends on that site. Consider how personal (or impersonal) your relationships are with those people:

- How many would you regard to be "highly personal"? How many are "highly impersonal"? (Perhaps you can rank them on a scale of 1 to 10.)

- Which factors noted in this section (unique, irreplaceable, interdependent, disclosing, and intrinsically rewarding) affect your appraisals?

- What percentage of your communication with these people occurs exclusively on Facebook? Through other mediated channels (phone, text, email)? Face to face? How does this ratio affect your friendships?

experience probably reveals that there's often a personal element in even the most impersonal situations. You might appreciate the unique sense of humor of a familiar blog poster or connect on a personal level with the person cutting your hair. And even the most tyrannical, demanding, by-the-book boss might show an occasional flash of humanity.

Just as there's a personal element in many impersonal settings, there is also an impersonal element in our relationships with the people we care most about. There are occasions when we don't want to be personal: when we're distracted, tired, busy, or just not interested. Sometimes all we want to know about certain friends is what they post on social media sites. In fact, interpersonal communication is rather like rich food—it's fine in moderation, but too much can make you uncomfortable.

Most of us don't have the time or energy to create highly personal relationships with everyone we encounter, either in person or via social media. In fact, the scarcity of qualitatively interpersonal communication contributes to its value. Like precious jewels and one-of-a-kind artwork, interpersonal relationships are special because of their scarcity.

COMMUNICATION PRINCIPLES AND MISCONCEPTIONS

Now that we've looked at definitions and approaches to communication, it's important to identify some principles of interpersonal interaction—and what communication can and can't accomplish.

Communication Principles

It's possible to draw several important conclusions about communication from what you have already learned in this chapter.

Communication Can Be Intentional or Unintentional Some communication is clearly intentional: You probably plan your words carefully before asking the boss for a raise or offering constructive criticism. Some scholars argue that only intentional messages like these qualify as communication. Others contend that even unintentional behavior is communicative. Suppose, for instance, that a friend overhears you muttering complaints to yourself. Even though you didn't intend for her to hear your remarks, they certainly did carry a message. In addition to these slips of the tongue, we unintentionally send many nonverbal messages. You might not be aware of your sour expression, impatient shifting, or sigh of boredom, but others view them nonetheless. Scholars have debated without reaching consensus about whether unintentional behavior should be considered communication, and it's unlikely that they will ever settle this issue.[36] In *Looking Out Looking In*, we will look at the communicative value of both intentional and unintentional behavior.

It's Impossible Not to Communicate   Because both intentional and unintentional behaviors send a message, many theorists agree that it is impossible not to communicate. Whatever you do—whether you speak or remain silent, confront or avoid, act emotional or keep a poker face—you provide information to others about your thoughts and feelings. In this sense, we are like transmitters that can't be shut off.

Of course, the people who decode your message may not interpret it accurately. They might take your kidding seriously or underestimate your feelings, for example. The message that you intend to convey may not even resemble the one that others infer from your actions. Thus, when we talk about "a communication breakdown" or "miscommunication," we rarely mean that communication has ended. Instead, we mean that it is inaccurate, ineffective, or unsatisfying.[37]

This explains why the best way to boost understanding is to discuss your intentions and your interpretations of the other person's behavior until you have negotiated a shared meaning. The perception-checking skills described in Chapter 4, the tips on clear language offered in Chapter 6, and the listening skills introduced in Chapter 8 will give you tools to boost the odds that the meanings of messages you send and receive are understandable to both you and others.

Communication Is Unrepeatable   Because communication is an ongoing process, it is impossible to repeat the same event. The friendly smile that worked so well when meeting a stranger last week might not succeed with the person you meet tomorrow. It might feel stale and artificial to you the second time around, or it might be wrong for the new person or occasion. Even with the same person, it's impossible to re-create an event. Why? Because neither you nor the other person is the same person. You've both lived longer. Your feelings about each other may have changed. You need not constantly invent new ways to act around familiar people, but you should realize that the "same" words and behavior are different each time they are spoken or performed.

Communication Is Irreversible   We sometimes wish that we could back up in time, erasing words or acts and replacing them with better alternatives. As the cartoon here points out, such reversal is impossible. Sometimes, further explanation can clear up another's confusion, or an apology can mollify another's hurt feelings. Other times no amount of explanation can erase the impression you have created. It is no more possible to "unreceive" a message than to "unsqueeze" a tube of toothpaste. The same is true of most electronic messages: Once you hit "send," they can't be taken back. Words said, messages sent, and deeds done are irretrievable.

"*We can pause, Stu—we can even try fast-forwarding— but we can never rewind.*"

Communication Has a Content and a Relational Dimension   Practically all exchanges operate on two levels. The **content dimension** involves the information being explicitly discussed: "Turn left at the next corner." "You can buy that for less online." "You're standing on my foot." In addition to this sort of obvious content, messages also have a **relational dimension** that expresses how you feel about the other person: whether you like or dislike the other person, feel in control or subordinate, feel comfortable or anxious, and so on.[38] For instance, consider how many different relational messages you could communicate by simply saying, "I'm busy tonight, but maybe some other time" in different ways.

Sometimes the content dimension of a message is all that matters. For example, you may not care much about how the customer service rep feels about you as long as you get a technician scheduled to fix your car. At other times, though, the relational dimension of a message is more important than the content under discussion (consider times when a customer service rep has spoken to you in a tone that seemed dismissive or rude). This explains why arguments can develop over apparently trivial subjects such as whose turn it is to wash the dishes or how to spend the weekend. In cases like this, what's really being tested is the nature of the relationship. Who's in control? How important are we to each other? Chapter 9 will explore these key relational issues in detail.

R. Jerome Ferraro/Getty Images

Communication Misconceptions

It's just as important to know what communication is *not* as to know what it is.[39] Avoiding the following misconceptions can save you a great deal of personal trouble.

More Communication Is Not Always Better   Whereas not communicating enough can cause problems, there are also situations when *too much* communication is a mistake. Sometimes excessive communication is simply unproductive, as when two people "talk a problem to death," going over the same ground again and again without making progress. As one communication book puts it, "More and more negative communication merely leads to more and more negative results."[40] Even when you aren't being critical, too much communication can backfire. Pestering a prospective employer after your job interview or texting too many "call me" messages can generate the opposite reaction from what you're seeking.

Meanings Are Not in Words   The biggest mistake we can make is to assume that *saying* something is the same thing as *communicating* it. As Chapter 4 explains, the words that make perfect sense to you can be perceived and interpreted in entirely different ways by others. Chapter 6 describes the most common types of verbal misunderstandings and suggests ways to minimize them. Chapter 8 introduces listening skills that help ensure that the way you receive messages matches the ideas that a speaker is trying to convey. As the old saying goes, "Words don't mean—*people* mean."

Successful Communication Doesn't Always Involve Shared Understanding   George Bernard Shaw once remarked, "The problem with communication . . . is the illusion that it has been accomplished." This observation may sound cynical, but research (and most likely your personal experience) demonstrates that misunderstandings are common.[41] In fact, evidence suggests that people who are well acquainted may be more likely to misunderstand one another than relative strangers.[42]

Mutual understanding can be one measure of successful communication,[43] but there are times when success comes from *not* completely understanding one another. For example, we are often deliberately vague in order to spare another's feelings. Imagine how you might reply when a friend asks, "What do you think about my new tattoo?" You might tactfully say, "Wow—that's really unusual," instead of honestly and clearly answering, "I think it's grotesque." In cases like this, we sacrifice clarity for the sake of kindness and to maintain our relationships. Some research suggests that satisfying relationships depend in part on flawed understanding. Couples who *think* their partners understand them are more satisfied with each other than those who *actually* understand what the other says and means.[44] In other words, more satisfying relationships can sometimes come from less-than-perfect understanding. Chapter 3 describes in detail the way we sometimes sacrifice clarity for the sake of maintaining relationships.

Communication Will Not Solve All Problems   Sometimes even the best-planned, best-timed communication won't solve a problem. Imagine, for example, that you ask an instructor to explain why you received a poor grade on a project that you believe deserved top marks. The instructor clearly outlines the reasons why you received the poor grade and sticks to that position after listening thoughtfully to your protests. Has communication solved the problem? Hardly.

Sometimes clear communication is even the *cause* of problems. Suppose, for example, that a friend asks you for an honest opinion of the $200 outfit she has just bought. Your clear and sincere answer, "I think it makes you look fat," might do more harm than good. Deciding when and how to self-disclose isn't always easy. See Chapter 3 for suggestions.

WHAT MAKES AN EFFECTIVE COMMUNICATOR?

It's easy to recognize good communicators and even easier to spot poor ones, but what characteristics distinguish effective communicators from their less successful counterparts?

Communication Competence Defined

Defining **communication competence** isn't as easy as it might seem. Although scholars struggle to agree on a precise definition, most would agree that competent communication involves achieving one's goals in a manner that, in most cases, maintains or enhances the relationship in which it occurs.[45] Put another way, competence seeks to be both *effective* and *appropriate*. You can probably think of people who achieve one of these goals at the expense of the other, such as the high-achieving businessperson who regularly ruffles feathers, or the kind and gracious person who doesn't stand up for herself or himself. Competence is a balancing act that requires looking out both for yourself and for others—sometimes a challenging task.[46]

The following characteristics typify a competent communicator.

There Is No Ideal Way to Communicate Your own experience shows that a variety of communication styles can be effective. Some very successful communicators are serious, whereas others use humor; some are gregarious, whereas others are quieter; and some are more straightforward, whereas others hint diplomatically. Just as there are many kinds of beautiful music or art, there are many kinds of competent communication. It certainly is possible to learn new, effective ways of communicating from observing models, but it would be a mistake to try to copy others in a way that doesn't reflect your own style or values.

∧ In the TV series *House of Cards*, the communication of conniving politician Frank Underwood (Kevin Spacey) is high in *effectiveness* (he almost always achieves his goals and gets his way) but low on *appropriateness* (he routinely damages others and his relationships with them). How would an impartial observer evaluate the moral dimensions of *your* communication?

Competence Is Situational Even within a culture or relationship, the specific communication that is competent in one setting might be a colossal blunder in another. The joking insults you routinely trade with one friend might offend a sensitive family member, and last Saturday night's romantic approach would most likely be out of place at work on Monday morning.

Because competent behavior varies so much from one situation and person to another, it's a mistake to think that communication competence is a trait that a person either has or does not have. It's more accurate to talk about *degrees* or *areas* of competence.[47] You might deal quite skillfully with peers, for example, but feel clumsy interacting with people much older or younger, wealthier or poorer, or more or less attractive than yourself. In fact, your competence with one person may vary from situation to situation. This means that it's an overgeneralization to say in a moment of distress, "I'm a terrible communicator!" when it's more accurate to say, "I didn't handle this situation very well, even though I'm better in others."

Competence Can Be Learned To some degree, biology is destiny when it comes to communication style.[48] Studies of identical and fraternal twins suggest that traits including sociability, anger, and relaxation seem to be partially a function of our genetic makeup. Some research suggests that certain personality traits predispose people towards particular competence skills.[49] For instance, those who are agreeable and conscientious by nature find it easier to be appropriate, and harder to be (and become) assertive and effective. Chapter 3 will have more to say about the role of neurobiology in communication traits.

Fortunately, biology isn't the only factor that shapes how we communicate. Communication competence is, to a great degree, a set of skills that anyone can learn. Skills training has been shown to help communicators in a variety of professional fields.[50] Research also shows that college students typically become more competent communicators over the course of their undergraduate studies.[51] In other words, your level of competence can improve through education and training, which means that reading this book and taking this course can help you become a more competent communicator.[52]

Characteristics of Competent Communicators

Although competent communication varies from one situation to another, scholars have identified several common denominators that characterize effective communication in most contexts.

A Wide Range of Behaviors   Effective communicators are able to choose their actions from a wide range of behaviors.[53] To understand the importance of having a large communication repertoire, imagine that someone you know repeatedly tells jokes—perhaps racist or sexist ones—that you find offensive. You could respond to these jokes in a number of ways:

- You could decide to say nothing, figuring that the risks of bringing the subject up would be greater than the benefits.

- You could ask a third party to say something to the joke teller about the offensiveness of the jokes.

- You could hint at your discomfort, hoping your friend would get the point.

- You could joke about your friend's insensitivity, counting on humor to soften the blow of your criticism.

- You could express your discomfort in a straightforward way, asking your friend to stop telling the offensive jokes, at least around you.

- You could even demand that your friend stop.

With this choice of responses at your disposal (and you can probably think of others as well), you could pick the one that has the best chance of success. But if you were able to use only one or two of these responses when raising a delicate issue—always keeping quiet or always hinting, for example—your chances of success would be much smaller. Indeed, many poor communicators are easy to spot by their limited range of responses. Some are chronic jokers. Others are always belligerent. Still others are quiet in almost every situation. Like a piano player who knows only one tune or a chef who can prepare only a few dishes, these people are forced to rely on a small range of responses again and again, whether or not they are successful.

Many people with disabilities have learned the value of having a repertoire of options available to manage unwanted offers of help.[54] Some of those options include performing a task quickly, before anyone has the chance to intervene; pretending not to hear the offer; accepting a well-intentioned invitation to avoid seeming rude or ungrateful; using humor to deflect a bid for help; declining a well-intentioned offer with thanks; and assertively refusing help from those who won't take no for an answer.

Ability to Choose the Most Appropriate Behavior   Simply possessing a large range of communication skills is no guarantee of success. It's also necessary to know which of these skills will work best in a particular situation. As the Artificial (un)Intelligence reading shows, a response that works well in one setting can flop miserably in another one.

Although it's impossible to say precisely how to act in every situation, you should consider at least three factors when choosing a response. The first factor is the communication *context*. The time and place will almost always influence how you act. Asking your boss for a raise or your lover for a kiss might produce good results if the time is right, but the identical request might backfire if your timing is poor. Likewise, the joke that would be ideal at a bachelor party would probably be inappropriate at a funeral.

Your *goal* will also shape the approach you take. Inviting a new neighbor over for a cup of coffee or dinner could be just the right approach if you want to encourage a friendship, but if you want to maintain your privacy, it might be wiser to be polite but cool. Likewise, your goal will determine your approach in situations in which you want to help another person. As you will learn in Chapter 8, sometimes offering advice is just what is needed. But when you want to help others develop the ability to solve problems on their own, it's better to withhold your own ideas and function as a sounding board to let them consider alternatives and choose their solutions.

Finally, your *knowledge of the other person* should shape the approach you take. If you're dealing with someone who is very sensitive or insecure, your response might be supportive and cautious. With an old and trusted friend, you might be blunt. The social niche of the other party can also influence how you communicate. For instance, you would probably act differently toward an 80-year-old person than you would toward a teenager. Likewise, there are times when it's appropriate to treat a man differently than a woman, even in this age of gender equity. And one study shows that using casual text language (such as "4" instead of "for") will be less successful when emailing your professor than it might be with your friends.[55]

Skill at Performing Behaviors   After you have chosen the most appropriate way to communicate, it's still necessary to perform the required skills effectively.[56] There is a big difference between knowing *about* a skill and being able to put it into practice. Simply being aware of alternatives isn't much help unless you can skillfully put these alternatives to work.

Just reading about communication skills in the following chapters won't guarantee that you can start using them flawlessly. As with any other skills— playing a musical instrument or learning a sport, for example—the road to competence in communication is not a short one. As you learn and practice the

ARTIFICIAL [UN]INTELLIGENCE AND COMMUNICATION [IN]COMPETENCE

Watson, the name for IBM's supercomputer best known for crushing *"Jeopardy!"* contestants at their own game, briefly went from "smart" to "smart ass" with the help of the Urban Dictionary.

According to Eric Brown, the "brains" behind Watson, he and his 35-person team wanted to get IBM's supercomputer to sound more like a real human. In Brown's mind, what better way to learn the intricacies of informal human communication and conversation than having Watson memorize the Urban Dictionary?

The Urban Dictionary, for those who don't know, is comprised of submissions from everyday people and regulated by volunteer editors, who are given an extremely small set of rules to maintain quality control. But for the most part, even with the help of human editors, the Urban Dictionary still turns out to be a rather profane place on the Web.

Watson may have learned the Urban Dictionary, but it never learned the all-important axiom, "There's a time and a place for everything." Watson simply couldn't distinguish polite discourse from profanity. Watson, unfortunately, learned all of the Urban Dictionary's bad habits, including throwing in overly-crass language at random points in its responses. Watson picked up similarly bad habits from reading Wikipedia.

In the end, Brown and his team were forced to remove the Urban Dictionary from Watson's vocabulary, and additionally developed a smart filter to keep Watson from swearing in the future.

For now, Watson will keep doing what it's great at: Helping hospitals diagnose sick patients based on their records and symptoms, and beating the snot out of game show participants. If Watson's brief stint with the Urban Dictionary teaches us anything, it's that artificial intelligence will take a long time to finally learn the complicated, ever-changing ins and outs of human communication.

Dave Smith

MindTap **ENHANCE ...**

your understanding by answering the following questions, either here or online.

1. Can you think of times when people have used "Urban Dictionary language" in settings where it wasn't appropriate?

2. On the other hand, can you think of times when people have used overly formal language in a situation that called for something more casual?

3. What kinds of guidelines should you follow when it comes to appropriate language use?

communication skills in the following pages, you can expect to pass through several stages,[57] shown in Figure 1.3.

Cognitive Complexity   Social scientists use the term **cognitive complexity** to describe the ability to construct a variety of frameworks for viewing an issue.[58] To understand how cognitive complexity can increase competence, imagine that a longtime friend seems to be angry with you. One possible explanation is that your friend is offended by something you've done. Another possibility is that something has happened in another part of your friend's life that is upsetting. Or perhaps nothing at all is wrong, and you're just being overly sensitive. Considering the issue from several angles might prevent you from overreacting or misunderstanding the situation, increasing the odds of finding a way to resolve the problem constructively. Chapter 4 discusses cognitive complexity—and ways to improve it—in greater detail.

Empathy   Seeing a situation from multiple points of view is important, but there's another step that goes beyond understanding different perspectives.

SKILL *Builder*

Stages in Learning Communication Skills

Learning any new skill requires moving through several levels of competence:

1. **Beginning Awareness.** This is the point at which you first learn that there is a new and better way of behaving. If you play tennis, for example, awareness might grow when you learn about a new way of serving that can improve your power and accuracy. In the area of communication, *Looking Out Looking In* should bring this sort of awareness to you.

2. **Awkwardness.** Just as you were awkward when you first tried to ride a bicycle or drive a car, your initial attempts at communicating in new ways may also be awkward. As the saying goes, "You have to be willing to look bad in order to get good."

3. **Skillfulness.** If you keep working at overcoming the awkwardness of your initial attempts, you'll be able to handle yourself well, although you will still need to think about what you're doing. As an interpersonal communicator, you can expect the stage of skillfulness to be marked by a great deal of thinking and planning, and also by increasingly good results.

4. **Integration.** Integration occurs when you're able to perform well without thinking about it. The behavior becomes automatic, a part of your repertoire.

◄ FIGURE 1.3
Stages in Learning
Communication Skills

Empathy involves feeling and experiencing another person's situation, almost as they do. This ability is so important that some researchers have labeled empathy the most important aspect of communication competence.[59] Chapters 4 and 8 introduce you to a set of skills that can boost your ability to empathize. For now, it's enough to note that getting a feel for how others view the world is a useful and important way to become a more effective communicator.

Self-Monitoring   Whereas increased cognitive complexity and empathy help you understand others better, self-monitoring is one way to understand yourself better. Psychologists use the term **self-monitoring** to describe the process of paying close attention to one's behavior and using these observations to shape the way one behaves. Self-monitors are able to separate a part of their consciousness and observe their behavior from a detached viewpoint, making observations such as:

"I'm making a fool of myself."

"I'd better speak up now."

"This approach is working well. I'll keep it up."

Although too much self-monitoring can be problematic (see Chapter 3), people who are aware of their behavior and the impression it makes are typically more skillful communicators than people who are low self-monitors.[60] For example, self-monitors are more accurate in judging others' emotional states, better at remembering information about others, less shy, and more assertive. By contrast, low self-monitors aren't able even to recognize their incompetence. One study revealed that poor communicators were blissfully ignorant of their shortcomings and more likely to overestimate their skill than were better communicators.[61] For example, experimental subjects who scored in the lowest quartile on joke-telling skills were more likely than their funnier counterparts to grossly overestimate their sense of humor.

Whereas low self-monitors may blunder through life, succeeding or failing without understanding why, high self-monitors have the detachment to ask themselves the question "How am I doing?" and to change their behavior if the answer isn't positive. This ability can be useful in both personal and professional settings. The President's Council of Economic Advisers maintains that greater "self-awareness, self-monitoring, and self-control" will help students be more successful when they enter the job market.[62]

Commitment   One feature that distinguishes effective communication—at least in qualitatively interpersonal relationships—is commitment. In other words, people who seem to care about relationships communicate better than those who don't.[63] This care shows up in at least two ways. The first is *commitment to the other person*. Concern for the other person is revealed in a variety of ways: a desire to spend time with him or her instead of rushing, a willingness to listen carefully instead of doing all the talking, the use of language that makes sense to the other person, and openness to change after hearing the other person's ideas. Effective communicators also *care about the message*. They appear sincere, seem to know what they are talking about, and demonstrate through words and deeds that they care about what they say.

How do you measure up as a competent communicator? Competence isn't a trait that people either have or do not have. Rather, it's a state that we

SKILL *Builder*

Check Your Competence

MindTap® PRACTICE … your competence as a communicator by answering the following questions, either here or online.

Other people are often the best judges of your competence as a communicator. They can also offer useful information about how to improve your communication. Find out for yourself by following these steps:

1. Choose a person with whom you have an important relationship.

2. In cooperation with this person, identify several contexts in which you communicate. For example, you might choose different situations such as "handling conflicts," "lending support to friends," or "expressing feelings."

3. For each situation, have your friend rate your competence by answering the following questions:

   a. Do you have a wide repertoire of response styles in this situation, or do you always respond in the same way?

   b. Are you able to choose the most effective way of behaving for the situation at hand?

   c. Are you skillful at performing behaviors? (Note that knowing how you want to behave isn't the same as being *able* to behave that way.)

   d. Do you communicate in a way that leaves others satisfied?

4. After reviewing your partner's answers, identify the situations in which your communication is most competent.

5. Choose a situation in which you would like to communicate more competently, and with the help of your partner:

   a. Determine whether your repertoire of behaviors needs to be expanded.

   b. Identify the ways in which you need to communicate more skillfully.

   c. Develop ways to monitor your behavior in the key situation to get feedback on your effectiveness.

achieve more or less frequently. A realistic goal, then, is not to become perfect, but rather to boost the percentage of time when you communicate in ways outlined in this section.

Competence in Intercultural Communication

Throughout history, most people lived and died within a few miles of where they were born. They rarely had much to do with people from different backgrounds. Today is a different story. To use a familiar metaphor, we live in a global village, our lives intertwined with people from very different personal histories and communication styles.

As our world becomes more multicultural, the likelihood of interacting with people from different parts of the world is greater than ever. Given this fact, it's important to realize that what qualifies as competent behavior in one culture might be completely inept, or even offensive, in another.[64] On an obvious level, customs like belching after a meal or appearing nude in public that might be appropriate in some parts of the world would be considered outrageous in others. But there are more subtle differences in competent

Looking at DIVERSITY

Igor Ristic: Competent Communication around the World

I was born in Bosnia and spent the first ten years of my life in Eastern Europe. I now live in the United States and have visited more than a dozen countries on five continents. The more of the world I experience, the more I'm inspired to learn how to communicate effectively within and between cultures.

Intercultural communication can be challenging. Take something as simple as customer service in restaurants. Waiters and waitresses in the United States make small talk with their customers, check in with them several times during a meal, and go to great lengths to be friendly and helpful. In contrast, most Eastern European servers quickly take an order, never interrupt diners during a meal, and drop off the bill as inconspicuously as possible. When I first came to the U.S., the friendliness of the wait staffs seemed unusual. Now when I return to Europe, I sometimes perceive their servers as impersonal and curt. Being an effective communicator requires that I remain

open-minded and understand the customs of each culture.

This isn't to suggest that Eastern Europeans aren't warm and friendly. In fact, when I talk with family members in Serbia, they often sit right next to me and drape an arm around my shoulder while we chat. After living in the U.S. for more than a decade, I've developed a strong sense of a "personal space bubble"—and I much prefer to sit facing others, at a distance, without touching, while holding a conversation. Those are things I never even thought about while growing up.

What I try to keep in mind is that cultural communication rules aren't "right" or "wrong"—they're simply different. Being a good communicator means I need to be aware of various cultural norms and adapt my communication style as much as possible.

"Competent Communication around the World" by Igor Ristic. Used with permission of author.

communication. For example, qualities like self-disclosing and speaking assertively that are valued in the United States are likely to be considered overly aggressive and insensitive in many Asian cultures, where subtlety and indirectness are considered important.[65]

Even within a single society, members of various co-cultures may have different notions of appropriate behavior. One study revealed that ideas of how good friends should communicate varied from one ethnic group to another.[66] As a group, Latinos valued relational support most highly, whereas African Americans valued respect and acceptance. Asian Americans prized a caring, positive exchange of ideas, and Anglo Americans prized friends who recognized their needs as individuals. Findings like these mean that there can be no surefire list of rules or tips that will guarantee your success as a communicator. They also mean that competent communicators are able to adapt their style to suit the individual and cultural preferences of others.[67]

National and ethnic differences aren't the only dimensions of culture. Within a society **co-cultures** have different communication practices. Consider just a few co-cultures:

- age (e.g., teen, senior citizen)
- occupation (e.g., fashion model, long-distance trucker)

- sexual orientation (e.g., lesbian, gay male)
- physical disability (e.g., wheelchair user, hearing-impaired)
- religion (e.g., evangelical Christian, Muslim)
- activity (e.g., biker, gamer)

Some scholars have even characterized men and women as belonging to different co-cultures, claiming that each gender's style of communication is distinct.[68] We'll have more to say about that topic throughout this book.

Communicating successfully with people from different cultural backgrounds calls for the same elements of competence outlined in what you have just read. But beyond these basic qualities, communication researchers have identified several other especially important ingredients of successful intercultural communication.[69]

Most obviously, it helps to know the rules of a specific culture. For example, the kind of self-deprecating humor that Americans are likely to find amusing may fall flat among Arabs from the Middle East.[70] But beyond knowing the specific rules of an individual culture, there are also attitudes and skills called "culture-general" that help communicators build relationships with people from other backgrounds.[71]

To illustrate the ingredients of culture-general communication competence, imagine you've just been hired to work in a Japanese-owned company in the United States that has manufacturing operations in Mexico and customers around the world. In your new job, you are surrounded by coworkers, supervisors, and clients who come from cultures and co-cultures that are different from your own. You are also required to make occasional trips abroad. How will you handle the communication demands of this position? Ideally, you'll possess the following attributes.

Motivation The desire to communicate successfully with strangers is an important start. For example, people who are high in willingness to communicate with people from other cultures report a greater number of friends from different backgrounds than those who are less willing to reach out.[72] Having the proper motivation is important in all communication, but particularly so in intercultural interactions, because they can be quite challenging.

Tolerance for Ambiguity Communicating with people from different backgrounds can be confusing. A tolerance for ambiguity makes it possible to accept, and even embrace, the often equivocal and sometimes downright incomprehensible messages that characterize intercultural communication.

If you happen to work with colleagues raised in traditional Native American co-cultures, you may find them much quieter and less outgoing than you are used to. Your first reaction might be to chalk up this reticence to a lack of friendliness. However, it may just be a reflection of a co-culture in which quietness is valued more than extraversion, and silence more than loquacity. In cross-cultural situations like this, ambiguity is a fact of life, and a challenge.

Open-Mindedness It's one thing to tolerate ambiguity; it's another to become open-minded about cultural differences. There is a natural tendency to view others' communication choices as "wrong" when they don't match our cultural upbringing. In some parts of the world, you may find that women are not regarded with the same attitude of equality that is common in the West. Likewise, in other cultures, you may be aghast at the casual tolerance of poverty beyond anything at home, or with practices of bribery that don't jibe with homegrown notions of what is ethical. In situations like these, principled communicators aren't likely to compromise deeply held beliefs about what is right. At the same time, competence requires an attitude that recognizes that people who behave differently are most likely following rules that have governed their whole lives. Chapter 4 offers more guidance on the challenges of viewing the world from others' perspectives.

Knowledge and Skill The rules and customs that work with one group might be quite different from those that succeed with another. For example, when traveling in Latin America, you are likely to find that meetings there usually don't begin or end at their scheduled time, and that it takes the participants quite a while to "get down to business." Rather than viewing your hosts as irresponsible and unproductive, you'll want to recognize that the meaning of time is not the same in all cultures. Likewise, the gestures others make, the distance they stand from you, and the eye contact they maintain have ambiguous meanings that you'll need to learn and follow.

Becoming interculturally competent requires *mindfulness*—awareness of your own behavior and that of others.[73] Communicators who lack this quality blunder through intercultural encounters *mindlessly*, oblivious of how their own behavior may confuse or offend others and how behavior that they consider weird may be simply different. When you're in a mindful state, you can use three strategies for moving toward a more competent style of intercultural communication:[74]

1. *Passive observation* involves noticing the behaviors of members of a different culture and using these insights to communicate in ways that are most effective.
2. *Active strategies* include reading, watching films, asking experts and members of the other culture how to behave, and taking academic courses related to intercultural communication and diversity.[75]
3. *Self-disclosure* involves volunteering personal information to people from the other culture with whom you want to communicate.

One type of self-disclosure is to confess your cultural ignorance: "This is very new to me. What's the right thing to do in this situation?" This approach is the riskiest of the three described here, because some cultures may not value candor and self-disclosure as much as others. Nevertheless, most people are pleased when strangers attempt to learn the practices of their culture, and they are usually more than willing to offer information and assistance.

MindTap° PRACTICE...
your skill at intercultural communication competence by completing the Concepts in Play activity online.

SUMMARY

Communication is essential on many levels. Besides satisfying practical needs, effective communication can enhance physical health and emotional well-being. Communication also creates our identities and satisfies social needs. The process of communication is not a linear one that people *do* to one another. Rather, communication is a transactional process in which participants create a relationship by simultaneously sending and receiving messages, many of which are distorted by various types of noise.

Interpersonal communication can be viewed quantitatively by the number of people involved, or qualitatively by the nature of interaction between them. In a qualitative sense, interpersonal relationships are unique, irreplaceable, interdependent, and intrinsically rewarding. Both personal and impersonal communication are useful, and most relationships have both elements.

Several principles guide how communication operates. Messages can be intentional or unintentional. It is impossible not to communicate. Communication is irreversible and unrepeatable. Messages have both content and relational dimensions. Some common misconceptions should be avoided when thinking about communication: meanings are not in words, but rather in people; more communication does not always make matters better; communication will not solve all problems; communication—at least effective communication—is not a natural ability.

Communication competence is the ability to get what you are seeking from others in a manner that maintains the relationship. Competence varies from one situation to another. The most competent communicators have a wide repertoire of behaviors, and they are able to choose the best behavior for a given situation and perform it skillfully. They are able to understand others' points of view and respond with empathy. They also monitor their own behavior and are committed to communicating successfully. In intercultural communication, competence involves having the right motivation, a tolerance for ambiguity, open-mindedness, and the knowledge and skill to communicate effectively.

KEY TERMS

channel
co-culture
cognitive complexity
communication competence
content dimension
decode
dyad
encode
environment
impersonal communication

instrumental goals
interpersonal communication
linear communication model
message
noise
receiver
relational dimension
self-monitoring
sender
transactional communication model

3

COMMUNICATION AND IDENTITY: CREATING AND PRESENTING THE SELF

AFTER STUDYING THE TOPICS IN THIS CHAPTER, YOU SHOULD BE ABLE TO:

1. Describe the relationship between self-concept, self-esteem, and communication.

2. Explain how self-fulfilling prophecies shape the self-concept and influence communication.

3. Compare and contrast the perceived self and the presenting self as they relate to impression management.

4. Describe the role that impression management plays in both face-to-face and mediated relationships.

5. Use the social penetration and Johari Window models to identify the nature of self-disclosing communication in one of your relationships.

6. Outline the potential benefits and risks of disclosing in a selected situation.

7. Assess the most competent mixture of candor and equivocation in a given situation.

Who are you? Take a moment now to answer this question. You'll need the following list as you read the rest of this chapter, so be sure to complete it now. Try to include all the characteristics that describe you:

Your moods or feelings (e.g., happy, angry, excited)
Your appearance (e.g., attractive, short)
Your social traits (e.g., friendly, shy)
Talents you have or do not have (e.g., musical, nonathletic)
Your intellectual capacity (e.g., smart, slow learner)
Your strong beliefs (e.g., religious, environmentalist)
Your social roles (e.g., parent, girlfriend)
Your physical condition (e.g., healthy, overweight)

Now look at what you've written. How did you define yourself? By career status or social role? Your temperament? Gender or sexual orientation? By your age? Your religion? Your occupation?

There are many ways of identifying yourself. List as many as you can. You'll probably see that the words you've chosen represent a profile of what you view as your most important characteristics. In other words, if you were required to describe the "real you," this list ought to be a good summary.

George Mayer/Bigstock

COMMUNICATION AND THE SELF

You might be wondering how this self-analysis is related to interpersonal communication. The short answer is that who you are both reflects and affects your communication with others. The long answer involves everything from biology to socialization to culture to gender. We'll begin with a look at two terms that are basic to the relationship between the self and communication.

Self-Concept and Self-Esteem

The list you created is at least a partial answer to the question "Who do you think you are?" It's likely that the phrases you chose generated some emotional responses—perhaps terms like "happy" or "sad," "confident" or "nervous." Replies like these show that how you *feel* about yourself is a big part of who you think you are. What we think and feel about ourselves are important components of the self that we'll examine now.

Self-Concept Who you think you are can be described as your **self-concept**: the relatively stable set of perceptions you hold of yourself. If a special mirror existed that reflected not only your physical features but also other aspects of yourself—emotional states, talents, likes, dislikes, values, roles, and so on—the reflection you'd see would be your self-concept. You probably recognize that the self-concept list you recorded earlier is only a partial one. To make the description complete, you'd have to keep adding items until your list ran into hundreds of words.

For most people this list dramatically illustrates just how fundamental the concept of self is. Even when the item being abandoned is an unpleasant one, it's often hard to give it up. And when asked to let go of their most central feelings or thoughts, most people balk. "I wouldn't be *me* without that," they insist. Of course, this proves our point: The concept of self is perhaps our most fundamental possession. Knowing who we are is essential because without a self-concept it would be impossible to relate to the world.

Self-Esteem While your self-concept describes who you think you are, **self-esteem** involves evaluations of self-worth. A hypothetical communicator's self-concept might include being quiet, argumentative, or self-controlled. His or her self-esteem would be determined by how he or she *felt* about these qualities. Consider these differing evaluations:

Quiet	"I'm a coward for not speaking up."
	versus
	"I enjoy listening more than talking."
Argumentative	"I'm pushy, and that's obnoxious."
	versus
	"I stand up for my beliefs."
Self-controlled	"I'm too cautious."
	versus
	"I think carefully before I say or do things."

People with high self-esteem tend to think well of others and expect to be accepted by them. On the other hand, those who dislike themselves are likely to believe that others won't like them either. Realistically or not, they imagine that others are constantly viewing them critically, and they accept these imagined or real criticisms as more proof that they are indeed unlikable people. Sometimes this low self-esteem is manifested in hostility toward others because the communicator takes the approach that the only way to look good is to put others down.

High self-esteem has obvious benefits, but it doesn't guarantee interpersonal success.[1] People with exaggerated self-esteem may *think* they make better impressions on others and have better friendships and romantic lives, but neither impartial observers nor objective tests verify these beliefs. It's easy to see how people with an inflated sense of self-worth could irritate others by

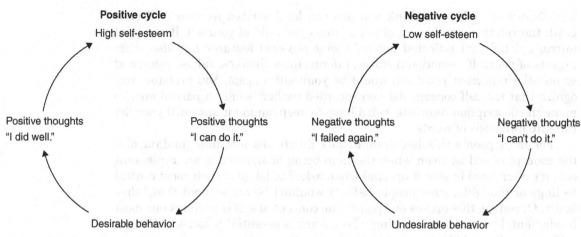

A FIGURE 3.1 The Relationship between Self-Esteem and Communication Behavior

coming across as condescending know-it-alls, especially when their self-worth is challenged.[2]

Despite these cautions, self-esteem *can* be the starting point for positive behaviors and interactions. Figure 3.1 shows the cycles that may begin from both positive and negative self-evaluations. These patterns often become self-fulfilling prophecies, as we'll discuss later in this chapter.

Biological and Social Roots of the Self

How did you become the kind of communicator you are? Were you born that way? Are you a product of your environment? As you'll now see, the correct answer to both of these questions is "yes."

PAUSE *and* REFLECT

Your Self-Esteem

MindTap® REFLECT... on your own self-esteem, either here or online.

Take a self-guided tour of your self-esteem provided by the National Association of Self-Esteem. As you explore, consider how the past and present have shaped your current level of self-esteem. Additionally, speculate about how your current level of self-esteem affects your own communication style and interpersonal relationships. You can find the link to this site by visiting CengageBrain.com to access the Speech Communication MindTap for *Looking Out Looking In*. The activity will take about 10 to 15 minutes.

Biology and the Self   Take another look at the "Who am I?" list you developed at the beginning of this chapter. You will almost certainly find some terms that describe your **personality**—characteristic ways that you think and behave across a variety of situations. Your personality tends to be stable throughout your life, and often it grows more pronounced over time.[3]

Research suggests that personality is formed in part by our genetic makeup.[4] For example, people who were judged shy as children still show a distinctive reaction in their brains as adults when they encounter new situations.[5] Some studies show that biology accounts for as much as half of communication-related personality traits such as extraversion,[6] shyness,[7] assertiveness,[8] verbal aggression,[9] and overall willingness to communicate.[10] In other words, to some degree, we come programmed to communicate in characteristic ways.

While you may have a disposition toward traits like shyness or aggressiveness, you can do a great deal to control how you actually communicate. More and more research suggests that personality is flexible, dynamic, and shaped by experiences.[11] Even shy people can learn how to reach out to others, and those with aggressive tendencies can learn to communicate in more sociable ways. One author put it this way: "Experiences can silence genes or activate them. Even shyness is like Silly Putty once life gets hold of it."[12] Throughout this book you will learn about communication skills that, with practice, you can build into your repertoire.

Socialization and the Self-Concept   How important are others in shaping our self-concept? Imagine growing up on a deserted island, with no one to talk to or share activities. How would you know how smart you are—or aren't? How would you gauge your attractiveness? How would you decide if you're short or tall, kind or mean, thin or heavy? Even if you could view your reflection in a mirror, you still wouldn't know how to evaluate your appearance without appraisals from others or people with whom to compare yourself. In fact, the messages we receive from the people in our lives play a central role in shaping how we regard ourselves.

Social scientists use the metaphor of a mirror to identify the process of **reflected appraisal**: the fact that each of us develops a self-concept that reflects the way we believe others see us. In other words, we are likely to feel less valuable, lovable, and capable to the degree that others have communicated ego-busting signals; and we will probably feel good about ourselves to the degree that others affirm our value.[13]

To illustrate this point further, let's start at the beginning. Children aren't born with any sense of identity. They learn to judge themselves only through the way others treat them. As children learn to speak and understand language, verbal messages contribute to a developing self-concept. Every day a child is bombarded with scores of appraisals about himself or herself. Some of these are positive: "You're so cute!" "I love you." "What a big girl." Other messages are negative: "What's the matter with you?" "Can't you do anything

Design Pics/Superstock

right?" "You're a bad boy." "Leave me alone. You're driving me crazy!" Evaluations like these are the mirror by which we know ourselves. Because children are trusting souls who have no other way of viewing themselves, they accept at face value both the positive and negative appraisals of the apparently all-knowing and all-powerful adults around them.

These same principles in the formation of the self-concept continue in later life, especially when messages come from what sociologists term **significant others**—people whose opinions we especially value. A look at the "ego boosters" and "ego busters" you will develop later in this chapter will show that the evaluations of a few especially important people can be powerful. Family members are the most obvious type of significant other, and their ego busters can be particularly hurtful as a result.[14] Others, though, can also be significant others: a special friend, a teacher, someone you dated, or perhaps an acquaintance whose opinion you value can leave an imprint on how you view yourself—sometimes for better, sometimes for worse.[15] To see the importance of significant others, ask yourself how you arrived at your opinion of yourself as a student, as a person attractive to others, as a competent worker, and you'll see that these self-evaluations were probably influenced by the way others regarded you.

The impact of significant others remains strong during adolescence. Inclusion in (or exclusion from) peer groups is a crucial factor in self-concept development for teenagers.[16] The good news is that parents who are understanding of their children's self-concepts during the adolescent years typically have better communication with their teens and can help them create a strong self-concept.[17] The influence of significant others becomes less powerful as people grow older. After most people approach the age of thirty, their self-concepts don't change radically, at least not without a conscious effort.[18]

So far we have looked at the way in which others' messages shape our self-concept. In addition to these messages, each of us forms our self-image by the process of **social comparison**: evaluating ourselves in terms of how we compare with others.

Two types of social comparison need highlighting. In the first type, we decide whether we are *superior* or *inferior* by comparing ourselves to others. Are we attractive or ugly? A success or failure? Intelligent or stupid? It depends on those against whom we measure ourselves.[19] For instance, research shows that young women who regularly compare themselves with ultra-thin media models develop negative appraisals of their own bodies.[20] In one study, young women's perceptions of their bodies changed for the worse after watching just thirty minutes of televised images of the "ideal" female form.[21] Men, too, who compare themselves to media-idealized male physiques evaluate their bodies negatively.[22] People also use others' online profiles as points of comparison, and they may feel less attractive after doing so.[23]

You'll probably never be as beautiful as a Hollywood star, as agile as a professional athlete, or as wealthy as a millionaire. When you consider the matter logically, these facts don't mean you're worthless. Nonetheless, many people judge themselves against unreasonable standards and suffer accordingly.[24] This is particularly true of people with perfectionistic tendencies, whose self-concepts have been shaped by demanding messages from significant others.[25] These distorted self-images can lead to serious behavioral disorders, such as depression, anorexia nervosa, and bulimia.[26] You'll read more about how to avoid placing perfectionistic demands on yourself in Chapter 5.

In addition to feelings of superiority and inferiority, social comparison provides a way to decide if we are the *same as* or *different from* others. A child who is interested in ballet and who lives in a setting where such preferences are regarded as weird will start to accept this label if there is no support from others. When at a dance camp, however, the child will likely flourish. Likewise, adults who want to improve the quality of their relationships but are surrounded by friends and family who don't recognize or acknowledge the importance of these matters may think of themselves as oddballs. Thus, it's easy to recognize that the **reference groups** against which we compare ourselves play an important role in shaping our view of ourselves.

You might argue that not every part of one's self-concept is shaped by others, insisting that certain objective facts are recognizable by self-observation. After all, nobody needs to tell a person that he is taller than others, speaks with an accent, has acne, and so on. These facts are obvious. Though it's true that some features of the self are immediately apparent, the *significance* we attach to them—the rank we assign them in the hierarchy of our list and the interpretation we give them—depends greatly on the opinions of others. After all, many of your features are readily observable, yet you don't find them important at all, because nobody has regarded them as significant.

By now you might be thinking, "It's not my fault that I've always been shy or insecure. Because I developed a picture of myself as a result of the way others have treated me, I can't help being what I am." Though it's true that to a certain extent you are a product of your environment, to believe that you are forever doomed to a poor self-concept would be a big mistake. Having held a poor self-image in the past is no reason for continuing to do so in the future. You *can* change your attitudes and behaviors, as you'll soon read.

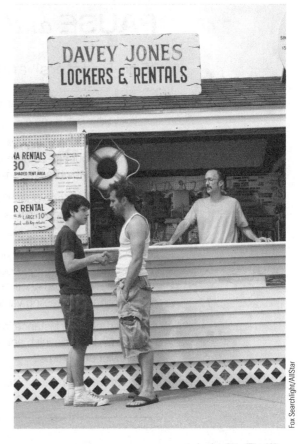

⋀ In the film *The Way Way Back*, shy, awkward Duncan (Liam James) endures a host of negative appraisals during his early adolescence, leading to low self-esteem. He then spends a summer working for fun-loving boss Owen (Sam Rockwell) who gives Duncan plenty of affirming messages. Can you think of significant others who have influenced how you think and feel about yourself? How have those messages affected the way you communicate with others?

PAUSE *and* REFLECT

"Ego Boosters" and "Ego Busters"

MindTap® REFLECT... on your own "ego boosters" and "ego busters" by answering the following questions, either here or online.

1. Recall someone you know or once knew who was an "ego booster"—who helped enhance your self-esteem by acting in a way that made you feel accepted, competent, worthwhile, important, appreciated, or loved.

2. Now recall an "ego buster" from your life—someone who acted in a large or small way to reduce your self-esteem. Recall how you felt after receiving the damaging message.

3. Now that you've thought about how others shape your self-concept, recall a time when *you* were an ego booster to someone else—when you intentionally or unintentionally boosted another's self-esteem. Look for a time when your actions left another person feeling valued, loved, needed, and so on.

4. Finally, recall an instance in which you were an ego buster for someone else. What did you do to diminish another's self-esteem? Were you aware of the effect of your behavior at the time?

After completing the exercise, you should begin to see the role communication plays in shaping the self-concept.

Characteristics of the Self-Concept

Now that you have a better idea of how your self-concept developed, we can look closer at some of its characteristics.

The Self-Concept Is Subjective   Although we tend to believe that our self-concept is accurate, in truth it may well be distorted. For example, researchers have found that there is no relationship between the way college students rate their ability as interpersonal communicators, public speakers, or listeners and their true effectiveness.[27] In all cases, the self-reported communication skill is higher than actual performance. In another study, college students were asked to rank themselves on their ability to get along with others.[28] Defying mathematical laws, all subjects—every last one of more than 800,000—put themselves in the top half of the population. Sixty percent rated themselves in the top 10 percent of the population, and an amazing 25 percent believed they were in the top 1 percent. Similarly, online daters often have a "foggy mirror"—that is, they see themselves more positively than others do.[29] This leads to inflated self-descriptions that don't always match what an objective third party might say about them.

Not all distortion of the self-concept is positive. Many people view themselves more harshly than the objective facts warrant. We have all experienced a temporary case of the "uglies," convinced that we look much worse than others assure us we do. Research confirms what common sense suggests: People are more critical of themselves when they are experiencing these negative moods than when they are feeling more positive.[30] Although we all suffer occasional bouts of self-doubt that affect our communication, some people suffer from long-term or even permanent states of excessive self-doubt and criticism.[31] It's easy to understand how this chronic condition can influence the way they approach and respond to others.

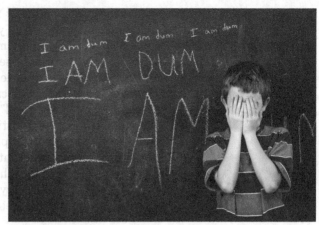

Distorted self-evaluations like these can occur for several reasons:

- *Obsolete information*. The effects of past failures in school or social relations can linger long after they have occurred, even though such events don't predict failure in the future. Likewise, your past successes don't guarantee future success.

- *Distorted feedback*. The remarks of overly critical parents, cruel friends, uncaring teachers, excessively demanding employers, or even memorable strangers can have a lasting effect. Other distorted messages are unrealistically positive. For instance, a child's inflated ego may be based on the praise of doting parents, and a boss's inflated ego may come from the praise of brownnosing subordinates.

- *Perfectionism*. From the time most of us learn to understand language, we are exposed to models who appear to be perfect. The implicit message is "A well-adjusted, successful person has no faults." Given this naive belief that everyone else is perfect and the knowledge that one isn't, it's easy to see how one's self-concept would suffer.

- *Social expectations*. Curiously, the perfectionist society to which we belong rewards those people who downplay the strengths we demand that they possess (or pretend to possess). We consider those who honestly appreciate their strengths to be "braggarts" or "egotists," confusing them with the people who boast about accomplishments they do not possess.[32] This convention leads most of us to talk freely about our shortcomings while downplaying our accomplishments.

After a while we begin to believe the types of statements we repeatedly make. The disparaging remarks are viewed as modesty and become part of our self-concept, and the strengths and accomplishments go unmentioned and are thus forgotten. And in the end, we see ourselves as much worse than we are. One way to avoid falling into the trap of becoming overly critical is to recognize your strengths rather than focusing exclusively on your shortcomings.

Scholars have coined the term *Internet-mediated reflected appraisal* to describe how communicators draw conclusions about themselves by considering how others view them online. [33] You might decide who you think you are (in part) by looking at how you portray yourself on social networking sites. Researchers asked participants to spend time reviewing their own Facebook profiles, then measured the participants' self-esteem. They found that participants felt better about themselves after looking at their Facebook pages.[34] In essence, the participants viewed their well-crafted profiles and thought, "This is how others see me—and I look pretty good!"

Of course, this raises questions about the validity of these self-appraisals. Facebook profiles are edited presentations that usually put a person's best foot forward. As you'll read later in this chapter, managing impressions via social media can lead to less-than-accurate portrayals and perceptions by the self and others. But at the very least, social networking sites can be a tool for helping people view themselves in the best light possible.

The Self-Concept Resists Change   Although we all change, there is a tendency to cling to an existing self-concept, even when evidence shows that it is obsolete. This tendency to seek and attend to information that conforms to an existing self-concept has been labeled **cognitive conservatism**.

This tendency toward cognitive conservatism leads us to seek out people who support our self-concept. For example, both college students and married couples with high self-esteem seek out partners who view them favorably, whereas those with negative self-esteem are more inclined to interact with people who view them unfavorably.[35] It appears that we are less concerned with learning the "truth" about ourselves than with reinforcing a familiar self-concept.

It's understandable why we're reluctant to revise a previously favorable self-concept. A student who did well in earlier years but now has failed to study might be unwilling to admit that the label "good scholar" no longer applies. Likewise, a previously industrious worker might resent a supervisor's mentioning increased absences and low productivity. These people aren't *lying* when they insist that they're doing well despite the facts to the contrary; they honestly believe that the old truths still hold, precisely because their self-concepts are so resistant to change.

Curiously, the tendency to cling to an outmoded self-perception also holds when the new self-perception would be more favorable than the old one. We recall a former student whom almost anyone would have regarded as beautiful, with physical features attractive enough to appear in any glamour magazine. Despite her appearance, in a class exercise, this woman characterized herself as "ordinary" and "unattractive." When questioned by her classmates, she described how as a child her teeth were extremely crooked and how she had worn braces for several years in her teens to correct this problem. During this time she was often teased by her friends, who never let her forget her "metal mouth," as she put it. Even though the braces had been off for two years, our student reported that she still saw herself as ugly and brushed aside our compliments by insisting that we were just saying these things to be nice—she knew how she *really* looked.

Communicators who are presented with information that contradicts their self-perception have two choices: They can either accept the new data and change their perception accordingly, or they can keep their original perception and in some way refute the new information. Because most communicators are reluctant to downgrade a favorable image of themselves, their tendency is to opt for refutation, either by discounting the information and rationalizing it away or by counterattacking the person who transmitted it. The problem of defensiveness is so great that we will examine it in detail in Chapter 11.

There are times when changing a distorted or obsolete self-concept can be a good thing. For example, you may view yourself as a less competent, desirable, and skilled person than the facts would suggest. Here are a few suggestions for embracing a more positive self-image.

1. **Have a realistic perception of yourself**. While some people have inaccurately inflated egos, others are their own worst critic. A periodic session of recognizing your strengths, such as you tried earlier in this chapter, is often a good way to put your strengths and weaknesses into perspective. It's also wise to surround yourself with supportive people who will give you the positive feedback you need and deserve.

2. **Have realistic expectations**. If you demand that you handle every act of communication perfectly, you're bound to be disappointed. And if you constantly compare yourself with gifted people, you're going to come up short. Rather than feel miserable because you're not as talented as an expert, realize that you probably are a better, wiser, or more skillful person than you used to be, and that this is a legitimate source of satisfaction.

3. **Have the will to change**. Often we say we want to change, when in fact we're simply not willing to do what's required (we'll discuss the fallacy of helplessness and ridding yourself of "can't" statements in Chapter 4). You *can* change in many ways, if only you are motivated to do so.

4. **Have the skill to change**. Trying isn't always enough. In some instances you would change if you knew how to do so. Seek out advice from books such as this one, or ask for suggestions from instructors, counselors, and other experts. Observing models can also be a powerful way to master new ways of communicating. Watch what people you admire do and say, not so that you can copy them, but so that you can adapt their behavior to fit your own personal style.

Culture, Gender, and Identity

We have already seen how experiences in the family, especially during childhood, shape our sense of who we are. Along with the messages we receive at home, many other forces mold our identity, and thus our communication, including age, physical ability/disability, sexual orientation, and socioeconomic status. Along with these forces, culture and gender are powerful forces that affect how we view ourselves and others and how we communicate. We will examine each of these forces now.

Culture   Although we seldom recognize the fact, our sense of self is shaped, often in subtle ways, by the culture in which we have been reared.[36] Most Western cultures are highly individualistic, whereas other traditional cultures—most Asian ones, for example—are much more collectivist. When asked to identify themselves, individualists in the United States, Canada, Australia, and Europe would probably respond by giving their first name, surname, street, town, and country. Many Asians do it the other way around.[37] If you ask Hindus for their identity, they will give you their caste and village as well as their name. The Sanskrit formula for identifying one's self begins with lineage and goes on to state family, house, and ends with one's personal name.[38] When members of different cultures were asked to create an "I am" list similar to the one you completed earlier in this chapter, those from collectivist cultures made far more group references than those from individualistic cultures.[39]

The difference between individualism and collectivism shows up in everyday interaction. Communication researcher Stella Ting-Toomey has developed a theory that explains cultural differences in important norms, such as honesty and directness.[40] She suggests that in individualistic Western cultures where there is a strong "I" orientation, the norm of speaking directly is honored, whereas in collectivistic cultures, where the main desire is to build connections between the self and others, indirect approaches that maintain harmony are considered more desirable. "I gotta be me" could be the motto of a Westerner, but "If I hurt you, I hurt myself" is closer to the Asian way of thinking.

You don't need to travel overseas to appreciate the influence of culture on the self. Within societies, co-cultural identity plays an important role in how we see ourselves and others. For example, ethnicity can have a powerful effect on how people think of themselves and how they communicate. Recall how you described yourself in the "Who Am I?" list you created when you began this chapter. If you are a member of a nondominant ethnic group, it's likely that you included your ethnicity in the most important parts of who you are. There's no surprise here: If society keeps reminding you that your ethnicity is important, then you begin to think of yourself in those terms. If you are part of the dominant majority, you probably aren't as conscious of your ethnicity. Nonetheless, it plays an important part in your self-concept. Being part of the majority increases the chances that you have a sense of belonging to the society in which you live and of entitlement to being treated fairly. Members of less privileged ethnic groups often don't have these feelings.

Sex and Gender   One way to appreciate the tremendous importance of gender on your sense of self is to imagine how your identity would be different if you had been born as a member of the other sex. Would you express your emotions in the same way? Deal with conflict? Relate to friends and strangers? The answer is quite likely "no."

From the earliest months of life, being male or female shapes the way others communicate with us, and thus our sense of self. Think about the first questions most people ask when a child is born. One of them is almost always "Is it a boy or a girl?" After most people know what the baby "is," they often behave accordingly.[41] They use different pronouns and often choose gender-related nicknames. With boys, comments often focus on size, strength, and activity; comments about girls more often address beauty, sweetness, and facial responsiveness. It's not surprising that these messages shape a child's sense of identity and how he or she will communicate. The implicit message is that some ways of behaving are masculine and others feminine. Little girls, for example, are more likely to be reinforced for acting "sweet" than are little boys.

Talking with LITTLE GIRLS

NeonShot/Bigstock

I went to a dinner party at a friend's home last weekend and met her five-year-old daughter for the first time. Little Maya was all curly brown hair, doe-like dark eyes, and adorable in her shiny pink nightgown. I wanted to squeal, "Maya, you're so cute! Look at you! Turn around and model that pretty ruffled gown, you gorgeous thing!"

But I didn't. I always bite my tongue when I meet little girls, restraining myself from my first impulse, which is to tell them how darn cute/pretty/beautiful/well-dressed/well-manicured/well-coiffed they are.

What's wrong with that? It's our culture's standard talking-to-little-girls icebreaker, isn't it? And why not give them a sincere compliment to boost their self-esteem?

15 to 18 percent of girls under 12 now wear mascara, eyeliner, and lipstick regularly; eating disorders are up and self-esteem is down; and 25 percent of young American women would rather win *America's Next Top Model* than the Nobel Peace Prize. Even bright, successful college women say they'd rather be hot than smart.

Teaching girls that their appearance is the first thing you notice tells them that looks are more important than anything. It sets them up for dieting at age 5 and foundation at age 11 and boob jobs at 17 and Botox at 23. That's why I force myself to talk to little girls as follows:

"Maya," I said, crouching down at her level, looking into her eyes, "very nice to meet you. Hey, what are you reading?" I asked. Her eyes got bigger, and the practiced, polite facial expression gave way to genuine excitement over this topic.

"What's your favorite book?" I asked.

"I'll go get it! Can I read it to you?"

Purplicious was Maya's pick and a new one to me, as Maya snuggled next to me on the sofa and proudly read aloud every word. Not once did we discuss clothes or hair or bodies or who was pretty. It's surprising how hard it is to stay away from those topics with little girls.

So, one tiny bit of opposition to a culture that sends all the wrong messages to our girls. One tiny nudge towards valuing female brains. One brief moment of intentional role modeling.

Try this the next time you meet a little girl. Ask her what she's reading. What does she like and dislike, and why? There are no wrong answers. You're just generating an intelligent conversation that respects her brain. For older girls, ask her about current events issues: pollution, wars, school budgets slashed. What bothers her out there in the world? How would she fix it if she had a magic wand?

Here's to changing the world, one little girl at a time.

Lisa Bloom

MindTap® ENHANCE... your understanding by answering the following questions, either here or online.

1. Do you think people talk differently to little girls than they talk to little boys? If so, offer examples.

2. What impact does communication with children have on the development of their self-concept and self-esteem?

3. Do you generally agree or disagree with the author's central point about talking to little girls? Explain why or why not.

The same principle operates in adulthood: A man who stands up for his beliefs might get approval for being "tough" or "persistent," whereas a woman who behaves in the same way could be described by critics as a "nag" or "bitch."[42] It's not hard to see how the gender roles and labels like these can have a profound effect on how men and women view themselves and on how they communicate.

Self-esteem is also influenced by gender. In a society that values competitiveness more in men than in women, it isn't surprising that the self-esteem of adolescent young men is closely related to having abilities that are superior in some way to those of their peers, whereas teenage women's self-worth is tied more closely to the success of their social relationships and verbal skills.[43] Research also suggests that young women struggle more with self-esteem issues than do young men. For example, the self-esteem of about two-thirds of the males in one study (ages 14 to 23) increased.[44] The same study revealed that about 57 percent of females in the same age group grew to feel *less* good about themselves.

Don't resign yourself to being a prisoner of expectations about your gender. Research demonstrates that our sense of self is shaped strongly by the people with whom we interact and by the contexts in which we communicate.[45] For example, a nonaggressive young man who might feel unwelcome and inept in a macho environment might gain new self-esteem by finding others who appreciate his style of communicating. A woman whose self-esteem is stifled by the limited expectations of bosses and coworkers can look for more hospitable places to work. Children usually can't choose the reference groups that shape their identities, but adults can.

The Self-Fulfilling Prophecy and Communication

The self-concept is such a powerful force on the personality that it not only determines how you see yourself in the present but also can actually influence your future behavior and that of others. Such occurrences come about through a phenomenon called the self-fulfilling prophecy.

A **self-fulfilling prophecy** occurs when a person's expectations of an event, and his or her subsequent behavior based on those expectations, make the event more likely to occur than would otherwise have been true.[46] A self-fulfilling prophecy involves four stages:

1. Holding an expectation (for yourself or for others)
2. Behaving in accordance with that expectation
3. Coming to pass of the expectation
4. Reinforcing the original expectation

You can see how this process operates by considering an example. Imagine you're scheduled to interview for a job you really want. You are nervous about how you'll do, and not at all sure you are really qualified for the position. You share your concerns with a professor who knows you well and a friend who works for the company. Both assure you that you're perfect for the job and that the firm would be lucky to have you as an employee. Based on these comments, you come to the interview feeling good about yourself. As a result, you speak with authority and sell yourself with confidence. The employers are clearly impressed, and you receive the job offer. Your conclusion: "My friend and professor were right. I'm the kind of person an employer would want!"

This example illustrates the four stages of a self-fulfilling prophecy. Thanks to the assurances of your professor and friend, your expectations about the interview were upbeat (Stage 1). Because of your optimistic attitude, you communicated confidently in the interview (Stage 2). Your confident behavior—along with your other qualifications—led to a job offer (Stage 3). Finally, the positive results reinforced your positive self-assessment, and you'll probably approach future interviews with greater assurance (Stage 4).

It's important to recognize the tremendous influence that self-fulfilling prophecies play in our lives. To a great extent we become what we believe. In this sense, we and those around us constantly create and re-create our self-concepts.

"I don't sing because I am happy. I am happy because I sing."

Types of Self-Fulfilling Prophecies There are two types of self-fulfilling prophecies. *Self-imposed prophecies* occur when your own expectations influence your behavior. In sports you've probably psyched yourself into playing either better or worse than usual, so that the only explanation for your unusual performance was your attitude. Similarly, you've probably faced an audience at one time or another with a fearful attitude and forgotten your remarks, not because you were unprepared, but because you said to yourself, "I know I'll blow it."

Research has demonstrated the power of self-imposed prophecies.[47] In one study, communicators who believed they were incompetent proved less likely than others to pursue rewarding relationships and more likely to sabotage their existing relationships than did people who were less critical of themselves.[48] On the other hand, students who perceived themselves as capable achieved more academically.[49] In another study, subjects who were sensitive to social rejection tended to expect rejection, perceive it where it might not have existed, and overreact to their exaggerated perceptions in ways that jeopardized the quality of their relationships.[50] Research also suggests that communicators who feel anxious about giving speeches seem to create self-fulfilling prophecies about doing poorly that cause them to perform less effectively.[51]

A second category of self-fulfilling prophecies is imposed by one person on another. A classic example was demonstrated by Robert Rosenthal and Lenore Jacobson in a study described in their book *Pygmalion in the Classroom.*[52] The experimenters told teachers that 20 percent of the children in a certain elementary school showed unusual potential for intellectual growth. The names of these 20 percent were drawn randomly. Eight months later, these "gifted" children showed significantly greater gains in IQ than did the remaining children, who had not been singled out for the teachers' attention. The change in the teachers' behavior toward these allegedly special students led to changes in the intellectual performance of these randomly selected children. Among other things, the teachers gave the "smart" students more

▲ The film *Divergent* depicts a dystopian society where citizens are pigeonholed into categories that shape their adult lives—in essence, an other-imposed prophecy. Sixteen-year-old Tris Prior (Shailene Woodley) doesn't fit those categories, so she sets out to define herself on her own terms. In doing so, she demonstrates the power of self-fulfilling prophecies to help us become the kind of person we choose. What are some other-imposed messages that shaped you in your formative years? Which of those did you accept and which did you reject?

time to answer questions, more feedback, and more praise. In other words, the selected children did better—not because they were any more intelligent than their classmates, but because their teachers held higher expectations for them and treated them accordingly.

This type of self-fulfilling prophecy has been shown to be a powerful force for shaping the self-concept and thus the behavior of people in a wide range of settings outside of schools.[53] In one study, a group of welders with relatively equal aptitudes began training. Everyone, including the trainer, was told that five of the welders had higher scores on an aptitude test—even though they were chosen randomly. All five finished at the top of the class. They had fewer absences and significantly higher final test scores. Most impressively, they learned the skills of their trade twice as quickly as those who weren't identified as being so talented. In another [54] study, military personnel who were randomly labeled as having high potential performed up to the expectations of their superiors. They were also more likely to volunteer for dangerous special duty.[55]

It's important to note that an observer must do more than just *believe* to create a self-fulfilling prophecy for the person who is the target of the expectations. The observer also must *communicate* that belief in order for the prediction to have any effect. If parents have faith in their children, but the kids aren't aware of that confidence, they won't be affected by their parents' expectations. If a boss has concerns about an employee's ability to do a job but keeps those concerns to herself, the employee won't be influenced. In this sense, the self-fulfilling prophecies imposed by one person on another are as much a communication phenomenon as a psychological one.

PRESENTING THE SELF: COMMUNICATION AS IMPRESSION MANAGEMENT

So far we have described how communication shapes the way communicators view themselves. We will now turn the tables and focus on the topic of **impression management**—the communication strategies that people use to influence how others view them.[56] You will see that many of our messages aim at creating a desired impression.

Public and Private Selves

To understand how impression management operates, we have to discuss the notion of self in more detail. So far we have referred to the "self" as if each of us had only one identity. In truth, each of us has several selves, some private and others public. Often these selves are quite different.

The **perceived self** is a reflection of the self-concept. Your perceived self is the person you believe yourself to be in moments of honest self-examination. We can call the perceived self "private," because you are unlikely to reveal all of it to another person. You can verify the private nature of the perceived self by reviewing the self-concept list you developed at the beginning of this chapter. If you were completely forthright when compiling that list, you'll probably find some elements of yourself there that you would not disclose to many people and some that you would not share with anyone. You might, for example, be reluctant to share some feelings about your appearance ("I think I'm rather unattractive"), your intelligence ("I'm smarter than most of my friends"), your goals ("The most important thing to me is becoming rich"), or your motives ("I care more about myself than about others").

In contrast to the perceived self, the **presenting self** is a public image—the way we want others to view us. The presenting self is sometimes called one's **face**. In most cases the presenting self that we seek to create is a socially approved image: diligent student, loving partner, conscientious worker, loyal friend, and so on. Social norms often create a gap between the perceived and presenting selves. In one study of college students, both men and women said their perceived selves included being "friendly" and "responsible." When it came to their public selves, the men wanted to be seen as "wild" and "strong," while the women presented themselves as "active" and "able."[57]

You can recognize the difference between public and private behaviors by recalling a time when you observed a driver, alone in his or her car, acting in ways that would never be acceptable in public. All of us engage in backstage ways of acting that we would never do in public. Just recall how you behave in front of the bathroom mirror when the door is locked, and you will appreciate the difference between public and private behaviors. If you knew that someone was watching, would you act differently?

Characteristics of Impression Management

Now that you have a sense of what impression management is, we can look at some characteristics of this process.

We Strive to Construct Multiple Identities It is an oversimplification to suggest that each of us uses impression management strategies to create just one identity. In the course of even a single day, most people perform a variety of roles: "respectful student," "joking friend," "friendly neighbor," and "helpful worker," to suggest just a few.

As you grew up you almost certainly changed characters as you interacted with your parents. In one context you acted as responsible adult ("You can trust me with the car!"), and in another context you were the helpless child ("I can't

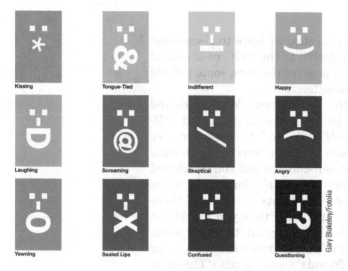

Kissing   Tongue-Tied   Indifferent   Happy

Laughing   Screaming   Skeptical   Angry

Yawning   Sealed Lips   Confused   Questioning

Gary Blakeley/Fotolia

find my socks!"). At some times—perhaps on birthdays or holidays—you were a dedicated family member, and at other times you may have played the role of rebel. Likewise, in romantic relationships we switch among many ways of behaving, depending on the context: friend, lover, business partner, scolding critic, apologetic child, and so on. And as you read in Chapter 1, the ability to shift styles from setting to setting and culture to culture is a feature of communication competence.

Impression Management Is Collaborative Sociologist Erving Goffman used a dramatistic metaphor to describe impression management.[58] He suggested that each of us is a kind of playwright who creates roles that reflect how we want others to see us, as well as a performer who acts out those roles. But unlike the audience for most forms of acting, our audience is made up of other actors who are trying to create their own characters. Impression-related communication can be viewed as a kind of process theater in which we collaborate with other actors to improvise scenes in which our characters mesh.

You can appreciate the collaborative nature of impression management by thinking about how you might handle a gripe with a friend or family member who has not returned your repeated calls to coordinate important details for a party. Suppose that you decide to raise the issue tactfully in an effort to avoid seeming like a nag (desired role for yourself: "nice person") and also to save the other person from the embarrassment of being confronted (hoping to avoid suggesting that the other person's role is "screw-up"). If your tactful bid is accepted, the dialogue might sound like this:

You: By the way, I've left a couple of messages on your cell. I'm not sure whether you've gotten them. We need to talk about the invitations before they go out tomorrow.

Other: Oh, sorry. I've been meaning to get back with you. It's just that I've been really busy lately with school and work.

You: That's okay. Could we talk about it now?

Other: How about I call you back in an hour?

You: Sure, no problem.

In this upbeat conversation, both you and the other person accepted one another's bids for identity as thoughtful, responsible friends. As a result, the conversation ran smoothly. Imagine, though, how differently the outcome would be if the other person didn't accept your presenting self:

You: By the way, I've left two messages on your cell. I'm not sure whether you've gotten them ...

Other: *(Defensively)* Okay, so I forgot. It's not that big a deal. You're not perfect yourself, you know!

PAUSE *and* REFLECT

Your Many Identities

MindTap REFLECT... on your many identities by keeping a record, either here or online.

You can get a sense of the many roles you try to create by keeping a record of the situations in which you communicate over a one- or two-day period. For each situation, identify a dramatic title to represent the image you try to create. A few examples might be "party animal," "helpful housekeeper," "wise older sibling," and "sophisticated film critic."

At this point you have the choice of persisting in trying to play the original role of "nice person": "Hey, I'm not mad at you, and I know I'm not perfect!" Or, you might switch to the new role of "unjustly accused person," responding with aggravation, "I never said I was perfect. But we're not talking about me here ..."

As this example illustrates, *collaboration* in impression management doesn't mean the same thing as *agreement*. The small issue of the phone message might mushroom into a fight in which you and the other person both adopt the role of combatants. The point here is that virtually all conversations provide an arena in which communicators construct their identities in response to the behavior of others. As you read in Chapter 1, communication isn't made up of discrete events that can be separated from one another. Instead, what happens at one moment is influenced by what each party brings to the interaction and what happened in their relationship up to that point.

Impression Management Can Be Deliberate or Unconscious   There's no doubt that sometimes we are highly aware of managing impressions. Most job interviews and first dates are clear examples of deliberate impression management. As noted in Chapter 1, high self-monitoring is usually helpful in these situations. But in other cases, we unconsciously act in ways that are really small public performances.[59] For example, experimental subjects expressed facial disgust in reaction to eating sandwiches laced with a supersaturated saltwater solution only when there was another person present. When they were alone, they made no faces while eating the same sandwiches.[60]

Another study showed that communicators engage in facial mimicry (such as smiling or looking sympathetic in response to another's message) in face-to-face settings only when their expressions can be seen by the other person. When they are speaking over the phone, and their reactions cannot be seen, they do not make the same expressions.[61] Studies like these suggest that most of our behavior is aimed at sending messages to others—in other words, impression management.

The experimental subjects described in the preceding paragraphs didn't consciously think, "Somebody is watching me eat this salty sandwich, so I'll make a face" or "Because I'm in a face-to-face conversation, I'll show I'm sympathetic by mimicking the facial expressions of my conversational partner." Decisions like these are often instantaneous and outside of our conscious awareness. In the same way, many of our choices about how to act in the array of daily interactions aren't highly considered strategic decisions. Rather, they rely on "scripts" that we have developed over time.

Despite the pervasiveness of impression management, it seems like an exaggeration to suggest that *all* behavior is aimed at making impressions. Young children certainly aren't strategic communicators. A baby spontaneously laughs when pleased and cries when sad or uncomfortable without any notion of creating an impression in others. Likewise, there are times when we, as adults, act spontaneously. Despite these exceptions, most people consciously or unconsciously communicate in ways that help construct desired identities for themselves and others.

Why Manage Impressions?

Why bother trying to shape others' opinions of you? Social scientists have identified several overlapping reasons.[62]

To Start and Manage Relationships Think about times when you have consciously and carefully managed your approach when meeting someone you would like to know better. You may do your best to appear charming and witty—or perhaps cool and suave. You don't need to be a phony to act this way; you simply are trying to show your best side. Once relationships are up and running, we still manage impressions—perhaps not as much, but often.

To Gain Compliance of Others We often manage our impressions to get others—both those we know and strangers—to act in ways we want. You might, for example, dress up for a visit to traffic court in the hope that your image (responsible citizen) will convince the judge to treat you sympathetically. You might chat sociably with neighbors you don't find especially interesting so that you can exchange favors or solve problems as they come up.

To Save Others' Face We often modify the way we present ourselves to support the way other people want to be seen. For example, able-bodied people often mask their discomfort upon encountering someone who is disabled by acting nonchalant or stressing similarities between themselves and the disabled person.[63] Young children who haven't learned about the importance of face-saving often embarrass their parents by behaving inappropriately ("Mommy, why is that man so fat?"), but by the time they enter school, behavior that might have been excusable or even amusing just isn't acceptable.

To Explore New Selves Sometimes we try on a new self in the same way we try on a different style of clothing: to see if it changes the way others view us and how we think and feel about ourselves. Toward this end, trying on new selves can be a means to self-improvement. For example, one study found that teens—especially lonely ones—who experimented with new identities online wound up reaching out more to people of different ages and cultural backgrounds than they did in their face-to-face lives. As a result, they actually increased their social competence.[64]

Face-to-Face Impression Management

In face-to-face interaction, communicators can manage their front in three ways: manner, appearance, and setting.[65] *Manner* consists of a communicator's words and nonverbal actions. Physicians, for example, display a wide variety of manners as they conduct physical examinations. Some are friendly and conversational, whereas others adopt a curt and impersonal approach. Much of a communicator's manner comes from what he or she says. A doctor who remembers details about your interests and hobbies is quite different from one who sticks to clinical questions. One who explains a medical procedure creates a different impression than another who reveals little information to the patient.

Along with the content of speech, nonverbal behaviors play a big role in creating impressions.[66] A doctor who greets you with a smile and a handshake comes across differently from one who gives nothing more than a curt nod. Manner varies widely in other professions and settings—professors, salespeople, hair stylists, and so on—and the impressions they create vary accordingly. The same principle holds in personal relationships. Your manner plays a major role in shaping how others view you. Chapters 6 and 7 will describe in detail how your words and nonverbal behaviors create impressions. Because you have to speak and act, the question isn't *whether* your manner sends a message, but rather *what* message it will send.

A second dimension of impression management is *appearance*—the personal items that people use to shape an image. Sometimes appearance is part of creating a professional image. A physician's white lab coat and a police officer's uniform both set the wearers apart as someone special. A tailored suit or a rumpled outfit creates very different impressions in the business world. Off the job, clothing is just as important. We choose clothing that sends a message about ourselves, sometimes trendy and sometimes traditional. Some people dress in ways that accent their sexuality, whereas others hide it. Clothing can say, "I'm an athlete," "I'm wealthy," or "I'm an environmentalist." Along with dress, other aspects of appearance play a strong role in impression management. Do you wear makeup? What is your hairstyle? Do you make an effort to look friendly and confident?

A final way to manage impressions is through the choice of *setting*—physical items that we use to influence how others view us. In modern Western society, the automobile is a major part of impression management. This explains why many people lust after cars that are far more expensive and powerful than they really need. A sporty convertible or fancy imported sedan doesn't just get drivers from one place to another; it also makes statements about the kind of people they are. The physical setting we choose and the way we arrange it are another important way to manage impressions. What colors do you choose for the place you live? What artwork? What music do you play? Of course, we choose a setting that we enjoy, but in many cases we create an environment that will present the desired front to others.

Online Impression Management

The preceding examples involve face-to-face interaction, but impression management is just as common and important in other types of communication.

At first glance, the technology of mediated communication seems to limit the potential for impression management. Texting, emailing, and blogging, for example, appear to lack the richness of other channels. They don't convey the tone of your voice, postures, gestures, or facial expressions. However, communication scholars recognize that what is missing in online communication can actually be an *advantage* for communicators who want to manage the impressions they make.[67]

Communicating online generally gives us more control over managing impressions than we have in face-to-face communication. As you read in Chapter 2, asynchronous forms of mediated communication like email, blogs, and web pages allow you to edit your messages until you create just the desired impression.[68] With email (and, to a lesser degree, with text messaging), you can compose difficult messages without forcing the receiver to respond immediately, and ignore others' messages rather than give an unpleasant response. Perhaps most important, when communicating via text-based technology, you generally don't have to worry about stammering or blushing, apparel or appearance, or any other unseen factor that might detract from the impression you want to create. (Photos, video, and streaming may be involved in some mediated communication—but you have choices about those as well.)

Of course, communicating via social media also allows strangers to change their age, history, personality, appearance, and other matters that would be impossible to hide in person.[69] A survey of one online dating site's participants found that 86 percent felt others misrepresented their physical appearance in their posted descriptions.[70] Online daters acknowledge the delicate task of balancing an ideal online identity against the "real" self behind their profile. Many admit they sometimes fudge facts about themselves—using outdated photos or "forgetting" information about their age, for instance. But they are less tolerant when prospective dates post inaccurate identities. For example, one date-seeker expressed resentment upon learning that a purported "hiker" hadn't hiked in years.[71] We'll talk about the ethics of such misrepresentations in the following section.

One study asked undergraduate Facebook users how they believe they come across in their profiles.[72] Most acknowledged that their self-presentations are highly positive—but not *too* positive. In general, they believed their profiles portrayed them as better than reality on certain dimensions (e.g., "funny," "adventurous," "outgoing"), accurately on other dimensions (e.g., "physically attractive," "creative"), and worse than reality on yet other dimensions

What I Instagrammed versus What Was Really Happening, Or, My Entire Life Is a Lie

I love Instagram. Whether I'm drinking a coffee, heading to the gym, or simply feeling in the mood for the occasional (okay, a little more than occasional) selfie, I love posting photos and interacting with other users.

Instagram, like all social media, is about presenting the ideal version of yourself. It's not *not* yourself per se.... It's more like, all the best parts of you displayed to the world and ignoring all the worst parts. So I, like most people, post the things that are going to reflect the best aspects of my life and personality.

Anyway, as a sort of confession: here is what I'm really doing in all those Instagrams versus what I presented to the world. Prepare to be shocked.

The Ultimate Selfie

Olivia muenter

What It Looks Like I'm Doing...

I just got back from vacation and thought I'd share my new, totally natural glow with all of you. I AM SO HAPPY BECAUSE MY LIFE IS TOTALLY AND COMPLETELY PERFECT. I took this photo one time. One time. This is how I look all the time. All. The. Time.

What I'm Actually Doing/ Thinking...

Do you want to know how many pictures I shot before I actually captured a photo that both accurately (and attractively) displayed how happy I was in this moment? 56. I hope you're judging me, because I am. Also, the entire epidermis of my forehead is peeling off in this photo because I didn't use sunscreen one day by the pool. Ah, cropping.

The Farmers Market Shot

Olivia muenter

What It Looks Like I'm Doing...

AH, PRODUCE! So bright. So fresh. So healthy. Perhaps I will throw some blueberries and spinach in my high-speed blender and create some juice to take to the office today. I only buy locally. And if you don't, I am judging you.

What I'm Actually Doing/ Thinking...

I wonder how long that fruit has been sitting there. I'm going to buy a blueberry muffin the size of my head instead.

The "I Am Productive" Shot

Olivia muenter

What It Looks Like I'm Doing...

What? You're not a morning person. How unfortunate. I start my day with green tea and fresh fruit every day, at the crack of dawn. I like to check my emails as the sun rises, right before I head to yoga.

What I'm Actually Doing/ Thinking...

I had to wake up at 7 A.M. because I had three assignments that I had quite literally left until the day that they were due. I have no recollection of whether I passed any of those assignments, but my memory is leaning toward no. P.S.: I hate mornings.

Olivia Muenter

MindTap ENHANCE... your understanding by answering the following questions, either here or online.

1. In what ways do you present yourself differently online than you do in person?

2. Have you ever carefully managed social media posts to portray yourself in a particular way, similar to what Olivia Muenter describes here?

3. Are there ethical boundaries that shouldn't be crossed when engaging in online impression management?

On the JOB

Managing Your Professional Identity

According to the *New York Times*, 70 percent of U.S. recruiters have rejected job candidates because of personal information online.[a] It's not hard to imagine how a careless image or post could scuttle your chances with a prospective employer.

To see how your online identity might help or harm your job prospects, start by plugging your name into one or more search engines. If the results might work against you, consider changing privacy settings on your profiles, customizing who can see certain updates and deleting unwanted information about yourself.[b]

Along with discovering unflattering information, you might be surprised to find that another person with the same name and an embarrassing profile pops up.

To minimize the chances of mistaken identity, consider distinguishing your professional self by including your middle name or middle initial on your résumé and all other information you post where online seekers might find it.

If you find potentially damaging information about yourself online and you can't remove it, consider seeking professional help to set the record straight. Services like www.reputation.com will monitor your online identity and take steps to protect your privacy and have damaging information removed.

Once you're on the job, recognize that your mediated messages are a powerful way to create and maintain your identity. Typos, brusque tone, and potentially offensive humor can be career-killers.[c]

("intelligent," "polite," "reliable"). It appears that the participants realized—perhaps intuitively—that their Facebook sites are an exercise in impression management.

Blogs, personal web pages, and profiles on social networking sites all provide opportunities for communicators to construct an identity.[73] Even the simple choice of a screen name ("lovemyporsche," "fun2bewith," "footballdude") says something about you and is likely to lead others to create impressions of you.[74] And interestingly, research shows that regularly viewing your own Facebook page can enhance your self-esteem.[75] This makes sense: Assuming you're carefully managing impressions on that site, it can be an ego-booster to remind yourself what you look like "at your best."

Impression Management and Honesty

After reading this far, you might think that impression management sounds like an academic label for manipulation or phoniness. There certainly are situations where impression management is dishonest. A manipulative date who pretends to be affectionate in order to gain sexual favors is clearly unethical and deceitful. So are job applicants who lie about academic records to get hired or salespeople who pretend to be dedicated to customer service when their real goal is to make a quick buck.

But managing impressions doesn't necessarily make you a liar. In fact, it is almost impossible to imagine how we could communicate effectively without making decisions about which front to present in one situation or another. It would be ludicrous to act the same way with strangers as you do with close friends, and nobody would show the same face to a two-year-old as he or she would to an adult.

Each of us has a repertoire of faces—a cast of characters—and part of being a competent communicator is choosing the best face for the situation. Consider a few examples:

- You offer to teach a friend a new skill: playing the guitar, operating a computer program, or sharpening up a tennis backhand. Your friend is making slow progress with the skill, and you find yourself growing impatient.

- You've been exchanging texts for several weeks with someone you met online, and the relationship is starting to turn romantic. You have a physical trait you haven't mentioned.

- At work you face a belligerent customer. You don't believe anyone has the right to treat you this way.

- A friend or family member makes a joke about your appearance that hurts your feelings. You aren't sure whether to make an issue of the joke or to pretend that it doesn't bother you.

In each of these situations—and in countless others every day—you have a choice about how to act. It is an oversimplification to say that there is only one honest way to behave in each circumstance and that every other response would be insincere and dishonest. Instead, impression management involves deciding which face—which part of yourself—to reveal. For example, when teaching a new skill, you choose to display the "patient" instead of the "impatient" side of yourself. In the same way, at work you have the option of acting defensive or nondefensive in difficult situations. With strangers, friends, or family you can choose whether to disclose your feelings. Which face to show to others is an important decision, but in any case you are sharing a real part of yourself. You may not be revealing everything, but as you will learn in the following section, complete self-disclosure is rarely appropriate.

SELF-DISCLOSURE IN RELATIONSHIPS

One way by which we judge the strength of our relationships is the amount of information we share with others. "We don't have any secrets," some people proudly claim. Opening up certainly is important. As you read in Chapter 1, disclosure is an ingredient in qualitatively interpersonal relationships. Given the obvious importance of self-disclosure, we need to look closer at the subject. Just what is it? When is it desirable? How can it best be done?

The best place to begin is with a definition. **Self-disclosure** is the process of deliberately revealing information about oneself that is significant and would not normally be known by others. Let's look closer at this definition. Self-disclosure must be *deliberate*. If you accidentally mention to a friend

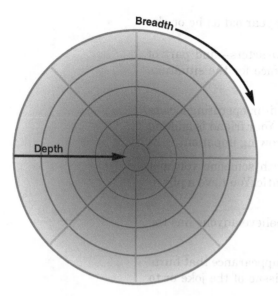

▲ FIGURE 3.2
Social Penetration Model

that you're thinking about quitting a job, or if your facial expression reveals irritation you wanted to hide, that doesn't qualify as self-disclosure. Besides being deliberate, the information must also be *significant*. Volunteering trivial facts, opinions, or feelings—that you like fudge, for example—hardly counts as disclosure. The third requirement is that the information being disclosed is *not known by others*. There's nothing noteworthy about telling others that you are depressed or elated if they already know that.

Models of Self-Disclosure

Although our definition of self-disclosure is helpful, it doesn't reveal the important fact that not all self-disclosure is equally revealing—that some disclosing messages tell more about us than others.

Social psychologists have described two ways in which communication can be more or less disclosing.[76] Their model of **social penetration** is pictured in Figure 3.2. The first dimension of self-disclosure in this model involves the **breadth** of information volunteered—the range of subjects being discussed. For example, the breadth of disclosure in your relationship with a coworker will expand as you begin revealing information about your life away from the job as well as on-the-job information. The second dimension of self-disclosure is the **depth** of information volunteered, the shift from relatively impersonal messages to more personal ones.

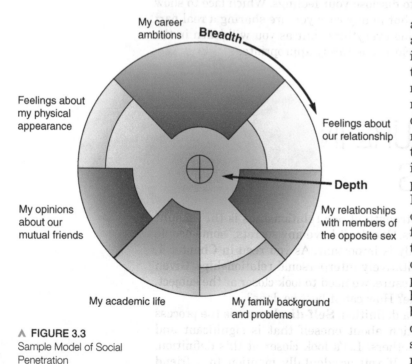

▲ FIGURE 3.3
Sample Model of Social Penetration

Depending on the breadth and depth of information shared, a relationship can be casual or intimate. In a casual relationship, the breadth may be great, but not the depth. A more intimate relationship is likely to have high depth in at least one area. The most intimate relationships are those in which disclosure is great in both breadth and depth. Social psychologists Irwin Altman and Dalmas Taylor see the development of a relationship as a progression from the periphery of their model to its center, a process that typically occurs over time. Each of your personal relationships probably has a different combination of breadth of subjects and depth of disclosure. Figure 3.3 pictures a student's self-disclosure in one relationship.

Looking at DIVERSITY

Lexie Lopez-Mayo: Culture, Gender, and Self-Disclosure

I was born in Mexico and have lived in the U.S. since I was ten. One of the things I've noticed about my Latin friends and family is that we tend to be more expressive and disclosing than many of my Euro-American friends. Of course there are exceptions to that rule, but overall I think people from my cultural background tend to reveal a lot. If we think it, we say it; if we feel it, we express it.

But culture isn't the only issue. Gender also plays a role. In my experience, Latin men easily express positive emotions, but they often hide negative feelings such as hurt and sadness. There's a strong cultural norm for Latinos to be tough, not admit failure, or show weakness—in other words, to be "macho."

I have other opportunities to see how culture and gender affect communication. My husband, who is African-American, is generally a laid-back, quiet kind of guy. However, when he's around his African-American buddies, he's much less reserved and much more disclosing. His language, volume, and mannerisms all change, and he becomes a lot more expressive.

And of course, personality plays a role in communication. I know quiet Latinas and disclosing Latinos, so culture doesn't always dictate how people express themselves. In the end, I think the way people communicate is influenced by who they are, where they're from, and whom they're with. In my case, I'm a highly expressive Latina who will tell just about anybody what I think, feel, and want!

"Culture, Gender, and Self-Disclosure" by Lexie Lopez-Mayo. Used with permission of author.

What makes the disclosure in some messages deeper than others? One way to measure depth is by how far it goes on two of the dimensions that define self-disclosure. Some revelations are certainly more *significant* than others. Consider the difference between saying "I love my family" and "I love you." Other revelations qualify as deep disclosure because they are *private*. Sharing a secret that you've told to only a few close friends is certainly a revealing act of self-disclosure, but it's even more revealing to divulge information that you've never told anyone. In general, facts ("I'm new in town") are more disclosing than clichés; opinions ("I really like it here") more than facts; and feelings ("… but I get a little lonely sometimes") more than opinions.

Another way to look at self-disclosure is by means of a device called the **Johari Window**.[77] (The window takes its name from the first names of its creators, Joseph Luft and Harry Ingham.) Imagine a frame like Figure 3.4 that contains everything there is to know about you: your likes and dislikes, your goals, your secrets, your needs—everything. This frame could be divided into information you know about yourself and things you don't know (Figure 3.5). It could also be split into things others know about you and things they don't know (Figure 3.6). Figure 3.7 reflects these divisions and has four parts.

Part 1 represents the information of which both you and the other person are aware. This part is your *open area*. Part 2 represents the *blind area*: information

Everything
about
you

∧ FIGURE 3.4

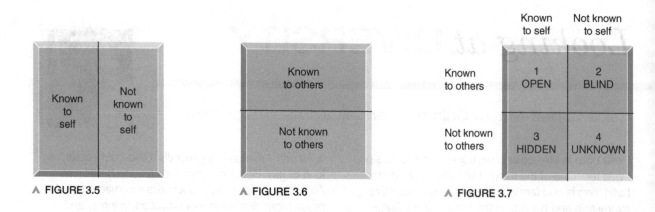

▲ FIGURE 3.5   ▲ FIGURE 3.6   ▲ FIGURE 3.7

of which you are unaware but of which the other person is aware. You learn about information in the blind area primarily through feedback from others. Part 3 represents your *hidden area*: information that you know but aren't willing to reveal to others. Items in this hidden area become public primarily through self-disclosure, which is the focus of this section. Part 4 represents information that is *unknown* to both you and others. At first the unknown area seems impossible to verify. After all, if neither you nor others know what it contains, how can you be sure it exists? We can deduce its existence because we are constantly discovering new things about ourselves. It is not unusual to discover, for example, that you have an unrecognized talent, strength, or weakness.

PAUSE *and* REFLECT

Building a Johari Window

MindTap® REFLECT... on your own communication by answering the following questions, either here or online.

You can use the Johari Window model to examine the level of self-disclosure in your own relationships.

1. Use the format described in this section to draw two Johari Windows representing the relationship between you and one other person. Remember to reverse one of the windows so that your open area and that of the other person face each other.

2. Describe which parts of yourself you keep in the hidden area. Explain your reasons for doing so. Describe the advantages or disadvantages or both of not disclosing these parts of yourself.

3. Look at the blind area of your model. Is this area large or small because of the amount of feedback (much or little) that you get from your partner or because of your willingness to receive the feedback that is offered?

4. Explain whether you are satisfied with the results illustrated by your answers. If you are not satisfied, explain what you can do to remedy the problem.

Benefits and Risks of Self-Disclosure

Occasionally we may blurt out a piece of revealing personal information, but most of the time our decision to self-disclose is conscious and deliberate. Communication researchers use the term **privacy management** to describe the choices people make to reveal or conceal information about themselves.[78] Those decisions are often made by weighing the pros and cons of self-disclosing. What are the risks and benefits of opening up?

Benefits of Self-Disclosure   There are several reasons why people choose to share personal information. As you read about each of them, see which apply to you.

Catharsis Sometimes you might disclose information in an effort to "get it off your chest." In a moment of candor, you might, for instance, reveal your regrets about having behaved badly in the past. Catharsis can provide mental and emotional relief—when handled properly.[79] Later in this chapter, you'll read guidelines for disclosing that increase the odds that you can achieve catharsis in a way that helps, instead of harms, relationships.

Reciprocity A well-documented conclusion from research is that one act of self-disclosure begets another.[80] There is no guarantee that your self-disclosures will trigger self-disclosures by others, but your own honesty can create a climate that makes others feel safer and perhaps even obligated to match your level of honesty. It's easy to imagine how telling a partner how you feel about the relationship ("I've been feeling bored lately …") would generate the same degree of candor ("You know, I've felt the same way!"). Reciprocity doesn't always occur on a turn-by-turn basis. Telling a friend today about your job-related problems might help her feel comfortable opening up to you later about her family history, when the time is right for this sort of disclosure.

Self-Clarification Sometimes you can clarify your beliefs, opinions, thoughts, attitudes, and feelings by talking about them with another person. This sort of "talking the problem out" occurs with psychotherapists, but it also goes on with others, all the way from good friends to bartenders or hairdressers.

Self-Validation If you disclose information ("I think I did the right thing …") with the hope of obtaining the listener's agreement, you are seeking validation of your behavior—confirmation of a belief that you hold about yourself. On a deeper level, this sort of self-validating disclosure seeks confirmation of important parts of your self-concept. Self-validation through self-disclosure is an important part of the "coming out" process through which gay people recognize their sexual preference and choose to integrate this knowledge into their personal, family, and social lives.[81]

Building and Maintaining Relationships Getting a relationship started requires some self-disclosure. Consider the role it plays in everything from a first date to a job interview (although the types of disclosures will be very different in these two contexts). Self-disclosure also plays a role in ongoing relational success.[82] For example, there is a strong relationship between the quality of self-disclosure and marital satisfaction.[83] The same principle applies in other personal relationships.

Social Influence Revealing personal information may increase your control over the other person and sometimes over the situation in which you and the other person find yourselves. For example, an employee who tells the boss that another firm has made overtures probably will have an increased chance of getting raises and improvements in working conditions.

Risks of Self-Disclosure While the benefits of disclosing are certainly important, opening up can also involve risks that make the decision to disclose a difficult and sometimes painful one.[84] The risks of self-disclosure fall into several categories.[85]

Rejection John Powell summed up the risks of disclosing in answering the question that forms the title of his book *Why Am I Afraid to Tell You Who I Am?*: "I am afraid to tell you who I am, because, if I tell you who I am, you may not like who I am, and that's all I have."[86] The fear of disapproval is powerful. Sometimes it is exaggerated and illogical, but there are real dangers in revealing personal information:

A: I'm starting to think of you as more than a friend. To tell the truth, I love you.
B: I think we should stop seeing one another.

Negative Impression Even if disclosure doesn't lead to total rejection, it can create a negative impression.
A: I've been thinking that we should get another dog.
B: To tell you the truth, I really don't like dogs. I haven't said so before because I know how much you love them.
A: Really? I can't imagine living with somebody who doesn't love dogs as much as I do.

"Since we're both being honest, I should tell you I have fleas."

Decrease in Relational Satisfaction Besides affecting others' opinions of you, disclosure can lead to a decrease in the satisfaction that comes from a relationship.

A: I need to tell you something. I really don't like it when you want to cuddle so much.
B: But I want to be close to you. ...

Loss of Influence Another risk of disclosure is a potential loss of influence in the relationship. Once you confess a secret weakness, your control over how the other person views you can be diminished.

A: *(Manager to employee)* I'd like to give you the weekend off, but to tell you the truth, I don't get to make any judgment calls around here. My boss makes all the decisions. In fact, he doesn't respect my opinions at all.

B: No kidding. I guess I know who to ask when I want to get anything done around here.

Hurting the Other Person Even if revealing hidden information leaves you feeling better, it might hurt others—cause them to be upset, for example. It's probably easy to imagine yourself in a situation like this:

A: I'm so ugly! I can't think of anything that will change the way I look.
B: Neither can I.

Guidelines for Self-Disclosure

By now it should be clear that deciding when and how much personal information to disclose is not a simple matter. The following guidelines can help you choose the level of self-disclosure that is appropriate in a given situation.

Is the Other Person Important to You? There are several ways in which someone might be important to you. Perhaps you have an ongoing relationship deep enough so that sharing significant parts of yourself justifies keeping your present level of togetherness intact. Or perhaps the person to whom you're considering disclosing is someone with whom you've previously related on a less personal level. But now you see a chance to grow closer, and disclosure may be the path toward developing that personal relationship.

Are the Amount and Type of Disclosure Appropriate? Some people have trouble with what's popularly known as "TMI"—sharing "too much information."[87] Classrooms are one setting where oversharing sometimes occurs. Communication researchers asked college students to report on self-disclosures they had heard in their classes.[88] While participants readily identified disclosures that helped the learning process (such as a student describing her heart condition in a physiology class), they also noted comments that crossed the line. In particular, participants objected to classroom self-disclosures that were too (a) frequent, (b) negative, (c) irrelevant to course materials, and (d) unexpected. (Take a moment and you can probably think of an example from each of these categories that you've encountered during a class.)

In general, it's wise not to divulge personal secrets in classroom discussions, with strangers, or on public Facebook postings, among other settings. Even students who appreciate self-disclosure from their teachers acknowledge that they don't want to hear too much, too often about their instructors' personal lives.[89] Of course, it's also possible to *withhold* too much information—perhaps in a counseling session or at a doctor's appointment, or in intimate relationships where nondisclosure might be regarded as deceit. The key is to recognize that there's a time and a place for engaging in, and refraining from, self-disclosure.

Is the Risk of Disclosing Reasonable? Take a realistic look at the potential risks of self-disclosure. Even if the probable benefits are great, opening yourself up to almost certain rejection may be asking for trouble. On the other

In Real Life

Appropriate and Inappropriate Self-Disclosure

Ramon has been working in an entry-level sales job for almost a year after graduating from the university. He likes the company, but he is growing frustrated at his lack of advancement. After much thought, he decides to share his concerns with his boss, Julie. Notice that Ramon's self-disclosure

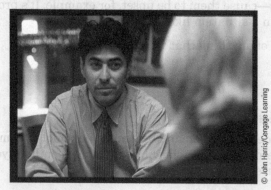

© John Harris/Cengage Learning

has the potential to enhance or jeopardize personal goals and relationships, depending on how well it follows the guidelines in these pages.

Ramon: Do you have a few minutes to talk?

Julie: Sure, no problem. Come on in.

Ramon: Do you mind if we close the door?

Julie: *(Looking a bit surprised)* Sure.

Ramon: I'd like to talk to you about the future.

Julie: The future?

Ramon: Well, it's been over a year since I started to work here. One of the things you told me in the interview back then was that people move up fast here …

Julie: Well, …

Ramon: …and I'm confused because I've been doing pretty much the same work since I was hired.

Julie: Well, we do think a lot of your work.

Ramon: I'm glad to hear that. But I'm starting to wonder how much of a chance I'll have to grow with this company. *(Ramon is disclosing his concerns about career advancement—a very appropriate topic to raise with his boss. There is some risk in this sort of disclosure, but given Ramon's apparently good standing with his boss, it seems reasonable.)*

Julie: I can understand that you're anxious about taking on more responsibility. I can tell you that you've got a good shot at advancing, if you can just hang in there for a little while.

Ramon: *(Impatiently)* That sounds good, but I've been waiting—longer than I expected to. I'm starting to wonder if some of the things I've heard around here are true.

hand, knowing that your partner is trustworthy and supportive makes the prospect of disclosing more reasonable.

Revealing personal thoughts and feelings can be especially risky on the job.[90] The politics of the workplace sometimes require communicators to keep feelings to themselves in order to accomplish both personal and organizational goals. You might, for example, find the opinions of a boss or customer personally offensive but decide to bite your tongue rather than risk losing your job or goodwill for the company.

In anticipating risks, be sure that you are realistic. It's sometimes easy to indulge in catastrophic expectations and imagine all sorts of disastrous consequences when in fact such horrors are unlikely to occur.

Will the Effect Be Constructive? Self-disclosure can be a vicious tool if it's not used carefully. Each person has a psychological "beltline." Below-the-belt

Julie: *(Suspiciously)* What kinds of things are you talking about, Ramon?

Ramon: Well, Bill and Latisha were telling me about some people who left here because they didn't get the promotions they were promised. *(Ramon discloses information that was told to him in confidence, jeopardizing the standing of two coworkers with Julie.)*

Julie: *(Firmly)* Ramon, I'm sure you understand that I can't talk about personnel decisions involving former employees. I can tell you that we try to give people all the challenges and rewards they deserve, though it can take a while.

Ramon: A year seems like more than "a while." I'm starting to think this company is more interested in having somebody with a Hispanic name on the payroll than giving me a real shot at promotion. *(Ramon's concern may be legitimate, but the sarcastic tone of his disclosure isn't constructive.)*

Julie: Look, I probably shouldn't be saying this, but I'm as frustrated as you are that it's taking so long to get a promotion arranged for you. I can tell you that there will be some personnel changes soon that will give you a good chance to make the kinds of changes you want. I think you can expect to see some changes in the next six weeks. *(Julie offers two items of self-disclosure that encourage Ramon to reciprocate.)*

Ramon: That's really good to hear! I have to tell you that I've started to think about other career options.

Not because I want to leave here, but because I just can't afford to stand still. I really need to start bringing home more money. I don't want to be one of those losers who still can't afford to buy his own house by the time he's forty. *(Ramon makes a big mistake disclosing his opinion about home ownership—a topic that has no relevance to the discussion at hand.)*

Julie: Gee, I'm still renting …

Ramon: Oh, I didn't mean that the way it sounded … *(But the damage from the inappropriate disclosure is already done.)*

Julie: Anyway, I'm glad you let me know about your concerns. I hope you can hang in there for just a little while longer.

Ramon: Sure. Six weeks, huh? I'll keep an eye on the calendar!

After the conversation, Julie still thinks Ramon is a candidate for promotion, but some of his inappropriate disclosures have left her with doubts about his maturity and good judgment, which she didn't have before they spoke. Julie makes a mental note to keep an eye on Ramon and to reconsider the amount of responsibility she gives him until he has demonstrated the ability to share his personal feelings and concerns more constructively.

MindTap® APPLY… this situation to your life by answering questions online.

jabs are a powerful way to disable another person, though usually at great cost to the relationship. It's important to consider the effects of your candor before opening up to others. Comments such as "I've always thought you were pretty unintelligent" or "Last year I made love to your best friend" can be devastating—to the listener, to the relationship, and to your self-esteem.

Is the Self-Disclosure Reciprocated?   The amount of personal information you reveal will usually depend on how much the other person reveals. As a rule, disclosure is a two-way street. For example, couples are happiest when their levels of openness are roughly equal.[91]

There are a few times when one-way disclosure is acceptable. Most of them involve formal, therapeutic relationships in which a client approaches a trained professional with the goal of resolving a problem. For instance, you wouldn't necessarily expect to hear about your doctor's personal ailments

SKILL *Builder*

Appropriate Self-Disclosure

MindTap® PRACTICE... your skill at appropriate self-disclosure either here or online.

Use the guidelines for self-disclosure in this section to develop one scenario where you might reveal a

self-disclosing message. Create a message of this type, and use the information in this chapter to discuss the advantages and disadvantages of sharing this message.

during a physical checkup—although it's been known to happen, sometimes to the chagrin of the patient.[92]

Do You Have a Moral Obligation to Disclose?

Sometimes we are morally obliged to disclose personal information. For example, surveys reveal that a majority of HIV-positive patients believe they have a duty to reveal their status to healthcare providers and partners, even when doing so risks their pride and dignity and can lead to being stigmatized.[93] Despite this prevailing belief, two decades of research has shown that 40 percent of persons testing positive for HIV did not reveal this result to their sexual partners.[94]

ALTERNATIVES TO SELF-DISCLOSURE

Although self-disclosure plays an important role in interpersonal relationships, it isn't the only type of communication available. To understand why complete honesty isn't always an easy or ideal choice, consider some familiar dilemmas:

- A new acquaintance is much more interested in becoming friends than you are. She invites you to a party this weekend. You aren't busy, but you don't want to go. What would you say?

- Your boss asks you what you think of his new wardrobe. You think it's cheap and flashy. Would you tell him?

- You're attracted to your best friend's mate, who has confessed that she or he feels the same way about you. You both agreed that you won't act on your feelings and that even bringing up the subject would make your friend feel terribly insecure. Now your friend has asked whether you're attracted at all to the mate. Would you tell the truth?

- You've just been given a large, extremely ugly painting as a gift by a relative who visits your home often. How would you respond to the question "Where will you put it?"

Although total honesty is desirable in principle, it can have potentially unpleasant consequences. It's tempting to avoid situations where self-disclosure would be difficult, but examples like the preceding ones show that evasion isn't always possible. Research and personal experience show that communicators—even those with the best intentions—aren't always completely honest when they find themselves in situations in which honesty would be uncomfortable.[95] Four common alternatives to self-disclosure are silence, lying, equivocating, and hinting. We will look closer at each one.

Silence

One alternative to self-disclosure is to keep your thoughts and feelings to yourself. You can get a sense of how much you rely on silence instead of disclosing by keeping a record of when you do and don't express your opinions. You're likely to find that withholding thoughts and feelings is a common approach for you. Telling the whole truth may be honest, but it can jeopardize you, the other person, and your relationship. Most thoughtful communicators would keep quiet rather than blurt out unsolicited opinions like "You look awful" or "You talk too much." Social scientists have found that people often make distinctions between "lies of omission" and "lies of commission"—and that saying nothing (omission) is usually judged less harshly than telling an outright lie (commission).[96] One study showed that, in the workplace, withholding information is often seen as a better alternative than lying or engaging in intentional deception.[97]

Lying

To most of us, lying appears to be a breach of ethics. Although lying to gain unfair advantage over an unknowing victim seems clearly wrong, another kind of mistruth—the "benevolent lie"—isn't so easy to dismiss as completely unethical. A **benevolent lie** is defined (at least by the teller) as unmalicious, or even helpful, to the person to whom it is told.

Whether or not they are innocent, benevolent lies are quite common, both in face-to-face and online relationships.[98] In research spanning four decades, a significant majority of people acknowledged that, even in their closest relationships, there are times when lying is justified.[99] In one study, 130 subjects were asked to keep track of the truthfulness of their everyday conversational statements.[100] Only 38.5 percent of these statements—slightly more than one-third—proved to be totally honest. In another experiment, subjects recorded their conversations over a two-day period and later counted their own deceptions. The average lie rate: three fibs for every ten minutes of conversation.[101]

Most people think that benevolent lies are told for the benefit of the recipient. In the study cited earlier, the majority of subjects claimed that such lying is "the right thing to do." Other research paints a less flattering picture of who benefits most from lying. One study found that two out of every three lies are told for "selfish reasons."[102] Table 3.1 identifies many of the reasons that people choose to lie—some more self-serving than others.

Research has shown that lying does, in fact, threaten relationships.[103] Not all lies are equally devastating, however. One study suggests that a liar's motives make a significant difference in whether the deception is perceived as acceptable

TABLE 3.1 Some Reasons for Lying

Reason	Example
Save face for others	"Don't worry—I'm sure nobody noticed that stain on your shirt."
Save face for self	"I wasn't looking at the files—I was accidentally in the wrong drawer."
Acquire resources	"Oh, *please* let me add this class. If I don't get in, I'll never graduate on time!"
Protect resources	"I'd like to lend you the money, but I'm short myself."
Initiate interaction	"Excuse me, I'm lost. Do you live around here?"
Be socially gracious	"No, I'm not bored—tell me more about your vacation."
Avoid conflict	"It's not a big deal. We can do it your way. Really."
Avoid interaction	"That sounds like fun, but I'm busy Saturday night."
Leave taking	"Oh, look what time it is! I've got to run!"

© Cengage Learning

by others.[104] If a lie appears to be self-serving and exploitive, it will most likely be treated as a relational transgression. On the other hand, if a mistruth seems aimed at sparing another's feelings, the chances of being forgiven increase.

Feelings like dismay and betrayal are greatest when the relationship is most intense, when the importance of the subject is high, and when there is previous suspicion that the other person isn't being completely honest. Of these three factors, the importance of the information lied about proved to be the key factor in provoking a relational crisis. We may be able to cope with "misdemeanor" lying, but "felonies" are a grave threat. In fact, the discovery of major deception can lead to the end of the relationship. More than two-thirds of the subjects in one study reported that their relationship had ended because they discovered a lie. Furthermore, they attributed the breakup directly to the lie.

The lesson here is clear: Lying about major parts of your relationship can have the gravest consequences. If preserving a relationship is important, honesty—at least about important matters—really does appear to be the best policy.

Equivocating

When faced with the dilemma of either lying or telling an unpleasant truth, communicators typically opt for a third approach—equivocation.[105] When a friend asks what you think of an awful outfit, you could say, "It's really unusual—one of a kind!" Likewise, if you are too angry to accept a friend's apology but don't want to appear petty, you might say, "Don't worry about it." One humorous set of suggestions shows how equivocation can help a reluctant business contact provide ambiguous references for an incompetent job applicant:

For a lazy worker: "You will be lucky to get this person to work for you." For someone with no talent: "I recommend this candidate with no qualifications."

For a candidate who should not be hired under any circumstances: "Waste no time hiring this person."

The value of equivocation becomes clear when you consider the alternatives. Consider the dilemma of what to say when you've been given an unwanted present—an ugly painting, for example—and the giver asks what you think of it. How can you respond? On one hand, you need to choose between telling the truth and lying. On the other hand, you have a choice of whether to make your response clear or vague. Figure 3.8 displays these choices. Among the choices, it's clear that Option 1—an equivocal, true response—is preferable to the others in several respects.

As one team of researchers put it, "equivocation is neither a false message nor a clear truth, but rather an alternative used precisely when both of these are to be avoided."[106]

Most people will usually choose to equivocate rather than tell a lie. In a series of experiments, subjects chose among telling a face-saving lie, telling the truth, and equivocating. Only 6 percent chose the lie, and only between 3 and 4 percent chose the hurtful truth. By contrast, more than 90 percent chose the equivocal response.[107] People *say* they prefer truth telling to equivocating, but given the choice, they prefer to finesse the truth.[108]

Equivocal

OPTION I: (Equivocal, True Message) "What an unusual painting! I've never seen anything like it!"	**OPTION II:** (Equivocal, False Message) "Thanks for the painting. I'll hang it as soon as I can find just the right place."
OPTION III: (Clear, True Message) "It's just not my kind of painting. I don't like the colors, the style, or the subject."	**OPTION IV:** (Clear, False Message) "What a beautiful painting! I love it."

True   False

Clear

▲ **FIGURE 3.8**
Dimensions of Truthfulness and Equivocation

© Cengage Learning

DILBERT BY SCOTT ADAMS

Direct Statement	Face-Saving Hint
I'm too busy to continue with this conversation.	I know you're busy; I better let you go.
Please don't smoke in here because it's bothering me.	I'm pretty sure that smoking isn't permitted here.
I'd like to invite you out for lunch, but I don't want to risk a "no" answer.	Gee, it's almost lunchtime. Have you ever eaten at that new Italian restaurant around the corner?

ETHICAL *Challenge*

Must We Always Tell the Truth?

"Is there really a Santa Claus?"
"Am I talking too much?"
"Isn't this the cutest baby you've ever seen?"
"Was it good for you?"

Questions like these often seem to invite answers that are less than totally honest. The research summarized in the "Alternatives to Self-Disclosure" section reveals that, at one time or another, virtually everyone avoids telling the complete truth. We seem to be caught between the time-honored commandment "Thou shall not lie" and the fact that everybody does seem to bend the truth, if only for altruistic reasons. What, then, are the ethics of honesty?

Philosopher Immanuel Kant had a clear answer: We may be able to evade unpleasant situations by keeping quiet, but we must always tell the complete truth when there is no way to avoid speaking up. He said that "truthfulness in statements which cannot be avoided is the formal duty of an individual . . . however great may be the disadvantage accruing to himself or another."[a] Kant's unbending position didn't make any exception for lies or equivocations told in the best interests of the receiver. In his moral code, lying is wrong—period.

Not all ethicists have shared Kant's rigid standards of truth telling. Utilitarian philosophers claim that the way to determine the morality of a behavior is to explore whether it leads to the greatest happiness for the greatest number of people. While encouraging truth-telling whenever possible, philosopher Sissela Bok offers some circumstances in which deception may be justified: doing good, avoiding harm, and protecting a larger truth.[b]

Bok is realistic enough to recognize that liars are prone to self-deceptive justifications. For this reason, she tempers her utilitarian position with a *test of publicity*. She suggests that we ask how others would respond if they knew that we were being untruthful. If most disinterested observers with all the facts supported untruthful speech as the best course, then it passes the test of publicity.

MindTap® APPLY... the ethical principles introduced here by answering the following questions, either here or online.

Submit your case for avoiding the truth to a "court of self-disclosure":

1. Recall recent situations in which you have used each of the following evasive approaches: lying, equivocating, and hinting.

2. Write an anonymous description of each situation, including a justification for your behavior, on a separate sheet of paper. Submit the cases to a panel of "judges" (most likely fellow students), who will evaluate the morality of these decisions.

Hinting

Hints are more direct than equivocal statements. Whereas an equivocal statement isn't necessarily aimed at changing others' behavior, a hint does aim to get a desired response from others.[109]

Hinting can spare others discomfort that comes with the undiluted truth. The face-saving value of hints explains why communicators are more likely to be indirect than fully disclosing when they deliver a potentially embarrassing message.[110] The success of a hint depends on the other person's ability to pick up the unexpressed message. Your subtle remarks might go right over the head of an insensitive receiver—or one who chooses not to respond. If this happens, you may decide to be more direct. If the costs of a direct message seem too high, however, you can withdraw without risk.

The Ethics of Evasion

It's easy to see why people choose hints, equivocations, and benevolent lies instead of complete self-disclosure. These strategies provide a way to manage difficult situations that is easier than the alternatives for both the speaker and the receiver of the message. In this sense, successful liars, equivocators, and hinters can be said to possess a certain kind of communicative competence. On the other hand, there are certainly times when honesty is the right approach, even if it's painful. At times like these, evaders could be viewed as lacking the competence or the integrity to handle a situation most effectively.

Are hints, benevolent lies, and equivocations ethical alternatives to self-disclosure? Some of the examples in these pages suggest that the answer is a qualified "yes." Many social scientists and philosophers agree. As the Ethical Challenge in this section shows, some argue that the morality of a speaker's *motives* for lying, not the lie itself, ought to be judged, and others ask whether the *effects* of a lie will be worth the deception.

Perhaps the right questions to ask are whether an indirect message is truly in the interests of the receiver and whether this sort of evasion is the only, or the best, way to behave in a given situation.

SUMMARY

The self-concept is a relatively stable set of perceptions that individuals hold about themselves. Self-esteem has to do with evaluations of self-worth. Some of the characteristics of the self are a result of inherited personality traits. In addition, the self-concept is created through messages from significant others—reflected appraisal—and through social comparison with reference groups. The self-concept is subjective and may vary from the way a person is perceived by others. Although the self evolves over time, the self-concept resists change. Other factors that affect the self-concept are culture and sex/gender. One's self-concept, as well as the self-concepts of others, can be changed through self-fulfilling prophecies.

Impression management consists of strategic communication designed to influence others' perceptions of an individual. Impression management aims at presenting to others one or more faces, which may be different from private, spontaneous behavior that occurs outside of others' presence. Communicators engage in creating an identity by managing their manner, appearance, and the settings in which they interact with others. Impression management occurs both in face-to-face and mediated communication. Because each person has a variety of faces that he or she can reveal, choosing which one to present need not be dishonest.

An important issue in interpersonal relationships is self-disclosure: honest, revealing messages about the self that are intentionally directed toward others. The social penetration model and the Johari Window are tools for describing our self-disclosure with others. Communicators disclose personal information for a variety of reasons and benefits: catharsis, reciprocity, self-clarification, self-validation, impression management, relationship maintenance and enhancement, and social influence. The risks of self-disclosure include the possibility of rejection, making a negative impression, a decline in relational satisfaction, a loss of influence, and hurting the other person. Four alternatives to self-disclosure are silence, lying, equivocating, and hinting. These can be ethical alternatives to self-disclosure; however, whether they are depends on the speaker's motives and the effects of the deception.

KEY TERMS

benevolent lie
breadth
cognitive conservatism
depth
face
impression management
Johari Window
perceived self
personality
presenting self

privacy management
reference groups
reflected appraisal
self-concept
self-disclosure
self-esteem
self-fulfilling prophecy
significant others
social comparison
social penetration

4

PERCEPTION: WHAT YOU SEE IS WHAT YOU GET

AFTER STUDYING THE TOPICS IN THIS CHAPTER, YOU
SHOULD BE ABLE TO:

1. Describe how the processes of selection, organization,
interpretation, and negotiation shape communication in
a given situation.

2. Explain how influences on perception affect
communication in a specific situation.

3. Analyze how common perception tendencies have
distorted your appraisals of another person, and hence
your communication. Use this information to present a
more accurate alternative set of perceptions.

4. Demonstrate how you might use the skill of perception
checking in a significant relationship.

5. Enhance your cognitive complexity by applying the
"pillow method" in a significant disagreement. Explain
how your expanded view of this situation might affect
your communication with the other(s) involved.

*S*tudy M. C. Escher's drawing *Relativity* seen here. It pictures a strange universe in which the inhabitants of each world exist at right angles, disconnected from one another's experience. This surreal vision provides a useful metaphor for challenges we encounter every day. Each of us experiences a different reality, and failing to understand other people's point of view can lead to problems on both practical and relational levels. But perceptual differences can enhance as well as interfere with relationships. By seeing the world through others' eyes, you can gain insights that are different—and often more valuable—than those arising out of your own experiences.

This chapter will help you deal with the challenge of communicating in the face of perceptual differences. We will begin by looking at some of the reasons why the world appears different to each of us. In our survey we'll explore several areas: how our psychological makeup, personal needs, interests, and biases shape our perceptions; the physiological factors that influence our view of the world; the social roles that affect our image of events; and the role that culture plays in creating our ideas of what behavior is proper. After examining the perceptual factors that can drive us apart, we'll look at two useful skills for bridging the perceptual gap.

THE PERCEPTION PROCESS

Our perception of the world around us is affected by who we are. A simple walk in the park would probably be a different experience for companions with different interests. A botanist might notice the vegetation; a fashion designer might pay attention to the way people are dressed; and an artist might be aware of the colors and forms of the people and surroundings. It's simply impossible to be aware of everything, no matter how attentive we might be. There's just too much going on. Because this ability to organize our perceptions is such a critical factor in our ability to function, we need to begin our study of perception by taking a closer look at this process. We can do so by examining the four steps by which we attach meaning to our experiences: selection, organization, interpretation, and negotiation.

Selection

Since we're exposed to more input than we can possibly manage, the first step in perception is the **selection** of which impressions we will attend to. Several factors cause us to notice some things and ignore others.

Stimuli that are *intense* often attract our attention. Something that is louder, larger, or brighter stands out. This explains why—other things being equal—we're more likely to remember extremely tall or short people, and why someone who laughs or talks loudly at a party attracts more attention (not always favorable) than do quiet guests.

Repetitious stimuli, repetitious stimuli, repetitious stimuli, repetitious stimuli, repetitious stimuli, repetitious stimuli also attract attention.[1] Just as a quiet but steadily dripping faucet can come to dominate our awareness, people to whom we're frequently exposed become noticeable.

ATTENTION IS ALSO FREQUENTLY RELATED TO contrast OR change IN STIMULATION. Put differently, unchanging people or things become less noticeable. This principle gives an explanation (excuse?) for why we take wonderful people for granted when we interact with them frequently. It's only when they stop being so wonderful or go away that we appreciate them.

Motives also determine what information we select from our environment. If you're anxious about being late for a date, you'll notice whatever clocks may be around you; and if you're hungry, you'll become aware of any restaurants, markets, and billboards advertising food in your path. Motives also determine how we perceive people. For example, someone on the lookout for a romantic adventure will be especially aware of attractive potential partners, whereas the same person at a different time might be oblivious to anyone but police or medical personnel in an emergency.

Selection isn't just a matter of attending to some stimuli: It also involves ignoring other cues. If, for example, you decide that someone is a terrific person, you may overlook his or her flaws. If you are focused on examples of unfair male bosses, you might not recognize unfair female bosses. For an interesting example of how we select some stimuli and ignore others, search "perception illusion" online and look for videos related to the work of researcher Daniel Simons.[2]

∧ FIGURE 4.1
© Cengage Learning

Organization

Along with selecting information from the environment, we must arrange it in some meaningful way. You can see how the principle of **organization** works by looking at Figure 4.1. You can view the picture either as one of a vase or as one of two twins, depending on whether you focus on the light or the dark areas. In instances such as this, we make sense of stimuli by noticing some data that stand out as a *figure* against a less striking *ground*. The "vase-face" drawing is interesting, because it allows us to choose between two sets of figure-ground relationships.

This principle of figure-ground organization operates in communication, too. Recall, for instance, how certain speech can suddenly stand out from a babble of voices. Sometimes the words are noticeable because they include your name, whereas at other times they might be spoken by a familiar voice.

Each of us can organize our impressions of other communicators using a number of schemes (called *perceptual schema* by social scientists). Sometimes we classify people according to their *appearance*: male or female, beautiful or ugly, heavy or thin, young or old, and so on. At other times we classify people according to their *social roles*: student, attorney, wife, etc. Another way we classify people is by their *interaction style*: friendly, helpful, aloof, and sarcastic are examples. In other cases we classify people by their *psychological traits* such as curious, nervous, and insecure. Finally, we can use others' *membership*, classifying them according to the group to which they belong: Democrat, immigrant, Christian, and so on.

The perceptual schemas we use shape the way we think about and communicate with others. If you've classified a professor, for example, as "friendly," you'll handle questions or problems one way; if you've classified a professor as "mean," your behavior will probably be quite different. What constructs do you use to classify the people you encounter in your life? Consider how your relationship might change if you used different schemas.

Stereotyping   After we've chosen an organizing scheme to classify people, we use that scheme to make generalizations and predictions about members of the groups who fit the categories we use. For example, if you're especially aware of gender, you might be alert to the differences between the way men and women behave or the way they are treated. If religion plays an important part in your life, you might think of members of your faith differently from others. If ethnicity is an important issue for you, you probably tune in to the differences between members of various ethnic groups. There's nothing wrong with generalizations as long as they are accurate. In fact, it would be impossible to get through life without them.

But when generalizations lose touch with reality, they lead to **stereotyping**—exaggerated generalizations associated with a categorizing system.[3] Stereotypes may be based on a kernel of truth, but they go beyond the facts at hand and make claims that usually have no valid basis.

You can begin to get a sense of your tendency to make generalizations and to stereotype by completing the following sentences:

1. Women are _____
2. Men are _____

3. Republicans are _____
4. Vegetarians are _____
5. Muslims are _____
6. Older people are _____

It's likely that you were able to complete each sentence without much hesitation. Does this mean you were stereotyping? You can answer this question by deciding whether your generalizations fit the three characteristics of stereotypes (we'll use "older people" as an example):

- *You often categorize people on the basis of an easily recognized characteristic.* Age is relatively simple to identify, so if you see someone who appears to be in her eighties, you might quickly categorize her as "elderly."

- *You ascribe a set of characteristics to most or all members of a category.* Based on your (limited) experiences with some elderly relatives, you conclude that older people have trouble hearing and are not mentally alert.

- *You apply the set of characteristics to any member of the group.* When you run into an elderly person at the store, you talk very loudly and slowly. Of course, that can be extremely annoying to energetic and sprightly older people who do not fit your stereotype.[4]

PAUSE *and* REFLECT

Your Perceptual Schema

MindTap® REFLECT . . . on your perceptual schema by answering the following questions, either here or online.

1. Identify which of the five general types of organizing schema (i.e., appearance, social roles, interaction style, psychological traits, or membership) you would use to classify people in each of the following contexts. After you've selected a primary organizing schema, offer a personal description within each type (e.g., attractive, roughly the same age as me).

   a. Spending time with new acquaintances at a party

   b. Socializing with fellow workers on the job

   c. Choosing teammates for an important class project

   d. Offering help to a stranded motorist

2. For each of the given contexts, consider:

   a. Other schema you might use.

   b. The consequences of using the schema you originally chose and the alternative you identified in the preceding step.

   c. In general, how might your relationships change if you used different constructs?

▲ The comedy *Dear White People* chronicles the challenges faced by the handful of black students at a fictitious Ivy League university. The film shines a humorous spotlight on the juggling act the students of color face retaining their unique identities while being stereotyped by the white majority. When do you stereotype others? How does that affect your relationships with people from different backgrounds?

Allstar Picture library

Once we buy into stereotypes, we often seek out isolated behaviors that support our inaccurate beliefs. For example, men and women in conflict often remember only behaviors of the other sex that fit their gender stereotypes.[5] They then point to these behaviors—which might not be representative of how the other person typically behaves—as "evidence" to suit their stereotypical and inaccurate claims: "Look! There you go criticizing me again. Typical for a woman!"

Stereotypes can plague interracial communication.[6] Surveys of college student attitudes show that many blacks characterize whites as "demanding" and "manipulative," whereas many whites characterize blacks as "loud" and "ostentatious." Stereotypes like these can hamper professional relationships as well as personal ones. For example, doctor–patient communication in the United States—particularly between white physicians and minority patients—can suffer from stereotyping on both sides. Physicians may fail to provide important information because they think their patients won't understand, and patients may not ask important questions because they believe their doctors don't have time for them. These kinds of expectations lead to self-fulfilling spirals and poorer health care.[7]

Stereotyping doesn't always arise from bad intentions. In some cases, careless generalizations can grow from good intentions, and even from a little bit of knowledge. For example, knowing that people raised in collectivistic cultures (see Chapter 3) tend to conform to group norms may lead you to mistakenly assume that anyone you meet from such a background is likely to be a selfless team player. But not all members of a group are equally collectivistic, or individualistic, for that matter. For example, a study of Americans of European and Latin descent showed differences within each group.[8] Some Latinos were more independent than some Euro Americans, and vice versa. Moreover, teens in Japan (a traditionally collectivist culture) say they often feel torn between collectivism and individualism, between time-honored traditions and contemporary trends.[9] As our world's "global village" becomes more connected by technology and media, generalizations about specific cultures are likely to become less accurate.

One way to avoid the kinds of communication problems that come from excessive stereotyping is to decategorize others, giving yourself a chance to treat them as individuals instead of assuming that they possess the same characteristics as every other member of the group to which you assign them. Consider how your communication with others might change if you moved some of their characteristics to the "background" and others to the "foreground" during your interactions.

Punctuation   The process of organizing goes beyond our generalized perceptions of people. We also can sequence our interactions with others in different ways, and this can have a powerful effect on our relationships. Communication theorists use the term **punctuation** to describe the determination of causes and effects in a series of interactions.[10] You can begin to understand how punctuation operates by visualizing a running quarrel between a husband and wife. The husband accuses the wife of being too demanding, whereas she complains that he is withdrawing from her. Notice that the order in which each partner punctuates this cycle affects how the quarrel looks. The husband begins by blaming the wife: "I withdraw because you're so demanding." The wife organizes the situation differently, starting with the husband: "I demand so much because you withdraw." These kinds of demand-withdraw arguments are frequent in intimate relationships.[11] After the cycle gets rolling, it is impossible to say which accusation is accurate. The answer depends on how the sentence is punctuated. Figure 4.2 illustrates how this process operates.

Differing punctuations can lead to a variety of communication problems. Notice how the following situations seem different depending on how they're punctuated:

"I don't like your friend because he never has anything to say."

"He doesn't talk to you because you act like you don't like him."

"I keep talking because you interrupt so much."

"I interrupt because you don't give me a chance to say what's on my mind."

The kind of finger-pointing that goes along with arguing over which punctuation scheme is correct will probably make matters worse. It's far more productive to recognize that a dispute can look different to each party and then move on to the more important question of "What can we do to make things better?"

THE INVESTIGATION

John Jonik

Interpretation

After we have selected and organized our perceptions, we interpret the information we've collected and sorted. **Interpretation**—attaching meaning to

Punctuation #1

Demanding ⟶ Withdrawing ⟶ Demanding ⟶ Withdrawing

Punctuation #2

Withdrawing ⟶ Demanding ⟶ Withdrawing ⟶ Demanding

◄ **FIGURE 4.2**
The Same Event Can Be
Punctuated in More Than
One Way

SKILL *Builder*

Punctuation Practice

MindTap® **PRACTICE …** your skill at different punctuation patterns by answering the following questions either here or online.

You can appreciate how different punctuation patterns can influence attitudes and behavior by following these directions.

1. Use the format pictured in Figure 4.2 to diagram the following situations from the point of view of both people involved. Consider how the differing punctuation patterns would affect the way the two people in each situation respond to one another.

   a. A father and daughter are growing more and more distant. The daughter withdraws because she interprets her father's coolness as rejection. The father views his daughter's aloofness as a rebuff and withdraws further.

   b. The relationship between two friends is becoming strained. One jokes to lighten up the tension, and the other becomes more tense.

   c. A dating couple is on the verge of breaking up. One partner frequently asks the other to show more affection. The other withdraws physical contact.

2. Now identify an ongoing difficult communication issue in your own life. Punctuate it in two ways: how you would punctuate it, and how the other person might punctuate it. Discuss how seeing the issue from the other person's point of view might change the way you communicate as you discuss the issue.

sense data—plays a role in virtually every interpersonal act. Is the person who smiles at you across a crowded room interested in romance or simply being polite? Is a friend's kidding a sign of affection or irritation? Should you take an invitation to "drop by any time" literally or not?

Several factors cause us to interpret an event in one way or another:

Degree of involvement with the other person. Two coworkers offer you the same excuse for why they were late to work. One is a close friend; the other is someone you barely know. Chances are good that you'll interpret your friend's excuse far more charitably.

Personal experience. What meanings have similar events held? If, for example, you've been gouged by landlords in the past, you might be skeptical about an apartment manager's assurances that careful housekeeping will assure you the refund of your cleaning deposit.

Assumptions about human behavior. "People generally do as little work as possible to get by." "In spite of their mistakes, people are doing the best they can." Beliefs like these will shape the way we interpret another's actions.

Attitudes. The attitudes we hold shape the way we make sense of others' behaviors. For example, what would you think if you overheard one man say "I love you" to another man? In one study, people with a high degree of homophobia (the fear of or discrimination against homosexuals) were likely to interpret this comment as an indication that the speaker was gay. Those with lower levels of homophobia were more likely to regard the affectionate statement as platonic rather than romantic.[12]

Expectations. Anticipation shapes interpretations.[13] As you read in Chapter 3, teachers who expect their students to do well will regard and treat those pupils differently. The same is true with our interpersonal interactions: Our expectations affect how we perceive and behave around others. We'll talk more about this common tendency later in the chapter.

Knowledge. If you know that a friend has just been jilted by a lover or been fired from a job, you'll interpret his aloof behavior differently than you would if you were unaware of what had happened. If you know that an instructor speaks sarcastically to all students, you won't be as likely to take her remarks personally.

Self-concept. When you're feeling insecure, the world is a very different place from the world you experience when you're feeling secure. For example, the recipient's self-concept is the most significant factor in determining whether people who are being teased interpret the teaser's motives as being friendly or hostile, and whether they respond with comfort or defensiveness.[14] The way we feel about ourselves strongly influences how we interpret others' behavior.

Relational satisfaction. The behavior that seems positive when you are happy with a partner might seem completely different when you are discontent with that person. For example, unsatisfied partners in a couple are more likely than satisfied partners to blame one another when things go wrong.[15] They are also more likely to believe that their partners are selfish and have negative intentions.

Although we have talked about selection, organization, and interpretation separately, the three phases of perception can occur in differing sequences. For example, a parent or babysitter's past interpretations (such as "Jason is a troublemaker") can influence future selections (his behavior becomes especially noticeable) and the organization of events (when there's a fight, the assumption is that Jason started it). As with all communication, perception is an ongoing process in which it is difficult to pin down beginnings and endings.

Negotiation

So far our discussion has focused on the components of perception—selection, organization, and interpretation—that take place in each individual's mind. But perception isn't just a solitary activity. A big part of sense-making occurs between and among people as they influence one another's perceptions and try to achieve a shared perspective. This process is known as **negotiation**.

It's rare to draw a conclusion about something or someone without comparing notes with others. Say for instance that you think a person you just met is attractive. It's likely that you'll ask friends for their opinions. If you hear negative appraisals, you might shift your initial perception—maybe not radically, but at least a bit. In one study that examined this process, college students rated the attractiveness of models in a series of photos.[16] Those who were able to see others' evaluations of the same photos slowly shifted their ratings to match the consensus. This suggests that beauty isn't just in the eye of the (individual) beholder—it's in the eyes of the (negotiating) beholders.

▲ In the film *Enough Said*, Eva (Julia Louis-Dreyfus) changes her positive appraisal of new boyfriend Albert (James Gandolfini) after hearing negative information about him from his ex-wife. Has your narrative opinion of another person shifted after receiving new input from others?

One way to understand how negotiation operates is to view interpersonal communication as an exchange of stories. Scholars call the stories we use to describe our personal world **narratives**.[17] Virtually every interpersonal situation can be described by more than one narrative. These narratives often differ. Ask two quarreling children why they're fighting, and they'll each describe how the other person is responsible for launching the conflict. Likewise, courtrooms are filled with opponents who tell very different narratives about who is the "villain" and who is the "hero." Conflict management is often a process of negotiating divergent perceptions of the same event.

When our narratives clash with those of others, we can either hang on to our own point of view and refuse to consider anyone else's (usually not productive) or we can try to negotiate a narrative that creates at least some common ground. Shared narratives provide the best chance for smooth communication. For example, romantic partners who celebrate their successful struggles against relational obstacles are happier than those who don't have this shared appreciation.[18] Likewise, couples who agree about the important turning points in their relationships are more satisfied than those who have different views of what incidents were most important.[19]

Shared narratives don't have to be accurate to be powerful. Couples who report being happily married after fifty or more years seem to collude in a relational narrative that doesn't jibe with the facts.[20] They agree that they rarely have conflict, although objective analysis reveals that they have had their share of struggles. Without overtly agreeing to do so, they choose to blame outside forces or unusual circumstances for problems instead of blaming each other. They offer the most charitable interpretations of each other's behavior, believing that their spouse acts with good intentions when things don't go well. They seem willing to forgive, or even forget, transgressions. Communication researcher Judy Pearson evaluates these findings:

> Should we conclude that happy couples have a poor grip on reality? Perhaps they do, but is the reality of one's marriage better known by outside onlookers than by the players themselves? The conclusion is evident. One key to a long happy marriage is to tell yourself and others that you have one and then to behave as though you do![21]

INFLUENCES ON PERCEPTION

Now that we've explored the processes by which we perceive, it's time to look at some of the influences that cause us to select, organize, interpret, and negotiate information.

Access to Information

We can only make sense of what we know, and none of us knows everything about even the closest people in our lives. When new information becomes available, your perceptions of others change. If you see your instructor only when she's teaching in the classroom, your conclusions about her will be based solely on her behaviors in that role. You might change your perception if you observe her in the roles of rush-hour driver, concert-goer, or grocery shopper. (Many of us have memories of running into our grade school teachers at the store and being shocked that they had lives outside of school.)

We often gain access to new information about others when their roles overlap. Consider how that might occur at an office party. A person's "office" and "party" roles are usually quite different— so at an offsite work celebration, you may see behaviors you hadn't expected. Similarly, when your sweetheart takes you home to meet the family, you might get to watch your partner playing "spoiled son" or "princess daughter" roles. If you've ever said, "I saw a whole new side of you tonight," chances are good it's because you gained access to information you didn't have before.

Social media can provide new information that can affect perceptions. That's why job hunters are encouraged to clean up their Internet profiles, being careful to manage the impressions they might make.[22] It's also why children and parents don't always want to be Facebook friends with each other.[23] Some roles are best kept private—or at least played to a select audience.

∧ *The Disappearance of Eleanor Rigby* is the collective title of three separate movies. Writer/director Ned Benson tells the same story from three different perspectives, titled *Him, Her,* and *Them.* How might an interpersonal relationship of yours look and sound different if told from your point of view, your partner's perspective, or your joint retelling of the story?

Physiological Influences

Another set of influences we need to examine involves our physical makeup. Within the wide range of human similarities, each of us perceives the world in a unique way because of physiological factors. In other words, although the same events exist "out there," each of us receives different images because of our unique perceptual hardware. Consider the long list of physiological factors that shapes our views of the world: the senses, age, health and fatigue, hunger, biological cycles, and psychological challenges.

The Senses   The differences in how each of us sees, hears, tastes, touches, and smells stimuli can affect interpersonal relationships. Consider the following everyday situations:

"Turn down that radio! It's going to make me go deaf."
"It's not too loud. If I turn it down, it will be impossible to hear it."

"It's freezing in here."
"Are you kidding? We'll suffocate if you turn up the heat!"

"Why don't you pass that truck? The highway is clear for a mile."
"I can't see that far, and I'm not going to get us killed."

These disputes aren't just over matters of opinion. The sensory data we receive are different. Differences in vision and hearing are the easiest to recognize, but other differences exist as well. There is evidence that identical foods taste differently to different individuals.[24] Scents that please some people repel others. Likewise, temperature variations that leave some of us uncomfortable are inconsequential to others. Recognizing these differences won't eliminate them, but it will make it easier to remember that the other person's preferences aren't crazy, just different.

Psychological Challenges   Some differences in perception are rooted in neurology. For instance, people with AD/HD (attention-deficit/hyperactivity disorder) are easily distracted from tasks and have difficulty delaying gratification. It's easy to imagine how those with AD/HD might find a long lecture boring and tedious, while other audience members are fascinated by the same lecture. People with bipolar disorder experience significant mood swings in which their perceptions of events, friends, and even family members shift dramatically. The National Institute of Mental Health estimates that between five and seven million Americans are affected by these two disorders alone—and many other psychological conditions influence people's perceptions.[25] It's important to remember that when others see and respond to the world differently than we do, there may be causes beyond those we immediately recognize.

Age   We experience the world differently throughout our lifetimes. Besides the obvious physical changes, age also alters perspective. Consider, for instance, how you've viewed your parents through the years. When you were a child, you probably thought they were all-knowing and flawless. As a teen, you may have viewed them as old-fashioned and mean. In adulthood, most people begin to regard their parents as knowledgeable and perhaps even wise.

Health and Fatigue   Recall the last time you came down with a cold, flu, or some other ailment. Do you remember how different you felt? You probably had much less energy. It's likely that you felt less sociable and that your thinking was slower than usual. These kinds of changes have a strong impact on how you relate to others. It's good to realize that someone else may be behaving differently because of illness. In the same way, it's important to let others know when you feel ill so that they can give you the understanding you need.

Just as being ill can affect your relationships, so can being overly tired. Trying to deal with important issues at such a time can get you into trouble. One study found that, when married couples don't sleep well, they have more negative perceptions of each other the following day, leading to more interpersonal discord.[26] Toward that end, a good night's sleep is an invaluable asset for managing interpersonal conflict. [27]

Hunger   People often get grumpy when they haven't eaten and get sleepy after stuffing themselves. Research confirms that lack of nutrition affects how we interact with others. In one study, teenagers who reported that their family did not get enough food to eat were almost three times as likely to have been suspended from school, almost twice as likely to have difficulty getting along with others, and four times as likely to have no friends.[28]

Biological Cycle   Are you a "morning person" or a "night person"? Most of us can answer this question easily, and there's a good physiological reason behind our response. Each of us is in a daily cycle in which all sorts of changes constantly occur, including body temperature, sexual drive, alertness, tolerance to stress, and mood.[29] Most of these changes are caused by hormonal cycles. For instance, adrenal hormones, which affect feelings of stress, are secreted at higher rates during some hours. In the same manner, the male and female sex hormones enter our systems at variable rates. We often aren't conscious of these changes, but they surely influence the way we relate to one another. After we're aware that our own daily cycles and those of others govern our feelings and behavior, it becomes possible to manage our lives so that we deal with important issues at the most effective times.

Cultural Differences

So far you have seen how physical factors can make the world a different place for each of us. But there's another kind of perceptual gap that often blocks communication—the gap between people from different backgrounds. Every culture has its own worldview, its own way of looking at the world. At times it's easy to forget that people everywhere don't see things the way we do.

Looking at DIVERSITY

Courtesy of Christa Kilvington

Christa Kilvington: Socioeconomic Stereotyping

What comes to mind when you hear the description "4.0 college student"? How about when you hear "welfare mom"? Most likely you get two very different mental pictures. Perhaps you imagine those kinds of people as complete opposites. And yet, I am both: A college student with straight-A grades who is also a single mother on public assistance. To some people, the combination doesn't fit. They figure that anyone smart enough to earn a 4.0 GPA shouldn't have ended up on welfare, or that anybody on welfare is probably too dumb and lazy to be in college and have straight-A grades.

The stereotypes people use to classify me shape the way they communicate. Most people who only know me from school and have no idea of my economic situation think of me as intelligent and ambitious—an academic standout. They speak to me formally and respectfully. Those who know me only by my income level—caseworkers, healthcare workers, grocery store clerks—tend to communicate with me in quite a different way. When I go to the welfare office, present my Medicaid card for a prescription, or pay for groceries with food stamps I am often treated as unintelligent, lazy, and dishonest. People speak to me in condescending and disrespectful tones.

Why do some people equate income level with intelligence? Why do they treat me and others differently based on our economic status? Why is it all right to treat people disrespectfully just because they are poor? Stereotypes exist for a reason, but it's important to go beyond them to find out each person's unique story. When you leave your mind open to the possibility that there is more to a person than meets the eye, that is when you grow as a person yourself.

"Socioeconomic Stereotyping" by Christa Kilvington. Used with permission of author.

The range of cultural differences is wide. In Middle Eastern countries, personal scents play an important role in interpersonal relationships. Arabs consistently breathe on people when they talk. As anthropologist Edward Hall explains:

> To smell one's friend is not only nice, but desirable, for to deny him your breath is to act ashamed. Americans, on the other hand, trained as they are not to breathe in people's faces, automatically communicate shame in trying to be polite. Who would expect that when our highest diplomats are putting on their best manners they are also communicating shame? Yet this is what occurs constantly, because diplomacy is not only "eyeball to eyeball" but breath to breath.

Even beliefs about the very value of talk differ from one culture to another.[30] Western cultures view talk as desirable and use it for social purposes as well as for task performance. Silence has a negative value in these cultures. It is likely to be interpreted as lack of interest, unwillingness to communicate, hostility, anxiety, shyness, or a sign of interpersonal incompatibility. Westerners are uncomfortable with silence, which they find embarrassing and awkward.

On the other hand, Asian cultures perceive talk differently. For thousands of years, Asian cultures have discouraged the expression of thoughts and feelings. Silence is valued, as Taoist sayings indicate: "In much talk there is great weariness," or "One who speaks does not know; one who knows does not speak." Unlike most North Americans, who are uncomfortable with silence, Japanese and Chinese believe that remaining quiet is the proper state when there is nothing to be said. In Asian cultures, a talkative person is often considered a show-off or insincere.

It's easy to see how these different views of speech and silence can lead to communication problems when people from different cultures meet. Both the talkative American and the silent Asian are behaving in ways they believe are proper, yet each views the other with disapproval and mistrust. This may require them to recognize and deal with their **ethnocentrism**—the attitude that one's own culture is superior to others. An ethnocentric person thinks—either privately or openly—that anyone who does not belong to his or her in-group is somehow strange, wrong, or even inferior. Travel writer Rick Steves describes how an ethnocentric point of view can interfere with respect for other cultural practices:

> … we [Americans] consider ourselves very clean and commonly criticize other cultures as dirty. In the bathtub we soak, clean, and rinse, all in the same water. (We would never wash our dishes that way.) A Japanese visitor, who uses clean water for each step, might find our way of bathing strange or even disgusting. Many cultures spit in public and blow their nose right onto the street. They couldn't imagine doing that into a small cloth, called a hanky, and storing that in their pocket to be used again and again. Too often we think of the world in terms of a pyramid of "civilized" (us) on the top and "primitive" groups on the bottom. If we measured things differently (maybe according to stress, loneliness, heart attacks, hours spent in traffic jams, or family togetherness) things stack up differently.

It isn't necessary to travel overseas to encounter differing cultural perspectives. Within this country there are many subcultures, and the members of each one have backgrounds that cause them to see things in different ways. Failure to recognize these differences can lead to unfortunate and unnecessary misunderstandings. For example, an uninformed Anglo teacher or police officer might interpret a lack of eye contact by a Latina as a sign of avoidance, or even dishonesty, when in fact this is the proper behavior in her culture for a female being addressed by an older man. To make direct eye contact in such a case would be considered undue brashness or even a sexual come-on.

It's encouraging to know that open-minded communicators can overcome preexisting stereotypes and learn to appreciate people from different backgrounds as individuals. In one study, college students who were introduced to strangers from different cultural backgrounds developed attitudes about their new conversational partners based more on their personal behavior than on preexisting expectations about how people from those backgrounds might behave.[31]

Social Roles

From the time we're born, each of us is indirectly taught a whole set of roles that we'll be expected to play. In one sense this set of prescribed parts is necessary because it enables a society to function smoothly and provides the security that comes from knowing what's expected of you. But in another sense, having roles defined in advance can lead to wide gaps in understanding. When roles become unquestioned and rigid, people tend to see the world from their own viewpoint, having no experiences that show them how other people see it. Let's look at how social roles affect our perception and communication.

⋀ In the TV series *Orange Is the New Black*, Laverne Cox plays the role of Sophia Burset, a transgender prisoner who has forsaken life as a husband and firefighter to become a woman. While never denying her personal history, the Burset character—and Cox in real life—refuses to be pigeonholed into traditional gender categories. Have gender stereotypes distorted your perception of others?

Gender Roles Although people use the terms *sex* and *gender* as if they were identical, there is an important difference.[32] *Sex* refers to biological characteristics of a male or female, whereas *gender* refers to the social and psychological dimensions of masculine and feminine behavior. A large body of research shows that males and females do perceive the world differently, for reasons ranging from genes to neurology to hormones.[33] However, even cognitive researchers who focus on biological differences between males and females acknowledge that societal gender roles and stereotypes affect perception dramatically.[34]

Gender roles are socially approved ways that men and women are expected to behave. Children learn the importance of gender roles by watching other people and by being exposed to media, as well as by receiving reinforcement.[35] After members of a society learn these customary roles, they tend to regard violations as unusual—or even undesirable.

Some theorists have suggested that stereotypical masculine and feminine behaviors are not opposite poles of a single continuum, but rather two separate sets of behavior.[36] With this view, an individual can act in a masculine manner or a feminine manner or exhibit both types of characteristics. The male–female

TABLE 4.1 Gender Roles

	MALE	FEMALE
Masculine	Masculine males	Masculine females
Feminine	Feminine males	Feminine females
Androgynous	Androgynous males	Androgynous females
Undifferentiated	Undifferentiated males	Undifferentiated female

dichotomy, then, is replaced with four psychological sex types: masculine, feminine, **androgynous** (combining masculine and feminine traits), and undifferentiated (neither masculine nor feminine traits). Combining the four psychological sex types with the traditional physiological sex types produces the eight categories listed in Table 4.1.

Each of these eight psychological sex types perceives interpersonal relationships differently. For example, masculine males may be likely to see their interpersonal relationships as opportunities for competitive interaction, as opportunities to win something. Feminine females often see their interpersonal relationships as opportunities to be nurturing, to express their feelings and emotions. Androgynous males and females, on the other hand, differ little in their perceptions of their interpersonal relationships.

Occupational Roles   The kind of work we do often influences our view of the world. Imagine five people taking a walk through the park. One, a botanist, is fascinated by the variety of trees and other plants. Another, a zoologist, is looking for interesting animals. The third, a meteorologist, keeps an eye on the sky, noticing changes in the weather. The fourth companion, a psychologist, is totally unaware of nature, instead concentrating on the interaction among the people in the park. The fifth person, a pickpocket, quickly takes advantage of the others' absorption to make some money. There are two lessons in this little scenario. The first, of course, is to watch your wallet carefully. The second is that our occupational roles shape our perceptions.

Even within the same occupational setting, the different roles that participants have can affect their perceptions. Consider a typical college classroom, for example. The experiences of the instructor and students often are dissimilar. Having dedicated a large part of their lives to their work, most instructors see their subject matter—whether French literature, physics, or communication—as vitally important. Students who are taking the course to satisfy a general education requirement may view the subject differently: maybe as one of many obstacles that stand between them and a degree, or perhaps as a chance to meet new people. Another difference centers on the amount of knowledge possessed by the parties. To an instructor who has taught the course many times, the material probably seems extremely simple, but to students encountering it for the first time, it may seem strange and confusing. We don't need to spell out the interpersonal strains and stresses that come from such differing perceptions.

Relational Roles   Think back to the "Who am I?" list you made in the opening of Chapter 3. It's likely your list included roles you play in relation to others: daughter, roommate, husband, friend, and so on. Roles like these don't just define who you are—they also affect your perception.

Take, for example, the role of parent. As most new mothers and fathers will attest, having a child alters the way they see the world. They might perceive their crying baby as a helpless soul in need of comfort, while nearby strangers have a less charitable appraisal. As the child grows, parents often pay more attention to the messages in the child's environment. One father we know said he never noticed how much football fans curse and swear until he took his six-year-old to a game with him. In other words, his role as father affected what he heard and how he interpreted it.

The roles involved in romantic love can also dramatically affect perception. These roles have many labels: partner, spouse, boyfriend/girlfriend, sweetheart, and so on. There are times when your affinity biases the way you perceive the object of your affection. You may see your sweetheart as more attractive than other people do, and perhaps you overlook some faults that others notice.[37] Your romantic role can also change the way you view others. One study found that when people are in love, they view other romantic candidates as less attractive than they normally would.[38]

Perhaps the most telltale sign of the effect of "love goggles" is when they come off. Many people have experienced breaking up with a romantic partner and wondering later, "What did I ever see in that person?" The answer—at least in part—is that you saw what your relational role led you to see.

PAUSE *and* REFLECT

Role Reversal

MindTap REFLECT . . . on new roles by answering the following questions, either here or online.

Walk a mile in another person's shoes. Find a group that is foreign to you, and try to become a member of it for a while.

1. If you're down on the police, see if your local department has a ride-along program where you can spend several hours on patrol with one or two officers.

2. If you think the present state of education is a mess, become a teacher yourself. Maybe an instructor will give you the chance to plan one or more classes.

3. If you're a political conservative, try getting involved in a liberal organization; if you're a liberal, check out the conservatives.

Whatever group you join, try to become part of it as best you can. Don't just observe. Get into the philosophy of your new role and see how it feels. You may gain a new appreciation for people you didn't understand.

COMMON TENDENCIES IN PERCEPTION

By now it's obvious that many factors affect the way we interpret the world. Social scientists use the term **attribution** to describe the process of explaining people's behavior.[39] We attribute meaning both to our own actions and to the actions of others, but we often use different yardsticks. Research has uncovered several perceptual tendencies that can lead to attribution errors.[40]

"Don't get me wrong, Ted. I like you, but you're not a special person. I'm a special person."

Jack Ziegler/Cartoonbank.com

We Judge Ourselves More Charitably Than We Judge Others

In an attempt to convince ourselves and others that the positive face we show to the world is true, we tend to judge ourselves in the most generous terms possible. Social scientists have labeled this tendency the **self-serving bias**.[41] When others suffer, we often blame the problem on their personal qualities. On the other hand, when we suffer, we blame the problem on forces outside ourselves. Consider a few examples:

When *they* botch a job, we might think they weren't listening well or trying hard enough; when *we* botch a job, the problem was unclear directions or not enough time.

When *he* lashes out angrily, we say he's being moody or too sensitive; when *we* lash out angrily, it's because of the pressure we've been under.

When *she* gets caught speeding, we say she should have been more careful; when *we* get caught speeding, we deny that we were driving too fast or we say, "Everybody does it."

When *she* uses profanity, it's because of a flaw in her character; when *we* swear, it's because the situation called for it.[42]

One study of "honest but hurtful" messages shows how self-serving bias can operate in romantic relationships.[43] Partners who deliver these candid messages tend to perceive them as helpful and constructive. When on the receiving end, however, the same messages are seen as hurtful and mean. In other words, "I'm a good sweetheart when I tell you the painful truth, but you're a bad sweetheart when you do the same to me."

We Cling to First Impressions

Labeling people according to our first impressions is an inevitable part of the perception process. These labels are a way of making quick interpretations:

"She seems cheerful"; "He appears sincere"; "They sound conceited." If such first impressions are accurate, they can be useful ways of deciding how to respond best to people in the future. Problems arise, however, when the labels we attach are inaccurate. After we form an opinion of someone, we tend to hang on to it and make any conflicting information fit our opinion.

Social scientists have coined the term **halo effect** to describe the tendency to form an overall positive impression of a person on the basis of one positive characteristic. One such characteristic is physical attractiveness, which can lead people to attribute all sorts of other virtues to the good-looking person.[44] For example, employment interviewers rate mediocre but attractive job applicants higher than their less attractive candidates.[45] And once employers form positive impressions, they often ask questions that confirm their image of the applicant.[46] For example, when an interviewer forms a positive impression, he might ask leading questions aimed at supporting his positive views ("What lessons did you learn from that setback?"), interpret answers in a positive light ("Ah, taking time away from school to travel was a good idea!"), encourage the applicant ("Good point!"), and sell the company's virtues ("I think you would like working here"). Likewise, applicants who create a negative first impression are operating under a cloud that may be impossible to dispel—a phenomenon sometimes referred to as "the devil effect."[47]

The power of first impressions is also important in personal relationships. A study of college roommates found that those who had positive initial impressions of each other were likely to have positive subsequent interactions, manage their conflicts constructively, and continue living together.[48] The converse was also true: Roommates who got off to a bad start tended to spiral negatively. This reinforces the wisdom and importance of the old adage, "You never get a second chance to make a first impression."

Given the almost unavoidable tendency to form first impressions, the best advice we can give is to keep an open mind and to be willing to change your opinion as events prove it mistaken.

We Assume That Others Are Similar to Us

In Chapter 3 you read one example of this principle: that people with low self-esteem imagine that others view them unfavorably, whereas people with high self-esteem imagine that others view them positively. The frequently mistaken assumption that others' views are similar to our own applies in a wide range of situations:

- You've heard a slightly raunchy joke that you think is pretty funny. You assume that it won't offend a somewhat straitlaced friend. It does.

- You've been bothered by an instructor's tendency to get off the subject during lectures. If you were an instructor, you'd want to know if anything you were doing was creating problems for your students, so you decide that your instructor will probably be grateful for some constructive criticism. Unfortunately, you're wrong.

- You lost your temper with a friend a week ago and said some things you regret. In fact, if someone said those things to you, you'd consider the relationship finished. Imagining that your friend feels the same way, you avoid making contact. In fact, your friend has avoided you because she thinks *you're* the one who wants to end things.

Examples like these show that others don't always think or feel the way we do and that assuming that similarities exist can lead to problems.[49] How can you find out the other person's real position? Sometimes by asking directly, sometimes by checking with others, and sometimes by making an educated guess after you've thought the matter out. All these alternatives are better than simply assuming that everyone would react as you do.

We Are Influenced by Our Expectations

Suppose you took a class and were told in advance that the instructor is terrific. Would this affect the way you perceive the teacher? Research shows that it almost certainly would. In one study, students who read positive comments about instructors on a website viewed those teachers as more credible and attractive than did students who were not exposed to the same comments.[50]

Expectations don't always lead to more positive appraisals. There are times when we raise our expectations so high that we are disappointed with the events that occur. If you are told that someone you are about to meet is extremely attractive, you may create a picture in your mind of a professional model, only to be let down when the person doesn't live up to your unrealistic expectations. What if you had been told that the person isn't very good-looking? In that case, you might have been pleasantly surprised by the person's appearance, and perhaps you would rate the person's attractiveness more positively. The point is, our expectations influence the way we see others, both positively and negatively—and that may lead to self-fulfilling prophecies.[51]

On the JOB

Sexual Harassment and Perception

Almost 50 years after the U.S. Civil Rights Act prohibited it, sexual harassment in the workplace remains a problem. Complaints of unwanted sexual advances and a hostile work environment have cost employers almost $50 million annually in recent years.[a]

Scholars have tried to understand why complaints of harassment persist when the law clearly prohibits behavior that creates a "hostile work environment." They have discovered that, while clear-cut examples of hostile sexism do exist, differing perceptions help explain many other incidents.

Not surprisingly, what constitutes harassment depends on gender: Women are more likely than men to rate a behavior as hostile and/or offensive.[b]

Perhaps more surprisingly, younger people (both men and women) are less likely than older people to regard a scenario as sexual harassment.

Along with age and sex, cultural background helps shape perceptions of harassment.[c] People from cultures with high power distance are less likely to perceive harassment than those from places with low power distance.

Findings like these don't excuse harassment, but they do help explain it. The more members of an organization understand one another's perceptions, the better the odds that unpleasant and unfortunate feelings of harassment will not arise.

We Are Influenced by the Obvious

The error of being influenced by what is most obvious is understandable. As you read at the beginning of this chapter, we select stimuli from our environment that are noticeable: intense, repetitive, unusual, or otherwise attention-grabbing. The problem is that the most obvious factor is not necessarily the only one—or the most significant one—for an event. For example:

- When two children (or adults, for that matter) fight, it may be a mistake to blame the one who lashes out first. Perhaps the other one was at least equally responsible, teasing or refusing to cooperate.

- You might complain about an acquaintance whose malicious gossiping or arguing has become a bother, forgetting that by putting up with such behavior in the past you have been at least partially responsible.

- You might blame an unhappy working situation on the boss, overlooking other factors beyond his or her control, such as a change in the economy, the policy of higher management, or demands of customers or other workers.

NBC/Allstar

⋀ On *The Voice*, judges use blind auditions in the opening rounds. On other performance shows, judges view contestants' appearance and sometimes even know their backstories before making an appraisal. Does that affect the judges' perceptions of the performer and the performance? Are there times when you would be better off knowing *less* about someone when making an evaluation?

PERCEPTION CHECKING

Serious problems can arise when people treat interpretations as if they were matters of fact. Like most people, you probably resent others jumping to conclusions about the reasons for your behavior.

"Why are you mad at me?" (Who said you were?)

"What's the matter with you?" (Who said anything was the matter?)

"Come on now. Tell the truth." (Who said you were lying?)

As you'll learn in Chapter 11, even if your interpretation is correct, a dogmatic, mind-reading statement is likely to generate defensiveness. The skill of **perception checking** provides a better way to handle your interpretations.[52]

Elements of Perception Checking

A complete perception check has three parts:

1. A description of the behavior you noticed
2. At least two possible interpretations of the behavior
3. A request for clarification about how to interpret the behavior

Perception checks for the preceding three examples would look like this:

"When you stomped out of the room and slammed the door," *(behavior)* "I wasn't sure whether you were mad at me" *(first interpretation)* "or just in a hurry." *(second interpretation)* "How *did* you feel?" *(request for clarification)*

"You haven't laughed much in the last couple of days." *(behavior)* "It makes me wonder whether something's bothering you" *(first interpretation)* "or whether you're just feeling quiet." *(second interpretation)* "What's up?" *(request for clarification)*

"You said you really liked the job I did." *(behavior)* "On the other hand, there was something about your voice that made me think you may not like it." *(first interpretation)* "Maybe it's just my imagination, though." *(second interpretation)* "How do you really feel?" *(request for clarification)*

Perception checking is a tool for helping you understand others accurately instead of assuming that your first interpretation is correct. Because its goal is mutual understanding, perception checking is a cooperative approach to communication. Besides leading to more accurate perceptions, it minimizes defensiveness by preserving the other person's face. Instead of saying, in effect, "I know what you're thinking ...," a perception check takes the more respectful approach that states or implies, "I know I'm not qualified to judge you without some help."

Perception-Checking Considerations

Like every communication skill outlined in *Looking Out Looking In*, perception checking isn't a mechanical formula that will work in every situation. As you develop the ability to check your perceptions, consider the following factors in deciding when and how to use this approach.

Completeness   Sometimes a perception check won't need all of the parts listed earlier to be effective:

"You haven't dropped by lately. Is anything the matter?" *(single interpretation combined with request for clarification)*

"I can't tell whether you're kidding me about being cheap or if you're serious." *(behavior combined with interpretations)* "Are you mad at me?"

"Are you sure you don't mind driving? I can use a ride if it's no trouble, but I don't want to take you out of your way." *(no need to describe behavior)*

Sometimes even the most skimpy perception check—a simple question like "What's going on?"—will do the job. You might also rely on other people to help you make sense of confusing behavior: "Rachelle has been awfully quiet lately. Do you know what's up?" A complete perception check is most necessary when the risk of sounding judgmental is highest.

Nonverbal Congruency   A perception check can succeed only if your nonverbal behavior reflects the open-mindedness of your words. An accusing tone of voice or a hostile glare will contradict the sincerely worded request for clarification, suggesting that you have already made up your mind about the other person's intentions.

Cultural Rules   The straightforward approach of perception checking has the best chance of working in what Chapter 6 identifies as *low-context cultures*: ones in which members use language as directly as possible. The dominant cultures of

In REAL LIFE

Perception Checking in Everyday Life

Perception checking only works if it is sincere and fits your personal style. The following examples show how perception checking sounds in everyday life and may help you find ways to use it when you are faced with ambiguous messages.

My Boss's Jokes

I get confused by my boss's sense of humor. Sometimes he jokes just to be funny, but other times he uses humor to make a point without coming right out and saying what's on his mind. Last week he was talking about the upcoming work schedule and he said with a laugh, "I own you all weekend!" I have a life besides work, so his comment left me worried.

I used a perception check to figure out what he meant: "Brad, when you told me 'I own you all weekend,' I wasn't sure whether you were kidding or whether you really expect me to work Saturday and Sunday. Were you serious?"

He kind of smiled and said, "No, I was just kidding. You only have to work Saturday and Sunday."

I still couldn't be sure whether or not he was serious, so I checked again: "You're kidding, right?"

My boss replied, "Well, I do need you at least one day, and two would be better." Once I figured out what he really meant, we worked out a schedule that had me work Friday evening and Saturday morning, which gave me the time off I needed.

If I hadn't used the perception check, I would have wound up worrying about being tied up all weekend, and getting mad at my boss for no good reason. I'm glad I spoke up.

My Dad's Affection

My father and I have a great relationship. A while back I picked him up at the airport after a week-long business trip and a long cross-country flight. On the way home, he was quiet—not his usual self. He said he was exhausted, which I understood. When we got home, he brightened up and started joking and playing with my younger brother. This left me feeling unhappy. I thought to myself, "Why is he so happy to see my brother when he hardly said a word to me?" I didn't say anything at the time. The next day I found myself feeling resentful toward my dad, and it showed. He said, "What's up with you?" But I was too embarrassed to say anything.

After learning this approach in class, I tried a perception check. I said, "Dad—when you were quiet on the way home after your business trip and then you perked up when you got home and saw Jaime, I wasn't sure what was up. I thought maybe you were happier to see him than me, or that maybe I'm imagining things. How come you said you were tired with me and then you perked up with Jaime?"

My dad felt awful. He said he was tired in the car, but once he got back to the house he was glad to be home and felt like a new man. I was too wrapped up in my mind to consider this alternative. Because I didn't use a perception check, I was unhappy and I started an unnecessary fight.

MindTap APPLY ... this situation to your life by answering questions online.

North America and Western Europe fit into this category, and members of these groups are most likely to appreciate perception checking. Members of *high-context cultures* (more common in Latin America and Asia), however, value social harmony over directness. High-context communicators are more likely to regard candid approaches like perception checking as potentially embarrassing, instead preferring less-direct ways of understanding one another. Thus, a "let's get this straight" perception check might work well with a Euro American manager who was raised to value directness, but could be a serious mistake with a Mexican American or Asian American boss who has spent most of his or her life in a high-context culture.

SKILL *Builder*

Perception Checking Practice

MindTap PRACTICE ... your perception-checking ability by answering the following questions either here or online.

Practice your perception-checking ability by developing three-part verifications for the following situations:

1. You made what you thought was an excellent suggestion to an instructor. The instructor looked uninterested but said she would check on the matter right away. Three weeks have passed, and nothing has changed.

2. A neighbor and good friend has not responded to your "Good morning" for three days in a row. This person is usually friendly.

3. You haven't received the usual weekly phone call from the folks back home in over a month. The last time you spoke, you had an argument about where to spend the holidays.

4. An old friend with whom you have shared the problems of your love life for years has recently changed behavior when around you. The formerly casual hugs and kisses have become longer and stronger, and the occasions where you "accidentally" brush up against each other have become more frequent.

Face Saving   Along with clarifying meaning, perception checking can sometimes be a face-saving way to raise an issue without directly threatening or attacking the other person. Consider these examples:

> "Are you planning on doing those dishes later, or did you forget that it's your turn?"

> "Am I boring you, or do you have something else on your mind?"

In the first case, you might have been quite confident that the other person had no intention of doing the dishes, and in the second that the other person was bored. Even so, a perception check is a less threatening way of pointing out their behavior than direct confrontation. Remember, one element of competent communication is the ability to choose the best option from a large repertoire, and perception checking can be a useful strategy at times.

EMPATHY, COGNITIVE COMPLEXITY, AND COMMUNICATION

Perception checking is a valuable tool for clarifying ambiguous messages, but ambiguity isn't the only cause of perceptual problems. Sometimes we understand what people mean without understanding why they believe as they do. At times like this, we are short on the vital ability to empathize.

AT FACEBOOK, CREATING EMPATHY

Of Facebook's 7,185 employees, Arturo Bejar may have the most difficult job: teaching the site's 1.3 billion users, especially its tens of millions of teenagers, how to be nice and respectful to one another.

Respectful? Online? Ha! That's never going to happen. Everyone knows that social media is an unwinnable game of who can be meaner. If Mr. Bejar thinks he can make Facebook users nice, he is—to borrow a popular Facebook comment—just stupid!

As the director of engineering for the Facebook Protect and Care team, he believes that most users are not trying to be mean and that they will retract a comment (and even feel bad about it) if they realize it has caused someone harm.

In other words, Mr. Bejar is trying to create empathy among Facebook users, in what used to happen in real settings like the playground, through social cues like crying and laughter. The company told me that each week eight million Facebook members use tools that allow users to report a harmful post or photo. Mr. Bejar's team designed these tools to let people know someone had hurt their feelings.

Teenagers are a particular focus, not just as victims of cyberbullying but because they sometimes lack the emotional maturity to handle negative posts. On Facebook, teenagers are presented with more options than just "it's embarrassing" when they want to remove a post. They are asked what's happening in the post, how they feel about it, and how sad they are. In addition, they are given a text box with a polite pre-written response that can be sent to the friend who hurt their feelings.

More often than not, the posts were not meant to hurt, but were jokes lost in digital translation. When Facebook asked people why they shared a post that hurt someone else, around 90 percent of respondents said they thought their friends would like the post or would think it was funny. Only 2 percent of users wanted to provoke or alarm someone else.

Researchers are looking at other ways to help users be more empathetic on social networks. Last year, Facebook borrowed ideas from Charles Darwin's 1872 book *The Expression of the Emotions in Man and Animals* to create stickers with facial expressions.

Next, Mr. Bejar said, his team is experimenting with sounds to help people convey how they feel. (Imagine sending someone the sound of a grunt, sigh, or a giggle to communicate your feelings about a post.)

Maybe this idea isn't that stupid after all.

Nick Bilton

MindTap ENHANCE ...
your understanding by answering the following questions, either here or online.

1. Have you ever been the object of a social media post that the creator apparently thought was funny but hurt your feelings? What factors played into the difference in perception?

2. Do you think the empathy tools identified in this reading can help people communicate more effectively on social networking sites? Would you use these tools if given the opportunity?

3. In general, do you think the use of social media enhances or detracts from interpersonal empathy? Offer examples to support your case.

Empathy

Empathy is the ability to re-create another person's perspective, to experience the world from the other's point of view. It may be impossible to ever experience another person's perspective completely, but with enough effort we can certainly gain a better idea of how the world appears to him or her.

As we'll use the term here, *empathy* involves three dimensions.[53] In one dimension, empathy involves *perspective taking*—an attempt to take on the viewpoint of another person. This requires a suspension of judgment so that for the moment you set aside your own opinions and try to understand the other person. Even a narcissist can be nudged to feel empathy for others by engaging in perspective-taking exercises.[54] Empathy also has an *emotional* dimension that helps us get closer to experiencing others' feelings: to gain a sense of their fear, joy, sadness, and so on. A third dimension of empathy is a genuine *concern* for the welfare of the other person. When we empathize, we go beyond just thinking and feeling as others do and genuinely care about their well-being.

Scores of recent studies show that humans are hardwired to empathize with others—it's built into our brains.[55] Best-selling author Daniel Goleman believes that cultivating this natural tendency toward empathy is the essence of "social intelligence."[56] The ability to empathize seems to exist in a rudimentary form in even the youngest children. Research sponsored by the National Institute of Mental Health revealed what many parents know from experience: Virtually from birth, infants become visibly upset when they hear another baby crying, and children who are a few months old cry when they observe another child in tears. Young children have trouble distinguishing others' distress from their own. If, for example, one child hurts his finger, another might put her own finger into her mouth as if she were feeling pain. Researchers report cases in which children who see their parents in tears wipe their own eyes, even though they are not crying.

Although children may have a basic capacity to empathize, studies with twins suggest that the degree to which we are born with the ability to sense how others are feeling seems to vary according to genetic factors.[57] Although some people may have an inborn edge, environmental experiences are the key to developing the ability to understand others. Specifically, the way in which parents communicate with their children seems to affect their ability to understand others' emotional states.[58] When parents point out to children the distress that others feel from their misbehavior ("Look how sad Jessica is because you took her toy. Wouldn't you be sad if someone took away your toys?"), those children gain

"How would you feel if the mouse did that to you?"

a greater appreciation that their acts have emotional consequences than when parents simply label such behavior as inappropriate ("That was a mean thing to do!"). Studies also show that allowing children to experience and manage frustrating events can help increase their empathic concern for others later in life.[59]

Culture plays an important role in our ability to understand the perspectives of others. Research shows that people raised in individualist cultures (which value independence) are often less adept at perspective-taking than those from collectivist cultures (which value interdependence).[60] In one study, Chinese and American players were paired together in a communication game that required the participants to take on the perspective of their partners. In all measures, the collectivist Chinese had greater success in perspective-taking than did their American counterparts. This isn't to suggest that one cultural orientation is better than the other; it only shows that culture shapes the way we perceive, understand, and empathize with others.

∧ In the television show *Undercover Boss*, high-ranking company officials in disguise take on the duties of lower-level employees in their organizations. The bosses usually gain a new appreciation and empathy for the challenges faced by their employees, both on the job and in their personal lives. Can you think of a supervisor who has forgotten what it's like to be on the bottom rung of a company? How do *you* regard and treat people who supply you with customer service?

It is easy to confuse empathy with **sympathy**, but the concepts are different. With sympathy, you view the other person's situation from *your* point of view. With empathy, you view it from *the other person's* perspective. Consider the difference between sympathizing and empathizing with an unwed mother or a homeless person. When you sympathize, it is the other person's confusion, joy, or pain. When you empathize, the experience becomes your own, at least for the moment. It's one thing to feel bad (or good) *for* someone; it's more profound to feel bad (or good) *with* someone. Nonetheless, empathy doesn't require you to *agree* with the other person. You can empathize with a difficult relative or a rude stranger without endorsing their behavior. Ultimately, all of us can profit from putting ourselves in anothers' shoes to better understand their worlds.

Cognitive Complexity

By now you can probably appreciate the value of empathy in boosting understanding and enhancing relationships. But how can we become more empathic? To answer that question, let's return to a feature of communication competence: cognitive complexity.

Cognitive Complexity and Communication

As noted in Chapter 1, cognitive complexity is the ability to construct a variety of frameworks for viewing an issue. Researchers have found that cognitive complexity increases the chances of satisfying communication in a variety of contexts, including marriage,[61] helping others who are feeling distressed,[62] being persuasive,[63] and career advancement.[64]

It was six men of Indostan

To learning much inclined,

Who went to see the elephant

Though all of them were blind

That each by observation

Might satisfy his mind.

The first approached the elephant

And, happening to fall

Against the broad and sturdy side,

At once began to bawl:

"Why, bless me! But the elephant

Is very much like a wall!"

The second, feeling of the tusk,

Cried: "Ho! What have we here

So very round and smooth and sharp?

To me, 'tis very clear,

This wonder of an elephant

Is very like a spear!"

The third approached the animal,

And, happening to take

The squirming trunk within his hands

Thus boldly up he spake:

"I see," quoth he, "the elephant

Is very like a snake!"

The fourth reached out his eager hand

And felt about the knee:

"What most this wondrous beast is like

Is very plain," quoth he:

"'Tis clear enough the elephant

Is very like a tree!"

The fifth who chanced to touch the ear

Said: "E'en the blindest man

Can tell what this resembles most—

Deny the fact who can:

This marvel of an elephant

Is very like a fan!"

The sixth no sooner had begun

About the beast to grope

Than, seizing on the swinging tail

That fell within his scope,

"I see," quoth he, "the elephant

Is very like a rope!"

And so these men of Indostan

Disputed loud and long,

Each in his own opinion

Exceeding stiff and strong;

Though each was partly in the right,

And all were in the wrong.

John G. Saxe

Not surprisingly, studies show a connection between cognitive complexity and empathy.[65] The relationship makes sense: The more ways you have to understand others and interpret their behaviors, the greater is the likelihood that you can see the world from their perspective. Cognitive complexity can also help people describe situations more thoroughly and less simplistically.[66] Interestingly, one study showed that cognitively complex people are better able to identify and understand when others are using sarcasm—an abstract form of communication that is sometimes lost on those with less mental acumen.[67] The good news is that cognitive complexity can be enhanced through training.[68] With that in mind, let's look at a skill that can help you achieve that goal.

Increasing Your Cognitive Complexity: The Pillow Method

The skill of perception checking discussed earlier in this chapter is a relatively quick, easy tool for clarifying potential misunderstandings, but some issues are too complex and serious to be handled with this approach. Writer Paul Reps describes a tool for boosting empathy when finding merit in another's position seems impossible.[69]

Developed by a group of Japanese schoolchildren, the **pillow method** gets its name from the fact that a problem has four sides and a middle, just like a pillow (Figure 4.3). As the following examples show, viewing an issue from each of these perspectives almost always leads to valuable insights—and in so doing enhances cognitive complexity.

Position 1: I'm Right, You're Wrong This is the perspective that we usually take when viewing an issue. We immediately see the virtues in our position and find fault with anyone who happens to disagree with us. Detailing this position takes little effort and provides little new information.

Position 2: You're Right, I'm Wrong At this point you switch perspectives and build the strongest possible arguments to explain how another

FIGURE 4.3
The Pillow Method

POSITION 1:
I'm right,
you're wrong

POSITION 3:
Both right,
both wrong

POSITION 5:
There's truth in
all perspectives

POSITION 4:
The issue isn't
important

POSITION 2:
You're right,
I'm wrong

person can view the issue differently from you. Besides identifying the strengths in the other's position, this is the time to play the devil's advocate and find flaws in your position. This requires discipline and a certain amount of courage, even though this is only an exercise, and you will soon be able to retreat to position 1 if you choose. But most people learn that switching perspectives reveals there is some merit to the other person's perspective.

ETHICAL *Challenge*

Empathy and the Golden Rule

Virtually everyone is familiar with the Golden Rule, which most of us learned in the form "Do unto others as you would have them do unto you." By obliging us to treat others as well as we would treat ourselves, this maxim seems to offer the foundation for a civil society in which everyone would behave with consideration.

Some ethicists have pointed out that the Golden Rule doesn't work well in situations where others don't want to be treated the same way you would. You may like to blast hip-hop music at top volume at 3 A.M., but appeals to the Golden Rule probably won't placate your neighbors who don't share your musical tastes or late-night hours. Likewise, just because you enjoy teasing banter, you aren't entitled to banter with others who might find this type of humor offensive or hurtful.

The Golden Rule presents special problems in cases of intercultural contacts, where norms for what is desirable vary dramatically. For example, most speakers from low-context cultures where English is the first language value honesty and explicit communication, but this level of candor would be offensive in the high-context cultures of Asia or the Middle East. A naive communicator following the Golden Rule might justify social blunders by claiming, "I was just communicating the way I'd like to be treated." This sort of ethnocentrism is a recipe for unsuccessful communication and perhaps for very unpleasant consequences.

In response to the challenge of differing wants, Milton Bennett proposed a "Platinum Rule": "Do unto others as they themselves would have done unto them." Unlike the Golden Rule, this rule requires us to understand how others think and what they want before we can determine how to act ethically.[a] Put differently, the Platinum Rule implies that empathy is a prerequisite for moral sensitivity.

Despite its initial appeal, the Platinum Rule poses its own problems. There are certainly cases where doing unto others what they want might compromise our own needs or even our ethical principles. It is easy to imagine cases in which the Platinum Rule would oblige us to cheat, steal, or lie on others' behalf.

Even if acting on the Platinum Rule is problematic, the benefit of thinking about it seems clear. An essential requirement for benign behavior is the ability to empathize, helping us recognize that what others want may be different than what we would want under the same circumstances.

MindTap® APPLY … the ethical principles introduced here by answering the following questions, either here or online.

Select one of your most important interpersonal relationships and consider the effects of applying the Golden Rule and the Platinum Rule.

1. Do you have enough information to apply the Golden Rule? What about the Platinum Rule? What communication might be necessary before you could put each rule into practice?

2. Which rule seems to be preferable?

There are some issues where it seems impossible to call the other position "right." Criminal behavior, deceit, and disloyalty often seem beyond justification. At times like these, it is possible to arrive at position 2 by realizing that the other person's behavior is understandable. For example, without approving, you may be able to understand how someone would resort to violence, tell lies, or cheat. Whatever the particulars, the goal of position 2 is to find some way of comprehending how anyone could behave in a way that you originally found impossible to defend.

Position 3: Both Right, Both Wrong From this position, you acknowledge the strengths and weaknesses of each person's arguments. If you have done a good job with position 2, it should be clear that there is some merit in both points of view, and that each side has its demerits. Taking a more evenhanded look at the issue can lead you to be less critical and more understanding of another's point of view.

Position 3 can also help you find the commonalities between your position and others'. Perhaps you've both been right to care so much about the issue, but both wrong to fail to recognize the other person's concerns. Perhaps there are underlying values that you both share and similar mistakes that you've both made. In any case, the perspective of position 3 should help you see that the issue isn't as much a matter of complete right and wrong as it first appeared to be.

Position 4: The Issue Isn't as Important as It Seems Although it is difficult to consider some issues unimportant, a little thought will show that most aren't as important as we make them out to be. The impact of even the most traumatic events—the death of a loved one or the breakup of a relationship, for example—usually lessens over time. The effects may not disappear, but we learn to accept them and get on with life. The importance of a dispute can also fade when you realize that you've let it overshadow other equally important parts of your relationship. It's easy to become so wrapped up in a dispute about one subject that you forget about the other ways in which you are close to the other person.

Position 5: There Is Truth in All Four Perspectives After completing the first four positions, a final step is to recognize that each of them has some merit. Although logic might suggest that it's impossible for a position to be both right and wrong, both important and unimportant, your own experience will show that there is some truth in each of the positions you have explored. After you have looked at an issue from these five perspectives, it is almost certain that you will gain new insights. These insights may not cause you to change your mind or even solve the problem at hand. Nonetheless, they can increase your understanding of the other person's position and thus improve the communication climate.

In Real Life

The Pillow Method in Action

Planning a Wedding

Background
Who would have thought that planning a wedding would be such a nightmare? My fiancé and I are struggling to decide whether we should have a large, festive wedding or a small, intimate one. I'm in favor of having a big, expensive ceremony and party. He wants a smaller, more affordable one.

Position 1: I'm Right, He's Wrong
I have a big family, and I would feel guilty not inviting everyone. Also, we have lots of friends who would really miss not being present to celebrate our special day. If we invite one friend or relative, I say we have to invite them all to avoid hurting anybody's feelings. Otherwise, where do you draw the line? As far as money goes, I say that you get married only once, and this is no time to scrimp. My parents are willing to help pay the expenses because they want our entire family to be there at the wedding.

Position 2: He's Right, I'm Wrong
My fiancé is right to say that we really don't have the funds to spend on a fancy wedding. Every dollar we spend on a lavish event will be one less dollar we have to buy a house, which we hope to do soon. My fiancé is right to say that a big wedding could postpone our house purchase for a year or two—maybe even longer, if real estate prices go up before we can buy. Even if my parents help pay for the event, our portion would still be more than we can afford. He's also right to say that no matter how many people we invite, someone is always going to be left out. It's just a case of where we draw the line. Finally, he's right to say that planning a big wedding will be a very stressful process.

Position 3: Both of Us Are Right, and Both Are Wrong
Both of us are right, and both are wrong. I'm right to want to include our extended families and friends on this joyous day, and I'm right to say that a special wedding would be a lifetime memory. He's right that doing so could still leave some hurt feelings and that it will postpone our house purchase. He also has a good point when he says that planning a big event could drive us crazy and distract us from the real importance of joining our lives.

Position 4: The Issue Isn't Important
After thinking about it, I've realized that getting married is different from being married. The decision about what kind of ceremony to have is important, but ultimately it won't affect the kind of marriage we have. How we behave after we're married will be much more important. And we are going to face a lot of decisions together—about children and jobs, for example—that will have much bigger consequences than this ceremony.

Position 5: There Is Truth in All Perspectives
Before using the pillow method to think through all sides of this issue, I was focused on getting my way. This attitude was creating some feelings between my fiancé and me that were not what we should be having as we faced this most important event. I've realized that if one or the other of us "wins" but the result is injured feelings, it won't be much of a victory. I don't know what kind of ceremony we will finally decide to have, but I'm determined to keep my focus on the really important goal of keeping our relationship positive and respectful.

MindTap APPLY ... this situation to your life by answering questions online.

SKILL *Builder*

Pillow Talk

MindTap® **PRACTICE** … your skill at applying the pillow method by answering the following questions either here or online.

Try using the pillow method in your life. It isn't easy, but after you begin to understand it, the payoff in increased understanding can be great.

1. Choose a person or viewpoint with whom or which you strongly disagree. If you've chosen a person, it's best to have him or her there with you, but if that's not possible, you can do it alone.

2. What disagreement should you choose? No doubt there are many in your life:

   Parent–child   Friend–friend

   Teacher–student   Nation–nation

   Employer–employee   Republican–Democrat

   Brother–sister

3. For each disagreement you choose, genuinely place yourself in each position on the pillow as you encounter it:

   a. Your position is correct, and your opponent's is wrong.

   b. Your opponent's position is correct, and yours is wrong.

   c. Both your positions are correct, and both are wrong.

   d. It isn't important which position is right or wrong.

   e. Finally, affirm the fact that there is truth in all four positions.

4. The more important the disagreement is to you, the harder it will be to accept positions 2 through 5 as valid, but the exercise will work only if you can suspend your present position and imagine how it would feel to hold the other ones.

5. How can you tell if you've been successful with the pillow method? The answer is simple: If, after going over all the steps, you can understand— not necessarily accept, but just understand—the other person's position, you've done it. After you've reached this *understanding*, do you notice any change in how you feel about the other person?

SUMMARY

There is more to the world "out there" than any person is capable of understanding. We make sense of our environment by the four-step process of selecting certain stimuli from the environment, organizing them into meaningful patterns, interpreting them in a manner that is shaped by a variety of factors, and negotiating them through narratives we share with others.

Many factors affect the way we select, organize, interpret, and negotiate information. Access to information plays an important role. So do physiological factors such as our senses, age, and health. Cultural background also influences the way we view the world, as do social roles. In addition to these factors, some common tendencies affect the way we assign meaning to others' behavior.

Perception checking can be a useful tool for verifying interpretations of others' behavior, instead of assuming that the first hunch is correct. A complete perception check includes a description of the other's behavior, at least two plausible interpretations of its meaning, and a request for clarification about what the behavior does mean.

Empathy is the ability to experience another person's point of view. Empathy differs from sympathy, because it involves seeing the situation from the other person's perspective rather than your own. Cognitive complexity is the ability to construct a variety of frameworks for understanding an issue. One means for boosting both empathy and cognitive complexity is the pillow method, which involves viewing an issue from five different perspectives.

KEY TERMS

androgynous
attribution
empathy
ethnocentrism
gender role
halo effect
interpretation
narrative
negotiation

organization
perception checking
pillow method
punctuation
selection
self-serving bias
stereotyping
sympathy

MindTap START ...

Explore this chapter's topics online.

5

EMOTIONS: FEELING, THINKING, AND COMMUNICATING

AFTER STUDYING THE TOPICS IN THIS CHAPTER, YOU SHOULD BE ABLE TO:

1. Describe how the four components of emotions affect the way you feel, and hence your communication, in an important situation.

2. Describe how the influences on emotional expression have affected your communication in an important relationship.

3. Apply the guidelines for effectively communicating emotions in an important situation.

4. Identify and dispute the fallacies that are creating debilitative emotions in an important situation. Explain how more rational thinking can lead to more constructive communication.

*I*t's impossible to talk about communication without acknowledging the importance of emotions. Think about it: Feeling confident can assist you in everything from giving a speech to asking for a date, whereas feeling insecure can ruin your chances. Feeling angry or defensive can spoil your time with others, whereas feeling and acting calm will help prevent or solve problems. The way you share or withhold your feelings of affection can affect the future of your relationships. On and on goes the list of feelings that influence how we interact with others: appreciation, loneliness, joy, insecurity, curiosity, irritation. The point is clear: Communication shapes our feelings, and feelings shape our communication.

The role of emotions in human affairs is apparent to social scientists and laypeople alike. Researchers coined the term **emotional intelligence (EQ)** to describe the ability to understand and manage one's own emotions and be sensitive to others' feelings.[1] Studies show that EQ is positively linked with self-esteem, life satisfaction, and self-acceptance,[2] as well as with healthy conflict management and relationships.[3] Some employers even use emotional intelligence measures as part of their personnel selection process.[4] Emotional intelligence is unquestionably vital to both personal and interpersonal success.

Stop for a moment and try to identify someone you know who is emotionally intelligent. Perhaps it's a family member who is in touch with a wide range of feelings without being overwhelmed by them, or a boss who makes wise and rational choices even under stress. Now think of a person who might be lacking emotional intelligence. Maybe it's a colleague who is uptight and dismissive about honest human feelings, or a friend who blows up at the smallest inconvenience. And finally, assess your own emotional intelligence. How well do *you* understand and manage your emotions, and how sensitive are you to others' feelings?

Because emotions play such an important role in virtually all types of relationships, this chapter looks closer at analyzing and expressing them. You will learn what feelings are and how to recognize them. You'll read guidelines about when and how to best share your feelings with others. Finally, we will explore how to enhance emotions that make communication more rewarding and decrease ones that interfere with effective relationships. In later chapters we'll discuss how to interpret others' emotional states, but for now we'll focus on identifying and expressing your own emotions.

⋀ In *The Big Bang Theory*, Sheldon Cooper (Jim Parsons) has a keen mind but lacks emotional intelligence. As a result, he often violates social rules and sometimes damages relationships. What is your level of emotional intelligence?

CBS/Photofest

WHAT ARE EMOTIONS?

Suppose that an extraterrestrial visitor asked you to explain emotions. How would you answer? You might start by saying that emotions are things that we feel. But this doesn't say much, because in turn you would probably describe feelings as synonymous with emotions. Social scientists generally agree that there are several components to the phenomena we label as feelings.[5]

Physiological Factors

When a person has strong emotions, many bodily changes occur.[6] For example, the physical components of fear include an increased heart rate, a rise in blood pressure, an increase in adrenaline secretions, an elevated blood sugar level, a slowing of digestion, and a dilation of the pupils. Marriage researcher John Gottman notes that symptoms like these also occur when couples are in intense conflicts.[7] He calls the condition "flooding" and has found that it impedes effective problem-solving. Some physiological changes are recognizable to the person having them: a churning stomach or tense jaw, for example. These cues can offer a significant clue to your emotions after you become aware of them.

Nonverbal Reactions

Not all physical changes that accompany emotions are internal. Feelings are often apparent by observable changes. Some of these changes involve a person's appearance: blushing, sweating, and so on. Other changes involve behavior: a distinctive facial expression, posture, gestures, different vocal tone and rate, and so on. And research confirms what might be guessed: nonverbal expressions of emotions become more pronounced under the influence of alcohol.[8] Alcohol serves as an emotion enhancer—sometimes for better, sometimes for worse.

Although it's reasonably easy to tell when someone is feeling a strong emotion, it's more difficult to be certain exactly what that emotion might be. A slumped posture and sigh may be a sign of sadness, or they may be a sign of fatigue. Likewise, trembling hands might indicate excitement, or they may indicate fear. As you'll learn in Chapter 7, nonverbal behavior is usually ambiguous, and it's dangerous to assume that it can be read with much accuracy.

Although we usually think of nonverbal behavior as the reaction to an emotional state, there may be times when the reverse is true—when nonverbal behavior actually *causes* an emotional state. In one study, subjects who were coached to smile actually reported feeling better, and when they altered their expressions to look unhappy, they felt worse than before.[9] Walking with an upbeat strut can stave off feelings of depression.[10] And "jumping for joy" is more than just an emotional reaction. Research suggests that the act of jumping up and down can actually trigger happiness.[11]

There's also a connection between verbalizing emotions and nonverbal reactions. One study showed that participants who generated words associated with pride and disappointment experienced a change in posture.[12] They unconsciously stood taller when talking about pride and slumped when using words for disappointment. The participants also experienced emotions associated with their words (e.g., feeling sad when speaking about disappointment). This reminds us that verbal and nonverbal expressions of emotion are often interconnected.

INTROVERTS: THOUGHTFUL, NOT SHY

As a card-carrying introvert, I am one of the many people whose personality confers on them a preference for the inner world of their own mind rather than the outer world of sociability. Our psychic opposites, extraverts, prefer schmoozing and social life because such activities boost their mood. They get bored by too much solitude.

Often confused with shyness, introversion does not imply social reticence or discomfort. Rather than being averse to social engagement, introverts become overwhelmed by too much of it, which explains why the introvert is ready to leave a party after an hour and the extravert gains steam as the night goes on. Extraverts are comfortable thinking as they speak. Introverts prefer slow-paced interactions that allow room for thought. Brainstorming does not work for them. Email does.

Like individuals, cultures have different styles. America is a noisy culture, unlike, for example, Finland, which values silence. Individualism, dominant in the United States and Germany, promotes the direct, fast-paced style of communication associated with extraversion. Collectivistic societies, such as those in East Asia, value privacy and restraint, qualities more characteristic of introverts.

"In verbal cultures, remaining silent presents a problem," report Anio Sallinen-Kuparinen, James McCroskey, and Virginia Richmond, who have studied communication styles in the United States and Finland. Perceptions of competence tend to be based on verbal behavior. An introvert who is silent in a group may actually be quite engaged—taking in what is said, thinking about it, waiting for a turn to speak—but will be seen in the United States as a poor communicator.

Introverts are not as mild-mannered as made out to be. They seethe and even will lash out at those who encroach upon or malign their personal comfort zones. Here are a few emotional buttons to avoid with your introverted companions.

- "'Why don't you like parties? Don't you like people?' is a common remark introverts hear," says Marti Laney, a psychologist and the author of *The Introvert Advantage*. "Usually we like people fine," she insists. "We just like them in small doses."

- Don't demand immediate feedback from an introvert. "Extraverts think we have answers but just aren't giving them," Laney says. "They don't understand we need time to formulate them" and often won't talk until a thought is suitably polished.

- Don't interrupt if an introvert does get to talking. Listen closely. "Being overlooked is a really big issue for introverts," Laney says. Introverts are unlikely to repeat themselves; they will not risk making the same mistake twice.

- Above all, "we hate people telling us how we can be more extraverted, as if that's the desired state," says Beth Buelow, a life and leadership coach for introverts. Many introverts are happy with the way they are. And if you're not, that's your problem.

Laurie Helgoe

MindTap ENHANCE ...

your understanding by answering the following questions, either here or online.

1. Given the descriptions in this reading, do you generally regard yourself as an introvert or an extravert? How does that affect your interpersonal communication with others?

2. Do you agree that introverts are misunderstood in this culture? If so, can you think of examples from your network of close friends and family?

3. What do you see as the primary differences between shyness and introversion?

Cognitive Interpretations

Although there may be situations in which physical behavior and emotional states are directly connected, in most situations the mind plays an important role in determining emotional states. As you read earlier, some physiological components of fear are a racing heart, perspiration, tense muscles, and elevated blood pressure. Interestingly enough, these symptoms are similar to the physical changes that accompany excitement, joy, and other positive emotions. In other words, if we were to measure the physical condition of someone having a strong emotion, we would have a hard time knowing whether that person was trembling with fear or quivering with excitement.

The recognition that the bodily components of most emotions are similar led some psychologists to conclude that the experience of fright, joy, or anger comes primarily from the label we give to the same physical symptoms at a given time.[13] Psychologist Philip Zimbardo offers a good example of this principle:

> I notice I'm perspiring while lecturing. From that I infer I am nervous. If it occurs often, I might even label myself a "nervous person." Once I have the label, the next question I must answer is "Why am I nervous?" Then I start to search for an appropriate explanation. I might notice some students leaving the room, or being inattentive. I am nervous because I'm not giving a good lecture. That makes me nervous. How do I know it's not good? Because I'm boring my audience. I am nervous because I am a boring lecturer and I want to be a good lecturer. I feel inadequate. Maybe I should open a delicatessen instead. Just then a student says, "It's hot in here, I'm perspiring and it makes it tough to concentrate on your lecture." Instantly, I'm no longer "nervous" or "boring."[14]

Zimbardo found that changing his interpretation of the event affected the way he felt about it. Social scientists refer to this process as **reappraisal**—rethinking the meaning of emotionally charged events in ways that alter their emotional impact.[15] Research shows that reappraisal is vastly superior to suppressing your feelings: It often leads to lower stress, higher self-esteem, and increased productivity.[16] Here are two examples:

- Your self-esteem has been shattered since you lost your job, particularly because some of your less-ambitious coworkers were not fired. You lack confidence as you look for new employment. You could reappraise the event as an opportunity to find a new position (or career) where your hard work and contributions will be better appreciated.

- A friend of yours says some malicious things about you behind your back. Although you are hurt, you decide his actions are a statement about *his* character, not yours—and that you'll demonstrate your character by not speaking poorly about him to others.

Reappraisal also has relational benefits. One study found that couples who regularly step back from their conflicts and reappraise them from a neutral perspective have higher levels of relational satisfaction.[17] In essence, these couples reduce the emotional impact of their disputes by looking at them rationally and dispassionately.

It's important to note that reappraisal is not about denying your feelings. Recognizing and acknowledging emotions such as anger, hurt, and grief (as well as happiness, love, and relief) are vital to psychological and relational health. However, when you're ready to move past difficult emotions, reappraisal can help. We'll take a closer look at using reappraisal to reduce debilitative emotions later in this chapter.

Verbal Expression

As you'll read in Chapter 7, nonverbal behavior is a powerful way of communicating emotion. In fact, nonverbal actions are better at conveying emotions than they are at conveying ideas. But sometimes words are necessary to express feelings. Saying "I'm really angry" is clearer and probably more helpful than stomping out of the room, and "I'm feeling nervous" might help explain a pained expression on your face. Putting emotions into words can help you manage them more effectively,[18] while leaving them unspoken can result in negative mental and even physiological effects.[19]

Some researchers believe there are several basic or primary emotions.[20] However, there isn't much agreement among scholars about what those emotions are, or about what makes them basic.[21] Moreover, emotions that are primary in one culture may not be primary in others, and some emotions have no direct equivalent in other cultures.[22] For example, "shame" is a central emotion in the Chinese experience,[23] whereas it's much less familiar to most people from Western cultures. Despite this debate, most scholars acknowledge that *anger, joy, fear,* and *sadness* are common and typical human emotions.

We experience most emotions with different degrees of intensity, and it's important to use language that represents these differences. Figure 5.1 illustrates this point clearly. To say you're "annoyed" when a friend breaks an important promise, for example, would probably be an understatement. In other cases, people chronically overstate the strength of their feelings. To them, everything is "wonderful" or "terrible." The problem with this sort of exaggeration is that when a truly intense emotion comes along, they have no words left to describe it adequately. If chocolate chip cookies from the local bakery are "unbelievably fantastic," how does it feel to fall in love?

Researchers have identified a wide range of problems that arise for people who aren't able to talk about emotions constructively, including social isolation, unsatisfying relationships, feelings of anxiety and depression, and misdirected aggression.[24] Furthermore, the way parents talk to their children about emotions has a powerful effect on the children's development. Studies identify two distinct parenting styles: "emotion coaching" and "emotion dismissing."[25] The coaching approach gives children skills for communicating about feelings in later life that lead to much more satisfying relationships. Children who grow up in families where parents dismiss emotions are at higher risk for behavior problems than those who are raised in families that practice emotion coaching.[26] Later in this chapter you will find some guidelines for effectively communicating about emotions.

Annoyed	Angry	Furious
Pensive	Sad	Grieving
Content	Happy	Ecstatic
Anxious	Afraid	Terrified
Liking	Loving	Adoring

∧ FIGURE 5.1
Intensity of Emotions

PAUSE *and* REFLECT

Recognizing Your Emotions

MindTap® REFLECT ... on your emotions by answering the following questions, either here or online.

Keep a three-day record of your feelings. You can do this by spending a few minutes each evening recalling what emotions you felt during the day, what other people were involved, and the circumstances in which the emotions occurred. To help make your emotions easier to review and reflect on, create a simple chart of your observations with the following headings: 1. Day, 2. Situation (time/place), 3. Emotion (primary/ mixed, mild/intense, physical sensation, thoughts, behaviors), 4. People involved, 5. Show and share feelings (why or why not?), 6. Subject or theme of the conversation.

At the end of the three-day period, you can understand the role that emotions play in your communication by answering the following questions:

1. How did you recognize the emotions you felt: through physiological stimuli, nonverbal behaviors, or cognitive processes?

2. Did you have any difficulty deciding which emotions you were feeling?

3. What emotions do you have most often? Are they primary or mixed? Mild or intense?

4. In what circumstances do you or don't you show your feelings? What factors influence your decision to show or not show your feelings? The type of feeling? The person or persons involved? The situation (time, place)? The subject that the feeling involves (money, sex, and so on)?

5. Consider one of the situations from the above question, during which you decided to show and share your feelings. What were the consequences? Were you satisfied with the outcome? If not, what can you do in the future to become more satisfied?

INFLUENCES ON EMOTIONAL EXPRESSION

Most people are reluctant to express their emotions, at least verbally. People are generally comfortable making statements of fact and often delight in expressing their opinion, but they balk at disclosing how they feel. Why do people hesitate to express their emotions? Let's look at several reasons.

Personality

There is an increasingly clear relationship between personality and the way we experience and communicate emotions.[27] For example, extraverted people— those with a tendency to be upbeat, optimistic, and to enjoy social contact— report more positive emotions in everyday life than less extraverted

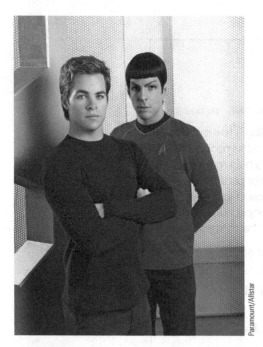

Paramount/Allstar

⋀ Unlike his hot-headed *Star Trek* colleague James T. Kirk (played here by Chris Pine), the iconic Mr. Spock (Zachary Quinto) suppresses his emotions. Being totally rational both helps and limits Spock's decision making. What are the pros and cons of emotions in your interpersonal encounters?

individuals.[28] Likewise, people with neurotic personalities (those with a tendency to worry, feel anxious, and be apprehensive) report more negative emotions in everyday life than less neurotic individuals. These personality traits are at least partially biological in nature.

Personality can be a powerful force, but it doesn't have to govern your communication satisfaction. For instance, people who are shy by nature can devise comfortable and effective strategies for reaching out. For example, the Internet has proven to be an effective way for reticent communicators to make contact, because it's been found to reduce social anxiety.[29] As described in Chapter 2, social media and computer dating services provide low-threat ways to approach others and get acquainted.[30]

Culture

People around the world generally experience the same emotions, but the same events can generate quite different feelings in different cultures.[31] The notion of eating snails might bring a smile of delight to some residents of France, whereas it would cause many North Americans to grimace in disgust. Culture also has an effect on how emotions are valued. One study found that Asian Americans and Hong Kong Chinese value "low arousal positive affect" (such as "calm") more than do European Americans, who tend to value "high arousal positive affect" (such as "excitement").[32] More specifically, the United States is known internationally as a "culture of cheerfulness." One author from Poland describes U.S. expressiveness this way: "Wow! Great! How nice! That's fantastic! I had a terrific time! It was wonderful! Have a nice day! Americans. So damned cheerful."[33]

There are also differences in the degree to which people in various cultures display their feelings. For example, social scientists have found support for the notion that people from warmer climates are more emotionally expressive than those who live in cooler climates.[34] Nearly 3,000 respondents representing 26 nationalities reported that people from the southern part of their countries were more emotionally expressive than were northerners.

One of the most significant factors that influences emotional expression is the position of a culture on the individualism-collectivism spectrum. Members of collectivistic cultures (such as Japan and India) prize harmony among members of their in-group and discourage expression of negative emotions that might upset relationships among people who belong to it. By contrast, members of highly individualistic cultures (such as the United States and Canada) feel comfortable revealing their emotions to people with whom they are close. It's easy to see how differences in display rules can lead to communication problems. For example, individualistic North Americans might view collectivistic Asians as less than candid, whereas Asians could easily regard North Americans as overly demonstrative.[35]

The phrase "I love you" offers an interesting case study of cultural differences in emotion expression. Researchers found that Americans say

"I love you" more frequently (and to more people) than do members of most other cultures.[36] It's not that love isn't a universal experience; rather, there are significant cultural differences about when, where, how often, and with whom the phrase should be used. For instance, Middle Easterners in the study said that "I love you" should only be expressed between spouses, and they warned that American men who use the phrase cavalierly with Middle Eastern women might be misinterpreted as making a marriage proposal. They were not alone: Study participants from a variety of backgrounds (e.g., Eastern Europe, India, Korea) said that they use the phrase quite sparingly, believing that its power and meaning would be lost if used too often. However, one factor was consistent across cultures: Women tend to say "I love you" more often than men. For more examples of the effect that gender has on emotion expression, read on.

Gender

Even within a culture, biological sex and gender roles often shape the ways in which men and women experience and express their emotions.[37] In fact, biological sex is the best predictor of the ability to detect and interpret emotional expressions—better than academic background, amount of foreign travel, cultural similarity, or ethnicity.[38] For example, research suggests that women are more attuned to emotions than men,[39] both within and across cultures.[40] A team of psychologists tested men's and women's recall of emotional images and found that females were 10 to 15 percent more accurate in remembering them. Furthermore, women's reactions to these emotion-producing stimuli were significantly more intense than men's.

Research on emotional expression suggests that there is at least some truth to the cultural stereotype of the unexpressive male and the more expressive female.[41] In face-to-face communication, one study showed that fathers mask their emotions more than mothers do, which leads their children to have more difficulty reading their fathers' emotional expressions.[42] In online communication, similar differences between male and female emotional expressiveness apply. For example, women are more likely than men to use emoticons, such as the symbol :), to express their feelings.[43] Women also express more affection on Facebook than do men.[44]

Zits used with the permission of the Zits Partnership, King Features Syndicate and the Cartoonist Group. All rights reserved.

The point is that while men and women generally experience the same emotions, there are some significant differences in the ways they express them.[45] These differences are due in large measure to social conventions, which we'll discuss now.

Social Conventions

In mainstream U.S. society, the unwritten rules of communication discourage the direct expression of most emotions.[46] Count the number of genuine emotional expressions that you hear over a two- or three-day period ("I'm angry"; "I feel embarrassed"), and you'll discover that emotional expressions are rare.

Looking at DIVERSITY

Todd Epaloose

Todd Epaloose: A Native American Perspective on Emotional Expression

Todd Epaloose was raised on the Zuñi pueblo in New Mexico. He spent part of his childhood on the reservation and part attending school in the city. He now lives in Albuquerque. As an urbanite who still spends time with his family on the reservation, Todd alternates between two worlds.

Zuñi and Anglo cultures are as different as night and day in the ways they treat communication about emotions. In mainstream U.S. culture, speaking up is accepted, or even approved. This is true from the time you are a child. Parents are proud when their child speaks up. Being quiet gets a child labeled as "shy," and is considered a problem.

In Zuñi culture, emotions are much less public. We are a private people, who consider a public display of feelings embarrassing. Self-control is considered a virtue. I think a lot of our emotional reticence comes from a respect for privacy. Your feelings are your own, and showing them to others is just as wrong as taking off your clothes in public. It's not that traditional Zuñis have fewer or less intense feelings than people in the city: It's just that there is less value placed on showing them in obvious ways.

The way we express affection is a good example of Zuñi attitudes and rules for sharing emotions. Our families are full of love. But someone from the city might not recognize this love, since it isn't displayed very much. There isn't a lot of hugging and kissing, even between

children and parents. Also, there isn't a lot of verbal expression: People don't say "I love you" to one another very much. We show our emotions by our actions: by helping one another, by caring for the people we love when they need us. That's enough to keep us happy.

I think some Native American emotional restraint might be helpful for people who are used to Anglo communication styles. Respecting others' privacy can be important: Some feelings are nobody else's business, and prying or demanding that they open up seems pushy and rude. Native American self-control can also add some civility to personal relationships. I'm not sure that "letting it all hang out" is always the best way.

One final word: I believe that in order to really understand the differences between emotional expression in Native American and Anglo cultures you have to live in both. If that isn't possible, at least realize that the familiar one isn't the only good approach. Try to respect what you don't understand.

"A Native American Perspective on Emotional Expression" by Todd Epaloose. Used with permission of author.

Not surprisingly, the emotions that people *do* share directly are usually positive ("I'm happy to say ..."; "I really enjoyed ..."). Communicators are reluctant to send messages that embarrass or threaten the "face" of others.[47] This is particularly true in the early stages of a new relationship, when a high ratio of positive-to-negative emotions is crucial to the relationship's development.[48] But even those in long-term relationships rarely express negative emotions directly. One study of married couples revealed that partners often share complimentary feelings ("I love you") or face-saving ones ("I'm sorry I yelled at you"). They also willingly disclose both positive and negative feelings about absent third parties ("I like Fred," "I'm uncomfortable around Gloria"). On the other hand, husbands and wives rarely verbalize face-threatening feelings ("I'm disappointed in you") or hostility ("I'm mad at you").[49]

Expression of emotions is also shaped by the requirements of many social roles. Researchers use the term **emotion labor** to describe situations in which managing and even suppressing emotions is both appropriate and necessary. Studies show that emotion labor is an important component of many if not most occupations (see the On the Job feature in this section for specific examples).

Social Media

Communicators generally express more emotion online than they do in person.[50] In some cases, that's good news. Those who have trouble sharing feelings face to face may find the freedom to do so behind the safety of a keyboard or touchscreen. Consider how it might be easier to type, rather than say, the words "I'm embarrassed" or "I love you."

Unfortunately, as discussed in Chapter 2, online disinhibition can also encourage emotional outbursts and tirades. This kind of venting can be hazardous to interpersonal relations, and it probably won't make you feel better. In a study of online "rant sites," volunteers who posted complaints felt angrier and less happy after doing so—the opposite of the catharsis the sites hope to provide.[51]

Social media can also feed emotional responses. For instance, regularly checking a romantic partner's Facebook site may spur feelings of jealousy, resulting in relational dissatisfaction.[52] The subtitle of one study asks this question: "Does Facebook Bring Out the Green-Eyed Monster of Jealousy?"[53] The short answer is "yes, it can"—especially when the viewer is already suspicious, and more so for women than men.[54] An unhealthy surveillance of loved ones—or former loved ones[55]—can take an emotional toll. We'll have more to say about jealousy and rumination later in this chapter.

The bottom line is that both senders and receivers experience emotions more intensely

"I'm not in one of my moods. I'm in one of your moods."

online. It's wise to keep this in mind before hitting send on emotionally charged messages, and before jumping to conclusions about ambiguous online information.

Emotional Contagion

Our emotions are influenced by the feelings of those around us through **emotional contagion**: the process by which emotions are transferred from one person to another.[56] As one commentator observed, "We catch feelings from one another as though they were some kind of social virus."[57] There is evidence that students catch the mood of their teachers,[58] customers are affected by the emotions of employees who serve them,[59] and husbands and wives directly influence each other's emotions.[60] In fact, studies show that our happiness (or unhappiness) can be affected by neighbors, friends of friends, or even total strangers.[61]

Emotional contagion can take place online as well as in person. In an analysis of millions of status updates on Facebook, researchers found that

On the JOB

Emotion Labor in the Workplace

The rules for expressing emotions on the job are clearly different from those in personal life. In intimate relationships (at least in mainstream Western culture), it's often important to tell friends, family, and loved ones exactly how you feel. In the workplace, however, it can be just as important to *conceal* emotions for the sake of clients, customers, coworkers, and supervisors—and also to protect your job.

Emotion labor—the process of managing and sometimes suppressing emotions—has been studied in a variety of occupational contexts. A few examples:

- If firefighters don't mask their emotions of fear, disgust, and stress, it will impede their ability to help the people whose lives they are trying to save. Emotion-management training is therefore vital for new firefighters.[a]

- Correctional officers at two minimum-security prisons described the tension of needing to be "warm, nurturing, and respectful" to inmates while also being "suspicious, strong, and tough." The officers acknowledged that it's taxing to manage competing emotions and juggle conflicting demands.[b]

- Money is an emotion-laden topic, which means that financial planners often engage in emotion labor. Researchers concluded that "relationships and communication with clients may indeed be more central to the work of financial planners than portfolio performance reports and changes in estate tax laws."[c]

While some of these occupations deal with life-and-death situations, emotion management is equally important in less intensive jobs. For instance, most customer-service positions require working with people who may express their dissatisfaction in angry and inappropriate ways ("I hate this store—I'm never shopping here again!"). In situations like these, it's usually unwise to "fight fire with fire," even if that's your natural impulse. Instead, competent on-the-job communicators can use the listening, defense-reducing, and conflict-management skills described in Chapters 8, 11, and 12.

It's not always easy to manage emotions, especially when you're feeling fearful, stressed, angry, or defensive. Nevertheless, doing the work of emotion labor is often vital for success on the job.

posts about rain—which is typically connected to negative moods—can have a ripple effect on readers.[62] Those exposed to their friends' rainy-day messages began posting more emotionally negative updates, even if it wasn't raining in their area. The good news is that positive posts are contagious too—at even greater rates. The researchers found that every positive status update led to 1.75 more positive posts by one's Facebook followers. It's important to recognize that communicating your emotional state—even online with people who may not know you well—can have an impact on the feelings and moods of others.

Most of us recognize the degree to which emotions are infectious. You can almost certainly recall instances when being around a calm person leaves you feeling more at peace, or when your previously sunny mood was spoiled by contact with a grouch. Researchers have demonstrated that this process occurs quickly and doesn't require much, if any, verbal communication.[63] In one study, two volunteers completed a survey that identified their moods. Then they sat quietly, facing each other for a two-minute period, ostensibly waiting for the researcher to return to the room. At the end of that time, they completed another emotional survey. Time after time, the brief exposure resulted in the less expressive partner's moods coming to resemble the moods of the more expressive one. It's easy to understand how emotions can be even more infectious with prolonged contact. In just a few months, the emotional responses of both dating couples and college roommates become dramatically more similar.[64]

GUIDELINES FOR EXPRESSING EMOTIONS

As you just read, there aren't any universal rules for the best way to communicate emotions. Personality, culture, gender roles, and social conventions all govern what approach will feel right to the people involved and what is most likely to work in a given situation. It's easy to think of times when it's *not* smart to express emotions clearly and directly. You usually can't chew out authority figures like difficult bosses or professors, and it's probably not wise to confront dangerous looking strangers who are bothering you.

Despite all the qualifiers and limitations, there will be times when you can benefit from communicating your feelings clearly and directly—even if you aren't normally an expressive person. When those times come, the following guidelines can help you explain how you feel.

A wide range of research supports the value of expressing emotions appropriately. On one hand, underexpression of feelings can lead to serious ailments. Inexpressive people—those who value rationality and self-control, try to control their feelings and impulses, and deny distress—are more likely to get a host of ailments, including cancer, asthma, and heart disease.[65]

Allstar Picture library

▲ Some might claim that 11-year-old Riley has it easy in the film *Inside Out* because her emotions come with names: Joy (voiced by Amy Poehler), Fear (Bill Hader), Disgust (Mindy Kaling), Anger (Lewis Black), and Sadness (Phyllis Smith). Of course, having these feelings doesn't mean she can always manage them well. Are you able to recognize your emotions when you experience them?

On the other hand, communicators who overexpress their negative feelings also suffer physiologically. When people lash out verbally, their blood pressure jumps an average of twenty points, and in some people it increases by as much as one hundred points.[66] The key to health, then, is to learn how to express emotions *constructively*.

Beyond the physiological benefits, another benefit of expressing emotions effectively is the chance of improving relationships.[67] As Chapter 3 explains, self-disclosure is one path (though not the only one) to intimacy. Even on the job, many managers and organizational researchers are contradicting generations of tradition by suggesting that constructively expressing emotions can lead to career success as well as help workers feel better.[68] Of course, the rules for expressing emotions in the workplace are usually more strict than those in personal relationships, so handle with care.[69]

Despite its benefits, expressing emotions effectively isn't a simple matter. It's obvious that showing every feeling of boredom, fear, anger, or frustration would get you into trouble. Even the indiscriminate sharing of positive feelings— love, affection, and so on—isn't always wise. But withholding emotions can be personally frustrating and can keep relationships from growing and prospering.

The following suggestions can help you decide when and how to express your emotions. Combined with the guidelines for self-disclosure in Chapter 2, they can improve the effectiveness of your emotional expression.

Recognize Your Feelings

Answering the question "How do you feel?" isn't as easy for some people as others. Some people (researchers call them "affectively oriented") are much more aware of their emotional states and use information about those emotional states when making important decisions.[70] By contrast, people with a low affective orientation usually aren't aware of their emotional states and tend to regard feelings as useless and unimportant information.

Beyond being *aware* of one's feelings, research shows that it's valuable to be able to *identify* one's emotions. Researchers have found that college students who can pinpoint the negative emotions they experience (such as "nervous," "angry," "sad," "ashamed," and "guilty") also have the best strategies for managing those emotions.[71] This explains why the ability to distinguish and label emotions is a vital component of emotional intelligence, both within and across cultures.[72]

As you read earlier in this chapter, feelings become recognizable in several ways. Physiological changes can be a clear sign of your feelings. Monitoring nonverbal behaviors is another excellent way to keep in touch with your emotions. You can also recognize your feelings by monitoring your thoughts as well as the verbal messages you send to others. It's not far from the verbal statement "I hate this!" to the realization that you're angry (or bored, nervous, or embarrassed).

Recognize the Difference between Feeling, Talking, and Acting

Just because you feel a certain way doesn't mean you must always talk about it, and talking about a feeling doesn't mean you must act on it. In fact, compelling evidence suggests that people who act out angry feelings—whether by lashing out, or even by hitting an inanimate punching bag—actually feel worse than those who experience anger without lashing out.[73]

Understanding the difference between having feelings and acting them out can help you express yourself constructively in tough situations. If, for instance, you recognize that you are upset with a friend, it becomes possible to explore exactly why you feel so upset. Sharing your feeling ("Sometimes I get so mad at you that I could scream") might open the door to resolving whatever is bothering you. Pretending that nothing is bothering you, or lashing out at the other person, is unlikely to diminish your resentful feelings, which can then go on to contaminate the relationship.

Expand Your Emotional Vocabulary

Most people suffer from impoverished emotional vocabularies. Ask them how they're feeling, and the response will almost always include the same terms: *good* or *bad*, *terrible* or *great*, and so on. Take a moment now to see how many feelings you can write down. After you've done your best, look at Table 5.1 and see which ones you've missed.

Many communicators think they are expressing feelings when, in fact, their statements are emotionally counterfeit. For example, it sounds emotionally revealing to say, "I feel like going to a show" or "I feel we've been seeing too much of each other." But in fact, neither of these statements has any emotional content. In the first sentence the word *feel* really stands for an intention: "I *want* to go to a show." In the second sentence the "feeling" is really a thought: "I *think* we've been seeing too much of each other." You can recognize the absence of emotion in each case by adding a genuine word of feeling to it. For instance, "I'm *bored*, and I want to go to a show" or "I think we've been seeing too much of each other, and I feel *confined*."

Relying on a small vocabulary to describe feelings is as limiting as relying on a small vocabulary to describe colors. To say that the ocean in all its moods, the sky as it varies from day to day, and the color of your true love's eyes are all "blue" tells only a fraction of the story. Likewise, it's overly broad to use a term like *good* or *great* to describe how you feel in situations as different as earning a high grade, finishing a marathon, and hearing the words "I love you" from a special person.

There are several ways to express a feeling verbally:[74]

- By using *single words*: "I'm angry" (or "excited," "depressed," "curious," and so on).

- By describing what's happening *to you*: "My stomach is tied in knots," "I'm on top of the world."

- By describing what you'd like *to do*: "I want to run away," "I'd like to give you a hug."

TABLE 5.1 Common Human Emotions

afraid	concerned	exhausted	hurried	nervous	sexy
aggravated	confident	fearful	hurt	numb	shaky
amazed	confused	fed	hysterical	optimistic	shocked
ambivalent	content	fidgety	impatient	paranoid	shy
angry	crazy	flattered	impressed	passionate	sorry
annoyed	defeated	foolish	inhibited	peaceful	strong
anxious	defensive	forlorn	insecure	pessimistic	subdued
apathetic	delighted	free	interested	playful	surprised
ashamed	depressed	friendly	intimidated	pleased	suspicious
bashful	detached	frustrated	irritable	possessive	tender
befuddled	devastated	furious	jealous	pressured	tense
bewildered	disappointed	glad	joyful	protective	terrified
bitter	disgusted	glum	lazy	puzzled	tired
bored	disturbed	grateful	lonely	refreshed	trapped
brave	ecstatic	happy	loving	regretful	ugly
calm	edgy	harassed	lukewarm	relieved	uneasy
cantankerous	elated	helpless	mad	resentful	up
carefree	embarrassed	high	mean	restless	vulnerable
cheerful	empty	hopeful	miserable	ridiculous	warm
cocky	enthusiastic	horrible	mixed	romantic	weak
cold	envious	hostile	mortified	sad	wonderful
comfortable	excited	humiliated	neglected	sentimental	worried

Sometimes communicators inaccurately minimize the strength of their feelings: "I'm a *little* unhappy" or "I'm *pretty* excited" or "I'm *sort of* confused." Of course, not all feelings are strong ones. We do feel degrees of sadness and joy, for example, but some people have a tendency to discount almost every feeling. Do you?

In other cases, communicators express feelings in a coded manner. This happens most often when the sender is uncomfortable about revealing the feeling in question. Some codes are verbal ones, as when the sender hints more or less subtly at the message.

For example, an indirect way to say "I'm lonesome" might be "I guess there's not much going on this weekend, so if you don't have any plans maybe you could text me and we could hang out." Such a message is so indirect that your real feeling may not be recognized. For this reason, people who send coded messages stand less of a chance of having their feelings understood—and their needs met.

If you do decide to express your feeling, you can be most clear by making sure that both you and your partner understand that your feeling is centered on a specific set of circumstances rather than being indicative of the whole relationship. Instead of saying "I resent you," say "I resent you when you don't keep your promises." Rather than saying "I'm bored with you," say "I'm bored when you talk about your money."

Share Multiple Feelings

The feeling you express often isn't the only one you're experiencing. For example, you might often express your anger but overlook the confusion, disappointment, frustration, sadness, or embarrassment that preceded it. To understand why, consider the following examples. For each one, ask yourself two questions: "How would I feel? What feelings might I express?"

> An out-of-town friend has promised to arrive at your place at six o'clock. When he hasn't arrived by nine, you are convinced that a terrible accident has occurred. Just as you pick up the phone to call the police and local hospitals, your friend breezes in the door with an offhand remark about getting a late start.

> A photo of you is posted by a friend on Facebook. On the one hand, you're flattered by your friend's display of affection for you. On the other hand, it's a picture that doesn't paint you in the best light. You wish the friend had asked first.

In situations like these, you would probably feel mixed emotions. Consider the case of the overdue friend. Your first reaction to his arrival would probably be relief: "Thank goodness, he's safe!" But you would also be likely to feel anger: "Why didn't he phone to tell me he'd be late?" The second example would probably leave you feeling pleased, embarrassed, and mad—all at the same time.

Despite the commonness of mixed emotions, we often communicate only one feeling—usually the most negative one. In both of the preceding examples, you might show only your anger, leaving the other person with little idea of the full range of your feelings. Consider the different reaction you would get by showing *all* of your emotions in these cases and in others.

Consider When and Where to Express Your Feelings

Often the first flush of a strong feeling is not the best time to speak out. If you're awakened by the racket caused by a noisy neighbor, storming over to complain might result in your saying things you'll regret later. In such a case, it's probably wiser to wait until you have thought out carefully how you might express your feelings in a way that would most likely be heard. Research shows that "imagined interactions" in advance of actual conversations can enhance relationships by allowing communicators to rehearse what they will say and to consider how others might respond.[75]

Even after you've waited for the first wave of strong feeling to subside, it's still important to choose the time that's best suited to the message. Being rushed or tired or disturbed by some other matter is probably a good reason for postponing the expression of your feeling. In the same manner, you ought to be sure that the recipient of your message is ready to hear you out before you begin. Sometimes that means checking the other person's mood before you start sharing emotions. In other cases, it's about calculating whether that person is relationally ready to hear sentiments such as "I love you." And when making personal disclosures, it's often a good idea to ensure a measure of privacy. (YouTube is filled with examples of people being embarrassed by public declarations of affection.)

There are also cases where you may choose to never express your feelings. Even if you're dying to tell an instructor that her lectures leave you bored to a stupor, you might decide it's best to answer her question "How's class going?"

SKILL *Builder*

Feelings and Phrases

MindTap® PRACTICE... communicating your feelings by answering the following questions either here or online.

You can try this exercise alone or with a group:

1. Choose a situation from column A and a receiver from column B.

2. Develop an approach for communicating your feelings for this combination.

3. Now create approaches for the same situation with other receivers from column B. How are the statements different?

4. Repeat the process with various combinations, using other situations from column A.

Column A: Situations

a. You receive a terse text message cancelling a date or appointment. It's the third time the other person has cancelled at the last minute.

b. The other person posts an inappropriate comment on your Facebook Wall.

c. The other person compliments you on your appearance, then says, "I hope I haven't embarrassed you."

d. The other person gives you a hug and says, "It's good to see you."

Column B: Receivers

An instructor

A family member (you decide which one)

A classmate you don't know well

Your best friend

with an innocuous "Okay." And even though you may be irritated by the arrogance of a police officer stopping you for speeding, the smartest approach might be to keep your feelings to yourself. In cases where you experience strong emotions but don't want to share them verbally (for whatever reason), writing your feelings and thoughts has been shown to have mental, physical, and emotional benefits.[76] For instance, one study found that writing about feelings of affection can actually reduce the writer's cholesterol level.[77]

Accept Responsibility for Your Feelings

It's important to make sure that your language reflects the fact that you're responsible for your feelings.[78] Instead of saying "You're making me angry," say "I'm getting angry." Instead of saying "You hurt my feelings," say "I feel

ETHICAL *Challenge*

Aristotle's Golden Mean

Almost two and a half millennia ago, the philosopher Aristotle examined the question of "moral virtue": What constitutes good behavior, and what ways of acting enable us to function effectively in the world? One important part of his examination addresses the management and expression of emotion: what he defines as "passions and actions."

According to Aristotle, an important dimension of virtuous behavior is moderation, which he defines as "an intermediate between excess and deficit … equidistant from the extremes … neither too much nor too little." He acknowledges that it isn't realistic or desirable for a passionate person to strive for the same type of behavior as a dispassionate person. After all, a world in which everyone felt and acted identically would be boring.

Instead of a "one-size-fits-all" approach to emotional expression, Aristotle urges communicators to moderate their own style, to be "intermediate not in the object, but relative to us." Following Aristotle's injunction, a person with a hot temper would strive to cool down, whereas a person who rarely expresses his or her feelings ought to aim at becoming more expressive. The result would still be two people with different styles, but each of whom behaved better than before seeking the golden mean.

According to Aristotle, moderation also means that emotions should be suited to the occasion: We should feel (and express) them "at the right times, with reference to the right objects, towards the right people, with the right motive, and in the right way." We can imagine times when even a normally restrained person could reasonably act with anger and times when a normally voluble person could reasonably behave with restraint. Even then, too much emotion (rage, for example) or too little emotion falls outside the range of virtue. In Aristotle's words, when it comes to "passions and actions … excess is a form of failure and so is deficit."

How would your emotional expression be different if you strived for moderation? Answer this question by identifying which parts of your emotional expression are most extreme, either in their intensity or their absence.

MindTap® APPLY … the ethical principles introduced here by answering the following questions, either here or online.

1. How might your relationships change if you acted more moderately?

2. Are there any situations in your life when more extreme forms of emotional expression are both moral and effective?

hurt when you do that." As you'll soon read, people don't make us like or dislike them, and believing that they do denies the responsibility that each of us has for our own emotions. Chapter 6 introduces "I" language, which offers a responsible way to express your feelings.

Be Mindful of the Communication Channel

As Chapter 1 explained, the channels we use to communicate make a difference in how others interpret our messages. This is particularly true when expressing emotions.

Communicators today have many more channel choices than they did a few decades ago, and the decision about when to use mediated channels—such as email, instant messaging, cell phones, social media sites, and blogging—call for a level of analysis that wasn't required in the past.[79] For instance, is it appropriate to signal your desire to end a relationship in a voice mail message? When is it acceptable to use CAPITAL LETTERS in a blog post to express displeasure? If you're excited about some good news, should you first tell your family and friends in person before publishing it on Facebook?

Most people intuitively recognize that the selection of a channel depends in part on the kind of message they're sending. In one survey, students identified which channel they would find best for delivering a variety of messages.[80] Most respondents said they would have little trouble expressing positive messages in person, but preferred mediated channels for negative messages.

"Flaming" is an extreme example of how mediated channels lend themselves to expressing negative emotions. The kind of civility that most people honor in other communication channels seems to have less of a hold on the Internet—certainly among strangers, but even among people who belong to the same personal networks. Before saying something you may later regret, it's worth remembering the principle stated in Chapter 1 that communication is irreversible. Once you hit the "Send" button, you can't retract an emotional outburst.

MANAGING EMOTIONS

Although feeling and expressing emotions usually adds to the quality of interpersonal relationships, not all feelings are beneficial. For instance, rage, depression, terror, and jealousy do little to help you feel better or improve your relationships. You will learn about tools to minimize these unproductive emotions. We'll also describe how to maximize the experience of positive emotions.

Facilitative and Debilitative Emotions

First, we need to make a distinction between **facilitative emotions**, which contribute to effective functioning, and **debilitative emotions**, which detract from effective functioning.

One difference between the two types is their *intensity*. For instance, a certain amount of anger or irritation can be constructive because it often provides the stimulus that leads you to improve the unsatisfying conditions. Rage, however, usually makes matters worse—especially when driving, as illustrated by the problems associated with "road rage."[81] The same holds true for fear. A little bit of fear before an important athletic contest or job interview might give you the boost that will improve your performance.[82] (Mellow athletes or employees usually don't do well.) But total terror is something else.

Not surprisingly, debilitative emotions like communication apprehension can lead to a variety of problems in personal, business, educational, and even medical settings.[83] When people become anxious, they generally speak less, which means that their needs aren't met; and when they do manage to speak up, they are less effective at communicating than their more confident counterparts.[84]

A second characteristic that distinguishes debilitative feelings from facilitative ones is their extended *duration*. Feeling depressed for a while after the breakup of a relationship or the loss of a job is natural, but spending the rest of your life grieving over your loss would accomplish nothing. In the same way, staying angry at someone for a wrong inflicted long ago can be just as punishing to you as to the wrongdoer. Social scientists call this **rumination**—dwelling persistently on negative thoughts that, in turn, intensify negative feelings. A substantial body of research confirms that rumination increases feelings of sadness, anxiety, jealousy, and depression[85] and makes them last longer.[86] Just as bad, people who ruminate are more likely to lash out with displaced aggression at innocent bystanders.[87]

Many debilitative emotions involve communication. Here are a few examples, offered by readers of *Looking Out Looking In*:

> When I first came to college, I had to leave my boyfriend. I was living with three girls, and for most of the first semester I was so lonesome and unhappy that I was a pretty terrible roommate.

> I got so frustrated with my overly critical boss that I lost my temper and quit one day. I told him what a horrible manager he was and walked off the job right then and there. Now I'm afraid to list my former boss as a reference, and I'm afraid my temper tantrum will make it harder for me to get a new job.

> I've had ongoing problems with my family, and sometimes I get so upset that I can't concentrate on my work or school, or even sleep well at night.

You will learn a method for dealing with debilitative feelings like these that can improve your effectiveness as a communicator. This method is based on the idea that one way to minimize debilitative feelings is to minimize unproductive thinking.

Sources of Debilitative Emotions

For most people, feelings seem to have a life of their own. You wish you could feel calm when approaching strangers, yet your voice quivers. You try to appear confident when asking for a raise, yet your eye twitches nervously. Where do feelings like these come from?

ʌ In the TV show *Revenge*, Emily Thorne (Emily VanCamp) feels driven to settle scores with people she believes have wronged her. Most observers would agree that while Emily's grievances may be justified, her desire for retribution is debilitating. What emotions typically accompany a desire for vengeance?

E4/Allstar

In REAL LIFE

Guidelines for Emotional Expression

After a long and frustrating search, Logan thinks he has found the ideal job that he wants and needs. The interview went well. As Logan was leaving, the interviewer said he was "very well qualified" and promised "You'll be hearing from us soon." That conversation took place almost two weeks ago, and Logan hasn't heard a word from the company.

The two transcripts below reflect very different ways of responding to this difficult situation. The first one ignores and the second one follows the Guidelines for Expressing Emotions described in this chapter. In each, Logan begins by *ruminating* about the employer's failure to get in touch as promised.

Ignoring Guidelines for Expressing Emotions

Logan doesn't explicitly recognize a single emotion he is experiencing, let alone any mixed emotions. Rather than accepting responsibility for his own feelings, he blames the employer for "driving me crazy."	"I can't believe those inconsiderate idiots! Who do they think they are, promising to call soon and then doing nothing? They're driving me crazy."
Logan jumps to the conclusion that a job offer isn't forthcoming, and lashes out without considering any alternatives.	"I give up. Since they aren't going to hire me, I'm going to call that interviewer and let her know what a screwed-up company they're running. I'll probably get her voice mail, but that's even better: That way I can say what's on my mind without getting nervous or being interrupted. They have no right to jerk me around like this, and I'm going to tell them just that." *(Angrily dials phone)*

Following Guidelines for Expressing Emotions

Logan identifies his mixture of feelings as a starting point for deciding what to do.	"I'm mad at the company for not keeping in touch like they promised. I'm also confused about whether I'm as qualified as I thought I was, and I'm starting to worry that maybe I didn't do as well in the interview as I thought. I'm also sorry I didn't ask her for a more specific time than 'soon.' And I'm really unsure about whether to give up, wait for them to call me, or reach out to the company and ask what's going on."

Physiology   One answer lies in our genetic makeup. As you read in Chapter 3, temperament is, to a large degree, inherited. Communication traits like shyness, verbal aggressiveness, and assertiveness are rooted in biology. Fortunately, biology isn't destiny. As you'll soon read, it is possible to overcome debilitative feelings.

Beyond heredity, cognitive scientists tell us that the cause of some debilitative feelings—especially those involving fight-or-flight responses—lies deep inside the brain, in an almond-sized cluster of interconnected structures

He recognizes the difference between what he would like to do (chew out the interviewer) and what is more appropriate and effective.	"If I'm not going to get the job, I'd like to chew out that interviewer for promising to call. But that would probably be a bad idea—burning my bridges, as my family would say."
Logan uses a perception check and considers sharing his feelings with the employer in a non-blaming way. He deliberately considers when and how to express himself, choosing email as the best channel to achieve his goals.	"Maybe I'll call her and say something like 'I'm confused. You said at the interview that I'd hear from you soon, but it's been almost two weeks now with no word.' I could ask whether I misunderstood (although I doubt that), or whether they need some more information from me. Let me think about that overnight. If the idea still sounds good in the morning, I'll call them."
Having decided to email the employer, Logan could use the face-saving methods described in Chapter 11 to compose his message. He could begin by speaking positively about his continued interest in the company, then raise his concern about not having heard from them, and then close by saying that he's looking forward to hearing back from them.	"Actually, an email would be better. I could edit my words until they're just right, and an email wouldn't put the interviewer on the spot like a phone call would."

MindTap APPLY ... this situation to your life by answering questions online.

called the amygdala (pronounced uh-MIG-duh-luh). The amygdala acts as a kind of sentinel that scans every experience, looking for threats. In literally a split second, it can sound an alarm that triggers a flood of physiological reactions: speeding heart rate, elevating blood pressure, heightening the senses, and preparing the muscles to react.[88]

This defense system has obvious value when we are confronted with real physical dangers, but in social situations the amygdala can hijack the brain, triggering emotions like fear and anger when there is no real threat. You might find yourself feeling uncomfortable when somebody stands too close to you or angry when someone cuts in front of you in line. As you'll soon read, thinking clearly is the way to avoid overreacting to events like these.

Emotional Memory   The source of some threats lies in what neuroscientists have termed our *emotional memory*. Seemingly harmless events can trigger debilitative feelings if they bear even a slight resemblance to troublesome experiences from the past. A few examples illustrate the point:

- Ever since being teased when he moved to a new elementary school, Darnell has been uncomfortable in unfamiliar situations.

- Alicia feels apprehensive around men, especially those with deep, booming voices. As a child, she was mistreated by a family member with a loud baritone voice.

- Miguel feels a wave of insecurity whenever he is around women who use the same perfume worn by a former lover who jilted him.

Self-Talk   Beyond neurobiology, what we think can have a profound effect on how we feel. It's common to say that strangers or your boss make you feel nervous, just as you would say that a bee sting makes you feel pain. The apparent similarities between physical and emotional discomforts become clear if you look at them like this:

EVENT	FEELING
Bee sting	Physical pain
Meeting strangers	Nervous feelings

When looking at your emotions in this way, you seem to have little control over how you feel. However, this apparent similarity between physical pain and emotional discomfort (or pleasure) isn't as great as it seems to be. Cognitive psychologists argue that it is not *events* such as meeting strangers or being jilted by a lover that cause people to feel bad, but rather the *beliefs they hold* about these events. As discussed earlier in the chapter, *reappraisal* involves changing our thoughts to help manage our emotions.

Albert Ellis, who developed an approach to reappraisal called *rational-emotive therapy*, tells a story that makes this point clear. Imagine yourself walking by a friend's house and seeing your friend stick his head out of a window and call you a string of vile names. (You supply the friend and the names.) Under these circumstances, it's likely that you would feel hurt and upset. Now imagine that instead of walking by a house, you are passing a mental institution. The same friend, who is obviously a patient there, shouts the same vile names at you. In this case, your feelings would probably be quite different—most likely sadness and pity.

You can see that in this story the activating event of being called names was the same in both cases, yet the emotional consequences were very different. The reason for your different feelings has to do with your thinking in each case. In the first case, you would most likely think that your friend was very angry with you; further, you might imagine that you must have done something terrible to deserve such a response. In the second case, you would probably assume that your friend had some psychological difficulty, and most likely you would feel sympathetic.

From this example you can start to see that it's the *interpretations* that people make of an event, during the process of **self-talk**, that determine their feelings.[89] Thus, the model for emotions looks like this:

EVENT	THOUGHT (SELF-TALK)	FEELING
Being called names	"I've done something wrong."	Hurt, upset
Being called names	"My friend must be sick."	Concern, sympathy

The same principle applies in more common situations. In job interviews, for example, people who become nervous are likely to use negative self-talk when they think about their performance: "I won't do well," "I don't know why I'm doing this."[90] In romantic relationships, thoughts shape satisfaction. The words "I love you" can be interpreted in a variety of ways. They could be taken at face value as a genuine expression of deep affection:

EVENT	THOUGHT (SELF-TALK)	FEELING
Hearing "I love you"	"This is a genuine statement."	Delight (perhaps)

The same words might be decoded as a sincere but mistaken declaration uttered in a moment of passion, an attempt to make the recipient feel better, or an attempt at manipulation. For example,

EVENT	THOUGHT (SELF-TALK)	FEELING
Hearing "I love you"	"She's just saying this to manipulate me."	Anger

In other words, our emotions are more a result of our thoughts than of the events we encounter. This takes us back to the reappraisal process described earlier in the chapter. It's possible to use self-talk to manage emotional responses. For instance, research shows that telling yourself "I am excited" instead of "Calm down" will generally lead to better performances in public speaking.[91] The words we use—even if they never leave our minds—can have a dramatic effect on how we manage our emotions.

PAUSE *and* REFLECT

Talking to Yourself

MindTap® REFLECT ... on how your thoughts shape your feelings by answering the following questions, either here or online.

You can become better at understanding how your thoughts shape your feelings by completing the following steps:

1. Take a few minutes to listen to the inner voice you use when thinking. Close your eyes now and listen to it. Did you hear the voice? Perhaps it was saying, "What voice? I don't have any voice...." Try again, and pay attention to what the voice is saying.

2. Now think about the following situations and imagine how you would react in each. How would you interpret them with your inner voice? What feelings would follow from each interpretation?

   a. While sitting on a bus, in class, or on the street, you notice an attractive person sneaking glances at you.

   b. During a lecture your professor asks the class "What do you think about this?" and looks toward you.

   c. You are telling friends about your vacation, and one yawns.

   d. You run into a friend on the street and ask how things are going. "Fine," she replies, and rushes off.

3. Now recall three recent times when you felt a strong emotion. For each one, recall the activating event and then the interpretation that led to your emotional reaction.

Irrational Thinking and Debilitative Emotions

Many debilitative emotions come from accepting a number of irrational thoughts—we'll call them *fallacies* here—that lead to illogical conclusions and in turn to debilitative emotions. We usually aren't aware of these thoughts, which makes them especially powerful.[92]

1. The Fallacy of Perfection   People who accept the **fallacy of perfection** believe that a worthwhile communicator should be able to handle every situation with complete confidence and skill.

Nobody is perfect. Given the desire to be valued and appreciated, it's tempting to try to *appear* flawless. But the costs of such deception are high. If others ever find you out, they'll see you as a phony. Even when your act isn't uncovered, it uses up a great deal of psychological energy and thus makes the rewards of approval less enjoyable.

Subscribing to the myth of perfection not only can keep others from liking you, but also can act as a force to diminish your own self-esteem. How can you like yourself when you don't measure up to the way you ought to be? It's liberating to comfortably accept the idea that you are not perfect.

2. The Fallacy of Approval   The **fallacy of approval** is based on the idea that it's not just desirable but vital to get the approval of virtually every person. People who accept this idea seek approval from others, even when they have to sacrifice their own principles and happiness to do so. Accepting this fallacy can lead to some ludicrous situations:

Carol and Mike Werner/Index Stock/Getty Images

> Feeling nervous because people you don't even like seem to disapprove of you
>
> Feeling apologetic when others are at fault
>
> Feeling embarrassed after behaving unnaturally to gain another's approval

The fallacy of approval is irrational because it implies that others will respect and like you more if you go out of your way to please them. Often this simply isn't true. Would *you* respect people who have compromised important values just to gain acceptance? Are you likely to think highly of people who repeatedly deny their own needs as a means of buying approval?

Don't misunderstand: Abandoning the fallacy of approval doesn't mean living a life of selfishness. It's still important to consider the needs of others and to meet them whenever possible. It's also pleasant—we might say even necessary—to strive for the respect of those people you value. The point here is that when you must abandon your own needs and principles in order to seek these goals, the price is too high.

3. The Fallacy of Shoulds   The **fallacy of shoulds** is the inability to distinguish between what is and what should be. You can see the difference by imagining a person who is full of complaints about the world:

> "There should be no rain on weekends."
>
> "People ought to live forever."
>
> "Money should grow on trees."
>
> "We should all be able to fly."

Complaints like these are obviously foolish. Yet many people torture themselves by engaging in this sort of irrational thinking when they confuse preferences with shoulds. They say and think things like this:

> "My friend should be more understanding."
>
> "She shouldn't be so inconsiderate."
>
> "They should be more friendly."
>
> "You should work harder."

The message in each of these cases is that you would *prefer* people to behave differently. Wishing that things were better is legitimate, and trying to change things may be a good idea, but it's unreasonable to *insist* that the world operate just as you want it to or to feel cheated when things aren't ideal.

CRITIC'S MATH

Larry David feels just like me and you when it comes to criticism.

You'd think he wouldn't. He co-created *Seinfeld*, the most successful sitcom of all time. His show *Curb Your Enthusiasm* is a smash success. He's been on the cover of *Rolling Stone* magazine. And yet, he still does the same math you and I do when it comes to critics.

What's critic's math? It's the formula most of us use when it comes to criticism. Here is an example of how it works:

> 1 insult + 1,000 compliments = 1 insult.

We need look no further than a story about Larry David in that *Rolling Stone* article to see it in action.

One night during his stay (in New York), David went to Yankee Stadium to see a game. His image went up on the big screen as *Curb Your Enthusiasm's* theme song played over the big speakers. An entire stadium of fans stood and cheered for the hopeless case from Brooklyn. It should have been a life-defining moment, the redemptive final scene in the biopic. But as it turned out, not so much. As David left the stadium, a guy drove by and yelled, "Larry, you suck!" "That's like, literally all he heard," David's friend says.

David spent the ride back from the Bronx obsessing over that moment. It was as if the other 50,000 people, the ones who loved him, didn't exist. "Who's that guy? What was that?" He asked. "Who would do that? Why would you say something like that?"

That's critic's math. One insult was able to erase an entire stadium of adulation. More than 50,000 people disappeared at the hand of one point of bitterness. Critic's math might be the most powerful magic on the planet.

There are three things you need to know about it:

1. *It doesn't instantly go away with success.* If right now you're thinking "If I sell a certain number of books or get a job promotion, I won't worry so much about what critic's think," you're wrong. Larry David is incredibly successful. If you have a hard time with critic's math with 10 followers on Twitter, you'll still have a hard time with it with 1 million followers. Don't chase success as a way to beat critic's math.

2. *Every time you believe critic's math, you make it more powerful.* Doubt and fear are like muscles. Every time you believe a lie it gets easier to believe the next time. It took Larry David a lifetime of critic's math to ignore a full stadium of fans.

3. *You're not the only one with a math problem.* You know which Amazon review for my book *Quitter* I think about the most? It's not the 95 5-star reviews the book got. It's the one 1-star review.

It's time you and me, and maybe even Larry David, let it go. Critic's math doesn't add up. In fact, it's all about subtraction. Subtracting compliments. Subtracting happiness. Subtracting joy.

Jon Acuff

MindTap ENHANCE ... your understanding by answering the following questions, either here or online.

1. Identify a time when you used "critic's math" in evaluating others' messages about you.

2. Reappraise the situation you identified in question 1, developing a more balanced response to the criticism. How does this reappraisal affect your emotions and your subsequent behavior?

Becoming obsessed with shoulds like these has three troublesome consequences. First, it leads to unnecessary unhappiness because people who are constantly dreaming about the ideal are seldom satisfied with what they have or who they are. Second, merely complaining without acting can keep you from doing anything to change unsatisfying conditions. Third, this sort of complaining can build a defensive climate with others, who will resent being nagged. It's much more effective to tell people about what you'd like than to preach. Say, "I wish you'd be more punctual" instead of "You should be on time." We'll discuss ways of avoiding defensive climates in Chapter 11.

4. The Fallacy of Overgeneralization   The **fallacy of overgeneralization** comprises two types. The first type of overgeneralization occurs when we base a belief on a limited amount of evidence. For instance, how many times have you found yourself saying something like this:

> "I'm so stupid! I can't even figure out how to download music on my phone."

> "Some friend I am! I forgot my best friend's birthday."

In cases like these, we focus on a limited type of shortcoming as if it represented everything about us. We forget that, along with encountering our difficulties, we have solved tough problems and that, though we're sometimes forgetful, at other times we're caring and thoughtful.

A second type of overgeneralization occurs when we *exaggerate* shortcomings:

> "You *never* listen to me."

> "You're *always* late."

> "I can't think of *anything*."

Absolute statements like these are almost always false and usually lead to discouragement or anger. You'll feel far better when you replace overgeneralizations with more accurate messages to yourself and others:

> "You often don't listen to me."

> "You've been late three times this week."

> "I haven't had any ideas I like today."

5. The Fallacy of Causation   The **fallacy of causation** is based on the irrational belief that emotions are caused by others rather than by your own self-talk.

This fallacy causes trouble in two ways. The first way plagues people who become overly cautious about communicating because they don't want to "cause" any pain or inconvenience for others. This attitude occurs in cases such as:

> Visiting friends or family out of a sense of obligation rather than a genuine desire to see them

> Keeping quiet when another person's behavior is bothering you

> Pretending to be attentive to a speaker when you are already late for an appointment or feeling ill

> Praising and reassuring others who ask for your opinion, even when your honest response would be negative

There's certainly no excuse for going out of your way to say things that will result in pain for others, and there will be times when you choose to inconvenience yourself to make life easier for those you care about. It's essential to realize, however, that it's an overstatement to say that you are the one who *causes* others' feelings. It's more accurate to say that they *respond* to your behavior with feelings of their own.

For example, consider how strange it sounds to suggest that you make others fall in love with you. Such a statement simply doesn't make sense. It would be closer to the truth to say that you act in one way or another, and someone might fall in love with you as a result. In the same way, it's incorrect to say that you *make* others angry, upset, or happy, for that matter. It's more accurate to say that others respond to your behavior.

The fallacy of causation also operates when we believe that others cause *our* emotions. Sometimes it certainly seems as if they do, either raising or lowering our spirits by their actions. But think about it for a moment: The same actions that will cause you happiness or unhappiness one day have little effect at other times. The insult or compliment that affected your mood strongly yesterday leaves you unaffected today. You certainly wouldn't feel some emotions without others' behavior, but your reaction, not their actions, determines how you feel.

6. The Fallacy of Helplessness The **fallacy of helplessness** suggests that satisfaction in life is determined by forces beyond your control. People who continuously see themselves as victims make such statements as:

> "There's no way a woman can get ahead in this society. It's a man's world, and the best thing I can do is to accept it."

> "I was born with a shy personality. I'd like to be more outgoing, but there's nothing I can do about that."

> "I can't tell my boss that she is putting too many demands on me. If I do, I might lose my job."

The mistake in statements like these becomes apparent after you realize that you can do many things if you really want to. Most "can't" statements can be more correctly rephrased either as "won't" statements ("I can't tell him what I think" becomes "I won't be honest with him") or as "don't know how" statements ("I can't carry on an interesting conversation" becomes "I don't know what to say"). After you've rephrased these inaccurate "can'ts," it becomes clear that they're either a matter of choice or an area that calls for your action—both quite different from saying that you're helpless.

7. The Fallacy of Catastrophic Expectations Fearful communicators who subscribe to the irrational **fallacy of catastrophic expectations** operate on the assumption that if something bad can possibly happen, it will. Typical catastrophic expectations include:

> "If I invite them to the party, they probably won't want to come."

> "If I speak up in order to try to resolve a conflict, things will probably get worse."

> "If I apply for the job I want, I probably won't be hired."

> "If I tell them how I really feel, they'll probably laugh at me."

After you start expecting catastrophic consequences, a self-fulfilling prophecy can begin to build. One study revealed that people who believed that their romantic partners would not change for the better were likely to behave in ways that contributed to the breakup of the relationship.[93]

Although it's naive to assume that all of your interactions with others will meet with success, it's just as naive to assume that you'll fail. One way to escape from the fallacy of catastrophic expectations is to think about the consequences that would follow even if you don't communicate successfully. Keeping in mind the folly of trying to be perfect and of living only for the approval of others, realize that failing in a given instance usually isn't as bad as it might seem. What if people do laugh at you? Suppose you don't get the job? What if others do get angry at your remarks? Are these matters really *that* serious?

Before moving on, we need to add a few thoughts about thinking and feeling. First, you should realize that thinking rationally won't completely eliminate debilitative emotions. Some debilitative emotions, after all, are very rational: grief over the death of someone you love, euphoria over getting a new job, and apprehension about the future of an important relationship after a serious fight, for example. Thinking rationally can eliminate many debilitative emotions from your life, but not all of them.

Minimizing Debilitative Emotions

How can you overcome irrational thinking? Social scientists and therapists have developed a simple yet effective approach.[94] When practiced conscientiously, it can help you cut down on the self-defeating thinking that leads to many debilitative emotions.

PAUSE *and* REFLECT

How Irrational Are You?

MindTap REFLECT … on your irrational thoughts by answering the following questions, either here or online.

1. Return to the situations described in the Talking to Yourself exercise earlier in this chapter. Examine each one to see whether your self-talk contains any irrational thoughts.

2. Keep a two- or three-day record of your debilitative emotions. Are any of them based on irrational thinking? Examine your conclusions, and see if you repeatedly use any of the fallacies described in the preceding section.

3. Take a class poll to see which fallacies are most popular. Also, discuss what subjects seem to stimulate most of this irrational thinking (e.g., schoolwork, dating, jobs, family).

Monitor Your Emotional Reactions The first step is to recognize when you're feeling debilitative emotions. (Of course, it's also nice to recognize pleasant emotions when they occur.) As we suggested earlier, one way to recognize emotions is through monitoring physiological responses: butterflies in the stomach, racing heart, hot flashes, and so on. Although such stimuli might be symptoms of food poisoning, more often they are symptoms of a strong emotion. You can also recognize certain ways of behaving that suggest your feelings: stomping instead of walking normally, being unusually quiet, or speaking in a sarcastic tone of voice are some examples.

It may seem strange to suggest that it's necessary to look for emotions—they ought to be immediately apparent. The fact is, however, that we often suffer from debilitative emotions for some time without noticing them. For example, at the end of a trying day you've probably caught yourself frowning and realized that you've been wearing that mask for some time without noticing it.

Note the Activating Event After you're aware of how you're feeling, the next step is to figure out what activating event triggered your response. Sometimes it is obvious. For instance, a common source of anger is being accused unfairly (or fairly) of foolish behavior; a common source of hurt is being rejected by somebody important to you. In other cases, however, the activating event isn't so apparent.

Sometimes there isn't a single activating event but rather a series of small events that finally builds toward a critical mass and triggers a debilitative emotion. This happens when you're trying to work or sleep and are continually annoyed by a string of interruptions, or when you suffer a series of small disappointments.

The best way to begin tracking down activating events is to notice the circumstances in which you have debilitative emotions. Perhaps they occur when you're around *specific people*. In other cases, you might be bothered by certain *types of individuals* because of their age, role, or background. Or perhaps certain *settings* stimulate unpleasant emotions: parties, work, school. Sometimes the *topic* of conversation is the factor that sets you off, whether it be politics, religion, sex, or some other subject.

Record Your Self-Talk This is the point at which you analyze the thoughts that are the link between the activating event and your feeling. If you're serious about getting rid of debilitative emotions, it's important to actually write down your self-talk when first learning to use this method. Putting your thoughts on paper will help you see whether they make any sense.

Monitoring your self-talk might be difficult at first. This is a new activity, and any new activity seems awkward. If you persevere, however, you'll

"So, when he says, 'What a good boy am I,' Jack is really reinforcing his self-esteem."

ZITS   BY JERRY SCOTT AND JIM BORGMAN

find that you will be able to identify the thoughts that lead to your debilitative emotions. After you get in the habit of recognizing this internal monologue, you'll be able to identify your thoughts quickly and easily.

Reappraise Your Irrational Beliefs   Reappraising your irrational beliefs is the key to success in the rational-emotive approach. Use the list of irrational fallacies in the preceding section to discover which of your internal statements are based on mistaken thinking.

You can do this most effectively by following three steps. First, decide whether each belief you've recorded is rational or irrational. Next, explain why the belief is rational or irrational. Finally, if the belief is irrational, you should write down an alternative way of thinking that is more rational and that can leave you feeling better when faced with the same activating event in the future.

Replacing self-defeating self-talk with more constructive thinking is an especially effective tool for improving self-confidence and relational communication.[95] Nonetheless, this approach triggers objections from some readers:

"The rational-emotive approach sounds like nothing more than trying to talk yourself out of feeling bad." This accusation is totally correct. After all, because we talk ourselves into feeling bad, what's wrong with talking ourselves out of feeling bad, especially when such feelings are based on irrational thoughts? Rationalizing may be an excuse and a self-deception, but there's nothing wrong with being rational.

"The kind of reappraising we just read sounds phony and unnatural. I don't talk to myself in sentences and paragraphs." There's no need to dispute your irrational beliefs in any special literary style. You can be just as colloquial as you want. The important thing is to clearly understand what thoughts led you

In REAL LIFE

Rational Thinking in Action

The following scenarios demonstrate how the rational thinking method described in this section applies in everyday challenges. Notice that thinking rationally doesn't eliminate debilitative emotions. Instead, it helps keep them in control, making effective communication more possible.

Situation 1: Dealing with Annoying Customers

Activating Event

I work in a shopping mall that swarms with tourists and locals. Our company's reputation is based on service, but lately I've been losing my patience with the customers. The store is busy from the second we open until we close. Many of the customers are rude, pushy, and demanding. Others expect me to be a tour guide, restaurant reviewer, medical consultant, and even a babysitter. I feel like I'm ready to explode.

Beliefs and Self-Talk

1. I'm sick of working with the public. People are really obnoxious!

2. The customers should be more patient and polite instead of treating me like a servant.

3. This work is driving me crazy! If I keep working here, I'm going to become as rude as the customers.

4. I can't quit: I could never find another job that pays this well.

Reappraising Irrational Beliefs

1. It's an overgeneralization to say that *all* people are obnoxious. Actually, most of the customers are fine. Some are even very nice. About 10 percent of them cause most of the trouble. Recognizing that most people are OK leaves me feeling less bitter.

2. It's true that obnoxious customers *should* be more polite, but it's unrealistic to expect that everybody will behave the way they ought to. After all, it's not a perfect world.

3. By saying that the customers are driving me crazy, I suggest that I have no control over the situation. I'm an adult, and I am able to keep a grip on myself.

into your debilitative emotions so that you can clearly reappraise them. While the approach is new to you, it's a good idea to write or talk out your thoughts in order to make them clear. After you've had some practice, you'll be able to do these steps in a quicker, less formal way.

"This approach is too cold and impersonal. It seems to aim at turning people into calculating, emotionless machines." This is simply not true. A rational thinker can still dream, hope, and love. There's nothing necessarily irrational about feelings like these. Basically rational people even indulge in a bit of irrational thinking once in a while, but they usually know what they're doing. Like healthy eaters who occasionally allow themselves a snack of junk food, rational thinkers occasionally indulge in irrational thoughts, knowing that they'll return to their healthy lifestyle soon with no real damage done.

"This technique promises too much. There's no chance I could rid myself of all unpleasant feelings, however nice that might be." We can answer this objection

I may not like the way some people behave, but it's my choice how to respond to them.

4. I'm not helpless. If the job is too unpleasant, I can quit. I probably wouldn't find another job that pays as well as this one, so I have to choose which is more important: money or peace of mind. It's my choice.

Situation 2: Meeting My Girlfriend's Family

Activating Event

Tracy and I are talking about marriage—maybe not soon, but eventually. Her family is very close, and they want to meet me. I'm sure I'll like them, but I am not sure what they will think about me. I was married once before, at a young age. It was a big mistake, and it didn't last. Furthermore, I was laid off two months ago, and I'm between jobs. The family is coming to town next week, and I am very nervous about what they will think of me.

Beliefs and Self-Talk

1. They've *got* to like me! This is a close family, and I'm doomed if they think I'm not right for Tracy.

2. No matter how sensibly I act, all they'll think of is my divorce and unemployment.

3. Maybe the family is right. Tracy deserves the best, and I'm certainly not that!

Reappraising Irrational Beliefs

1. The family's approval is definitely important. Still, my relationship with Tracy doesn't depend on it. She's already said that she's committed to me, no matter what they think. The sensible approach is to say I *want* their approval, but I don't *need* it.

2. I'm expecting the absolute worst if I think that I'm doomed no matter what happens when we meet. There is a chance that they will dislike me, but there's also a chance that things will work out fine. There's no point in dwelling on catastrophes.

3. Just because I've had an imperfect past doesn't mean I'm wrong for Tracy. I've learned from my past mistakes, and I am committed to living a good life. I know I can be the kind of husband she deserves, even though I'm not perfect.

> **MindTap® APPLY ...** this situation to your life by answering questions online.

by agreeing that rational-emotive thinking probably won't totally solve your emotional problems. What it can do is reduce their number, intensity, and duration. This method is not the answer to all your problems, but it can make a significant difference—which is not a bad accomplishment.

Maximizing Facilitative Emotions

Reducing debilitative emotions is only part of the emotional health equation. Contemporary scholars maintain that fostering positive emotions is just as important as minimizing negative ones. Whether it's called "learned optimism"[96] or "positivity,"[97] the approach is similar to what we've outlined in this section. If thoughts cause feelings, then positive thoughts can cause positive feelings. Ruminating on the good rather than the bad in life can enhance one's emotional, relational, and even physical health.[98]

SKILL *Builder*

Rational Thinking

1. Return to the diary of irrational thoughts you recorded in the previous Pause and Reflect exercise. Dispute the self-talk in each case, and write a more rational interpretation of the event.

2. Now try out your ability to think rationally on the spot. You can do this by acting out the scenes listed after step 4. You'll need three players for each one: a subject, the subject's "little voice"—his or her thoughts—and a second party.

3. Play out each scene by having the subject and second party interact while the "little voice" stands just behind the subject and says what the subject is probably thinking. For example, in a scene where the subject is asking an instructor to reconsider a low grade, the little voice might say, "I hope I haven't made things worse by bringing this up. Maybe he'll lower the grade after rereading the test. I'm such an idiot! Why didn't I keep quiet?"

4. Whenever the little voice expresses an irrational thought, the observers who are watching the skit should call out, "Foul." At this point the action should stop while the group discusses the irrational thought and suggests a more rational line of self-talk. The players should then replay the scene with the little voice speaking in a more rational way.

Here are some possible scenes (of course, you can invent others as well):

a. Two people are just beginning their first date.

b. A potential employee has just begun a job interview.

c. A teacher or boss is criticizing the subject for showing up late.

d. A student and instructor run across each other in the supermarket.

It's unrealistic to think that you'll have a positive emotional response to every event. The key according to researcher Barbara Fredrickson is to leave plenty of room to enjoy and savor positive emotional experiences.[99] And even though you can't dictate all the events of your life, you have the power to reappraise them. Clichés such as "look on the bright side" and "have an attitude of gratitude" may not be comforting when delivered by others, but they can serve as helpful self-reminders. You can regard challenging situations as growth opportunities. You can focus on what you gained rather than what you lost. You can choose compassion over contempt. The difference between "That really hurt me" and "I found out how strong and capable I really am" is often a matter of mindset—and positive emotions follow positive appraisals.

Many people find it easier to focus on their negative emotional experiences. It often takes mindful effort to pay attention to and express pleasurable feelings in close relationships. Here are ten emotions that Frederickson's research identifies as basic to positivity: *joy, gratitude, serenity, interest, hope, pride, amusement, inspiration, awe,* and *love.* How many have you experienced recently? How often do you express these emotions to people who matter? Is it possible that you felt but can't recall them? Identifying and then talking or writing about your positive emotional experiences can lead to greater personal and interpersonal satisfaction.

SUMMARY

Emotions have several dimensions. They are signaled by internal physiological changes, manifested by nonverbal reactions, and defined in most cases by cognitive interpretations. We can use this information to make choices about whether or not to verbalize our feelings.

There are several reasons why people do not verbalize many of the emotions they feel. Some people have personalities that are less prone toward emotional expression. Culture and gender also have an effect on the emotions we do and don't share with others. Social rules and roles discourage the expression of some feelings, particularly negative ones. Social media may also increase the intensity of emotions for both message senders and receivers. Finally, contagion can lead us to experience emotions that we might not otherwise have had.

Because total expression of emotions is not appropriate, several guidelines help define when and how to express emotions effectively. Expanding your emotional vocabulary, becoming more self-aware, and expressing mixed feelings are important. Recognizing the difference between feeling, thinking, and acting, as well as accepting responsibility for feelings instead of blaming them on others, lead to better reactions. Choosing the proper time and place to share feelings is also important, as is choosing the best channel for expressing emotions.

Whereas some emotions are facilitative, others are debilitative and inhibit effective functioning. Many of these debilitative emotions are biological reactions rooted in the amygdala portion of the brain, but their negative impact can be altered through rational thinking. It is often possible to communicate more confidently and effectively by identifying troublesome emotions, identifying the activating event and self-talk that triggered them, and reappraising any irrational thoughts with a more logical analysis of the situation. It is also important to identify and enjoy facilitative emotions.

KEY TERMS

debilitative emotions
emotional contagion
emotional intelligence (EQ)
emotion labor
facilitative emotions
fallacy of approval
fallacy of catastrophic expectations
fallacy of causation

fallacy of helplessness
fallacy of overgeneralization
fallacy of perfection
fallacy of shoulds
reappraisal
rumination
self-talk

MindTap® START …
Explore this chapter's topics online.

HERE ARE THE TOPICS DISCUSSED IN THIS CHAPTER:

6

LANGUAGE: BARRIER AND BRIDGE

AFTER STUDYING THE TOPICS IN THIS CHAPTER, YOU SHOULD BE ABLE TO:

1. Analyze a real or potential misunderstanding in terms of semantic or pragmatic rules.

2. Describe how the principles presented in the section of this chapter titled "The Impact of Language" operate in your life.

3. Construct a message at the optimal level of specificity or vagueness for a given situation.

4. Recast "you" statements into "I" or "we" statements to reflect your responsibility for the content of messages.

5. Rephrase disruptive statements in less inflammatory terms.

6. In a given situation, analyze how gender or cultural differences (or both) may affect the quality of interaction.

*T*he problems that began with Babel continue today. Sometimes it seems as if none of us speaks the same language. Yet despite its frustrations and challenges, language is clearly a marvelous tool. It is the gift that allows us to communicate in a way that no other animals appear to match. Without language, we would be more ignorant, ineffectual, and isolated.

In this chapter, we explore the nature of language, looking at how to take advantage of its strengths and minimize its weaknesses. After a quick explanation of the symbolic nature of language, we examine the sources of language-based misunderstandings. We then move beyond the challenges of simply understanding one another and explore how the language we use affects the climate of interpersonal relationships. Finally, we broaden our focus even more to look at how linguistic practices shape the attitudes of entire cultures.

jorisvo/Shutterstock.com

Now the whole world had one language and a common speech.

As men moved eastward, they found a plain in Shinar and settled there.

They said to each other, "Come, let's make bricks and bake them thoroughly." They used brick instead of stone, and tar for mortar.

Then they said, "Come, let us build ourselves a city, with a tower that reaches to the heavens, so that we may make a name for ourselves and not be scattered over the face of the whole earth."

But the Lord came down to see the city and the tower that the men were building.

The Lord said, "If as one people speaking the same language they have begun to do this, then nothing they plan to do will be impossible for them.

Come, let us go down and confuse their language so they will not understand each other."

So the Lord scattered them from there over all the earth, and they stopped building the city.

That is why it was called Babel—because there the Lord confused the language of the whole world.

Genesis 11:1–9

LANGUAGE IS SYMBOLIC

In the natural world, signs have a direct connection with the things they represent. For example, smoke is a sign that something's burning, and a high fever is a sign of illness. There's nothing arbitrary about the relationship between natural signs and the things they represent. Nobody made them up, and they exist independently of human opinions.

In human language, the connection between signs and the things they represent isn't so direct. Instead, language is *symbolic*: There's only an arbitrary connection between words and the ideas or things to which they refer. For example, there is nothing particularly fivelike in the number five. The word represents the number of fingers on your hand only because English speakers agree that it does. To a speaker of French, the symbol *cinq* would convey the same meaning; to a computer programmer, the same value would be represented by the coded symbol 101.

Even sign language, as "spoken" by most hearing-impaired people, is symbolic in nature and not the pantomime it might seem. Because this form of communication is symbolic and not literal, hundreds of sign languages around the world have evolved independently whenever significant numbers of hearing-impaired people are in contact.[1] These distinct languages include American Sign Language, British Sign Language, French Sign Language, Danish Sign Language, Chinese Sign Language—even Australian Aboriginal and Mayan Sign Languages.

The symbolic nature of language is a blessing. It enables us to communicate in ways that wouldn't otherwise be possible about ideas, reasons, the past, the future, and things not present. Without symbolic language, none of this would be possible. However, the indirect relationship between symbols and the things they represent leads to communication problems only hinted about in the tower of Babel story.

If everyone used symbols in the same way, then language would be much easier to manage and understand—but your own experience shows that this isn't always the case. Messages that seem perfectly clear to you prove confusing or misleading to others. You tell the hairstylist to "take a little off the top" and are stunned to discover that her definition of "a little" was equivalent to your definition of "a lot." You have a heated argument about the merits of *feminism* without realizing that you and the other person have been using the word to represent entirely

"What part of oil lamp next to double squiggle over ox don't you understand?"

different ideas. Misunderstandings like these remind us that meanings are in people, not in words.

In Washington, DC, an uproar developed when the city's ombudsman, David Howard, used the word *niggardly* to describe an approach to budgeting.[2] Howard, who is white, was accused by some African American critics of uttering an unforgivable racial slur. His defenders pointed out that the word, which means "miserly," is derived from Scandinavian languages and has no link to the racial slur it resembles. Even though the criticisms eventually died away, they illustrate that the meanings that people associate with words—correctly or not—have far more significance than do their dictionary definitions.

UNDERSTANDINGS AND MISUNDERSTANDINGS

Language is rather like plumbing: We pay the most attention to it when something goes wrong. But the problems that arise from misunderstandings aren't always immediately apparent, and they occur more often than we imagine. Most people vastly overestimate how well their explanations get through and how well they understand others.[3] Because misunderstandings are the greatest cause of concern for most people who study language, we'll begin our study by looking at sets of rules we use to understand—and sometimes misunderstand—one another's speech.

Understanding Words: Semantic Rules

Semantic rules reflect the ways in which users of a language assign meaning to a particular linguistic symbol, usually a word. Semantic rules make it possible for us to agree that "bikes" are for riding and "books" are for reading, and they help us know who we will and won't encounter when we use rooms marked "men" or "women." Without semantic rules, communication would be impossible because each of us would use symbols in unique ways, without sharing meaning. Semantic misunderstandings arise when people assign different meanings to the same words. We will look at some of the most common ones.

Equivocation   Equivocal statements can be interpreted in more than one way. As you read in Chapter 3, equivocation can be a strategic alternative to blunt disclosure. It's easier to say "That tattoo is really unusual" than to say "That tattoo is really ugly." Sometimes we use **equivocal language** without realizing that ambiguous statements can be have more than one meaning. Consider a few amusing examples from news headlines:

Family Catches Fire Just in Time

Man Stuck on Toilet; Stool Suspected

20-Year Friendship Ends at the Altar

Trees Can Break Wind

Some equivocal misunderstandings can be embarrassing. As one woman recalls: "In the fourth grade the teacher asked the class what a period was. I raised my hand and shared everything I had learned about girls getting their period. But he was talking about the dot at the end of a sentence. Oops!"[4]

Other equivocal statements can be even more troubling. A nurse gave one of her patients a scare when she told him that he "wouldn't be needing" his robe, books, and shaving materials anymore. The patient became quiet and moody. When the nurse inquired about the odd behavior, she discovered that the poor man had interpreted her statement to mean he was going to die soon. In fact, the nurse meant he would be going home.

It's difficult to catch every equivocal statement and clarify it while speaking. For this reason, the responsibility for interpreting statements accurately rests in large part with the receiver.

"Be honest with me, Roger. By 'mid-course correction' you mean divorce, don't you."

Feedback of one sort or another—for example, the kind of perception checking introduced in Chapter 4 and the paraphrasing described in Chapter 8—can help clear up misunderstandings.

Relative Language   **Relative words** gain their meaning by comparison. For example, do you attend a large or small school? This depends on what you compare it to. Alongside a huge state university, your school may not seem big, but compared with a small college, it may seem quite large. Relative words such as *fast* and *slow*, *smart* and *stupid*, *short* and *long* are clearly defined only through comparison.

Some relative terms are so common that we mistakenly assume they have a clear meaning. For instance, if a friend told you it's "likely" she'll show up at your party tonight, what are the chances she's going to come? In one study, students were asked to assign percentages to such terms as *doubtful*, *toss-up*, *likely*, *probable*, *good chance*, and *unlikely*.[5] There was a tremendous variation in the meaning of most of these terms. For example, the responses for *probable* ranged from 0 to 99 percent. *Good chance* fell between 35 percent and 90 percent, whereas *unlikely* fell between 0 and 40 percent.

One way to make words more measurable is to turn them into numbers. Healthcare practitioners have learned that patients often use vague descriptions when describing their pain: "It hurts a little"; "I'm pretty sore." The use of a numeric pain scale can give a more precise response—and lead to a better diagnosis.[6] When patients are asked to rank their pain from 1 to 10, with 10 being the most severe pain they've ever experienced, the number 7 is much more concrete and specific than "It aches a bit." The same technique can be used when asking people to rate anything from the movies they've seen to their job satisfaction.

Static Evaluation   "Mark is a nervous guy." "Mia is short-tempered." "You can always count on Ming." Statements that contain or imply the word *is* lead to the mistaken assumption that people are consistent and unchanging—an incorrect belief known as **static evaluation**. Instead of labeling Mark as permanently and totally nervous, it would be more accurate to outline the particular situations in which he behaves nervously. The same goes for Mia, Ming, and the rest of us: We are more changeable than the way static, everyday language describes us.

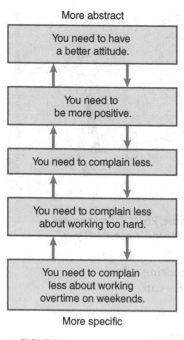

More abstract

You need to have
a better attitude.

You need to
be more positive.

You need to complain less.

You need to complain less
about working too hard.

You need to complain
less about working
overtime on weekends.

More specific

⋀ **FIGURE 6.1**
Abstraction Ladder

Abstraction When it comes to describing problems, goals, appreciation, and requests, some language is more specific than others. **Abstract language** is vague in nature, whereas **behavioral language**—as its name implies—refers to specific things that people say or do. The **abstraction ladder** in Figure 6.1 illustrates how the same phenomenon can be described at various levels of specificity and abstraction. Notice how the ladder's bottom-rung description is more concrete and behavioral, and thus it is probably clearer than the top rung's abstract injunction to develop a "better attitude."

We use higher-level abstractions all the time. For instance, rather than saying "Thanks for washing the dishes," "Thanks for vacuuming the rug," or "Thanks for making the bed," it's easier to say "Thanks for cleaning up." In such everyday situations, abstractions are a useful kind of verbal shorthand.

Although verbal shorthand like this can be useful, highly abstract language can lead to blanket judgments and stereotyping: "Marriage counselors are worthless," "Skateboarders are delinquents," or "Men are no good." Overly abstract expressions like these can cause people to *think* in generalities, ignoring uniqueness. As you learned in Chapter 4, stereotyping can injure interpersonal relationships because it categorizes and evaluates people in ways that may not be accurate.

You can appreciate the value of behavioral descriptions by looking at the examples in Table 6.1. Notice how much more clearly the behavioral descriptions explain the speaker's thoughts than do the vaguer terms.

TABLE 6.1 Abstract versus Behavioral Descriptions

	Abstract Description	Behavioral Description			Remarks
		Who Is Involved	In What Circumstances	Specific Behaviors	
Problem	I talk too much.	People I find intimidating	When I want them to like me	I talk (mostly about myself) instead of giving them a chance to speak or asking about their lives.	Behavioral description more clearly identifies behaviors to change.
Goal	I want to be more constructive.	My roommate	When we talk about household duties	Instead of finding fault with her ideas, suggest alternatives that might work.	Behavioral description clearly outlines how to act; abstract description doesn't.
Appreciation	"You've really been helpful lately."	Deliver to fellow worker	"When I've had to take time off work because of personal problems …"	"… you took my shifts without complaining."	Give both abstract and behavioral descriptions for best results.
Request	"Clean up your act!"	Deliver to target person	"When we're around my family …"	"… please don't tell jokes that involve sex."	Behavioral description specifies behavior.

SKILL *Builder*

Down-to-Earth Language

MindTap® PRACTICE ... your skill at nonabstract language by answering the following questions either here or online.

You can appreciate the value of nonabstract language by translating the following into behavioral terms:

1. An abstract goal for improving your interpersonal communication (e.g., "be more assertive" or "stop being so sarcastic").

2. A complaint you have about another person (e.g., that he or she is "selfish" or "insensitive").

3. A request for someone to change (e.g., "I wish you'd be more punctual" or "Try to be more positive").

4. An appreciation you could share with another person (e.g., "Thanks for being so helpful" or "I appreciate your patience").

In each case, describe the person or persons involved, the circumstances in which the behavior occurs, and the precise behaviors involved. What differences can you expect when you use behavioral descriptions like the ones you have created here?

Understanding Structure: Syntactic Rules

Syntactic rules govern the grammar of a language. You can appreciate how syntax contributes to the meaning of a statement by considering two versions of a letter:

Version 1

Dear John:

I want a man who knows what love is all about. You are generous, kind, thoughtful. People who are not like you admit to being useless and inferior. You have ruined me for other men. I yearn for you. I have no feelings whatsoever when we're apart. I can be forever happy—will you let me be yours?

Mary

Version 2

Dear John:

I want a man who knows what love is. All about you are generous, kind, thoughtful people, who are not like you. Admit to being useless and inferior. You have ruined me. For other men, I yearn. For you, I have no feelings whatsoever. When we're apart, I can be forever happy. Will you let me be?

Yours,
Mary

Semantic rules don't explain why these letters send virtually opposite messages. There's no ambiguity about the meaning of the words they contain: *love, kind, thoughtful,* and so on. The opposite meanings of the letters came from their different syntax.

Although most of us aren't able to describe the syntactic rules that govern our language, it's easy to recognize their existence when they are violated. A humorous example is the way the character Yoda speaks in the *Star Wars* movies. Phrases such as "The dark side are they" or "Your father he is" often elicit a chuckle because they bend syntactical norms. Sometimes, however, apparently ungrammatical speech is simply following a different set of syntactic rules, reflecting regional or co-cultural dialects. Linguists believe it is crucial to view such dialects as *different* rather than *deficient* forms of English.[7]

"I never said 'I love you.' I said 'I love ya.'
Big difference!"

Understanding Context: Pragmatic Rules

Semantic and syntactic problems don't account for all misunderstandings.[8] To appreciate a different type of communication challenge, imagine how a young female employee might struggle to make sense of her older male boss's statement, "You look very pretty today." She almost certainly would understand the meaning of the words, and the syntax is perfectly clear. Still, the boss's message could be interpreted in several ways. Was the remark a simple compliment? A come-on? Did it contain the suggestion that she didn't look nice other days?

If the boss and employee share the same interpretation of the message, their communication would be smooth. But if they bring different perspectives to interpreting it, a problem exists. Table 6.2 shows several ways in which different perspectives of the boss and employee would lead to their attaching different meanings to the same words.

TABLE 6.2 Pragmatic Rules Govern the Use and Meaning of a Statement

	Boss	Employee
Statement	"You look very nice today."	
Self-Concept "Who am I?" "Who is s/he?"	Friendly guy	Woman determined to succeed on own merits
Episode "What's going on in this exchange?"	Casual conversation	Possible come-on by boss?
Relationship "Who are we to one another?"	Boss who treats employees like family members	Subordinate employee, dependent on boss's approval for advancement
Culture "What does my background say about the meaning here?"	Euro-American, raised in United States	Latina, raised in South America

Adapted from Pearce, W. B. & Cronen, V. (1980). Communication, action, and meaning. New York: Praeger; and Griffin, E. (2012). A first look at communication theory (8th ed.). New York: McGraw-Hill.

In situations like this one, we rely on **pragmatic rules** to decide how to interpret messages in a given context. Pragmatic rules govern the way speech operates in everyday interaction. You can't look up pragmatic rules in any dictionary. They are almost always unstated, but they are just as important as semantic and syntactic rules in helping us make sense of one another's messages.

The best way to appreciate how pragmatic rules operate is to think of communication as a kind of cooperative game. Like all games, success depends on all of the players understanding and following the same set of rules. This is why communication scholars use the term *coordination* to describe the way conversation operates when everyone involved uses the same set of pragmatic rules.[9]

Some pragmatic rules are shared by most people in a culture. In North America, for instance, competent communicators understand that the question "How's it going?" usually isn't really a request for information. Anyone familiar with the rules of conversation knows that the proper answer is something like "Pretty good. How's it going with you?" Likewise, most people understand the pragmatic rule that says that "Would you like a drink?" means "Would you like an alcoholic beverage?" whereas "Would you like something to drink?" is a more open-ended question.

Besides following cultural rules, people in individual relationships create their own sets of pragmatic rules. Consider the use of humor: The teasing and jokes you exchange with gusto with one friend might be considered tasteless or offensive in another relationship.[10] For instance, imagine an email message typed in CAPITAL LETTERS and filled with CURSE WORDS, INSULTS, NAME-CALLING, and EXCLAMATION MARKS!!! How would you interpret such a message? An outside observer may consider this an example of "flaming" and be appalled, when in fact the message might be a fun-loving case of "verbal jousting" between buddies.[11] If you have a good friend whom you call by a less-than-tasteful nickname as a term of endearment, then you understand the concept. Keep in mind, however, that those who aren't privy to your relationship's pragmatic rules are likely to misunderstand you, so you'll want to be wise about when and where to use these personal codes.

Allstar Picture library

⋀ In *The Imitation Game*, Alan Turing (Benedict Cumberbatch) is a genius when it comes to breaking Nazi battle codes, but he has trouble understanding the pragmatic rules of everyday speech. He misses the linguistic nuances that are an essential part of jokes, sarcasm, and flirting. Are there times when you misunderstand others' messages because you take them too literally? Have you ever been misunderstood for similar reasons?

THE IMPACT OF LANGUAGE

So far we have focused on language only as a medium for helping communicators understand one another. But along with this important function, language can shape our perceptions of the world around us and reflect the attitudes we hold toward one another.

PAUSE *and* REFLECT

Your Linguistic Rules

MindTap° REFLECT ... on linguistic rules by answering the following questions, either here or online.

To what extent do linguistic rules affect your understanding of and relationships with others? Explore this question by following these steps:

1. Recall a time when you encountered someone whose speech violated the syntactic rules that you are used to. What was your impression of this person? To what degree was this impression influenced by her or his failure to follow familiar linguistic rules? Consider whether this impression was or was not valid.

2. Recall at least one misunderstanding that arose when you and another person followed different semantic rules. Use hindsight to consider whether this misunderstanding (and others like it) could be avoided. If semantic misunderstandings can be minimized, explain what approaches might be useful.

3. Identify at least two pragmatic rules that govern the use of language in one of your relationships. Share these rules with other students. Do they use language in the same way as you and your relational partner?

Naming and Identity

"What's in a name?" Juliet asked rhetorically. If Romeo had been a social scientist, he would have answered "A great deal."

Research has demonstrated that names are more than just a simple means of identification. Names shape the way others think of us, the way we view ourselves, and the way we act. For more than a century, researchers have studied the impact of rare and unique names on the people who bear them.[12] Early studies claimed that people with unusual names suffered everything from psychological and emotional disturbance to failure in college. More recent studies have shown that people often have negative appraisals not only of unusual names but also of unusual name spellings.[13] Of course, what makes a name (and its spelling) unusual changes with time. In 1900, the twenty most popular names for baby girls in the United States included Bertha, Mildred, and Ethel. By 2013, the top twenty names included Madison, Ava, and Isabella—names that would have been highly unusual a century earlier.[14]

Names are one way to shape and reinforce a child's personal identity. Naming a baby after a family member (e.g., "Junior" or "Trey") can create a connection between the youngster and his or her namesake. Name choice can also be a powerful way to make a statement about cultural identity. For example, in recent decades a large percentage of names given to African American babies have been distinctive to that co-culture.[15] In California, more than 40 percent of black girls born in a recent period had names that not a single white baby born in the entire state was given. Researchers suggest that

FINDING THE WORDS
TO TALK ABOUT DISABILITY

William came home from school a few weeks back and he said, "Mom." He said it as a sentence, the way he does when he has something important to tell me. And then again, "Mom. My friend Ashley is not good at listening. And she screams."

William is three. He attends a local public preschool, and he's in an "integrated" classroom, which is to say, a classroom where typically developing children learn and play alongside children with special needs. Three years ago, William's older sister Penny was in the same classroom. Penny has Trisomy 21, also known as Down syndrome, and that third chromosome impacts nearly every aspect of her development. She wears braces to support her flat feet and weak ankles. When she was in preschool, she relied on sign language in addition to spoken words to communicate.

But just because I have a daughter with a disability doesn't mean that I know how to talk about disabilities with my children. When Penny was first born, I found myself in a maze of words that had never mattered to me before—abnormality, disability, high-risk pregnancy, genetic counseling, special needs. It became easier with time. I started to use "people-first" language, calling her a baby with Down syndrome instead of a Down's baby. I substituted "normal" with "typical" when it came to describing other children. In my subsequent pregnancies, I talked about the "chance" of having another child with Down syndrome instead of the "risk."

And over time, the words became more than politically correct attempts

DenysKuvaiev/Bigstock

to support my new identity as the mother of a child with a disability. Over time, the words became reality. I really did see Penny as a child first, with Down syndrome as a descriptive but secondary marker. I really did come to believe that individuals with disabilities were not people to be pitied or people in need of help but rather human beings who were just like me. Our particularities were different, but I came to understand that we all have limitations and places of vulnerability and need, and we all have possibilities for joy and relationships and self-giving.

I was delighted when William was accepted, via lottery, into the integrated preschool class. But I wondered if I would be able to put words to his experience. I wondered if I would be able to talk about disability in a way that was honest and positive, in a way that built bridges instead of creating categories or judgments. So when William told me that Ashley doesn't listen well and screams, I took a deep breath.

I said, "Maybe she hasn't learned how to listen yet." He nodded. And then I asked, "What is Ashley good at?"

He tilted his head. "Playin' games and runnin' around."

"What are you good at?"

"Listening."

"What's hard for you?"

"Coloring."

That was the end of our conversation. William has talked about Ashley since then, but only because he tells me things about his friend—that she takes the bus, that they pretend to do cooking together, that he wanted to have a sticker chart with prizes just like her. As far as William is concerned, Ashley is just another kid in his class. There are some things that are hard for her. There are some things she's good at. Just like him.

Eventually William will realize that many aspects of our culture—from language to legislation—erect walls between kids like him and kids like Ashley. But I hope that growing up with a sister with Down syndrome and going to school alongside boys and girls who have different challenges than he does will open his eyes, and his heart, to understanding our common humanity. I hope he will grow up with an ability to see beyond labels, to trust that he has something to offer to everyone he meets, but that he also has something to receive from them.

Amy Julia Becker

MindTap® ENHANCE . . . your understanding by answering the following questions, either here or online.

1. What communication principles did the author use when talking with her son William about his friend Ashley? How did they shape William's attitudes and behaviors?

2. What labels have you seen used for people that affect, positively or negatively, the way that others view them and treat them?

3. Are there ways you can adapt your language to reclassify others more constructively?

Paramount/Allstar

∧ The high school movie *Mean Girls* captures the role of linguistic convergence in defining and maintaining in-groups. Cady (Linsday Lohan) learns quickly that if she's going to fit in with the popular "Plastics" at her school, she'll have to adopt their language, including terms such as "fetch," "word vomit," and "fugly." Does your language reflect the groups to which you belong?

distinctive names like these are a symbol of solidarity with the African American community. Conversely, choosing a less distinctive name can be a way of integrating the baby into the majority culture.

Affiliation

Besides shaping an individual's identity, speech can build and demonstrate solidarity with others. Research has demonstrated that communicators are attracted to others whose style of speaking is similar to theirs.[16] Likewise, communicators who want to show affiliation with one another adapt their speech in a variety of ways, including their choice of vocabulary, rate of talking, number and placement of pauses, and level of politeness—a process known as *speech accommodation*.[17] Adolescents who all adopt the same vocabulary of slang words and speech mannerisms illustrate the principle of linguistic solidarity. The same process works among members of other groups ranging from street gangs to military personnel. Communication researchers call the process of adapting one's speech style to match that of others **convergence**. One study even showed that adopting the swearing patterns of bosses and coworkers can help people feel connected on the job (see the On the Job sidebar in this chapter for more about swearing in the workplace).[18]

In one study, the likelihood of mutual romantic interest increased when conversational partners' use of pronouns, articles, conjunctions, prepositions, and negations matched.[19] The same study revealed that when couples used similar language styles while instant messaging, the chances of their relationship continuing increased by almost 50 percent. The researchers speculate that unconscious language-style matching relates to how much each is paying attention to what the other says. Another study found that members of online communities often develop a shared language and conversational style, and their affiliation with each other can be seen in increased uses of the pronoun *we*.[20]

When two or more people feel equally positive about one another, their linguistic convergence will be mutual. But when communicators want or need approval, they often adapt their speech to accommodate the other person's style, trying to say the "right thing" or speak in a way that will help them fit in. We see this process when immigrants who want to gain the rewards of material success in a new culture strive to master the host language. Likewise, employees who seek advancement tend to speak more like their bosses.

The principle of speech accommodation works in reverse, too. Communicators who want to set themselves apart from others adopt the strategy of **divergence**, speaking in a way that emphasizes their differences from others. For example, members of an ethnic group, even though fluent in the dominant language, might use their own dialect as a way of showing solidarity with one another—a sort of "us against them" strategy. The same behavior can occur across ethnic lines, such as teens who adopt the slang of particular subcultures to show divergence with adults and convergence with their peers.[21]

Of course, communicators need to be careful about when—and when not—to converge their language with others. Most of us can remember the embarrassment of hearing a parent using youthful slang and thinking, "You're too old to be saying that—quit trying to sound like us." On a more serious level, using ethnic or racial epithets when you're not a member of that in-group can be inappropriate and even offensive. One of the pragmatic goals of divergence is the creation of norms about who has the "right" to use certain words and who does not.

Power and Politeness

Communication researchers have identified several language patterns that add to or detract from a speaker's power to influence others. Notice the difference between these two statements from an employee to a manager:

> "Excuse me, sir. I hate to say this, but I ... uh ... I guess I won't be able to finish the project on time. I had a personal emergency, and ... well ... it was just impossible to finish it by today. I'll have it on your desk on Monday, OK?"

> "I won't be able to finish the project on time. I had a personal emergency, and it was impossible to finish it by today. I'll have it on your desk Monday."

Whether or not the boss finds the excuse acceptable, it's clear that the tone of the second one is more confident, whereas the tone of the first is apologetic and uncertain. Table 6.3 identifies several **powerless speech mannerisms** illustrated in the statements you just read. Some studies have shown that

Table 6.3 Examples of Powerless Language

Hedges	"I'm *kinda* disappointed ..." "I *think* we should ..." "I *guess* I'd like to ..."
Hesitations	"*Uh*, can I have a minute of your time?" "*Well*, we could try this idea ..." "I wish you would—*er*—try to be on time."
Intensifiers	"I'm *really* glad to see you." "I'm not *very* hungry."
Polite forms	"Excuse me, *sir* ..."
Tag questions	"It's about time we got started, *isn't it*?" "*Don't you think* we should give it another try?"
Disclaimers	"*I probably shouldn't say this, but* ..." "*I'm not really sure, but* ..."
Rising inflections	See the reading "The Way You Talk Can Hurt You?" in Chapter 7.

speakers whose talk is free of these mannerisms are rated as more competent, dynamic, and attractive than speakers who sound powerless.[22] Powerful speech can help candidates in job interviews. Employers rate applicants who use a powerful style as more competent and employable than candidates who speak less forcefully.[23] One study revealed that even a single type of powerless speech mannerism can make a person appear less authoritative or socially attractive.[24]

A *disclaimer* is a type of powerless speech that attempts to distance a speaker from remarks that might be unwelcome. For example, you might preface a critical message by saying "I don't mean to sound judgmental, but ..." and then go on to express your disapproval. One study showed that disclaimers actually *increase* negative judgments.[25] For instance, the phrase "I don't mean to sound arrogant ..." followed by a high-handed comment led subjects to regard the speaker as *more* arrogant. Disclaimers involving other negative qualities such as laziness and selfishness produced similar results. It seems that disclaimers backfire because they sensitize listeners to look for—and find—precisely the qualities that the speaker is trying to disavow.

Some scholars question the label "powerless" because tentative and indirect speech styles can sometimes achieve goals better than more assertive approaches.[26] For example, less forceful approaches can be attempts at **politeness**: communicating in ways that save face for both senders and receivers. Politeness is valued is some cultures more than others.[27] In Japan, for instance, saving face for others is an important goal, so communicators there tend to speak in ambiguous terms and use hedge words and qualifiers. Traditional Mexican culture, with its strong emphasis on cooperation, also uses hedging to smooth over interpersonal relationships. By not taking a firm stand with their speech language, Mexicans avoid making others feel ill at ease. The Korean culture represents yet another people who prefer "indirect" speech (e.g., "perhaps," "could be") over "direct" speech.

Even in cultures that value assertiveness, language that is *too* powerful may intimidate or annoy others. Consider these two different approaches to handling a common situation:

> "Excuse me. My baby is having a little trouble getting to sleep. Would you mind turning down the music just a little?"

> "My baby can't sleep because your music is too loud. You need to turn it down."

The more polite, if less powerful, approach would probably produce better results than the stronger statement. How can this fact be reconciled with the research on powerful language? As noted in Chapter 1, interpersonal competence is a balance between effectiveness and appropriateness. If you come across as too powerful, you may get what you're seeking in the short term but alienate the other person in ways that will make your relationship more difficult in the long term. Furthermore, a statement that is *too* powerful can convey relational messages of disrespect and superiority, which are just as likely to antagonize others as to gain their compliance.

In some situations, polite, less apparently powerful forms of speech can even enhance a speaker's effectiveness.[28] For example, a boss might say to an assistant, "Would you mind making copies of this document? In truth, both the boss and secretary know that this is an order and not a request, but the questioning form is more considerate and leaves the assistant feeling better about the boss.[29] The importance of achieving both content and relational goals helps explain why a mixture of powerful speech and polite speech is usually most effective.[30]

Disruptive Language

Not all linguistic problems come from misunderstandings. Sometimes people understand one another perfectly and still wind up in a conflict. Of course, not all disagreements can, or should be, avoided. But eliminating three linguistic habits from your communication repertoire can minimize the kind of disagreements that don't need to happen, allowing you to save your energy for the unavoidable and important disagreements.

Fact–Opinion Confusion Factual statements are claims that can be verified as true or false. By contrast, opinion statements are based on the speaker's beliefs. Unlike factual statements, they can never be proved or disproved. Consider a few examples of the difference between factual and opinion statements:

Fact	Opinion
You forgot my birthday.	You don't care about me.
You keep interrupting me.	You're a control freak.
You tell a lot of ethnic jokes.	You're a bigot.

On the JOB

Swearing in the Workplace

Swearing may offend some people, but it serves a variety of communication functions.[a] It's a way to express emotions and to let others know how strongly you feel. It can be a compliment ("that was #$&@ing terrific!") or a harsh insult. Swearing can even be a term of endearment.

Swearing on the job can be especially problematic.[b] Communication researchers investigated the effects of swearing in work settings. Not surprisingly, their research shows that the more formal the situation, the more negative the appraisal. The chosen swear word also makes a difference: "F-bombs" have been rated as more inappropriate than other less-volatile terms. Relational history also is important: Hearers who are surprised by a speaker's swearing are likely to deem the person as incompetent.

Despite its downside, swearing can have its place at work. Stanford University professor Robert Sutton notes that choosing *not* to swear can actually violate the norms of some organizations.[c] He maintains that swearing on rare occasions can be effective for the shock value. (The fact that Sutton authored a book called *The No Asshole Rule* suggests he practices what he preaches.)

But even Sutton adds a cautionary note about swearing on the job: "If you are not sure, don't do it." The rules of interpersonal competence apply: Analyze and adapt to your audience, and engage in self-monitoring. And when in doubt, err on the side of restraint.

When factual and opinion statements are set side by side like this, the difference is clear. In everyday conversation, however, we often present our opinions as if they were facts, and in doing so we invite an unnecessary argument. For example:

"That was a dumb thing to say!"

"Spending that much on a pair of shoes is a waste of money!"

"You can't get a fair shake in this country unless you're a white male."

Notice how much less antagonistic each statement would be if it were prefaced by a qualifier that takes responsibility for the opinion such as "I believe ...," "In my opinion ...," or "It seems to me...." We'll discuss the importance of responsible "I" language later in this chapter.

Fact-Inference Confusion Problems also arise when we confuse factual statements with inferential statements—conclusions arrived at from an interpretation of evidence.

Arguments often result when we label our inferences as facts:

A: Why are you mad at me?

B: I'm not mad at you. Why have you been so insecure lately?

A: I'm not insecure. It's just that you've been so critical.

B: What do you mean, "critical"? I haven't been critical....

Instead of trying to read the other person's mind, a far better course is to use the skill of perception checking that you learned in Chapter 4: Identify the observable behaviors (facts) that have caught your attention and describe one or more possible interpretations that you have drawn from them. After describing this train of thought, ask the other person to comment on the accuracy of your interpretation.

"When you didn't return my phone call *(fact)*, I got the idea that you're mad at me *(interpretation)*. Are you?" *(question)*

"You've been asking me whether I still love you a lot lately *(fact)*, and that makes me think you're feeling insecure *(inference)*. Or maybe I'm behaving differently. What's on your mind?" *(question)*

Emotive Language

Comedian George Carlin described how we editorialize when he observed that "anybody driving slower than you is an idiot, and anyone going faster than you is a maniac."

Emotive language seems to describe something but actually announces the speaker's attitude toward it. If you approve of a friend's roundabout approach to a difficult subject, you might call her "tactful"; if you don't approve of it, you might accuse her of "beating around the bush." Whether the approach is good or bad is more a matter of opinion than of fact, although this difference is obscured by emotive language.

You can appreciate how emotive words are really statements of opinion when you consider these examples:

If you approve, say	If you disapprove, say
thrifty	cheap
traditional	old-fashioned
extravert	loudmouth
cautious	cowardly
progressive	radical
information	propaganda
military victory	massacre
eccentric	crazy

The best way to avoid arguments involving emotive words is to describe the person, thing, or idea you are discussing in neutral terms and to label your opinions as such. Instead of saying "Quit making sexist remarks," say "I really don't like it when you call us 'girls' instead of 'women.'" These behavioral statements not only are more accurate but also have a much better chance of being well received by others.

The Language of Responsibility

Besides providing a way to make the content of a message clear or obscure, language reflects the speakers' willingness to take responsibility for their beliefs and feelings. This acceptance or rejection of responsibility says a great deal about the speaker and can shape the tone of a relationship. To see how, read on.

PAUSE *and* REFLECT

Conjugating "Irregular Verbs"

MindTap REFLECT ... on your usage of emotive language by answering the following questions, either here or online.

The technique is simple: Just take an action or personality trait and show how it can be viewed either favorably or unfavorably, according to the label it's given and the person who is engaging in the behavior. For example:

I'm casual. (most favorable)

You're a little careless. (less favorable)

He's a slob. (least favorable)

Or try this one:

I'm thrifty. (most favorable)

You're money conscious. (less favorable)

She's a tightwad. (least favorable)

Notice how these labels display the self-serving bias discussed in Chapter 3, as well as the principle that we're usually less charitable when describing others' behavior than our own.

1. Try a few conjugations yourself, using the following statements:

   a. I'm tactful.

   b. I'm conservative.

   c. I'm quiet.

   d. I'm relaxed.

   e. My child is high-spirited.

   f. I have high self-esteem.

2. Now recall at least two situations in which you used emotive language as if it was a description of fact and not an opinion. A good way to recall these situations is to think of a recent disagreement and imagine how the other people involved might have described it differently than you.

"It" Statements   Notice the difference between the sentences of each set:

"It bothers me when you're late."
"I'm worried when you're late."

"It's nice to see you."
"I'm glad to see you."

"It's a boring class."

"I'm bored in the class."

As the name implies, **"it" statements** replace the personal pronoun *I* with the less immediate word *it*. By contrast, **"I" language** clearly identifies the speaker as the source of a message. Communicators who use "it" statements avoid responsibility for ownership of a message, attributing it instead to some unidentified source. This habit isn't just imprecise—more important, it is an unconscious way to avoid taking a position.

Dreamworks/Allstar

"But" Statements   Statements that take the form "X-but-Y" can be confusing. A closer look at **"but" statements** explains why. In each sentence, the word *but* cancels the thought that precedes it:

> "You're really a great person, but I think we ought to stop seeing each other."

> "You've done good work for us, but we're going to have to let you go."

> "This paper has some good ideas, but I'm giving it a D grade because it's late."

These "buts" often are a strategy for wrapping the speaker's real but unpleasant message between more palatable ideas in a psychological sandwich. This approach can be a face-saving strategy worth using at times. When the goal is to be absolutely clear, however, the most responsible approach is to deliver the positive and negative messages separately so they both get heard.

"I" and "You" Language   We've seen that "I" language is a way of accepting responsibility for a message. In contrast, **"you" language** expresses a judgment of the other person. Positive judgments ("You look great today!") rarely cause problems, but notice how each of the following critical "you" statements implies that the subject of the complaint is doing something wrong:

> "You left this place a mess!"

> "You didn't keep your promise!"

> "You're really crude sometimes!"

It's easy to see why "you" language can arouse defensiveness. A "you" statement implies that the speaker is qualified to judge the target—not an idea that most listeners are willing to accept, even when the judgment is correct.

Fortunately, "I" language provides a more accurate and less provocative way to express a complaint.[31] "I" language shows that the speaker takes responsibility for the complaint by describing his or her reaction to the other's

⋀ In *The Help*, white 1960s socialites use a positive-sounding title—"The Home Help Sanitation Initiative"—to try to enact a policy that reinforces their prejudices against black housekeepers. Abstract and ambiguous language can sometimes obscure the truth. Can you think of words, labels, or titles that overstate (or understate) the actions of the people involved?

Silver-John/Bigstock

behavior without making any judgments about its worth. Here are some "I" language alternatives for the examples offered above:

> "I don't want to be responsible for all of the cleaning in the apartment."

> "I'm angry that I was on time and you weren't."

> "I don't like when you tell off-color jokes in front of my parents."

The In Real Life feature in this section shows what "I" language sounds like as part of a conversation.

Despite its obvious advantages, even the best-constructed and delivered "I" message won't always succeed. As author and "I" language advocate Thomas Gordon acknowledges, "Nobody welcomes hearing that his behavior is causing someone a problem, no matter how the message is phrased."[32] Furthermore, "I" language in large doses can start to sound egotistical. Research shows that self-absorbed people, also known as "conversational narcissists," can be identified by their constant use of first-person singular pronouns.[33] For this reason, "I" language works best in moderation. Chapter 11 will discuss how to use "I" language effectively as a central component of the assertive message format.

"We" Language   One way to avoid overuse of "I" language is to consider the pronoun *we*. **"We" language** implies that the issue is the concern and responsibility of both the speaker and receiver of a message. Consider a few examples:

> "We need to figure out a budget that doesn't bankrupt us."

> "I think we have a problem. We can't seem to talk about your friends without fighting."

> "We aren't doing a very good job of keeping the place clean, are we?"

It's easy to see how "we" language can help build a constructive climate. It suggests a kind of "we're in this together" orientation that reflects the transactional nature of communication. People who use first-person plural pronouns signal their closeness, commonality, and cohesiveness with others.[34] For example, couples who use "we" language are more satisfied and manage conflict better than those who rely more heavily on "I" and "you" language.[35] In another study, strangers who were required to use the pronoun "we" instead of the phrase "you and I" in their interactions felt closer to one another.[36]

On the other hand, "we" statements aren't always appropriate. Sometimes using this pronoun sounds presumptuous and demanding because it suggests that you are speaking for the other person as well as yourself. [37] It's easy to imagine someone responding to your statement "We have a problem …" by saying "Maybe you have a problem, but don't tell me I do!"

Given the pros and cons of both "I" language and "we" language, what advice can we give about the most effective pronouns to use in interpersonal communication? Researchers have found that "I" and "we" combinations (e.g., "I think that we …" or "I would like to see us …") have a good chance of being received favorably.[38] Because too much of any pronoun comes across

TABLE 6.4 Pronoun Use and Its Effects

	ADVANTAGES	DISADVANTAGES	TIPS
"I" language	Takes responsibility for personal thoughts, feelings, and wants. Less defense-provoking than evaluative "you" language.	Can be perceived as egotistical, narcissistic, and self-absorbed.	Use "I" messages when the other person doesn't perceive a problem. Combine "I" with "we" language.
"We" language	Signals inclusion, immediacy, cohesiveness, and commitment.	Can speak improperly for others.	Combine with "I" language. Use in group settings to enhance unity. Avoid when expressing personal thoughts, feelings, and wants.
"You" language	Signals other orientation, particularly when the topic is positive.	Can sound evaluative and judgmental, particularly during confrontations.	Use "I" language during confrontations. Use "you" language when praising or including others.

as inappropriate, combining pronouns is generally a good idea. If your "I" language reflects your position without being overly self-absorbed, your "you" language shows concern for others without judging them, and your "we" language includes others without speaking for them, you will probably come as close as possible to the ideal use of pronouns. Table 6.4 summarizes the advantages and disadvantages of each type of language and offers suggestions for approaches that have a good chance of success.

SKILL *Builder*

Practicing "I" Language

MindTap® PRACTICE ... your skill at delivering "I" messages by answering the following questions either here or online.

You can develop your skill at delivering "I" messages by following these steps:

1. Visualize situations in your life when you have, or might have, sent each of the following messages:

   You're not telling me the truth!
   You think only of yourself!
   Don't be so touchy!
   Quit fooling around!
   You don't understand a word I'm saying!

2. Write alternatives to each statement using "I" language.

3. Think of three "you" statements you might make to people in your life. Transform each of these statements into "I" language and rehearse them with a classmate.

In REAL LIFE

"I" and "You" Language on the Job

For some time, Rebecca has been frustrated by her fellow worker Tom's frequent absences from the job. She hasn't spoken up because she likes Tom and also because she doesn't want to sound like a complainer. Lately, though, Tom's absences have become longer and more frequent. Today he extended his half-hour lunch an extra 45 minutes. When he returns to the office, Rebecca confronts him with her gripe using "you" language:

© Jason Harris/Cengage Learning

Rebecca: Where have you been? You were due back at 12:30, and it's almost 1:30 now.

Tom: *(Surprised by Rebecca's angry tone, which she has never used before with him)* I had a few errands to run. What's the problem?

Rebecca: We all have errands to run, Tom. But it's not fair for you to do yours on company time.

Tom: *(Feeling defensive after hearing Rebecca's accusation)* I don't see why you have to worry about how I do my job. Beth [their boss] hasn't complained, so why should you worry?

Rebecca: Beth hasn't complained because all of us have been covering for you. You should appreciate what a tight spot we're in, making excuses every time you come in late or leave early. *(Again, Rebecca uses "you" language to tell Tom how he should think and act.)*

Tom: *(Now too defensive to consider Rebecca's concerns)* Hey, I thought we all covered for one another here. What about the time last year when I worked late for a week so you could go to your cousin's wedding in San Antonio?

Rebecca: That's different! Nobody was lying then. When you take off, I have to make up stories about where you are. You're putting me in a very difficult spot, Tom, and it's not fair. You can't count on me to keep covering for you.

GENDER AND LANGUAGE

So far we have discussed language use as if it were identical for both sexes. Some popular writers and researchers believe that men and women speak in distinct ways, as if they are from different cultures.[39] Other scholars suggest that the differences are few and mostly not significant.[40] What are the similarities and differences between male and female language use?

Content

The first research on conversational topics and gender was conducted more than two generations ago. Despite the changes in male and female roles since then, the results of several studies are remarkably similar.[41] In these studies, women and men ranging in age from 17 to 80 described the range of topics each discussed with friends of the same sex. Certain topics were common

Tom: *(Feeling guilty but too angry from Rebecca's judgments and threat to acknowledge his mistakes)* Fine. I'll never ask you for a favor again. Sorry to put you out.

Rebecca may have succeeded in reducing Tom's lateness, but her choice of "you" language left him feeling defensive and angry. The climate in the office is likely to be more strained—hardly the outcome Rebecca was seeking.

Here's how she could have handled the same issue using "I" language to describe her problem instead of blaming Tom.

Rebecca: Tom, I need to talk to you about a problem. *(Notice how Rebecca identifies the problem as hers instead of attacking Tom.)*

Tom: What's up?

Rebecca: You know how you come in late to work sometimes or take long lunch hours?

Tom: *(Sensing trouble ahead and sounding wary)* Yeah?

Rebecca: Well, I need to tell you that it's putting me in a tight spot. *(Rebecca describes the problem in*

behavioral terms and then goes on to express her feeling.) When Beth asks where you are, I don't want to say you're not here because that might get you in trouble. So sometimes I make excuses or even lie. But Beth is sounding suspicious of my excuses, and I'm worried about that.

Tom: *(Feeling defensive because he knows he's guilty but also sympathetic to Rebecca's position)* I don't want you to get in trouble. It's just that I've got to take care of a lot of personal business.

Rebecca: I know, Tom. I just want you to understand that it's getting impossible for me to cover for you.

Tom: Yeah, OK. Thanks for helping out.

Notice how "I" language made it possible for Rebecca to confront Tom honestly but without blaming or attacking him personally. Even if Tom doesn't change, Rebecca has gotten the problem off her chest, and she can feel proud that she did so in a way that didn't sound ugly or annoying.

MindTap® APPLY ... this situation to your life by answering questions online.

---

to both men and women: work, movies, and television. Both men and women tended to reserve discussions of sex and sexuality for members of the same sex.

The differences between the men and women in these studies were more striking than the similarities. Female friends spent much more time discussing personal and domestic subjects; relationship problems; family, health and reproductive matters; weight; food and clothing; men; and other women. Men, on the other hand, were more likely to discuss music, current events, sports, business, and other men. Both men and women were equally likely to discuss personal appearance, sex, and dating in same-sex conversations. True to one common stereotype, women were more likely to gossip about close

"Sometimes I think he can understand every word we're saying."

friends and family. By contrast, men spent more time gossiping about sports figures and media personalities. Women's gossip was no more derogatory than men's. Many of these differences still appear in analyses of gender differences in online topics (see "Gender" in Chapter 2).[42]

These differences can lead to frustration when men and women try to converse with one another.[43] Researchers report that *trivial* is the word often used by both men and women to describe topics discussed by the opposite sex. "I want to talk about important things," a woman might say, "like how we're getting along. All he wants to do is talk about the news or what we'll do this weekend." Likewise, some men complain that women ask for and offer more details than necessary and focus too often on feelings and emotions.

Reasons for Communicating

Both men and women, at least in the dominant cultures of North America, use language to build and maintain social relationships. Regardless of the sex of the communicators, the goals of almost all ordinary conversations include making the conversation enjoyable by being friendly, showing interest in what the other person says, and talking about topics that interest the other person.[44] *How* men and women accomplish these goals is often different, though. Although most communicators try to make their interaction enjoyable, men are more likely than women to emphasize making conversation fun. Their discussions involve a greater amount of joking and good-natured teasing.

By contrast, women's discussions tend to involve feelings, relationships, and personal problems.[45] In fact, communication researcher Julia Wood flatly states that "for women, talk *is* the essence of relationships."[46] When members of a group of women were surveyed to find out what kinds of satisfaction they gained from talking with their friends, the most common theme mentioned was a feeling of empathy—"To know you're not alone," as some put it.[47] Whereas men commonly described same-sex conversations as something they *liked*, women described their same-sex conversations as a kind of contact they *needed*. The characteristically female orientation for relational communication is supported by studies of married couples showing that wives spend proportionately more time than husbands communicating in ways that help maintain their relationship.[48]

Conversational Style

Women tend to behave somewhat differently in conversations than do men, although the differences aren't as dramatic as you might imagine.[49] For instance, the popular myth that women are more talkative than men doesn't hold up under scientific scrutiny—researchers have found that men and women speak roughly the same number of words per day.[50]

One way to analyze gender-linked language differences is to observe men and women talking with each other. Communication scholar Anthony Mulac found that in mixed-sex conversations, men are more likely than women to use sentence fragments ("Nice photo"), judgmental adjectives ("Reading can be a drag"), directives ("Think of some more"), and "I" references ("I have a lot to do").[51] Women are more likely to use intensive adverbs ("He's *really* interested"), emotional references ("If he really cared about you ..."), uncertainty verbs

("It seems to me …"), and relational maintenance questions ("How was your day?"). Differences like these are consistent with studies showing that men's speech is characteristically more direct, succinct, and task-oriented. By contrast, women's speech is more typically indirect, elaborate, and focused on relationships.[52]

Women often use statements showing support for the other person, demonstrations of equality, and efforts to keep the conversation going.[53] With these goals, it's not surprising that traditionally female speech often contains statements of sympathy and empathy: "I've felt just like that myself," "The same thing happened to me!" Women are also inclined to ask questions that invite the other person to share information: "How did you feel about that?" "What did you do next?" The importance of nurturing a relationship also explains why female speech is often somewhat tentative. Saying, "This is just my opinion …" is less likely to put off a conversational partner than a more definite "Here's what I think…."

An accommodating style isn't always a disadvantage. One study found that female authors often use less-powerful language when writing for a female audience and that this approach is particularly effective in health-focused magazines.[54] Another study revealed that women who spoke tentatively were actually more persuasive with men than those who used more powerful speech.[55]

As you read in Chapter 2, gender differences in language use and conversational topics show up vividly in online communication. The language of social media also shapes the way some people talk in person. For instance, clipped versions of words that are popular in texting and tweeting ("adorb" "presh," "probs") have found their way into face-to-face interactions. Research suggests that women (typically younger ones) are more likely than men to use these jargon shortcuts in conversations.[56]

Nongender Variables

The link between gender and language use isn't as clear-cut as it might seem. Several research reviews have found that the ways women and men communicate are more similar than different. For example, one analysis of more than 1,200 research studies found that only 1 percent of variance in communication behavior resulted from gender difference.[57] According to this review, there is no significant difference between male speech and female speech in areas such as use of qualifiers ("I guess" or "This is just my opinion"), tag questions, and vocal fluency.[58] Another meta-analysis involving more than 3,000 participants found that women were only slightly more likely than men to use tentative speech.[59] Finally, researchers looked for sex differences in adults' talkativeness, affiliative speech, and assertive speech—and found negligible differences in every instance.[60] In essence, these studies found that men's and women's speech is far more similar than different.

Some on-the-job research shows that male and female supervisors in similar positions behave the same way and are equally effective. In light of this research, which shows considerable similarities and relatively minor differences between the sexes, one communication scholar suggests that the "Men are from Mars, women are from Venus" metaphor should be replaced by the notion that "Men are from North Dakota, women are from South Dakota."[61]

A growing body of research explains some of the apparent contradictions between the similarities and differences between male speech and female speech. Research has revealed other factors that influence language use as much or more than does gender.[62] For example, social philosophy plays a role. Feminist wives talk longer than their partners, whereas nonfeminist wives speak less than their partners. In addition, cooperative or competitive orientations of speakers have more influence on how they interact than does their gender.[63] The speaker's occupation also influences speaking style. For example, male day-care teachers' speech to their students resembles the language of female teachers more closely than it resembles the language of fathers at home. And female farm operators working in a male-dominated profession often use more masculine language patterns by swearing and talking "tough as nails."[64]

Another powerful force that influences the way individual men and women speak is their gender role. Recall the gender roles described in Chapter 4: masculine, feminine, and androgynous. Remember that these gender roles don't necessarily line up neatly with biological sex. There are "masculine" females, "feminine" males, and androgynous communicators who combine traditionally masculine and feminine characteristics. These gender roles can influence a communicator's style more than his or her biological sex. For example, one study revealed that masculine subjects used significantly more dominance language than did either feminine or androgynous subjects.[65] Feminine subjects expressed slightly more submissive behaviors and more equivalence behaviors than did the androgynous subjects, and their submissiveness and equivalence were much greater than those of the masculine subjects, regardless of their biological sex. And in gay and lesbian relationships, the conversational styles of partners reflect power differences in the relationship (e.g., who is earning more money) more than the biological sex of the communicators.[66]

While there are differences in male and female speech patterns, they may not be as great as some popular books suggest—and some of them may not result from biological sex at all. In practical terms, the best approach is to recognize that differences in communication style—whether they come from biological sex, gender, culture, or individual factors—present both challenges and opportunities. We need to take different styles into account but not exaggerate or use them to stigmatize one another.

PAUSE *and* REFLECT

Exploring Gender Differences in Communication

MindTap® REFLECT ... on exploring gender differences in communication by answering the following questions, either here or online.

As noted, some pop-culture writers claim that the communication styles of men and women are so different that "men are from Mars, women are from Venus." Others say the differences aren't that dramatic, and that a more apt metaphor would be "men are from North Dakota, women are from South Dakota." From your experience, which metaphor seems more accurate? If your answer is "neither," create another geographical metaphor to describe your experience. Be sure to provide examples.

CULTURE AND LANGUAGE

Anyone who has tried to translate ideas from one language to another knows that conveying the same meaning isn't always easy.[67] Sometimes the results of a bungled translation can be amusing. For example, the American manufacturers of Pet milk unknowingly introduced their product in French-speaking markets without realizing that the word *pet* in French means "to break wind."[68] Likewise, the English-speaking representative of a U.S. soft drink manufacturer naively drew laughs from Mexican customers when she offered free samples of Fresca soda pop. In Mexican slang, the word *fresca* means "lesbian."

Even choosing the right words during translation won't guarantee that non-native speakers will use an unfamiliar language correctly. For example, Japanese insurance companies warn their policyholders who are visiting the United States to avoid their cultural tendency to say "Excuse me" or "I'm sorry" if they are involved in a traffic accident.[69] In Japan, apologizing is a traditional way to express goodwill and maintain social harmony, even if the person offering the apology is not at fault. But in the United States an apology can be taken as an admission of fault and result in Japanese tourists being wrongly held responsible for accidents.

Difficult as it may be, translation is only a small part of the differences in communication between members of different cultures. Differences in the way language is used and the worldview that a language creates make communicating across cultures a challenging task.

Verbal Communication Styles

Using language is more than just choosing a particular group of words to convey an idea. Each language has its own unique style that distinguishes it from others. Matters such as the amount of formality or informality, precision or vagueness, and brevity or detail are major ingredients in speaking competently. And when a communicator tries to use the verbal style from one culture in a different one, problems are likely to arise.[70]

One way in which verbal styles vary is in their *directness*. Anthropologist Edward Hall identified two distinct cultural ways of using language.[71] **Low-context cultures** generally value using language to express thoughts, feelings, and ideas as directly as possible. Low-context communicators look for the meaning of a statement in the words spoken. By contrast, **high-context cultures** value using language to maintain social harmony. Rather than upset others by speaking directly, high-context communicators learn to discover meaning from the context in which a message is delivered: the nonverbal behaviors of the speaker, the history of the relationship, and the general social rules that govern interaction between people. Table 6.5 summarizes some key differences between the way low- and high-context cultures use language.

North American culture falls toward the low-context end of the scale. Residents of the United States and Canada value straight talk and grow impatient with "beating around the bush." By contrast, most Asian and Middle Eastern cultures fall toward the high-context end of the scale. In many Asian cultures, for example, maintaining harmony is important, so communicators

TABLE 6.5 Low- and High-Context Communication Styles

LOW CONTEXT	HIGH CONTEXT
Majority of information carried in explicit cues. High reliance on explicit verbal messages.	Important information not always expressed explicitly. Clues carried in the situational context (time, place, relationship).
Self-expression valued. Communicators state opinions and desires directly and strive to persuade others to accept their own viewpoint.	Relational harmony valued and maintained by indirect expression of opinions. Communicators abstain from saying "no" directly.
Clear, eloquent speech considered praiseworthy. Verbal fluency admired.	Communicators talk "around" the point, allowing the other to fill in the missing pieces. Ambiguity and use of silence admired.

Looking at DIVERSITY

Courtesy of Pilar Bernal de Pheils

Pilar Bernal de Pheils: Speaking the Patient's Language

A native of Colombia, Pilar Bernal de Pheils is a clinical professor in the School of Nursing at the University of California San Francisco. She supervises nurse practitioners in training at both San Francisco's Mission Neighborhood Health Center and Women's Community Clinic.

I work in a setting where linguistic and cultural barriers make communication especially challenging. At the Mission Neighborhood Health Center, almost all of our patients are monolingual Spanish speakers from under-served backgrounds. Most were born outside the USA, and very few have received anything beyond a basic education. Many seek help for medical and psychoso-cial issues that require linguistic and cultural sensitivity.

Everyone on our clinic staff is bilingual, which is important for the population we serve. Serious prob-lems can occur when patients don't have the benefit of a healthcare provider or translator who can under-stand and speak their language fluently.

It can be especially dangerous to *think* you under-stand another language when you don't know the nuances. For example, one common phrase Latino patients use to express the sensation of bloating is "Estoy inflamada." The literal translation is "I am inflamed," but that doesn't capture what the patient

is trying to describe. A provider or trainee who lacks a good grasp of the language could misunderstand the patient and misdiagnose the problem.

I remind my trainees to keep humble, both because their linguistic skills may not be as good as they may think, and because overconfidence can cause patients to feel intimidated. I also train my students to ask "Tell me more" as a way of increasing the odds that they will understand what our patients are trying to explain. And because the stakes are so high, it's important to provide a skilled professional translator when a staff member is not fluent in medical Spanish. It's expensive and time consuming, but in the end the results justify the costs.

It's hard enough for both patients and healthcare providers to communicate effectively under any circumstances, but the differences escalate when different languages are involved. Both attitude and skill are essential to bridge the gap.

will avoid speaking directly if that would threaten another person's face. For this reason, Japanese and Koreans are less likely than Americans to offer a clear "no" to an undesirable request. Instead they will probably use roundabout expressions such as "I agree with you in principle, but ..." or "I sympathize with you...."

The same sort of clash between directness and indirectness can aggravate problems between straight-talking, low-context Israelis, who value speaking directly, and Arabs, whose high-context culture stresses smooth interaction. It's easy to imagine how the clash of cultural styles could lead to misunderstandings and conflicts between Israelis and their Palestinian neighbors. Israelis could view the Palestinians as evasive, whereas the Palestinians could view the Israelis as insensitive and blunt.

It's worth noting that even generally straight-talking residents of the United States raised in the low-context Euro-American tradition often rely on context to make their point. When you decline an unwanted invitation by saying, "I can't make it," it's likely that both you and the other person know that the choice of attending isn't really beyond your control. If your goal was to be perfectly clear, you might say, "I don't want to get together." As Chapter 3 explains in detail, we often equivocate precisely because we want to obscure our true thoughts and feelings.

Besides their degrees of clarity and vagueness, language styles can also vary across cultures in being *elaborate* or *succinct*. Speakers of Arabic, for instance, commonly use language that is much richer and more expressive than that of most communicators who use English. Strong assertions and exaggerations that would sound ridiculous in English are a common feature of Arabic. This contrast in linguistic styles can lead to misunderstandings between people from different backgrounds. As one observer put it:

> First, an Arab feels compelled to overassert in almost all types of communication because others expect him [or her] to. If an Arab says exactly what he [or she] means without the expected assertion, other Arabs may still think that he [or she] means the opposite. For example, a simple "no" by a guest to the host's requests to eat more or drink more will not suffice. To convey the meaning that he [or she] is actually full, the guest must keep repeating "no" several times, coupling it with an oath such as "By God" or "I swear to God." Second, an Arab often fails to realize that others, particularly foreigners, may mean exactly what they say even though their language is simple. To the Arabs, a simple "no" may mean the indirectly expressed consent and encouragement of a coquettish woman. On the other hand, a simple consent may mean the rejection of a hypocritical politician.*

Succinctness is most extreme in cultures where silence is valued. In many Native American cultures, for example, the favored way to handle ambiguous social situations is to remain quiet.[72] In contrasting this silent style to the talkativeness that is common in mainstream American cultures when people first meet, it's easy to imagine how the first encounter between an Apache or Navajo and an Anglo might feel uncomfortable to both people.

A third way in which languages differ from one culture to another involves *formality* and *informality*. The informal approach that characterizes relationships in countries such as the United States, Canada, and Australia,

---

* Almaney, A. & Alwan, A. (1982). Communicating with the Arabs. Prospect Heights, IL: Waveland.

as well as the Scandinavian countries, is quite different from the great concern for using proper speech in many parts of Asia and Africa. Formality isn't so much a matter of using correct grammar as of defining social position. In Korea, for example, the language reflects the Confucian system of relational hierarchies.[73] It has special vocabularies for different sexes, different levels of social status, different degrees of intimacy, and different types of social occasions. For example, there are different degrees of formality for speaking with old friends, nonacquaintances whose background one knows, and complete strangers. When you contrast these sorts of distinctions with the casual friendliness that many North Americans use even when talking with complete strangers, it's easy to see how a Korean might view communicators in the United States as boorish and how an American might view communicators in Korea as stiff and unfriendly.

Language and Worldview

Different linguistic styles are important, but there may be even more-important differences that separate speakers of various languages. For almost 150 years, theorists have put forth the notion of **linguistic relativity**: that the worldview of a culture is shaped and reflected by the language its members speak.[74] The best-known example of linguistic relativity is the notion that Eskimos have a large number of words (estimated at everything from seventeen to one hundred) for what we simply call *snow*. Different terms are used to describe conditions such as a driving blizzard, crusty ice, and light powder. This example suggests how linguistic relativity operates. The need to survive in an Arctic environment led Eskimos to make distinctions that would be unimportant to residents of warmer environments, and after the language makes these distinctions, speakers are more likely to see the world in ways that match the broader vocabulary.

Even though there is some doubt that Eskimos really have so many words for snow,[75] other examples do seem to support the principle of linguistic relativity.[76] For instance, bilingual speakers seem to think differently when they change languages. In one study, French American people were asked to interpret a series of pictures. When they described the pictures in French, their descriptions were far more romantic and emotional than when they described the pictures in English. Likewise, when students in Hong Kong were asked to complete a values test, they expressed more traditional Chinese values when they answered in Cantonese than when they answered in English. In Israel, both Arab and Jewish students saw greater distinctions between their group and "outsiders" when using their native language than when they used English, a neutral tongue for them. Examples like these show the power of language to shape cultural identity—sometimes for better and sometimes for worse.

The best-known declaration of linguistic relativity is the **Sapir-Whorf hypothesis** credited to Edward Sapir and Benjamin Whorf.[77] Following Sapir's theory, Whorf observed that the language spoken by Hopi Native Americans represents a view of reality that is dramatically different from that of more-familiar tongues. For example, the Hopi language makes no distinction between nouns and verbs. Therefore, the people who speak it describe the entire world as being constantly in process. Whereas in English we use nouns to characterize

LANGUAGE AND HERITAGE

"Mi'ja, it's me. Call me when you wake up." It was a message left on my phone machine from a friend. But when I heard that word mi'ja, a pain squeezed my heart. My father was the only one who ever called me this. Because his death is so recent, the word overwhelmed me and filled me with grief.

Mi'ja (MEE-ha) from *mi hija* (me ee-HA). The words translate as "my daughter." Daughter, my daughter, daughter of mine: They're all stiff and clumsy, and have nothing of the intimacy and warmth of the word *mi'ja*—"daughter of my heart," maybe. Perhaps a more accurate translation of *mi'ja* is "I love you." Sometimes a word can be translated into more than a meaning. In it is the translation of a worldview, a way of looking at things, and,

Jupiterimages/Photodisc/Getty Images

yes, even a way of accepting what others might not perceive as beautiful. *Urraca*, for example, instead of "grackle." Two ways of looking at a black bird. One sings, the other cackles. Or, *tocayola*, your name-twin, and therefore, your friend. Or the beautiful *estrenar*, which means to wear something for the first time.

There is no word in English for the thrill and pride of wearing something new.

Spanish gives me a way of looking at myself and the world in a new way. For those of us living between worlds, our job in the universe is to help others see with more than their eyes during this period of chaotic transition.

Sandra Cisneros

MindTap **ENHANCE ...** your understanding by answering the following questions, either here or online.

1. Can you think of words and names that others use for you that denote their relationship with you, similar to how hearing the word *Mi'ja* led Sandra Cisneros to think of her father?

2. If you know another language, describe how certain concepts are difficult to translate from one language to another. Discuss the role that *culture* plays in this phenomenon.

people or objects as being fixed or constant, Hopi view them more as verbs, constantly changing. In this sense, English represents much of the world rather like a snapshot camera, whereas Hopi language represents the world more like a motion picture.

Some languages contain terms that have no English equivalents.[78] For example, consider a few words in other languages:

nemawashi (Japanese): The process of informally feeling out all of the people involved with an issue before making a decision.

lagniappe (French/Creole): An extra gift given in a transaction that wasn't expected by the terms of a contract.

lao (Mandarin): A respectful term used for older people, showing their importance in the family and in society.

"The Eskimos have eighty-seven words for snow and not one for malpractice."

dharma (Sanskrit): Each person's unique, ideal path in life and knowledge of how to find it.

koyaanisquatsi (Hopi): Nature out of balance; a way of life so crazy it calls for a new way of living.

A premise of linguistic relativity is that our words don't just *reflect* how we see the world; they also *affect* how we see it. The language we use shapes our perception of things, others, and ourselves. Studies examining the effects of "fat talk" demonstrate this principle.[79] People who regularly put concerns about their weight into words ("I'm so fat"; "My butt is huge") reinforce a poor body image. Researchers identified three particular signs that fat talk is doing harm: (1) when it's used routinely and compulsively; (2) when it involves constant comparisons with others; and (3) when it includes guilt words like "should" and "ought" ("I really should drop some weight"). As you read in Chapter 3, a steady diet of negative self-appraisals and social comparison can turn into a destructive cycle of thoughts, words, and behaviors.

The effects of language on a speaker's thoughts and feelings can also be seen in a study conducted at the University of Bristol.[80] Researchers asked participants to speak aloud three types of words: swear words, euphemisms for swear words (such as saying "the F-word" instead the actual term), and neutral words. When swearing, participants had much stronger physiological stress responses than when they used euphemistic or neutral terms. The researchers see this as an example of linguistic relativity: "Taboo words become directly associated with emotional centers in the brain. Accordingly, taboo words can evoke strong emotions even when they are uttered without any desire to offend." In other words, the language we use has an impact on our minds—sometimes in ways we don't even realize.

SUMMARY

Language is both a marvelous communication tool and the source of many interpersonal problems. Every language is a collection of symbols governed by a variety of rules: semantic, syntactic, and pragmatic.

Terms used to name people influence the way the people are regarded. The terms used to name speakers and the language they use reflect the level of affiliation of a speaker toward others. Language patterns also reflect and shape a speaker's perceived power.

Some language habits—such as confusing facts with opinions or inferences and using emotive terms—can lead to unnecessary disharmony in interpersonal relationships. Language also acknowledges or avoids the speaker's acceptance of responsibility for his or her thoughts and feelings.

There are some differences in the ways men and women speak. The content of their conversations varies, as do their reasons for communicating and their conversational styles. However, not all differences in language use can be accounted for by the speaker's biological sex. Gender roles, occupation, social philosophy, and orientation toward problem solving also influence people's use of language.

Different languages often shape and reflect the views of a culture. Some cultures value directness, brevity, and the succinct use of language, whereas others value indirect or elaborate forms of speech. In some societies, formality is important, whereas others value informality. Beyond these differences, there is evidence to support linguistic relativism—the notion that language exerts a strong influence on the worldview of the people who speak it.

KEY TERMS

abstraction ladder
abstract language
behavioral language
"but" statements
convergence
divergence
emotive language
equivocal language
high-context cultures
"I" language
"it" statements
linguistic relativity

low-context cultures
politeness
powerless speech mannerisms
pragmatic rules
relative words
Sapir-Whorf hypothesis
semantic rules
static evaluation
syntactic rules
"we" language
"you" language

START ...

Explore this chapter's
topics online.

7

NONVERBAL COMMUNICATION: MESSAGES BEYOND WORDS

AFTER STUDYING THE TOPICS IN THIS CHAPTER, YOU SHOULD BE ABLE TO:

1. Explain the defining characteristics of nonverbal communication.

2. List and offer examples of each type of nonverbal message introduced in this chapter.

3. In a given situation, recognize your own nonverbal behavior and its relational significance.

4. Monitor and manage your nonverbal cues in ways that achieve your goals.

5. Share appropriately your interpretation of another's nonverbal behavior with that person.

What's going on in the photo seen here? You don't need to be a mind reader to recognize that, along with whatever words are being spoken, other messages are being expressed here. Some social scientists have argued that 93 percent of the emotional impact of a message comes from nonverbal cues. Others have reasoned more convincingly that the figure is closer to 65 percent.[1] Whatever the precise figure, the point remains: Nonverbal communication plays an important role in how we make sense of one another's behavior.

Recall a recent exchange in one of your important relationships. What kinds of nonverbal behaviors might an observer notice? What might those behaviors say about your relationship?

Image Source/Alamy

CHARACTERISTICS OF NONVERBAL COMMUNICATION

As you read this chapter, you'll become acquainted with the field of nonverbal communication: the way we express ourselves—not by what we say but rather by what we do.

Nonverbal Communication Defined

We need to begin our study of nonverbal communication by defining that term. At first this might seem like a simple task: If *non* means "not" and *verbal* means "words," then *nonverbal communication* means "communicating without words." In fact, this literal definition isn't completely accurate. For instance, most communication scholars do not define American Sign Language as nonverbal even though the messages are unspoken. On the other hand, you'll soon read that certain aspects of the voice aren't really verbal, although they are vocal. (Can you think of any? Table 7.1 will help.)

For our purposes, we'll define **nonverbal communication** as "messages expressed by nonlinguistic means." This rules out sign languages and written

TABLE 7.1 Types of Communication

	VOCAL COMMUNICATION	NONVOCAL COMMUNICATION
Verbal Communication	Spoken words	Written words
Nonverbal Communication	Vocal tone, rate, pitch, volume, etc.	Gestures, movement, appearance, facial expression, touch, etc.

words, but it includes messages transmitted by vocal means that don't involve language—such as sighs, laughs, throat clearing, and other assorted noises. In addition, our definition allows us to explore the nonlinguistic dimensions of the spoken word—volume, rate, pitch, and so on. It also encompasses more abstract factors such as physical appearance, the environment in which we communicate, how close or far we stand from each other, and the way we use time. And, of course, it includes the features most people think of when they consider nonverbal communication: body language, gestures, facial expression, and eye contact.

Nonverbal Skills Are Vital

It's hard to overemphasize the importance of effective nonverbal expression and the ability to read and respond to others' nonverbal behavior.[2] Nonverbal encoding and decoding skills are a strong predictor of popularity, attractiveness, and socioemotional well-being.[3] Good nonverbal communicators are more persuasive than people who are less skilled, and they have a greater chance of success in settings ranging from careers to poker games to romance. Nonverbal sensitivity is a major part of the "emotional intelligence" described in Chapter 5, and researchers have come to recognize that it is impossible to study spoken language without paying attention to its nonverbal dimensions.[4]

All Behavior Has Communicative Value

Suppose you tried not to communicate any messages at all. What would you do? Stop talking? Close your eyes? Curl up into a ball? Leave the room? You can probably see that even these behaviors communicate messages—that you're avoiding contact. One study demonstrated this fact.[5] When communicators were told not to express nonverbal clues, others viewed them as dull, withdrawn, uneasy, aloof, and deceptive. This impossibility of not communicating is extremely important to understand because it means that each of us is a kind of transmitter that cannot be shut off. No matter what we do, we give off information about ourselves.[6]

Stop for a moment and examine yourself as you read this. If someone were observing you now, what nonverbal clues would that person get about how you're feeling? Are you sitting forward or reclining back? Is your posture tense or relaxed? Are your eyes wide open, or do they keep closing? What does your facial expression communicate? Can you make your face expressionless? Don't people with expressionless faces communicate something to you?

Of course, we don't always intend to send nonverbal messages. Unintentional nonverbal behaviors differ from intentional ones.[7] For example, we often stammer, blush, frown, and sweat without meaning to do so. Whether or not our nonverbal behavior is intentional, others recognize it and make

20th Century Fox/Allstar

▲ Simian characters in *The Dawn of the Planet of the Apes* behave in ways that are recognizable to moviegoers. Their emotions are easy to gauge from their facial expressions, gestures, and body language, without a word being said. What nonverbal cues can you use to make informed guesses about how others are feeling?

interpretations about us based on their observations. Some theorists argue that unintentional behavior may provide information but that it shouldn't count as communication.[8] We draw the boundaries of nonverbal communication more broadly, suggesting that even unconscious and unintentional behavior conveys messages and thus is worth studying as communication.

Nonverbal Communication Is Primarily Relational

Some nonverbal messages serve utilitarian functions. For example, a police officer directs the flow of traffic, and a team of street surveyors uses hand motions to coordinate its work. But nonverbal communication more commonly expresses the kinds of relational (rather than content) messages discussed in Chapter 1 and the kinds of identity messages that you read about in Chapter 3.[9]

Consider, for example, the role of nonverbal communication in *impression management*.[10] Chapter 3 discussed how we strive to create an image of ourselves as we want others to view us. Nonverbal communication plays an important role in this process—in many cases more important than verbal communication. For instance, think what happens when you attend a party where you are likely to meet strangers you would like to get to know better. Instead of managing impressions verbally ("Hi! I'm attractive, friendly, and easygoing"), you behave in ways that will present this image. You might smile a lot and perhaps try to strike a relaxed pose. It's also likely that you dress carefully—even if that requires looking as though you hadn't given a lot of attention to your appearance.

Along with impression management, nonverbal communication *reflects and shapes the kinds of relationships we have with others*. Think about the wide range of ways you could behave when greeting another person. You could wave, shake hands, nod, smile, clap the other person on the back, give a hug, or avoid all contact. Each one of these decisions would send a message about the nature of your relationship with the other person. Within romantic relationships, nonverbal behaviors are especially important. For example, displays of affection such as sitting close, holding hands, and giving affectionate gazes are strongly connected to satisfaction and commitment in romantic relationships.[11]

Nonverbal communication performs a third valuable social function: *conveying emotions* that we may be unwilling or unable to express—or ones that we may not even be aware of. In fact, nonverbal communication is much better suited to expressing attitudes and feelings than ideas. You can prove this by imagining how you could express each item on the following list nonverbally:

a. You're tired.
b. You're in favor of capital punishment.
c. You're attracted to another person in the group.
d. You think prayer in the schools should be allowed.
e. You're angry at someone in the room.

This experiment shows that, short of charades, nonverbal messages are much better at expressing attitudes and emotions (a, c, and e) than other sorts of messages (b and d). Among other limitations, nonverbal messages can't convey:

Simple matters of fact ("The book was written in 1997.")

The past or future tenses ("I was happy yesterday"; "I'll be out of town next week.")

An imaginary idea ("What would it be like if ...")

Conditional statements ("If I don't get a job, I'll have to move out.")

Nonverbal Communication Occurs in Mediated Messages

As you read in Chapter 2, face-to-face communication is richer in nonverbal cues than mediated messages. Despite that fact, there is plenty of nonverbal information available when we use technology to communicate. Video calls obviously provide nonverbal information, as do photos on social networking sites. However, even text-based electronic communication has nonverbal features.

The most obvious way to represent nonverbal expressions in type is with *emoticons*, using keyboard characters like these:

- :-) Basic smile

- ;-) Wink and grin

- :-(Frown

- :-@ Screaming, swearing, very angry

- :-/ or :-\ Skeptical

- :-O Surprised, yelling, realization of an error

Many programs now turn these keystroke combinations into graphic icons, known as *emoji*. Emoticons and emoji can clarify the meaning that isn't evident from words alone.[12] For example, see how each graphic below creates a different meaning for the same statement:

- You are driving me crazy 😁

- You are driving me crazy 😠

- You are driving me crazy 😍

Just like their in-person counterparts, emoticons and emoji are ambiguous and can communicate a variety of nonverbal messages.[13] A smiley face could mean "I'm really happy," "I'm only kidding," or "I just zinged you." The same is true of other online communication markers.[14] Exclamation marks (sometimes more than one!!!) can be used at the end of sentences, or even by themselves, to denote a variety of emotional states. Ellipses (…) at the end of a phrase can signal displeasure, thoughtfulness, or bemusement. They can also be turn-taking signals, similar to what might be conveyed nonverbally with your face or with pauses during in-person conversations. And "lexical surrogates" such as "hmmm" or "ooooh" have meanings ranging from delight to disapproval. Paralinguistic markers like these are best understood within their communicative and relational contexts.

Not only does the content of a nonverbal message matter, but when it is sent matters as well.[15] If you've ever been upset by a friend who hasn't responded punctually to one of your texts, then you know the role that timeliness plays in mediated interpersonal communication. We'll talk more about *chronemics* later in this chapter, but here we want to note that time management is a vital feature of online interaction. It's also a good example of the principle that you cannot *not* communicate. Communicators have expectations about when others should reply to their posts, emails, and text messages, and delays can be perceived negatively.

Although nonverbal information can be communicated online, constant use of electronic channels can dull the perception of nonverbal cues. A group of preteens in one study was cut off from all forms of electronic communication for five days at camp.[16] Interaction with their peers during that period took place exclusively in person. When compared with a control group that was free to use electronic devices during that same period, those who were restricted from technology dramatically improved their ability to recognize others' nonverbal cues of emotion. This serves as a reminder that in-person communication offers greater access to important nonverbal cues than is available through most modes of electronic interaction.

Nonverbal Communication Serves Many Functions

Just because this chapter focuses on nonverbal communication, don't get the idea that our words and our actions are unrelated. Quite the opposite is true: Verbal and nonverbal communication are interconnected elements in every act of communication. (See Table 7.2 for a comparison of verbal and nonverbal communication.) Nonverbal behaviors can operate in several relationships with verbal behaviors.

Repeating   If someone asked you for directions to the nearest drugstore, you might say, "North of here about two blocks," **repeating** your instructions

TABLE 7.2 Some Differences between Verbal and Nonverbal Communication

	VERBAL COMMUNICATION	NONVERBAL COMMUNICATION
Complexity	One dimension (words only)	Multiple dimensions (voice, posture, gestures, distance, etc.)
Flow	Intermittent (speaking and silence alternate)	Continuous (it's impossible to not communicate nonverbally)
Clarity	Less subject to misinterpretation	More ambiguous
Impact	Has less impact when verbal and nonverbal cues are contradictory	Has stronger impact when verbal and nonverbal cues are contradictory
Intentionality	Usually deliberate	Often unintentional

nonverbally by pointing north. This sort of repetition isn't just decorative: People remember comments accompanied by gestures more than those made with words alone.[17]

Complementing Even when it doesn't repeat language, nonverbal behavior can reinforce what's been said. **Complementing** nonverbal behaviors match the thoughts and emotions the communicator is expressing linguistically. You can appreciate the value of this function by imagining the difference between saying "Thank you" with a sincere facial expression and tone of voice and saying the same words in a deadpan manner.

Substituting When a friend asks "What's up?" you might shrug your shoulders instead of answering in words. Many facial expressions operate as substitutes for speech. It's easy to recognize expressions that function like verbal interjections and say "Gosh," "Really?," "Oh, please!," and so on.[18] Nonverbal **substituting** can be useful when communicators are reluctant to express their feelings in words. Faced with a message you find disagreeable, you might sigh, roll your eyes, or yawn when speaking out would not be appropriate. Likewise, a parent who wants a child to stop being disruptive at a party can flash a glare across the room without saying a word (and what child doesn't know the power of "the look" from Mom or Dad?).

Accenting Just as we use italics to emphasize an idea in print, we use nonverbal devices to emphasize oral messages. Pointing an accusing finger adds emphasis to criticism (as well as probably creating defensiveness in the receiver). **Accenting** certain words with the voice ("It was *your* idea!") is another way to add nonverbal emphasis.

Regulating Nonverbal behaviors can serve a **regulating** function by influencing the flow of verbal communication.[19] We can regulate conversations nonverbally by nodding (indicating "I understand" or "keep going"), looking away (signaling a lack of attention), or moving toward the door (communicating a desire to end the conversation). Of course, most of us have learned the hard way that nonverbal signals like these don't guarantee that the other party will pay attention to, interpret, or respond to them in the ways we had hoped.

Contradicting People often express **contradicting** messages in their verbal and nonverbal behaviors. A common example of this sort of **mixed message** is the experience we've all had of hearing someone with a red face and bulging veins yelling, "Angry? No, I'm not angry!" In situations like these, we tend to believe the nonverbal message instead of the words.[20] A humorous illustration of this concept can be seen in the Cingular cell phone commercial "Mother Love" (available on popular video sites). A mother and daughter appear to be having an argument with raised voices, flailing arms, and scowling faces. Careful listening to their words, however, reveals that they're slinging compliments and praise at each other, including the phrases "I really like it!" and "I love you!" What makes the commercial amusing is that their verbal and nonverbal messages don't match—and it's easy to believe they're angry rather than happy, no matter what their words say.

She dresses in flags
comes on
like a mack truck
she paints
her eyelids green
and her mouth
is a loud speaker rasping out
profanity
at cocktail parties
she is everywhere
like a sheep dog
working a flock
nipping at your sleeve
spilling your drink
bestowing
wet sloppy kisses
but i
have received
secret messages
carefully written
from the shy
quiet woman
who hides
in this
bizarre
gaudy castle

Ric Masten

© SuperStock/SuperStock

Nonverbal Communication Offers Deception Clues

When message senders are telling lies, their nonverbal behavior sometimes gives them away. Inadvertent signals of deception—often called **leakage**—can come through a variety of nonverbal channels.

Some of these channels are more revealing than others. Facial expressions offer important information,[21] but deceivers also pay more attention to monitoring these cues in an attempt to maintain a "poker face." More reliable is pupil dilation, a physiological response that can't easily be controlled.[22] Speech patterns also offer a variety of leakage clues.[23] In one experiment, subjects

TABLE 7.3 Leakage of Nonverbal Cues to Deception

Deception Cues Are More Likely When the Deceiver

Wants to hide emotions being felt at the moment

Feels strongly about the information being hidden

Feels apprehensive or guilty about the deception

Gets little enjoyment from being deceptive

Has not had time to rehearse the lie in advance

Knows there are severe punishments for being caught

Based on Ekman, P. (2001). Telling lies. New York: Norton.

who were encouraged to be deceitful made more speech errors, spoke for shorter periods of time, and had a lower rate of speech than did others who were encouraged to express themselves honestly. Another experiment revealed that the pitch of a liar's voice tends to be higher than that of a truth teller. Liars leak nonverbal cues of deception in some situations more than others. Table 7.3 outlines some conditions under which leakage is more likely.

A variety of self-help books and seminars claim that liars can be easily identified by monitoring their nonverbal cues, but scientific research doesn't support that notion. Communication scholars Judee Burgoon and Tim Levine have studied deception detection for years. In their review of decades of research on the subject, they came up with what they call "Deception Detection 101"—three findings that have been repeatedly supported in studies.[24] They are:

- We are accurate in detecting deception only slightly more than half the time—in other words, only a shade better than what we could achieve with a coin flip.

- We overestimate our abilities to detect other's lies—in other words, we're not as good at catching deception as we think we are.

- We have a strong tendency to judge others' messages as truthful—in other words, we want to believe people wouldn't lie to us (which biases our ability to detect deceit).

As one writer put it, "There is no unique telltale signal for a fib. Pinocchio's nose just doesn't exist, and that makes liars difficult to spot."[25] Moreover, some popular prescriptions about liars' nonverbal behaviors simply aren't accurate.

∧ In the TV series *The Americans*, Russian spies Philip (Matthew Rhys) and Elizabeth (Keri Russell) must carefully monitor their nonverbal cues so as not to give away their identities. This means paying close attention to every detail—their apparel, eye contact, proxemics, accents—in an attempt to seem "American" (and happily married). What do your nonverbal cues reveal about where and how you were raised? In what ways do you change those cues depending on the situation?

For instance, conventional wisdom suggests that liars avert their gaze and fidget more than nonliars. Research, however, shows just the opposite: Liars often sustain *more* eye contact and fidget *less*, in part because they believe that to do otherwise might look deceitful.[26] While it's possible to make some generalizations about the nonverbal tendencies of liars, caution should be exercised in making evaluations of others' truth telling based on limited and ambiguous nonverbal cues.[27]

Nonverbal Communication Is Ambiguous

You learned in Chapter 5 that verbal messages are open to multiple interpretations, but nonverbal messages are even more ambiguous. For example, consider the photo seen here. What do you think is the relationship between the people in it? Can you be sure? Or consider the example of a wink: In one study, college students interpreted this nonverbal signal as meaning a variety of things, including an expression of thanks, a sign of friendliness, a measure of insecurity, a sexual come-on, and an eye problem.[28]

Even the most common nonverbal behavior can be ambiguous. A group of Safeway supermarket employees filed grievances over the company's "Superior Service" policy that required workers to smile and make eye contact with customers. The grocery clerks reported that some customers took the friendly greetings as come-ons.[29] Although nonverbal behavior can be very revealing, it can have so many possible meanings that it's impossible to be certain which interpretation is correct. Law-enforcement officials in California discouraged one motorist group from publicizing a set of hand signals drivers

could use to signal one another with messages such as "Danger ahead" or "There's a problem with your car." They warned that hand signs could be misinterpreted as gang signs that would provoke violent reactions.[30]

The ambiguous nature of nonverbal behavior becomes clear in the area of courtship and sexuality. Does a kiss mean "I like you a lot" or "I want to have sex"? Does pulling away from a romantic partner mean "Stop now" or "Keep trying"? Communication researchers explored this question by surveying one hundred college students about sexual consent in twelve dating scenarios in order to discover under what conditions verbal approaches (for example, "Do you want to have sex with me?") were considered preferable to nonverbal indicators (such as kissing as an indicator of a desire to have sex).[31] In every scenario, verbal consent was seen as less ambiguous than nonverbal consent. This doesn't mean that romantic partners don't rely on nonverbal signals; many of the respondents indicated that they interpret nonverbal cues (such as kissing) as signs of sexual willingness. However, nonverbal cues were far less likely to be misunderstood when accompanied by verbal cues.

Some people have more difficulty decoding nonverbal signals than do others. For people with a syndrome called *nonverbal learning disorder* (NVLD), reading facial expressions, tone of voice, and other cues is dramatically more difficult.[32] Because of a processing deficit in the right hemisphere of the brain, people with NVLD have trouble making sense of many nonverbal cues. Humor or sarcasm can be especially difficult to understand for people—especially children—with NVLD. For example, if they learn the right way to introduce themselves to an unfamiliar adult (by shaking hands and saying "Pleased to meet you"), they may attempt the same response in a group of children where it might be viewed as odd or "nerdy." When peers do give them subtle feedback, such as raised eyebrows, they miss the information completely and therefore cannot modify their behavior next time.[33]

Even for those of us who don't suffer from NVLD, the ambiguity of nonverbal behavior can be frustrating. The perception-checking skill you learned in Chapter 4 can be a useful tool for figuring out what meanings you can accurately attach to confusing cues.

PAUSE *and* REFLECT

Body Language

MindTap® REFLECT ... on body language by answering the following questions, either here or online.

This exercise will both increase your skill in observing nonverbal behavior and show you the dangers of being too sure that you're a perfect reader of body language. Begin by choosing a partner from your class. You can try the exercise either in or out of class, and the period of time over which you do it is flexible—from a single class period to several days. Follow these directions:

1. For the first period of time (however long you decide to make it), observe the way your partner behaves. Notice movements, mannerisms, postures, style of dress, and so on. To remember your observations, jot them down. If you're doing this exercise out of class over an extended period of time, there's no need to let your observations interfere with whatever you'd normally be doing: Your only job here is to compile a list of your partner's behaviors. In this step, you should be careful *not to interpret* your partner's behaviors—just record what you see.

2. At the end of the time period, share what you've seen with your partner, who should do the same with you.

3. For the next period of time, your job not only is to observe your partner's behavior but also to *interpret* it. This time in your conference you should tell your partner what you thought his or her behaviors revealed. For example, does careless dressing suggest oversleeping, loss of interest in appearance, or the desire to feel more comfortable? If you noticed frequent yawning, did you think this meant boredom, fatigue after a late night, or sleepiness after a big meal? Don't feel bad if your guesses weren't all correct. Remember that nonverbal clues tend to be ambiguous. You may be surprised how checking out the nonverbal clues you observe can help build a relationship with another person.

INFLUENCES ON NONVERBAL COMMUNICATION

The way we communicate nonverbally is influenced to a certain degree by biological sex and to a great degree by the way we are socialized. To learn more about these influences, read on.

Gender

It's easy to identify stereotypical differences in male and female styles of nonverbal communication. Just think about exaggerated caricatures of macho men and delicate women that appear from time to time. Many jokes, as well as humorous films and plays, have been created around the results that arise when characters try to act like members of the opposite sex.

Although few of us behave like stereotypically masculine or feminine movie characters, there are recognizable differences in the way men and women look and act. Some of the most obvious differences are physiological: height, depth and volume of the voice, and so on. Other differences are rooted more in socialization. In general, females are usually more nonverbally expressive, and they are better at recognizing others' nonverbal behavior.[34] More specifically, research shows that, compared to men, women smile more; use more facial expression; use more head, hand, and arm gestures (but less expansive gestures); touch others more; stand closer to others; are more vocally expressive; and make more eye contact.[35]

After looking at differences like these, it might seem as if men and women communicate in radically different ways. In fact, men's and women's nonverbal communication is more similar than different in many respects.[36] Differences like the ones described in the preceding paragraph are noticeable, but they are outweighed by the similar rules we follow in areas such as making eye contact, posture, gestures, and so on. You can prove this by imagining what it would be like to use radically different nonverbal rules: standing only an inch away from others, sniffing strangers, or tapping the forehead of someone when you want his or her attention. Moreover, male–female nonverbal differences are less pronounced in conversations involving gay and lesbian participants.[37] Gender certainly has an influence on nonverbal style, but the differences are often a matter of degree rather than kind.

Culture

Cultures have different nonverbal languages as well as verbal ones.[38] Fiorello LaGuardia, legendary mayor of New York from 1933 to 1945, was fluent in English, Italian, and Yiddish. Researchers who watched films of his campaign speeches found that they could tell with the sound turned off which language he was speaking by noticing the changes in his nonverbal behavior.[39]

Some nonverbal behaviors have different meanings from culture to culture. The OK gesture made by joining the tips of thumb and forefinger to form a circle is a cheery affirmation to most Americans, but it has less positive meanings in other parts of the world.[40] In France and Belgium, it means "You're worth zero." In Greece and Turkey, it is a vulgar sexual invitation, usually meant as an insult. Given this sort of cross-cultural ambiguity, it's easy to imagine how an innocent tourist might wind up in serious trouble.

Culture also affects how nonverbal cues are monitored. In Japan, for instance, people tend to look to the eyes for emotional cues, whereas Americans and Europeans focus on the mouth.[41] These differences can be seen in the text-based emoticons used in these cultures. American emoticons focus on mouth expressions, while Japanese emoticons feature the eyes. (Search for "Western and Eastern emoticons" in your browser for examples.)

Even though we recognize that differences exist in the nonverbal rules of different cultures, subtle differences can damage relationships without the parties ever recognizing exactly what has gone wrong. Anthropologist Edward Hall points out that, whereas Americans are comfortable conducting business at a distance of roughly 4 feet, people from the Middle East stand much closer.[42] It is easy to visualize the awkward advance-and-retreat pattern that might occur when two diplomats or businesspeople from these cultures meet. The Middle Easterner would probably keep moving forward to close the gap, whereas the American would continually back away. Both would feel uncomfortable, probably without knowing why.

Like distance, patterns of eye contact vary around the world.[43] A direct gaze is considered appropriate, if not imperative, for speakers seeking power in Latin America, the Arab world, and southern Europe. However, Asians, Indians, Pakistanis, and northern Europeans gaze at a listener peripherally or not at all out of respect rather than a lack of interest.[44] In either case, deviations from the norm are likely to make a listener uncomfortable.

The use of time depends greatly on culture.[45] Some cultures (e.g., North American, German, and Swiss) tend to be **monochronic**, emphasizing punctuality, schedules, and completing one task at a time. Other cultures (e.g., South American, Mediterranean, and Arab) are more **polychronic**, with flexible schedules in which multiple tasks are pursued at the same time.[46] One psychologist discovered the difference between North and South American attitudes when teaching at a university in Brazil.[47] He found that some Brazilian students arrived halfway through a two-hour class and most of them stayed put and kept asking questions when the class was scheduled to end. A half-hour after the official end of the class, the psychologist finally closed off discussion because there was no indication that the students intended to leave. This flexibility of time is quite different from what is common in most North American colleges!

As Table 7.4 shows, differences in cultural rules can lead to misunderstandings. For example, observations have shown that black women in all-black groups are nonverbally more expressive and interrupt one another

kosmos111/Shutterstock.com

TABLE 7.4 Cultural Differences in Nonverbal Communication Can Lead to Misunderstandings

Behaviors that have one meaning for members of the same culture or co-culture can be interpreted differently by members of other groups.

BEHAVIOR	PROBABLE IN-GROUP PERCEPTION	POSSIBLE OUT-GROUP PERCEPTION
Avoidance of direct eye contact (Latino/Latina)	Used to communicate attentiveness or respect	A sign of inattentiveness; direct eye contact is preferred
Aggressively challenging a point with which one disagrees (African American)	Acceptable means of dialogue; not regarded as verbal abuse or a precursor to violence	Arguments are viewed as inappropriate and a sign of potential imminent violence
Use of finger gestures to beckon others (Asian)	Appropriate if used by adults for children, but highly offensive if directed at adults	Appropriate gesture to use with both children and adults
Silence (Native American)	Sign of respect, thoughtfulness, and/or uncertainty/ambiguity	Interpreted as boredom, disagreement, or refusal to participate
Touch (Latino/Latina)	Normal and appropriate for interpersonal interactions	Deemed appropriate for some intimate or friendly interactions; otherwise perceived as a violation of personal space
Public display of intense emotions (African American)	Accepted and valued as measure of expressiveness; appropriate in most settings	Violates expectations for self-controlled public behaviors; inappropriate in most public settings
Touching or holding hands of same-sex friends (Asian)	Acceptable in behavior that signifies closeness in platonic relationships	Perceived as inappropriate, especially for male friends

more than white women in all-white groups. This doesn't mean that black women always feel more intensely than their white counterparts. A more likely explanation is that the two groups follow different cultural rules. One study found that in racially mixed groups both black and white women moved closer to each others' style.[48] This nonverbal convergence shows that skilled communicators can adapt their behavior when interacting with members of other cultures or subcultures in order to make the exchange smoother and more effective.

Despite the many cultural differences, some nonverbal behaviors have the same meanings around the world. Smiles and laughter are universal signals of positive emotions, for example, whereas sour expressions are universal signals of displeasure.[49] Charles Darwin believed that expressions like these are the result of evolution, functioning as survival mechanisms that allowed early humans to convey emotional states before the development of language. The innateness of some facial expressions becomes even clearer when we examine the behavior of children who are born with impaired hearing and sight.[50] Despite a lack of social learning, these children often display a broad range of expression. They smile, laugh, and cry in ways that are similar to those of seeing and hearing children. In other words, nonverbal behavior—like much of our communication—is influenced by both our genetic heritage and our culture.

TYPES OF NONVERBAL COMMUNICATION

Keeping the characteristics of nonverbal communication in mind, let's look at some of the ways we communicate in addition to words.

Body Movement

The first area of nonverbal communication we'll discuss is the broad field of **kinesics**, or body position and motion. In this section, we'll explore the role that body orientation, posture, gestures, facial expressions, and eye contact play in our relationships with one another.

Body Orientation   We'll start with **body orientation**—the degree to which we face toward or away from someone with our body, feet, and head. To understand how this kind of physical positioning communicates nonverbal messages, imagine that you and a friend are in the middle of a conversation when a third person approaches and wants to join you. You're not especially glad to see this person, but you don't want to sound rude by asking him to leave. By turning your body slightly away from the intruder, you can make your feelings very clear. The nonverbal message here is "We're interested in each other right now and don't want to include you in our conversation." The general rule is that facing someone directly signals your interest and facing away signals a desire to avoid involvement.

You can learn a good deal about how people feel by observing the way people position themselves. The next time you're in a crowded place where people can choose whom to face directly, try noticing who seems to be included in the action and who is being subtly shut out. And in the same way, pay attention to your own body orientation. You may be surprised to discover that you're avoiding a certain person without being conscious of it or that at times you're "turning your back" on people altogether. If this is the case, it may be helpful to figure out why.

Posture   Another way we communicate nonverbally is through **posture**. To see if this is true, stop reading for a moment and notice how you're sitting. What does your position say nonverbally about how you feel? Are there any other people near you now? What messages do you get from their current posture? By paying attention to the postures of those around you, as well as your own, you'll find another channel of nonverbal communication that can furnish information about how people feel about themselves and one another.

An indication of how much posture communicates is shown by our language. It's full of expressions that link emotional states with body postures:

I won't take this lying down! (Nor will I stand for it!)

I feel the weight of the world on my shoulders.

He's a real slouch in the office (but he's no slouch on the basketball court).

She's been sitting on that project for weeks.

Posture may be the least ambiguous type of nonverbal behavior. In one study, 176 computer-generated mannequin figures were created, and observers were asked to assign emotions to particular postural configurations. The raters had more than 90-percent agreement on postures that were connected with anger, sadness, and happiness.[51] Some postures seem easier to interpret than others. Disgust was the emotion that was hardest to identify from body posture, and some raters thought that surprise and happiness had similar postural configurations.

Tension and relaxation offer other postural keys to feelings. We take relaxed postures in nonthreatening situations and tighten up in threatening situations.[52] Based on this observation, we can tell a good deal about how others feel simply by watching how tense or loose they seem to be. For example, tenseness is a way of detecting status differences: The lower-status person is generally the more rigid and tense-appearing one, and the higher-status person appears more relaxed. Research shows that adopting a high-status pose—such as putting your feet up on a desk with hands clasped behind your head—can actually lead to increased feelings of power.[53]

Gestures Movements of the hands and arms—**gestures**—are an important type of nonverbal communication. Some social scientists claim that a language of gestures was the first form of human communication, preceding speech by tens of thousands of years.[54]

The most common forms of gestures are what social scientists call **illustrators**—movements that accompany speech but don't stand on their own.[55] For instance, if someone on a street corner asked you how to get to a restaurant across town, you might offer street names and addresses—but all the while you'd probably point with your fingers and gesture with your hands to illustrate how to get there. Remove the words from your directions and it's unlikely that the other person would ever find the restaurant. Think also of people who like to "talk with their hands," gesturing vigorously even when they're conversing on the phone and can't be seen by the other party. Research shows that North Americans use illustrators more often when they are emotionally aroused—trying to explain ideas that are difficult to put into words when they are furious, horrified, agitated, distressed, or excited.[56] Studies also show that it is easier to comprehend and learn a second language when it is accompanied by illustrators and other nonverbal cues.[57]

A second type of gestures is **emblems**—deliberate nonverbal behaviors that have a precise meaning and are known to virtually everyone within a cultural group. Unlike illustrators, emblems can stand on their own and often function as replacements for words. For example, all North Americans know that a head nod means "Yes," a head shake means "No," a wave means "Hello" or "Goodbye," and a hand to the ear means "I can't hear you." And almost every Westerner over the age of seven knows the meaning of a raised middle finger. It's important to remember, however, that the meanings of emblems like these are not universal. For instance, the "thumbs-up" sign means "good" in the United States but is an obscene gesture in Iraq and several other countries.[58]

A third type of gestures is **adaptors**—unconscious bodily movements in response to the environment. For instance, shivering when it's cold and folding your arms to get warmer are examples of adaptors. Of course, sometimes we cross our arms when we're feeling "cold" toward another person—and thus adaptors can reveal the climate of our relationships. In particular, self-touching behaviors—sometimes called **manipulators**—are often a sign of discomfort, such as fiddling with your hands or rubbing your arms during an interview.[59] But not *all* fidgeting signals uneasiness. People also are likely to engage in self-touching when relaxed. When they let down their guard (either alone or with friends), they will be more likely to fiddle with an earlobe, twirl a strand of hair, or clean their fingernails. Whether or not the fidgeter is hiding something, observers are likely to interpret these behaviors as a signal of dishonesty. Because not all fidgeters are dishonest, it's important not to jump to conclusions about the meaning of adaptors.

Actually, *too few* gestures may be just as significant an indicator of mixed messages as *too many*.[60] Limited gesturing may signal a lack of interest, sadness, boredom, or low enthusiasm. Illustrators also decrease whenever someone is cautious about speaking. For these reasons, a careful observer will look for either an increase or a decrease in the usual level of gestures.

On the JOB

Nonverbal Communication in Job Interviews

The old adage "You never get a second chance to make a first impression" is never truer than in job interviews. The impression you make in the first few minutes of this crucial conversation can define the way a prospective employer views you—and thus the path of your career. Research highlights the vital role that nonverbal communication plays in shaping how interviewers regard job applicants.[a]

Here's a look at three specific behaviors that have been the subject of studies on employment interviewing:

- *Handshaking*. In American culture, most professional interactions begin with a handshake. As simple as this ritual might seem, research shows that the quality of a handshake is related to interviewer hiring recommendations. Handshakes should be firm and energetic without being overpowering—and this holds true for both men and women.[b]

- *Attire and Appearance*. Being well dressed and properly groomed is basic to interview success. A business-appropriate appearance enhances perceptions of a candidate's credibility and social skills. A rule of thumb is that it's better to err on the side of formality than casualness, and conservative colors and fashion are preferable to being flashy.[c]

- *Smiling*. While it may seem obvious, one study found that "authentically smiling interviewees were judged to be more suitable and were more likely to be short-listed and selected for the job."[d] The word *authentically* is important—judges in the study made negative appraisals of plastered-on smiles that didn't seem genuine. The key is to smile naturally and regularly, exhibiting a friendly and pleasant demeanor.

It's easy to imagine how other nonverbal cues discussed in this chapter (e.g., eye contact, posture, tone of voice, etc.) are vital in making a good impression in a job interview. For more information, consult the myriad books and websites devoted to employment interviewing. You can also visit your school's career-development center or perhaps even take a course in interviewing. In every case, you'll be coached that what you do and how you look is as important as what you say in a job interview.

THE EYES HAVE IT

Look inside your kitchen cabinet and odds are you have a collection of old friends gazing back at you—the Quaker Oats man, the Sun-Maid girl, Aunt Jemima, and maybe a Keebler elf or two. The reason they are there may have more do with your subconscious craving for eye contact than the taste of the products.

In a study published in the journal *Environment and Behavior*, researchers at Cornell University manipulated the gaze of the cartoon rabbit on Trix cereal boxes and found that adult subjects were more likely to choose Trix over competing brands if the rabbit was looking at them rather than away.

"Making eye contact even with a character on a cereal box inspires powerful feelings of connection," said Brian Wansink, one of the study's authors.

This follows a flurry of recent research on the magnetic and mesmeric nature of eye contact and its essential role in developing emotional stability and social fluency. Studies show that newborns instinctively lock eyes with their caregivers. Researchers have also found that children and adults who avoid or are denied eye contact are more likely to suffer from depression and feelings of isolation as well as exhibit antisocial traits such as callousness. This is alarming in a society where people increasingly spend more time looking at their mobile devices than at one another.

Eye contact makes us more socially aware and empathetic. It allows us to make sense of our relationships and social orientation. Avoiding eye contact out of fear or insecurity, or breaking eye contact to read a text, check email, or play Candy Crush, degrades your social facility and emotional intelligence.

Researchers at Northwestern University found that patients of doctors who made more eye contact had better health, adhered more to medical advice and were more likely to seek treatment for future problems. Not surprisingly, doctors who brought laptops into the examining room made less eye contact.

"Eye contact is a really good surrogate for where attention is and the level of accord building in a relationship," said Enid Montague, a professor of engineering and medicine at Northwestern who used video recordings of 100 patient visits to a primary care clinic for her analysis. "We found eye contact leads to significantly better patient outcomes."

Which brings us back to the Quaker Oats man and Aunt Jemima gazing out of your kitchen cabinet—not to mention Chef Boyardee, Cap'n Crunch, Uncle Ben, and the Gerber baby. It's probably no accident that these brands have endured while some competing brands with fancy fonts and clever graphics—but no eye contact—have fallen by the wayside.

Kate Murphy

MindTap **ENHANCE …**
your understanding by answering the following questions, either here or online.

1. Observe the degree of eye contact others use when they engage with you. Based on your experience, what is the optimal level of eye contact in varying types of relationships and contexts?

2. Pay attention to your level of eye contact in important personal relationships. How might adjusting this level change the nature of your interactions?

228

Face and Eyes   The face and eyes are probably the most noticed parts of the body, but this doesn't mean that their nonverbal messages are the easiest to read. The face is a tremendously complicated channel of expression for several reasons.

First, it's difficult to describe the number and kind of expressions we produce with our face and eyes. Researchers have found that there are at least eight distinguishable positions of the eyebrows and forehead, eight of the eyes and lids, and ten for the lower face.[61] When you multiply this complexity by the number of emotions we feel, you can see why it's almost impossible to compile a dictionary of facial expressions and their corresponding emotions.

Second, facial expressions are difficult to understand because of the speed with which they can change. For example, slow-motion films show **microexpressions** fleeting across a subject's face in as short a time as it takes to blink an eye.[62] Without being aware, liars may leak how they genuinely feel through brief furrows of the brow, pursing of the lips, or crinkling around the eyes.[63] Microexpressions like these are more likely to occur during what's known as "high-stakes" lying, such as when there are severe punishments for being caught.[64] Keep in mind that slow-motion recordings and trained professionals are often required to pick up these brief deception cues.

Despite the complex way in which the face shows emotions, you can still pick up clues by watching faces carefully. One of the easiest ways is to look for expressions that seem too exaggerated to be true. For instance, genuine facial expressions usually last no longer than five seconds—anything more and we start to doubt they are real (contestants in pageants with smiles plastered on their faces often come across as "fake" or "plastic").[65] Another way to detect feelings is to watch others' expressions when they aren't likely to be thinking about their appearance. We've all had the experience of glancing into another car while stopped in a traffic jam, or of looking around at a sporting event, and seeing expressions that the wearer would probably never show in more guarded moments.

The eyes can send several kinds of messages. Meeting someone's glance with your eyes is usually a sign of involvement, whereas looking away is often a sign of a desire to avoid contact. This principle has a practical application in commerce: Customers leave larger tips when their servers (male and female) maintain eye contact with them.[66] Research also shows that communicators who make direct eye contact are far more likely to get others to comply with their requests than are those who make evasive glances.[67] We'll see later in this chapter how the same principle holds true with touching others—which is why the term *eye contact* is relevant. A sense of connection leads to compliance.

Another kind of message the eyes communicate is a positive or negative attitude.[68] When someone looks toward us with the proper facial expression, we get a clear message that the looker is interested in us—hence the expression "making eyes." At the same time, when our long glances toward someone else are avoided, we can be pretty sure that the other person isn't as interested in a relationship as we are. (Of course, there are all sorts of courtship games in which the receiver of a glance pretends not to notice any message by glancing away yet signals interest with some other part of the body.) The eyes can also communicate both dominance and submission.[69] We've all played the game of trying to stare down somebody, and there are times when downcast eyes are a sign of giving in.

Looking at DIVERSITY

Annie Donnellon: Blindness and Nonverbal Cues

I have been blind since birth, so I've never had access to many of the nonverbal cues that sighted people use. In fact, I think that "sightlings" (a pet name for my friends who are sighted) take for granted how much of their meaning comes through nonverbal channels. When I recently took an interpersonal communication course, the material on nonverbal communication was in some ways a foreign language to me.

For instance, I felt a bit left out when the class discussed things like body movement, eye contact, and facial expressions. I understand how these cues work, but I haven't experienced many of them myself. I have never "stared someone down" or "shot a look" at anyone (at least not intentionally!). While I know that some people "talk with their hands," that's something I've never witnessed and rarely do.

When the subject turned to paralanguage, I was back on familiar territory. I listen very carefully to the way people speak to figure out what they're thinking and feeling. My family and friends tell me I'm more tuned in to these issues than most sightlings are. It's typical for me to ask "Are you okay today?" when friends send messages that seem mixed. They may say everything's fine, but their voice often tells a different story.

I'm a singer and performer, and some of my biggest frustrations have come from well-meaning teachers who coach me on my nonverbals. I remember one acting instructor asking me, "How do you think your character would express herself nonverbally

in this scene?" and I thought to myself "I have no idea." People who are sighted may think that anger cues like clenched fists, rigid posture, or shrugged shoulders are "natural" expressions, but I believe that many of them are learned by watching others.

Let me pass along some keys that can help make communication smoother and more effective. It's important to mention your name when starting a conversation with people who are blind: Don't assume they can figure out who you are from your voice. At the end of a conversation, please say that you're leaving. I often feel embarrassed when I'm talking to someone, only to find out that they walked away mid-sentence.

Most important: Clue in visually-impaired people when something is going on that they can't see. Often at my sorority meetings, something will happen that everyone is laughing about, but I'm left out of the loop because I can't see the nonverbal cues. Over the years my friends and family have learned that whispering a quick description of the events helps me feel more a part of the interaction.

The interpersonal course I took was an enriching experience for me, my professor, and my classmates. I think we learned a lot from each other—especially about the vital and complex role of nonverbal communication in interpersonal relationships.

"Blindness and Nonverbal Cues" by Annie Donnellon. Used with permission of author.

Voice

The voice is another channel of nonverbal communication. Social scientists use the term **paralanguage** to describe nonverbal, vocal messages. The way a message is spoken can give the same word or words many meanings. For example, note how many meanings come from a single sentence just by shifting the emphasis from one word to another:

This is a fantastic communication book. (Not just any book, but *this* one in particular.)

This is a *fantastic* communication book. (This book is superior, exciting.)

This is a fantastic *communication* book. (The book is good as far as communication goes; it may not be so great as literature or drama.)

This is a fantastic communication *book*. (It's not a play or album; it's a book.)

There are many other ways we communicate paralinguistically through tone, rate, pitch, volume—even through pauses. Consider two types of pauses that can lead to communication snags. The first is the *unintentional pause*—those times when people stop to collect their thoughts before deciding how best to continue their verbal message. It's no surprise that liars tend to have more unintentional pauses than truth tellers, as they often make up stories on the fly.[70] When people pause at length after being asked a delicate question ("Did you like the gift I bought you?"), it might mean they're buying time to come up with a face-saving—and perhaps less-than-honest—response.

A second type of pause is the *vocalized pause*. These range from disfluencies such as "um," "er," and "uh" to filler words that are used habitually such as "like," "okay," and "ya know." Research shows that vocalized pauses reduce a person's perceived credibility[71] and negatively affect perceptions of candidates in job interviews.[72] When Caroline Kennedy was considering running for the Senate, her press tour interviews were filled with vocalized pauses. In one case she used "ya know" 142 times in a single interview with *The New York Times*. Although this wasn't the reason she decided not to run for office, many commentators noted that it certainly didn't help her professional image.[73]

Researchers have identified the power of paralanguage through the use of content-free speech—ordinary speech that has been electronically manipulated so that the words are unintelligible but the paralanguage remains unaffected. (Hearing a foreign language that you don't understand has the same effect.) Subjects who hear content-free speech can consistently recognize the emotion being expressed as well as identify its strength.[74] Young children respond to the paralanguage of adults, warming up to those who speak warmly and shying away from those who speak in a less-friendly manner.[75]

Paralanguage can affect behavior in many ways, some of which are rather surprising. Researchers have discovered that communicators are most likely to comply with requests delivered by speakers whose rate was similar to their own: People who spoke rapidly responded most favorably to rapid talkers, whereas slow speakers preferred others whose rate was also slow.[76] Besides complying with same-rate speakers, listeners also feel more positively about people who speak at their own rate.

Sarcasm is one instance in which we use both emphasis and tone of voice to change a statement's meaning to the opposite of its verbal message. Experience this reversal yourself with the following three statements. First say them literally and then sarcastically.

"Thanks a lot!"

"I really had a wonderful time on my blind date."

"There's nothing I like better than lima beans."

As they do with other nonverbal messages, people often ignore or misinterpret the vocal nuances of sarcasm. Members of certain groups—children, people with weak intellectual skills, and poor listeners—are more likely to misunderstand sarcastic messages than others.[77] In one study, children younger than age ten lacked the linguistic sophistication to tell when a message was sarcastic.[78]

The Way You Talk Can Hurt You?

Women have a distinctive style of speaking: "I was shopping last night? And I saw this wonderful dress? It was so black and slinky?" It's hard to convey intonation in print, but the question marks indicate a rise in pitch at the end of the sentence, as in a question. Many women, especially younger women, use this intonation in declarative sentences: "This is Sally Jones? I have an appointment with Dr. Smith? And I'd like to change it to another day?"

I cringe when I hear this. The rising intonation sounds timid and lacking in self-confidence; the speaker seems to be asking for approval or permission to speak when there's no need to. She should make her point straightforwardly, in an assertion that drops in pitch as it ends.

And I worry that rising intonation harms women. It gets them taken less seriously than they should be in public debates; it encourages salesmen and car mechanics to cheat them when they wouldn't try cheating a man.

A woman friend who studies languages says I've got it wrong. Unlike men, who use conversation to fight for status, she tells me, women see it as cooperative. And they use rising pitch to convey this to their audience. Their tone encourages the supportive interjections, such as "Uh-huh," "Exactly," and "I know what you mean," with which women far more than men interlard each other's speech. And it asks listeners to contribute their ideas on the speaker's topic.

At the very least, women's use of rising intonation involves an ambiguity. It uses a sound that in other contexts conveys timidity, for a very different purpose. Given this ambiguity, we shouldn't be surprised if female speakers who are trying to be cooperative are often heard as hesitant.

It's clearly idiotic to treat conversation as a contest, as so many men do. We'd all benefit from a more cooperative approach. But we need a new symbol to express this, one with no connotations of weakness.

If we find this symbol, we can all, men and women, speak in friendly but firm tones. We can tell anecdotes without lecturing but also without seeming to kowtow. When we call the doctor's, we can say: "This is Sally (or Sam) Jones." (No question about it.) "I have an appointment with Dr. Smith." (I'm reminding you of a fact.) "And I'd like to change it to another day." (Now, can you help me?)

Thomas Hurka

MindTap® ENHANCE …

your understanding by answering the following questions, either here or online.

1. Can you identify people in your life who speak the way the author describes in this reading? If so, what is your reaction to them?

2. Describe the role that tone of voice plays in getting you to comply with requests and directives from others.

3. Are there changes you might consider making in your paralanguage to become a more effective communicator?

Some vocal factors are perceived more positively than others. For example, communicators who speak loudly and without hesitations are viewed as more confident than those who pause and speak quietly.[79] People with more-attractive voices are rated more highly than those with less-attractive voices.[80] Just what makes a voice attractive can vary. As Figure 7.1 shows, culture can make a difference. Surveys show that there are both similarities and differences between what Mexicans and Americans view as the ideal voice. Accent plays an important role in shaping perceptions. Generally speaking, accents that identify a speaker's membership in a group lead to more positive evaluations (if the group is high status) or to negative evaluations (if the group is low status).[81]

Touch

Shortly after her husband was elected U.S. president, First Lady Michelle Obama violated diplomatic protocol by returning the hug of Great Britain's Queen Elizabeth II. Some observers were appalled, and others delighted. Regardless of their reaction, everyone would have agreed that touch is a powerful way of communicating.

Social scientists use the word **haptics** to describe the study of touching. Touch can communicate many messages and signal a variety of relationships, such as the following:[82]

Functional and professional (dental exam, haircut)

Social and polite (handshake)

Friendship and warmth (clap on back, Spanish *abrazo*)

Sexual arousal (some kisses, strokes)

Aggression (shoves, slaps)

Some nonverbal behaviors occur in several types of relationships. A kiss, for example, can mean anything from a polite but superficial greeting to the most intense arousal. What makes a given touch more or less intense? Researchers have suggested several factors:

Which part of the body does the touching

Which part of the body is touched

How long the touch lasts

How much pressure is used

Whether there is movement after contact is made

Whether anyone else is present

The situation in which the touch occurs

The relationship between the people involved[83]

From this list you can see that there is, indeed, a complex language of touch. Because nonverbal messages are inherently ambiguous, it's no surprise that this language can often be misunderstood. Is a hug playful or suggestive of stronger feelings? Is a touch on the shoulder a friendly gesture or an

MEXICAN IDEAL SPEAKER'S VOICE

Medium in pitch
Medium in rate
Loud in volume

Clear enunciation
Well-modulated
Without regional accent
Cheerful

Firm
Low in pitch
Somewhat slow with pauses

U.S. IDEAL SPEAKER'S VOICE

Λ **FIGURE 7.1**
A Comparison of the Ideal Speakers' Voice Types in Mexico and the United States

Adapted from "Communicative Power: Gender and Culture as Determinants of the Ideal Voice," in *Women and Communicative Power: Theory, Research and Practice*, edited by Carol A. Valentine and Nancy Hoar. ©1988 by SCA. Reprinted by permission.

attempt at domination? The ambiguity of nonverbal behavior often leads to serious problems.

Touch plays a powerful role in shaping how we respond to others. For instance, in a laboratory task, subjects evaluated partners more positively when they were touched (appropriately, of course) by them.[84] Besides increasing liking, touch also increases compliance. A restaurant server's fleeting touches on the hand and shoulder result in larger tips.[85] Touching customers in a store increases their shopping time, their evaluation of the store, and also the amount of shopping.[86] When an offer to try samples of a product is accompanied by a touch, customers are more likely to try the sample and buy the product.[87]

Some of the most pronounced benefits of touching occur in medicine and the health and helping professions. For example, patients are more likely to take their medicines when physicians give a slight touch while prescribing.[88] Massage can help premature children gain weight, help colicky children to sleep better, improve the mood of depressed adolescents, and boost the immune function of cancer and HIV patients.[89] Research shows that touch between therapists and clients has the potential to encourage a variety of beneficial changes: more self-disclosure, better client self-acceptance, and more positive client–therapist relationships.[90]

Touch also has an impact in school. Students are twice as likely to volunteer and speak up in class if they have received supportive touch on the back or arm from their teacher.[91] Even athletes benefit from touch. One study of National Basketball Association players revealed that the "touchiest" teams had the most successful records while the lowest-scoring teams had the least amount of touch among teammates.[92]

Of course, touch must be culturally appropriate. Furthermore, touching by itself is no guarantee of success, and too much contact can be bothersome, annoying, or even downright creepy. But research confirms that appropriate contact can enhance your success.

PAUSE *and* REFLECT

The Rules of Touch

MindTap° REFLECT . . . on the rules that govern touch by answering the following questions, either here or online.

Like most types of nonverbal behavior, touching is governed by cultural and social rules. Imagine that you are writing a guidebook for visitors from another culture. Describe the rules that govern touching in the following relationships. In each case, describe how the gender of the participants also affects the rules.

1. An adult and a five-year-old child

2. An adult and a twelve-year-old

3. Two good friends

4. Boss and employee

Appearance

Whether or not we're aware of the fact, how we look sends messages to others. There are two dimensions to appearance: physical attractiveness and clothing.

Physical Attractiveness   There is little dispute that people who are deemed physically attractive receive many social benefits.[93] For example, females who are perceived as attractive have more dates, receive higher grades in college, persuade males with greater ease, and receive lighter court sentences. Both men and women perceived by others as attractive are rated as being more sensitive, kind, strong, sociable, and interesting than their less-fortunate brothers and sisters.

The influence of physical attractiveness begins early in life.[94] Preschoolers were shown photographs of children their own age and asked to choose potential friends and enemies. The researchers found that children as young as three agreed as to who was attractive and unattractive. Furthermore, the children valued their attractive counterparts—both of the same and the opposite sex—more highly. Teachers also are affected by students' attractiveness. Physically attractive students are usually judged more favorably—as being more intelligent, friendly, and popular—than their less-attractive counterparts.[95] Teacher–student assessments work in both directions—research shows that physically attractive professors receive higher evaluations from their students.[96]

Physical attractiveness is also an asset in the professional world, affecting hiring, promotion, and performance evaluation decisions.[97] This bias has been referred to as "lookism" and can lead to the same kinds of prejudice as racism and sexism.[98] For instance, research shows that women gain an 8 percent wage bonus for above-average looks; they pay a 4 percent wage penalty for below-average appearance. For men, the attractiveness wage bonus is only 4 percent; however, the penalty for below-average looks is a full 13 percent. Occasionally physical attractiveness has a negative effect: Interviewers may turn down good-looking candidates because they're perceived as threats.[99] While attractiveness generally gets rewarded, glamorous beauty can be intimidating.[100]

Fortunately, attractiveness is something we can control without having to call a plastic surgeon. If you aren't totally gorgeous or handsome, don't despair: Evidence suggests that, as we get to know more about people and like them, we start to regard them as better looking.[101] Moreover, we view others as beautiful or ugly not just on the basis of their "original equipment" but also on the basis of how they use that equipment. Posture, gestures, facial expressions, and other behaviors can increase the physical attractiveness of an otherwise unremarkable person. Finally, the way we dress can make a significant difference in the way others perceive us, as you'll now see.

Warren Brothers/Allstar

˄ When his wife dumps him, Cal Weaver (Steve Carrell) turns to hunky Jacob Palmer (Ryan Gosling) for advice about how to act to attract women in *Crazy, Stupid Love*. Jacob overhauls Cal's appearance: shoes, shirts, suits, jeans, hair. And as happens in the movies, Cal emerges with a new sense of confidence and dating success. How much does your appearance affect how you feel about yourself? Can it change the way you interact with others?

Clothing   Besides being a means of protecting us from the elements, cloth-ing is a means of communicating nonverbally. One writer has suggested that clothing conveys at least ten types of messages to others:[102]

    Economic background

    Economic level

    Educational background

    Educational level

    Level of sophistication

    Level of success

    Moral character

    Social background

    Social position

    Trustworthiness

Research shows that we do make assumptions about people based on their clothing.[103] For example, experimenters dressed in uniforms resembling police officers were more successful than those dressed in civilian clothing in requesting pedestrians to pick up litter and in persuading them to lend money to an overparked motorist. Likewise, solicitors wearing sheriff's and nurse's uniforms increased the level of contributions to law-enforcement and healthcare campaigns. We are also more likely to follow the lead of those in more formal attire when it comes to violating social rules. Eighty-three percent of the pedestrians in one study copied the action of a jaywalker dressed in higher-status clothing who violated a "wait" crossing signal, whereas only 48 percent followed a confederate dressed in lower-status clothing.

George Doyle/Stockbyte/Getty Images

Physical Space

Proxemics is the study of the way people and ani-mals use space. There are at least two dimensions of proxemics: distance and territoriality.

Distance   Each of us carries around a sort of invis-ible bubble of personal space wherever we go. We think of the area inside this bubble as our private ter-ritory—almost as much a part of us as our own bod-ies. To appreciate this, take a moment to complete the "Distance Makes a Difference" exercise in this sec-tion. As you move closer to your partner, the distance between your bubbles narrows and at a certain point disappears altogether: Your space has been invaded, and this is the point at which you probably feel uncomfortable. As you move away again, your partner retreats out of your bubble, and you feel more relaxed.

    Of course, if you were to try this experiment with someone very close to you—a romantic partner, for example—you might not have felt any discomfort at all, even while touching. The reason is that our willingness to get close to others—physically as well as emotionally—varies according to the person we're with and the situation we're in. And it's precisely the distance that we voluntarily put between ourselves and others that gives a nonverbal clue about our feelings and the nature of the relationship.

As you read earlier in this chapter, appropriate proxemic distances differ from culture to culture. Anthropologist Edward T. Hall has defined four distances that most North Americans use in their everyday lives.[104] He says we choose a particular distance depending on how we feel toward the other person at a given time, the context of the conversation, and our interpersonal goals.

- The first of Hall's four spatial zones begins with skin contact and ranges out to about 18 inches. We usually use **intimate distance** with people who are emotionally the closest to us and then mostly in private situations—making love, caressing, comforting, protecting.

- The second spatial zone, **personal distance**, ranges from 18 inches at its closest point to 4 feet at its farthest. Its closer range is the distance at which most couples stand in public. The far range runs from about 2½ to 4 feet. As Hall puts it, at this distance we can keep someone "at arm's length." This choice of words suggests the type of communication that goes on at this range: The contacts are still reasonably close, but they're much less personal than the ones that occur a foot or so closer.

- The third spatial zone, **social distance**, ranges from 4 to about 12 feet. Within it are the kinds of communication that usually occur in business. Its closer range, from 4 to 7 feet, is the distance at which conversations usually occur between salespeople and customers and between people who work together. We use the far range of social distance—7 to 12 feet—for more formal and impersonal situations. Sitting at this distance signals a far different and less-relaxed type of conversation than would pulling a chair around to the boss's side of the desk and sitting only three or so feet away.

- **Public distance** is Hall's term for the farthest zone, running outward from 12 feet. The closer range of public distance is the one that most teachers use in the classroom. In the farther ranges of public space—25 feet and beyond—two-way communication is almost impossible. In some cases, it's necessary for speakers to use public distance because of the size of their audience, but we can assume that anyone who voluntarily chooses to use it when he or she could be closer is not interested in having a dialogue.

Choosing the optimal distance can have a powerful effect on how we regard others and how we respond to them. For example, students are more satisfied with teachers who reduce the distance between themselves and their classes. They also are more satisfied with a course itself, and they are more likely to follow a teacher's instructions.[105] Likewise, medical patients are more satisfied with physicians who operate at the closer end of the social distance zone.[106]

Territoriality   Whereas personal space is the invisible bubble we carry around as an extension of our physical being, **territory** remains stationary.

PAUSE *and* REFLECT

Distance Makes a Difference

MindTap® REFLECT … on how distance makes a difference in communication by answering the following questions, either here or online.

1. Choose a partner, and go to opposite sides of the room and face each other.

2. Very slowly begin walking toward each other while carrying on a conversation. You might simply talk about how you feel as you follow the exercise. As you move closer, try to be aware of any change in your feelings. Continue moving slowly toward each other until you are only an inch or so apart. Remember how you feel at this point.

3. Now, while still facing each other, back up until you're at a comfortable distance for carrying on your conversation.

4. Share your feelings with each other or the whole group.

Any geographical area such as a work area, room, house, or other physical space to which we assume some kind of "rights" is our territory. What's interesting about territoriality is that there is no real basis for the assumption of proprietary rights of "owning" many areas, but the feeling of ownership exists nonetheless. Your room at home probably feels like yours whether you're there or not, unlike personal space, which is carried around with you. In the same way, you may feel proprietary about the seat you always occupy in class, even though you have no illusions about owning that piece of furniture.[107]

The way people use space can communicate a good deal about power and status.[108] Generally, we grant people with higher status more personal territory and greater privacy. We knock before entering the boss's office, whereas she can usually walk into our work area without hesitating. In traditional schools, professors have offices, dining rooms, and even toilets that are private, whereas students, who are presumably less important, have no such sanctuaries. Among the military, greater space and privacy usually come with rank: Privates sleep forty to a barrack, sergeants have their own private rooms, and generals have government-provided houses.

Physical Environment

Physical settings, architecture, and interior design affect our communication. The impressions that home designs communicate can be remarkably revealing. Researchers showed students slides of the insides or outsides of twelve upper-middle-class homes and then asked them to infer the personality of the owners from their impressions.[109] The students were especially accurate after glancing at interior photos. The decorating schemes communicated information about the homeowners' intellectualism, politeness, maturity, optimism, tenseness, willingness to take adventures, and family orientations. The home exteriors also gave viewers accurate perceptions of the owners' artistic interests, graciousness, privacy, and quietness.

Besides communicating information about the designer, an environment can shape the kind of interaction that takes place in it. In one experiment, subjects working in a "beautiful" room were more positive and energetic than those working in "average" or "ugly" spaces.[110] In another experiment, students perceived professors who occupied well-decorated offices as being more credible than those occupying less-attractive offices.[111] Doctors have shaped environments to improve the quality of interaction with their patients. Simply removing a doctor's desk makes patients feel almost five times more at ease during office visits.[112] In another study, redesigning a convalescent ward of a hospital greatly increased the interaction between patients. In the old design, seats were placed shoulder to shoulder around the edges of the ward. By grouping the seats around small tables so that patients faced each other at a comfortable distance, the amount of conversations doubled. And in office cubicles, occupants who face out (rather than in) send the message that they're open to communication—and it also allows them to better protect their work's confidentiality.[113]

Time

Social scientists use the term **chronemics** to describe the study of how humans use and structure time. The way we handle time can express both intentional and unintentional messages.[114] For instance, sending a delayed response—or no response at all—to a work email can create the impression of untrustworthiness, especially from a subordinate or peer.[115]

In a culture that values time highly, waiting can be an indicator of status. "Important" people (whose time is supposedly more valuable than that of others) may be seen by appointment only, whereas it is acceptable to intrude without notice on lesser beings. A related rule is that low-status people must never make high-status people wait. It would be a serious mistake to show up late for a job interview, whereas the interviewer might keep you cooling your heels in the lobby. Important people are often whisked to the head of a restaurant or airport line, while presumably less-exalted masses are forced to wait their turn.

Time can be a marker not only of power and status but also of relationships. Research shows that the amount of time spent with a relational partner sends important messages about valuing that person.[116] In one study analyzing 20 nonverbal behaviors, "spending time together" was the most powerful predictor of both relational satisfaction and perceived interpersonal understanding.[117] Time is also measured and valued in mediated communication. Studies show that the length of time it takes for someone to respond to email messages or to postings in virtual groups has a strong correlation with perceptions of that person.[118] As you might guess, quick responses get positive appraisals, while tardy or neglected replies can have an adverse effect on trust and effectiveness in virtual groups.[119]

In REAL LIFE

Recognizing Nonverbal Cues

You can appreciate how nonverbal cues reflect attitudes by reading the following transcript twice. The first time, imagine that Kim's nonverbal behavior signals that she is glad to meet Stacy and looking forward to getting to know Stacy better. For your second reading, imagine that Kim feels just the opposite: She is put off by Stacy and feels uncomfortable around her.

© John Harris/Cengage Learning

Think about all the ways Kim's nonverbal behaviors might change, depending on her attitude toward Stacy. Even though she speaks the same words, imagine how her posture, gestures, facial expressions, voice, and use of distance might differ and how these nonverbal cues would reflect her feelings about her new neighbor.

Stacy: Hi. I'm new here. Just moved into Unit 14 yesterday. My name's Stacy. (*Extends her hand, ready to shake*)

Kim: Hi! I'm Kim. I'm your next-door neighbor in number 12.

Stacy: Great! This looks like a nice place.

Kim: It is. Everybody's friendly, and we all get along really well.

Stacy: (*Glancing down at a magazine in Kim's mail*) Hmmm. *American Songwriter*. Are you a musician?

Kim: Yeah, I'm a singer-songwriter. Mostly acoustic. I play around town. Nothing too big yet, but I'm hoping …

Stacy: (*Excitedly*) Whoa! I'm a musician too!

Kim: Really!

Stacy: Yeah. I play rhythm guitar with The Festering Sores. Have you heard of us?

Kim: Yeah, I think so.

Stacy: Well, you'll have to come hear us some time. And maybe we could even jam together, since we're both guitarists.

Kim: That would be interesting!

Stacy: Wow! I can already tell I'm going to like it here. Hey … what's the attitude around here about pets?

Kim: They're pretty strict about the "No dogs or cats" policy.

Stacy: No problem! Jezebel isn't either.

Kim: Well, what is Jezebel?

Stacy: (*Proudly*) She's a green iguana. A real beauty.

Kim: You're kidding, right?

Stacy: Nope. You'll probably meet her one of these days. In fact, she's kind of a runaway, so you might find her in your place if you leave the door open. Especially when the weather cools down. (*Semi-kidding*) She really likes to snuggle up to a warm body.

Kim: Well, I'm more of a bird person, so …

Stacy: She makes friends with everybody. You'll love her!

Kim: Look, I've gotta run. I'm already late for a practice session.

Stacy: I'll see you around. Really glad we're gonna be neighbors!

Kim: Me too.

MindTap® APPLY … this situation to your life by answering questions online.

SUMMARY

Nonverbal communication consists of messages expressed by nonlinguistic means such as body movement, vocal characteristics, touch, appearance, physical space, physical environment, and time.

Nonverbal skills are vital for competent communicators. Nonverbal communication is pervasive; in fact, it is impossible to not send nonverbal messages. Although many nonverbal behaviors are universal, their use is affected by both culture and gender. Most nonverbal communication reveals attitudes and feelings; in contrast, verbal communication is better suited to expressing ideas. Even mediated messages carry nonverbal cues. Nonverbal communication serves many functions. It can repeat, complement, substitute for, accent, regulate, and contradict verbal communication. When presented with conflicting verbal and nonverbal messages, communicators are more likely to rely on the nonverbal ones. For this reason, nonverbal cues are important in detecting deception. It's necessary to exercise caution in interpreting such cues, however, because nonverbal communication is ambiguous.

KEY TERMS

accenting
adaptors
body orientation
chronemics
complementing
contradicting
emblems
gestures
haptics
illustrators
intimate distance
kinesics
leakage
manipulators
microexpression

mixed message
monochronic
nonverbal communication
paralanguage
personal distance
polychronic
posture
proxemics
public distance
regulating
repeating
social distance
substituting
territory

8

LISTENING: MORE THAN MEETS THE EAR

AFTER STUDYING THE TOPICS IN THIS CHAPTER, YOU SHOULD BE ABLE TO:

1. Identify the situations in which you listen mindfully and those when you listen mindlessly and then evaluate the appropriateness of each style in a given situation.

2. Identify the circumstances in which you listen ineffectively and the poor listening habits you use in these circumstances.

3. Identify the response styles you commonly use when listening to others.

4. Demonstrate a combination of listening styles you could use to respond effectively in a given situation.

I have just

wandered back

into our conversation

and find

that you

are still

rattling on

about something

or other

i think i must

have been gone

at least

twenty minutes

and you

never missed me

now this might say

something

about my acting ability

or it might say

something about

your sensitivity

one thing

troubles me tho

when it

is my turn

iStockphoto.com/Nancy Louie

to rattle on

for twenty minutes

which I

have been known to do

have you

been missing too.

Ric Masten

Poem "Conversations" from *Dragonflies, Codfish & Frogs* by Ric Masten. Copyright © Sunflower Ink, Palo Colorado Road, Carmel, CA 93923. Reprinted with permission.

Ric Masten's poem here shows there's more to listening than gazing politely at a speaker and nodding your head. As you will soon learn, listening is a demanding and complex activity—and just as important as speaking in the communication process.

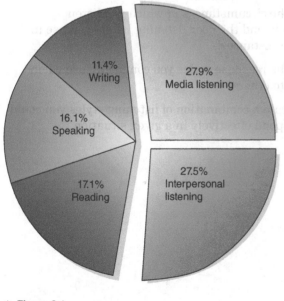

Λ Figure 8.1
Time Devoted to Communication Activities

11.4% Writing

27.9% Media listening

16.1% Speaking

17.1% Reading

27.5% Interpersonal listening

If we use frequency as a measure, then listening easily qualifies as the most important kind of communication. We spend more time listening to others than in any other type of communication. One study (summarized in Figure 8.1) revealed that college students spend about 11 percent of their communicating time writing, 16 percent speaking, and 17 percent reading—but more than 55 percent listening.[1] On the job, listening is just as important. Studies show that most employees of major corporations in North America spend about 60 percent of each workday listening to others.[2]

Besides being the most frequent form of communication, listening is at least as important as speaking in terms of making relationships work. In committed relationships, listening to personal information in everyday conversations is considered a vital ingredient of satisfaction.[3] In one survey, marital counselors identified "failing to take the other's perspective when listening" as one of the most frequent communication problems in the couples with whom they worked.[4]

When a group of adults was asked what communication skills were most important in family and social settings, listening was ranked first.[5]

The *International Journal of Listening* devoted an entire issue to exploring various contexts in which listening skills are crucial, including education,[6] health care,[7] religion,[8] and the business world.[9] When working adults were asked to name the most common communication behavior they observed in their place of business, "listening" topped the list.[10] The On the Job box in the following section explores in detail the vital role listening plays in the workplace.

This chapter will explore the nature of listening. After defining listening, we will examine the elements that make up the listening process and look at challenges that come with becoming a better listener. Finally, you will read about a variety of listening response styles that you can use to better understand and even help others.

LISTENING DEFINED

So far we've used the term *listening* as if it needs no explanation. Actually, there's more to this concept than you might think. We will define **listening**— at least the interpersonal type—as the process of making sense of others' messages.

Traditional approaches to listening focus on the reception of *spoken* messages. However, we've broadened the definition to include messages of all sorts because much of contemporary listening takes place through mediated channels, some of which involve the written word. Consider times you've said something like, "I was talking with a friend, and she told me … "—and the conversation you recount actually took place via texting, emailing, or instant messaging. Chapter 2 describes how social support can be offered through blogs, Facebook posts, and other social media (for example, see the reading "Texting to Save Lives" later in this chapter). We'll continue to focus on spoken messages in this chapter (beginning with our discussion of "hearing" below), but recognize that "listening" in contemporary society involves more than meets the ear.

Hearing versus Listening

People often think of hearing and listening as the same thing, but they are quite different. *Hearing* is the process in which sound waves strike the eardrum and cause vibrations that are transmitted to the brain. (You'll read more about hearing in the following section.) *Listening* occurs when the brain reconstructs these electrochemical impulses into a representation of the original sound and then gives them meaning. Barring illness, injury, or cotton plugs, you can't stop hearing.[11] Your ears will pick up sound waves and transmit them to your brain whether you want them to or not.

Listening, however, isn't automatic. People hear all the time without listening. Sometimes we automatically and unconsciously block out irritating sounds, such as a neighbor's lawnmower or the roar of nearby traffic. We also stop listening when we find a subject unimportant or uninteresting.

Self-Assessment

Your Listening Skills
Before reading any further, take an online quiz to check your listening skills. You can complete this activity by visiting www. CengageBrain.com to access the Speech Communication MindTap for *Looking Out Looking In.*

Boring stories, TV commercials, and nagging complaints are common examples of messages we may hear but tune out.

Mindless Listening

When we move beyond hearing and start to listen, researchers note that we process information in two very different ways—sometimes referred to as the *dual-process theory*.[12] Social scientists use the terms *mindless* and *mindful* to describe these different ways of listening.[13] **Mindless listening** occurs when we react to others' messages automatically and routinely, without much mental investment. Words such as *superficial* and *cursory* describe mindless listening better than terms like *ponder* and *contemplate*.

While the term *mindless* may sound negative, this sort of low-level information processing is a potentially valuable type of communication because it frees us to focus our minds on messages that require our careful attention.[14] Given the number of messages to which we're exposed, it's impractical to listen carefully and thoughtfully 100 percent of the time. It's also unrealistic to devote your attention to long-winded stories, idle chatter, or remarks you've heard many times before. The only realistic way to manage the onslaught of messages is to be "lazy" toward many of them. In situations like these, we forgo careful analysis and fall back on the schemas—and sometimes the stereotypes—described in Chapter 4 to make sense of a message. If you stop right now and recall the messages you have heard today, it's likely that you processed most of them mindlessly.

On the JOB

Listening in the Workplace

Being an effective speaker is important in career success, but good listening skills are just as vital. A study examining the link between listening and career success revealed that better listeners rose to higher levels in their organizations.[a] When human resource executives across the country were asked to identify skills of the ideal manager, the ability to listen effectively ranked at the top of the list.[b] In problem-solving groups, effective listeners are judged as having the most leadership skills.[c]

Listening is just as important in careers that involve cold facts as in ones that involve lots of one-on-one interaction. For example, a survey of more than 90,000 accountants identified effective listening as the most important communication skill for professionals entering that field.[d] When a diverse group of senior executives was asked what skills are most

important on the job, listening was identified more often than any other skill, including technical competence, computer knowledge, creativity, and administrative talent.[e]

Just because businesspeople believe listening is important doesn't mean they do it well. A survey in which 144 managers were asked to rate their listening skills illustrates this point. Astonishingly, not one of the managers described himself or herself as a "poor" or "very poor" listener, whereas 94 percent rated themselves as "good" or "very good."[f] The favorable self-ratings contrasted sharply with the perceptions of the managers' subordinates, many of whom said their bosses' listening skills were weak. Of course, managers aren't the only people whose listening needs work—all of us could stand to improve our skills.

Mindful Listening

By contrast, **mindful listening** involves giving careful and thoughtful attention and responses to the messages we receive. You tend to listen mindfully when a message is important to you and also when someone you care about is speaking about a matter that is important to him or her. Think of how your ears perk up when someone starts talking about your money ("The repairs will cost me how much?") or how you tune in carefully when a close friend tells you about the loss of a loved one. In situations like these, you want to give the message sender your complete and undivided attention.

Sometimes we respond mindlessly to information that deserves—and even demands—our mindful attention. Ellen Langer's determination to study mindfulness began when her grandmother complained about headaches coming from a "snake crawling around" beneath her skull. The doctors quickly diagnosed the problem as senility—after all, they reasoned, senility comes with old age and makes people talk nonsense. In fact, the grandmother had a brain tumor that eventually took her life. The event made a deep impression on Langer:

> For years afterward I kept thinking about the doctors' reactions to my grandmother's complaints, and about our reactions to the doctors. They went through the motions of diagnosis, but were not open to what they were hearing. Mindsets about senility interfered. We did not question the doctors; mindsets about experts interfered.[15]

Most of our daily decisions about whether to listen mindfully don't have life-and-death consequences, but the point should be clear: There are times when we need to consciously and carefully listen to what others are telling us. That kind of mindful listening will be the focus of the remainder of this chapter.

ELEMENTS IN THE LISTENING PROCESS

By now, you can begin to see that there is more to listening than sitting quietly while another person speaks. In truth, listening is a process that consists of five elements: hearing, attending, understanding, responding, and remembering.[16]

Hearing

As we have already discussed, **hearing** is the physiological dimension of listening. It occurs when sound waves strike the ear at a certain frequency and loudness. Hearing is influenced by a variety of factors, including background noise. If there are other loud noises, especially at the same frequency as the message we are trying to hear, we find it difficult to sort out the important signals from the background. Hearing is also affected by auditory fatigue, a temporary loss of hearing caused by continuous exposure to the same tone or loudness. If you spend an evening at a loud party, you may have trouble hearing well, even after getting away from the crowd. If you are exposed to loud noise often enough, permanent hearing loss can result—as many rock musicians and fans can attest.

For many communicators, the challenge of hearing is even more difficult as a result of physiological problems. In the United States alone, more than 31 million people communicate with some degree of hearing loss.[17] One study revealed that, on any given day, one-fourth to one-third of the children in a typical classroom do not hear normally.[18] As a competent communicator, you need to recognize when you may be speaking to someone with a hearing loss and adjust your approach accordingly.

Attending

Whereas hearing is a physiological process, **attending** is a psychological one and is part of the process of selection described in Chapter 4. We would go crazy if we attended to every sound we hear, so we filter out some messages and focus on others. Needs, wants, desires, and interests determine what is attended to. It is not surprising that research shows we attend most carefully to messages when there's a payoff for doing so.[19] If you're planning to see a movie, you'll listen to a friend's description more carefully than you would have otherwise. And when you want to get better acquainted with others, you'll pay careful attention to almost anything they say in hopes of improving the relationship.

It is surprising, though, that attending helps more than the listener; it also helps the message sender. Participants in one study viewed brief

"One of my strengths as an employee is my ability to multitask."

Barbara Smaller/Cartoonbank.com

movie segments and then described them to listeners who varied in their degree of attentiveness to the speakers. Later on, the researchers tested the speakers' long-term recall of details from the movie segments. Those who had recounted the movie to attentive listeners remembered more details of the film.[20]

Understanding

Understanding occurs when we make sense of a message. It is possible to hear and attend to a message without understanding it at all. And, of course, it's possible to misunderstand a message. Communication researchers use the term **listening fidelity** to describe the degree of congruence between what a listener understands and what the message sender was attempting to communicate.[21] This chapter describes the many reasons why we misunderstand others—and why they misunderstand us. It also outlines skills that will help you improve your understanding of others.

Responding

Responding to a message consists of giving observable feedback to the speaker. Although listeners don't always respond visibly to a speaker, research suggests they should do so more often. One study of 195 critical incidents in banking and medical settings showed that a major difference between effective and ineffective listening was the kind of feedback offered.[22] Good listeners show they are attentive by nonverbal behaviors such as keeping eye contact and reacting with appropriate facial expressions—which was of particular importance to children in one study who were asked to evaluate "good" versus "bad" listeners.[23] Verbal behavior—answering questions and exchanging ideas, for example—also demonstrates attention. [24] It's easy to imagine how other responses would signal less-effective listening. A slumped posture, bored expression, and yawning send a clear message that you are not tuned in to the speaker.

Adding responsiveness to our listening model demonstrates a fact that we discussed in Chapter 1: Communication is *transactional* in nature. Listening isn't just a passive activity. As listeners, we are active participants in a communication transaction. At the same time that we receive messages, we also send them. Responding is such an integral part of good listening that we'll devote an entire section to listening responses in the second half of this chapter.

Remembering

Remembering is the ability to recall information. If we don't remember a message, listening is hardly worth the effort. Research suggests that most people remember only about 50 percent of what they hear immediately after hearing it.[25] Within 8 hours, the 50 percent remembered drops to about 35 percent. After two months, the average recall is only about 25 percent of the original message. Given the amount of information we process every day—from teachers, friends, the radio, TV, cell phones, and other sources—the residual message (what we remember) is a small fraction of what we hear. You can begin to get a sense of how tough it is to listen effectively by trying the following Pause and Reflect "Listening Breakdowns" exercise.

Looking at DIVERSITY

Austin Lee

Seungcheol Austin Lee

Culture and Listening Responses

As a researcher who also teaches courses in intercultural communication, I pay close attention to the impact of culture on interpersonal interaction. It's easy to see how culture affects factors such as nonverbal cues and language style. It's not quite as simple to see the role culture plays in people's listening styles. Over the years, however, I've made a few observations.

I was born and raised in South Korea, where power distance is an important ingredient in communication patterns. People in roles of authority—parents, teachers, employers—are treated with great respect and deference. This affects listening styles—and more particularly, listening responses. A person with low power will usually listen silently to a person in authority. To ask questions or offer suggestions might be perceived as an inappropriate challenge. On the other hand, people in high power positions are likely to offer listening responses such as analyzing, advising, and judging. In fact, they would probably view such responses as their obligation.

When I came to the United States as a graduate student, I learned that remaining silent during conversations can create the wrong impression. Some of my professors thought I was passive and uninterested because I was listening silently when I was trying to show respect. They expected me to offer suggestions and feedback. This wasn't easy as it contradicted deep-rooted norms of my culture.

Another cultural difference I have noticed is about interruptions. When I stumble with words, Americans are less likely to help me out by suggesting the word or phrase that I'm searching for, while Koreans are willing to jump in and fill in the blanks, and even complete the sentence for me. In American culture, interruptions may be perceived as an attempt to take over the floor. But in a collectivistic society like Korea, people show their connectedness with good-natured interruptions to help the conversation flow. But again, this only happens when talking to peers or subordinates. Most Koreans wouldn't dare interrupt when a higher-up is talking.

"Culture and Listening Responses" by Austin Lee. Used with permission of author.

PAUSE *and* REFLECT

Listening Breakdowns

MindTap® **REFLECT ...** on listening breakdowns by answering the following questions, either here or online.

You can overcome believing in some common myths about listening by recalling specific instances when:

1. You heard another person's message but did not attend to it.

2. You attended to a message but forgot it almost immediately.

3. You attended to and remembered a message but did not understand it accurately.

4. You understood a message but did not respond sufficiently to convey your understanding to the sender.

5. You failed to remember some or all of an important message.

THE CHALLENGE OF LISTENING

It's easy to acknowledge that listening is important and to describe the steps in the listening process. What's difficult is to actually become a better listener. This section will describe the challenges that listeners must face and overcome to become more effective communicators. We'll look at various types of ineffective listening, then we'll explore the many reasons we don't listen better. As you read this material, think to yourself, "How many of these describe *me?*" The first step to becoming a better listener is to recognize areas that need improvement.

Types of Ineffective Listening

Your own experience will probably confirm the fact that poor listening is all too common. Although a certain amount of ineffective listening is inescapable and sometimes even understandable, it's important to be aware of these types of problems so you can avoid them when listening well really counts.

Pseudolistening Whereas mindless listening may be a private matter, **pseudolistening** is an imitation of the real thing—an act put on to fool the speaker. Pseudolisteners give the appearance of being attentive: They look you in the eye; they may even nod and smile. But the show of attention is a polite façade because their minds are somewhere else. Paradoxically, pseudolistening can take more effort than simply tuning out the other person.

Stage-Hogging Stage-hogs (sometimes called *conversational narcissists*) try to turn the topic of conversations to themselves instead of showing interest in the speaker.[26] One **stage-hogging** strategy is a *shift-response*—changing the focus of the conversation from the speaker to the narcissist: "You think your math class is tough? You ought to try my physics class!" Interruptions are another hallmark of stage-hogging. Besides preventing the listener from learning potentially valuable information, they can damage the relationship between the interrupter and the speaker. For example, applicants who interrupt the questions of employment interviewers are likely to be rated less favorably than applicants who wait until the interviewer has finished speaking before they respond.[27]

Selective Listening Selective listeners respond only to the parts of your remarks that interest them, rejecting everything else. Sometimes **selective listening** is legitimate, as when we screen out radio commercials and music and keep an ear cocked for a weather report or an announcement of the time. Selective listening is less appropriate in personal settings when obvious inattention can be a slap in the face to the other person. Consider how you feel when listeners perk up only when the topic relates to them.

Insulated Listening Insulated listeners are almost the opposite of their selective cousins just described. Instead of looking for specific information, these people avoid it. Whenever a topic arises that they'd rather not deal with, those who use **insulated listening** simply fail to hear or acknowledge it. You remind them about a problem, and they'll nod or answer you—and then promptly ignore or forget what you've just said.

Defensive Listening Defensive listeners take others' remarks as personal attacks. The teenager who perceives her parents' questions about her friends and activities as distrustful snooping uses **defensive listening**, as do touchy parents who view any questioning by their children as a threat to their authority and parental wisdom.

Ambushing Ambushers listen carefully to you, but only because they're collecting information that they'll use to attack what you say. The technique of a cross-examining prosecution attorney is a good example of **ambushing**. Needless to say, using this kind of strategy will justifiably initiate defensiveness in the other person.

Insensitive Listening   Those who use **insensitive listening** respond to the superficial content in a message but miss the more important emotional information that may not be expressed directly. "How's it going?" an insensitive listener might ask. When you reply by saying "Oh, okay I guess" in a dejected tone, he or she responds "Well, great!" Insensitive listeners tend to ignore the nonverbal cues described in Chapter 7 and lack the empathy described in Chapter 4.

Why We Don't Listen Better

After thinking about the styles of ineffective listening described previously, most people begin to see that they listen carefully only a small percentage of the time. Sad as it may be, it's impossible to listen well *all* of the time for several reasons that we'll outline here.

Message Overload   It's especially difficult to focus on messages—even important ones—when you are bombarded by information. Face-to-face messages come from friends, family, work, and school. Personal media—text messages, phone calls, emails, and instant messages—demand your attention. Along with these personal channels, we are awash in messages from mass media. This deluge of communication has made the challenge of attending tougher than at any time in human history.[28]

Tristar/Allstar

Preoccupation   Another reason we don't always listen carefully is that we're often wrapped up in personal concerns that seem more important than the messages that others are sending. It's difficult to pay attention to someone else when you're worrying about an upcoming exam or thinking about the great time you plan to have over the next weekend.

▲ In *The Devil Wears Prada*, the domineering boss Miranda Priestly (Meryl Streep) is a model of ineffective listening. She attends only to things that matter to her ("The details of your incompetence do not interest me") and does so insensitively ("Bore someone else with your questions"). She also interrupts, rolls her eyes, and walks out on her subordinates in mid-conversation. Do you know people who "listen" this way? How do you react to them?

Rapid Thought   Listening carefully is also difficult for a physiological reason. Although we're capable of understanding speech at rates of 600 words per minute, the average person only speaks between 100 and 150 words per minute.[29] Thus, we have mental "spare time" while someone is talking. The temptation is to use this time in ways that don't relate to the speaker's ideas: thinking about personal interests, daydreaming, planning a rebuttal, and so on. The trick to effective listening is to use this spare time to understand the speaker's ideas better rather than to let your attention wander.

Effort   Listening effectively is hard work. The physical changes that occur during careful listening show the effort it takes: the heart rate quickens,

Darrin Henry/Bigstock

respiration increases, and body temperature rises.[30] Notice that these changes are similar to the body's reaction to physical effort. This is no coincidence. Listening carefully to a speaker can be just as taxing as a workout—which is why some people choose not to make the effort.[31] If you've come home exhausted after an evening of listening intently to a friend in need, you know how draining the process can be.

External Noise The physical world in which we live often presents distractions that make it difficult to pay attention to others. Consider, for example, how the efficiency of your listening decreases when you are seated in a crowded, hot, stuffy room surrounded by others talking next to you and traffic noises outside. It's not surprising that noisy classrooms often make learning difficult for students.[32] In such circumstances, even the best intentions aren't enough to ensure clear understanding.

Faulty Assumptions We often make faulty assumptions that lead us to believe we're listening attentively when quite the opposite is true. When the subject is a familiar one, it's easy to tune out because you think you've heard it all before. A related problem arises when you assume that a speaker's thoughts are too simple or too obvious to deserve careful attention when, in fact, they do. At other times just the opposite occurs. You think that another's comments are too complex to be understood (as in some lectures), so you give up trying to make sense of them.

Lack of Apparent Advantages It often seems that there's more to gain by speaking than by listening. When business consultant Nancy Kline asked some of her clients why they interrupted their colleagues, these are the reasons she heard:

> My idea is better than theirs.
>
> If I don't interrupt them, I'll never get to say my idea.
>
> I know what they are about to say.
>
> They don't need to finish their thoughts since mine are better.
>
> Nothing about their idea will improve with further development.
>
> It is more important for me to get recognized than it is to hear their idea.
>
> I am more important than they are.[33]

Even if some of these thoughts are true, the egotism behind them is stunning. Furthermore, nonlisteners are likely to find that the people they cut off are less likely to treat their ideas with respect. Like defensiveness, listening is often reciprocal. You get what you give.

Lack of Training Even if we want to listen well, we're often hampered by a lack of training. A common but mistaken belief is that listening is like breathing—an activity that people do well naturally. "After all," the common belief goes, "I've been listening since I was a child. I don't need to study the subject

TABLE 8.1 Comparison of Communication Activities

	LISTENING	SPEAKING	READING	WRITING
Learned	First	Second	Third	Fourth
Used	Most	Next to most	Next to least	Least
Taught	Least	Next to least	Next to most	Most

in school." The truth is that listening is a skill much like speaking: Virtually everybody does it, though few people do it well. Unfortunately, there is no connection between how competently most communicators *think* they listen and how competent they really are in their ability to understand others.[34] The good news is that listening can be improved through instruction and training.[35] Despite this fact, the amount of time spent teaching listening is far less than that spent on other types of communication. Table 8.1 reflects this upside-down arrangement.

Hearing Problems Sometimes a person's listening ability suffers from a physiological hearing problem. In such cases, both the person with the problem and others can become frustrated at the ineffective communication that results. One survey explored the feelings of adults who have spouses with hearing loss. Nearly two-thirds of the respondents said they feel annoyed when their partner can't hear them clearly. Almost one-quarter said that beyond just being annoyed, they felt ignored, hurt, or sad. Many of the respondents believe their spouses are in denial about their condition, which makes the problem even more frustrating.[36] If you suspect that you or someone you know suffers from a hearing loss, then it's wise to have a physician or audiologist perform an examination.

Meeting the Challenge of Listening

After reading the previous section, you might decide that listening well is next to impossible. Fortunately, with the right combination of attitude and skill, you can indeed listen better. The following guidelines will show you how.

Talk Less Zeno of Citium put it most succinctly: "We have been given two ears and but a single mouth, in order that we may hear more and talk less." If your true goal is to understand the speaker, avoid the tendency to hog the stage and shift the conversation to your ideas. Talking less doesn't mean you must remain completely silent. As you'll soon read, giving feedback that clarifies your understanding and seeks new

Auremar/Bigstock

information is an important way to understand a speaker. Nonetheless, most of us talk too much when we're claiming to understand others. Other cultures, including many Native American ones, value listening at least as much as talking.[37] You can appreciate the value of this approach by trying the "Talking Stick" Pause and Reflect exercise.

Get Rid of Distractions Some distractions are external: ringing telephones, radio or television programs, friends dropping in, and so on. Other distractions are internal: preoccupation with your own problems, an empty stomach, and so on. If the information you're seeking is really important, do everything possible to eliminate the internal and external distractions that interfere with careful listening. This might mean turning off the TV, shutting off your cell phone, or moving to a quiet room where you won't be bothered by the lure of the computer, the work on your desk, or the food on the counter.

PAUSE *and* REFLECT

Speaking and Listening with a "Talking Stick"

MindTap® REFLECT ... on using a "talking stick" by completing the activity and answering the following questions, either here or online.

PART I:

Explore the benefits of talking less and listening more by using a "talking stick." This exercise is based on the Native American tradition of "council." Gather a group from your class and join in a circle in a quiet room. Designate a particular object as the talking stick. (Almost any easily held object will do.) Participants will then pass the object around the circle. The rules of the talking stick circle are precise. Each person may speak only:

1. When holding the stick

2. For as long as he or she holds the stick

3. Without interruption from anyone else in the circle

When a member is through speaking, the stick passes to the left, and the speaker surrendering the stick must wait until it has made its way around the circle before speaking again.

PART II:

After each member of the group has had the chance to speak, discuss how this experience differed from more common approaches to listening. What desirable parts of the talking stick circle do you think could be introduced into everyday conversations?

Don't Judge Prematurely   Most people would agree that it's essential to understand a speaker's ideas before judging them. However, all of us are guilty of forming snap judgments, evaluating others before hearing them out. This tendency is greatest when the speaker's ideas conflict with our own. Conversations that ought to be exchanges of ideas turn into verbal battles, with the "opponents" trying to ambush one another in order to win a victory. It's also tempting to judge prematurely when others criticize you, even when those criticisms may contain valuable truths and when understanding them may lead to a change for the better. Even if there is no criticism or disagreement, we tend to evaluate others based on sketchy first impressions, forming snap judgments that aren't at all valid. The lesson contained in these negative examples is clear: Listen first. Make sure you understand. *Then* evaluate.

Look for Key Ideas   It's easy to lose patience with long-winded speakers who never seem to get to the point—or *have* a point, for that matter. Nonetheless, most people do have a central idea. By using your ability to think more quickly than the speaker can talk, you may be able to extract the central idea from the surrounding mass of words you're hearing. If you can't figure out what the speaker is driving at, you can always use a variety of response skills, which we'll examine now.

TYPES OF LISTENING RESPONSES

Of the five components of listening (hearing, attending, understanding, responding, and remembering), *responding* lets us know how well others are tuned in to what we're saying. Think for a moment of someone you consider a good listener. Why did you choose that person? It's probably because of the way she or he responds while you are speaking: making eye contact and nodding when you're talking, staying attentive while you're telling an important story, reacting with an exclamation when you say something startling, expressing empathy and support when you're hurting, and offering another perspective or advice when you ask for it.[38]

The rest of this chapter will describe a variety of response styles. We'll begin by describing responses that are focused on gathering more information to better understand the speaker. By chapter's end, our focus will be on listening responses that offer a speaker our assessment and direction.

Prompting

In some cases, the best response a listener can give is a small nudge to keep the speaker talking. **Prompting** involves using silences and brief statements of encouragement to draw others out. Besides helping you better understand

TEXTING TO SAVE LIVES

Crisis Text Line is the first national, 24/7 crisis-intervention hotline to conduct its conversations exclusively by text message. The majority of their clients are teens, and the range of issues for which they offer help include dating and domestic abuse, eating disorders, self-injury, GLBT challenges, veterans' problems, and suicide.

Counselors have found that adolescents often open up via text messaging in ways they don't through other channels. In this description, note how the counselors use some of the listening response skills described in this chapter—prompting, questioning, paraphrasing, and supporting.

Depression is common among teens, and its consequences are volatile: suicide is the third leading cause of death for Americans between the ages of ten and twenty-four. In that same age group, the use of text messaging is near-universal. The average adolescent sends almost two thousand text messages a month. They contact their friends more by text than by phone or e-mail or instant-message or even face-to-face conversations. For teens, texting isn't a novel form of communication; it's the default.

The act of writing, even if the product consists of only a hundred and forty characters composed with one's thumbs, forces a kind of real-time distillation of emotional chaos. The young people who contact Crisis Text Line might be doing so between classes, while waiting in line for the bus, or before soccer practice. In addition, more than ninety-eight percent of text messages are opened; they are four times more likely to be read by the recipient than e-mails. If you are a distressed teen or a counselor, you know that what you say will be read.

Counselors are trained to put texters at ease and not to jump too quickly into a problem-solving mode. Open-ended questions are good; "why" questions are bad. Also bad: making assumptions about the texter's gender or sexual orientation, sounding like a robot, using language that a young person might not know. Techniques that are encouraged include validation ("What a tough situation"); "tentafiers" ("Do you mind if I ask you …"); strength identification ("You're a great brother for being so worried about him"); and empathetic responses ("It sounds like you're feeling anxious because of all these rumors"). The implicit theory is that in a conversation people are naturally inclined to fill silences.

Often, the conversations are about minor-seeming problems—fights with friends, academic pressure from parents—and the bar for helpfulness is quite low. "A lot of times, when chatting with young people, it's clear that they just need someone to listen to them," one counsellor told me. "Sometimes it's obvious. They'll say, 'Thanks for listening. Nobody ever does that,' and at other times it's less explicit; they just want to get everything out, and they provide you with a very, very detailed account."

The etiquette encouraged for counsellors can be surprising. When an agitated friend texts me bad news (a breakup, a layoff, a sudden rent increase), my instinct is to find a positive response to the predicament ("But you didn't even like him!" "Now you can finally go freelance!" "MOVE!"). But this is precisely what one is not supposed to do when communicating with a teenager in crisis. Instead, counsellors are trained to deploy language that at first seems inflammatory: "You must be devastated" is a common refrain; so is "That sounds like torture." The idea is to validate texters' feelings and respond in a way that doesn't belittle them.

Alice Gregory

MindTap ENHANCE … your understanding by answering the following questions, either here or online.

1. What advantages might arise from using texting to seek help?

2. Which strategies described in this reading might prove helpful to you if/when you seek help?

3. Which strategies could you use when others seek your help?

the speaker, prompting can also help others clarify their thoughts and feelings. Consider this example:

Pablo: Julie's dad is selling a complete computer system for only $600, but if I want it, I have to buy it now. He's got another interested buyer. It's a great deal, but buying it would wipe out my savings. At the rate I spend money, it would take me a year to save up this much again.

Tim: Uh-huh.

Pablo: I wouldn't be able to take that ski trip over winter break … but I sure could save time with my schoolwork … and do a better job, too.

Tim: That's for sure.

Pablo: Do you think I should buy it?

Tim: I don't know. What do you think?

Pablo: I just can't decide.

Tim: *(Silence)*

Pablo: I'm going to do it. I'll never get a deal like this again.

In cases like this, your prompting can be a catalyst to help others find their own answers. Prompting will work best when it's done sincerely. Your non-verbal behaviors—eye contact, posture, facial expression, tone of voice—have to show that you are concerned with the other person's problem. Mechanical prompting is likely to irritate instead of help.

Questioning

It's easy to understand why **questioning** has been called "the most popular piece of language."[39] Asking for information can help both the person doing the asking and the one providing answers.[40]

Questioning can help you, the asker, in at least three ways. Most obviously, the answers you get can fill in facts and details that will sharpen your understanding ("Did he give you any reasons for doing that?" "What happened next?"). Also, by asking questions you can learn what others are thinking and feeling ("What's on your mind?" "Are you mad at me?") as well as what they might want ("Are you asking me to apologize?").

Besides being useful to the person doing the asking, questions can also be a tool for the one who answers. As people in the helping professions know, questions can encourage self-discovery. You can use questions to encourage others to explore their thoughts and feelings. "So, what do you see as your options?" may prompt an employee to come up with creative problem-solving alternatives. "What would be your ideal solution?" might help a friend get in touch with various wants and needs. Most important is that encouraging discovery rather than dispensing advice indicates you have faith in others' ability to think for themselves. This may be the best message that you can communicate as an effective listener.

Despite their apparent benefits, not all questions are equally helpful. Whereas **sincere questions** are aimed at understanding others, **counterfeit questions** are aimed at sending a message, not receiving one. Counterfeit questions come in several varieties:

- *Questions that trap the speaker*. When your friend says, "You didn't like that movie, did you?," you're being backed into a corner. It's clear that your friend disapproves, so the question leaves you with two choices: You can disagree and defend your position, or you can devalue your reaction by lying or equivocating—"I guess it wasn't perfect." Consider how much easier it would be to respond to the sincere question, "What did you think of the movie?"

- *A tag question*. Phrases like "did you?" or "isn't that right?" at the end of a question can be a tip-off that the asker is looking for agreement, not information. Although some tag questions are genuine requests for confirmation, counterfeit ones are used to coerce agreement: "You said you'd call at 5 o'clock, but you forgot, didn't you?" Similarly, leading questions that begin with "Don't you," such as "Don't you think he would make a good boss?," direct others toward a desired response. As a simple solution, changing "Don't you?" to "Do you?" makes the question less leading.

- *Questions that make statements*. "Are you *finally* off the phone?" is more of a statement than a question—a fact unlikely to be lost on the targeted person. Emphasizing certain words can also turn a question into a statement: "You lent money to *Tony*?" We also use questions to offer advice. The person who asks "Are you going to stand up to him and give him what he deserves?" clearly has stated an opinion about what should be done.

- *Questions that carry hidden agendas*. "Are you busy Friday night?" is a dangerous question to answer. If you say "No," thinking the person has something fun in mind, you won't like hearing "Good, because I need help moving my piano." Obviously, such questions are not designed to enhance understanding. They are setups for the proposal that follows. Other examples include "Will you do me a favor?" and "If I tell you what happened, will you promise not to get mad?" Wise communicators answer questions that mask hidden agendas cautiously, with responses like "It depends" or "Let me hear what you have in mind before I answer."

- *Questions that seek "correct" answers*. Most of us have been victims of questioners who want to hear only a particular response. "Which shoes do you think I should wear?" can be a sincere question—unless the asker has a predetermined preference. When this happens, the asker isn't interested in listening to contrary opinions, and "incorrect" responses get shot down. Some of these questions may venture into delicate territory. "Honey, do you think I look fat?" can be a request for a "correct" answer.

- *Questions based on unchecked assumptions*. "Why aren't you listening to me?" assumes that the other person isn't paying attention. "What's the matter?" assumes that something is wrong. As Chapter 4 explains, perception checking is a much better way of checking out assumptions. As you recall, a perception check offers a description and interpretations followed by a sincere request for clarification: "When you kept looking over at the TV, I thought you weren't listening to me, but maybe I was wrong. Were you paying attention?"

Paraphrasing

For all its value, questioning won't always help you understand or help others. For example, consider what might happen when you ask for directions to a friend's home. Suppose that you've received these instructions: "Drive about a mile and then turn left at the traffic signal." Now imagine that a few common problems exist in this simple message. First, suppose that your friend's idea of "about a mile" differs from yours: Your mental picture of the distance is actually closer to 2 miles, whereas your friend's is closer to 300 yards. Next, consider that "traffic signal" really means "stop sign"; after all, it's common for us to think one thing and say another. Keeping these problems in mind, suppose that you tried to verify your understanding of the directions by asking, "After I turn at the signal, how far should I go?" to which your friend replies that the house is the third from the corner. Clearly, if you parted after this exchange, you would encounter a lot of frustration before finding the elusive residence.

Because questioning doesn't always provide the information you need, consider another kind of listening response—one that would tell you whether you understood what had already been said before you asked additional questions. This type of feedback involves restating in your own words the message you thought the speaker just sent, without adding anything new. Statements that reword the listener's interpretation of a message are commonly termed **paraphrasing**. If the listener in the preceding scenario had offered this paraphrase—"You're telling me to drive down to the traffic light by the high school and turn toward the mountains, is that it?"—it probably would have led the speaker to clarify the message.

The key to success in paraphrasing is to restate the other person's comments in your own words as a way of cross-checking the information. If you simply repeat the other person's comments verbatim, you will sound foolish—and you still might be misunderstanding what has been said. Notice the difference between simply parroting a statement and true paraphrasing:

> **Speaker:** I'd like to go, but I can't afford it.
> **Parroting:** You'd like to go, but you can't afford it.
> **Paraphrasing:** So if we could find a way to pay for you, you'd be willing to come. Is that right?

> **Speaker:** You look awful!
> **Parroting:** You think I look terrible.
> **Paraphrasing:** Sounds like you think I've put on too much weight.

There are two levels at which you can paraphrase messages. The first involves paraphrasing *factual information* that will help you understand the other person's ideas more clearly. At the most basic level, this sort of reflecting can prevent frustrating mix-ups: "So you want to meet *this* Tuesday, not next week, right?"

You can also paraphrase *personal information*: "So my joking makes you think I don't care about your problem." This sort of nondefensive response

In REAL LIFE

Paraphrasing on the Job

This conversation between two coworkers shows how paraphrasing can help people solve their own problems. Notice how Jill comes to a conclusion without Mark's advice. Notice also how the paraphrasing sounds natural when combined with sincere questions and other helping styles.

© Jason Harris/Cengage Learning

Jill: I've had the strangest feeling about John *(their boss)* lately.

Mark: What's that? *(A simple question invites Jill to go on.)*

Jill: I'm starting to think maybe he has this thing about women—or maybe it's just about me.

Mark: You mean he's coming on to you? *(Mark paraphrases what he thinks Jill has said.)*

Jill Oh, no, not at all! But it seems like he doesn't take women—or at least me—seriously. *(Jill corrects Mark's misunderstanding and explains herself.)*

Mark What do you mean? *(Mark asks another simple question to get more information.)*

Jill Well, whenever we're in a meeting or just talking around the office and he asks for ideas, he always seems to pick men. He gives orders to women—men, too—but he never asks the women to say what they think.

Mark So you think maybe he doesn't take women seriously, is that it? *(Mark paraphrases Jill's last statement.)*

Jill He sure doesn't seem interested in their ideas. But that doesn't mean he's a total woman hater. I know he counts on some women in the office. Teresa has been here forever, and he's always saying he couldn't live without her. And when Brenda got the new computer system up and running last month, I know he appreciated that. He gave her a day off and told everybody how she saved our lives.

Mark Now you sound confused. *(Mark reflects her apparent feeling.)*

Jill I *am* confused. I don't think it's just my imagination. I mean I'm a good producer, but he has never—not once—asked me for my ideas about how to

---

may be difficult when you are under attack, but it can short-circuit defensive arguments. Chapter 11 will explain in more detail how to use paraphrasing when you're being criticized.

Paraphrasing personal information can also be a tool for helping others, as the In Real Life transcript in this chapter shows.[41] Reflecting the speaker's thoughts and feelings (instead of judging or analyzing, for example) shows your involvement and concern. The nonevaluative nature of paraphrasing encourages the problem holder to discuss the matter further. Reflecting thoughts and feelings allows the problem holder to unload more of the concerns he or she has been carrying around, often leading to the relief that comes from catharsis. Finally, paraphrasing helps the problem holder to sort out the problem. The clarity that comes from this sort of perspective can improve sales or anything. And I can't remember a time when he's asked any other women. But maybe I'm overreacting.

Mark You're not positive whether you're right, but I can tell that this has you concerned. *(Mark paraphrases both Jill's central theme and her feeling.)*

Jill Yes. But I don't know what to do about it.

Mark Maybe you should … *(Starts to offer advice but catches himself and decides to ask a question instead.)* So what are your choices?

Jill Well, I could just ask him if he's aware that he never asks women's opinions. But that might sound too aggressive and angry.

Mark And you're not angry? *(Tries to clarify how Jill is feeling.)*

Jill Not really. I don't know whether I should be angry because he's not taking ideas seriously, or whether he just doesn't take my ideas seriously, or whether it's nothing at all.

Mark So you're mostly confused. *(Reflects Jill's apparent feeling again.)*

Jill Yes! I don't know where I stand with John, and not being sure is starting to get to me. I wish I knew what he thinks of me. Maybe I could just tell him I'm confused about what is going on here and ask him to clear it up. But what if it's nothing? Then I'll look insecure.

Mark *(Mark thinks Jill should confront the boss, but he isn't positive that this is the best approach, so he paraphrases what Jill seems to be saying.)* And that would make you look bad.

Jill I'm afraid maybe it would. I wonder if I could talk it over with anybody else in the office and get their ideas …

Mark: … see what they think …

Jill Yeah. Maybe I could ask Brenda. She's easy to talk to, and I do respect her judgment. Maybe she could give me some ideas about how to handle this.

Mark Sounds like you're comfortable with talking to Brenda first. *(Paraphrases)*

Jill *(Warming to the idea)* Yes! Then if it's nothing, I can calm down. But if I do need to talk to John, I'll know I'm doing the right thing.

Mark Great. Let me know how it goes.

> MindTap® APPLY … this situation to your life by answering questions online.

make it possible to find solutions that weren't apparent before. These features make paraphrasing a vital skill in the human services professions, leadership training, and even hostage negotiation.[42]

Effective paraphrasing is a skill that takes time to develop. You can make your paraphrasing sound more natural by taking any of three approaches, depending on the situation:

1. Change the speaker's wording:

   Speaker: Bilingual education is just another failed idea of bleeding-heart liberals.

   Paraphrase: Let me see if I've got this right. You're mad because you think bilingual ed sounds good, but it doesn't work?

2. Offer an example of what you think the speaker is talking about:

    Speaker: Lee is such a jerk. I can't believe the way he acted last night.

    Paraphrase: You think those jokes were pretty offensive, huh?

3. Reflect the underlying theme of the speaker's remarks:

    Paraphrase: You keep reminding me to be careful. Sounds like you're worried that something might happen to me. Am I right?

Paraphrasing won't always be accurate. However, expressing your restatement tentatively gives the other person a chance to make a correction. (Note how the examples end with questions in an attempt to confirm if the paraphrase was accurate.)

Because it's an unfamiliar way of responding, paraphrasing may feel awkward at first, but if you start by paraphrasing occasionally and then gradually increase the frequency of such responses, you can begin to learn the benefits. You can begin practicing paraphrasing by trying the Skill Builder in this section.

There are several factors to consider before you decide to paraphrase:

1. **Is the issue complex enough?** If you're fixing dinner, and someone wants to know when it will be ready, it would be exasperating to hear, "You're interested in knowing when we'll be eating."
2. **Do you have the necessary time and concern?** Paraphrasing can take a good deal of time. Therefore, if you're in a hurry, it's wise to avoid starting a conversation you won't be able to finish. Even more important than time is concern. Paraphrasing that comes across as mechanical or insincere reflecting can do more harm than good.[43]
3. **Can you withhold judgment?** Use paraphrasing only if you are willing to focus on the speaker's message without injecting your own judgments. It can be tempting to rephrase others' comments in a way that leads them toward the position you think is best without ever clearly stating your intentions.
4. **Is your paraphrasing in proportion to other responses?** Paraphrasing can become annoying when it's overused. This is especially true if you suddenly add this approach to your style. A far better way to use paraphrasing is to gradually introduce it into your repertoire.

Supporting

There are times when other people want to hear more than a reflection of how *they* feel; they would like to know how *you* feel for and about them. **Supporting** reveals a listener's solidarity with the speaker's situation. One scholar describes supporting as "expressions of care, concern, affection, and interest, especially during times of stress or upset."[44]

There are several types of listening responses that can provide support:

Empathizing	"I can understand why you'd be upset about this."
	"Yeah, that class was tough for me, too."
Agreement	"You're right—the landlord is being unfair."
	"Sounds like the job is a perfect match for you."

Offers to help	"I'm here if you need me."
	"I'd be happy to study with you for the next test if you'd like."
Praise	"Wow—you did a fantastic job!"
	"You're a terrific person, and if she doesn't recognize it, that's her problem!"
Reassurance	"The worst part seems to be over. It will probably get easier from here."
	"I'm sure you'll do a great job."

SKILL *Builder*

Paraphrasing Practice

MindTap® **PRACTICE . . .** your skill at paraphrasing by completing the exercise and answering the following questions, either here or online.

This exercise will help you see that it is possible to understand someone who disagrees with you without arguing or sacrificing your point of view.

1. Work in groups of three. Designate one person as A, another as B, and the third as C, the observer.

2. Find a topic on which person A and person B apparently disagree—a current events topic, a philosophical or moral issue, or perhaps simply a matter of personal taste.

3. Person A begins by making a personal statement on the subject, while person B listens without interruption, and person C observes. If person B responds before person A is done speaking, person C's job is to act as a referee, allowing person A to continue.

4. When person A has completed his or her statement, person B's job is to then paraphrase the statement. Person B should offer a clean paraphrase, in no way indicating agreement or disagreement with A's remarks. If person B offers an opinion within the paraphrase, person C's job is to

act as a referee and remind them about the rules of the exercise.

5. Person A then responds by telling person B whether the response was accurate, sticking with the content of the message rather than criticizing person B's performance. If there was some misunderstanding, person A should clarify the message, and B should offer a revised paraphrase of his or her new understanding of the statement. Again, person C's role is to observe and act as a neutral referee if the conversation diverts from the rules of the exercise. This process should continue until everyone is sure that B understands A's statement.

6. Now it's B's turn to respond to A's statement and for A to help the process of understanding by correcting B. Person C will again perform the role of neutral observer. This process continues until all partners are satisfied that they have explained themselves fully and have been heard by their partners.

7. Now, person C should switch places with person A and have an opportunity to send a message to and receive a message from person B, repeating steps 2, 3, and 4 above.

8. After this exercise is complete, answer reflection questions online.

> Adam (Joseph Gordon-Levitt) receives a variety of listening responses—some more helpful than others—from friends, family, and professionals as he battles cancer in the movie 50/50. These range from nondirective empathizing to highly directive advice. What kinds of listening responses do you offer when someone you know is hurting? What kind of responses do you like to receive when you're the one struggling?

It's easy to identify what effective support *doesn't* sound like. Some scholars have called these messages "cold comfort."[45] As the following examples suggest, you're probably *not* being supportive if you:

- *Deny others the right to their feelings.* Consider the stock remark "Don't worry about it." Although it may be intended as a reassuring comment, the underlying message is that the speaker wants the person to feel differently. The irony is that the suggestion probably won't work—after all, it's unlikely that people can or will stop worrying just because you tell them to do so.[46] Research about such responses is clear: "Messages that explicitly acknowledge, elaborate, and legitimize the feelings and perspective of a distressed person are perceived as more helpful messages than those which only implicitly recognize or deny the feelings and perspective of the other."[47]

- *Minimize the significance of the situation.* Consider the times you've been told, "Hey, it's only ___." You can probably fill in the blank in a variety of ways: "a job," "her opinion," "a test," "puppy love," "a party." To someone who has been the victim of verbal abuse, the hurtful message isn't "just words"; to a child who didn't get an invitation, it isn't "just a party"; to a worker who has been chewed out by the boss, it isn't "just a job."

- *Focus on "then and there" rather than "here and now."* Although it is sometimes true that "you'll feel better tomorrow," it sometimes isn't. Even if the prediction that "ten years from now you won't remember her name" proves correct, it provides little comfort to someone experiencing heartbreak today.

- *Cast judgment.* It usually isn't encouraging to hear "You know, it's your own fault—you really shouldn't have done that" after you've confessed to making a poor decision. As you'll learn in Chapter 11, evaluative and condescending statements are more likely to engender defensiveness than to help people change for the better.

- *Focus on yourself.* It can be tempting to talk at length about a similar experience you've encountered ("I know exactly how you feel. Something like that happened to me...."). While your intent might be to show empathy, research shows that such messages aren't perceived as helpful because they draw attention away from the distressed person.[48]

- *Defend yourself.* When your response to others' concerns is to defend yourself ("Don't blame me; I've done my part"), it's clear that you are more concerned with yourself than with supporting the other person.

How often do people fail to provide appropriate supportive responses? One survey of mourners who had recently suffered from the death of a loved one reported that 80 percent of the statements made to them were unhelpful.[49] Nearly half of the "helpful" statements were advice: "You've got to get out more." "Don't question God's will." Despite their frequency, these suggestions were helpful only 3 percent of the time. Far more helpful were expressions that acknowledged the mourner's feelings, such as "This must be so hard—I know how much she meant to you." Chapter 9 will describe other ways to supply social support to the people in your life.

When handled correctly, supporting responses *can* be helpful. Guidelines for effective support include:

1. **Recognize that you can support another person's struggles without approving of his or her decisions**. Suppose, for instance, that a friend has decided to quit a job that you think she should keep. You could still be supportive by saying, "I know you've given this a lot of thought and that you're doing what you think is best." Responses like this can provide face-saving support without compromising your principles.[50]

2. **Monitor the other person's reaction to your support**. If it doesn't seem to help, consider other types of responses that let him or her explore the issue.

3. **Realize that support may not always be welcome**. In one survey, some people reported occasions when social support wasn't necessary because they felt capable of handling the problem themselves.[51] Many regarded uninvited support as an intrusion, and some said it left them feeling more nervous than before. The majority of respondents expressed a preference for being in control of whether their distressing situation should be discussed with even the most helpful friend.

4. **Make sure you're ready for the consequences.** Talking about a difficult event may reduce distress for the speaker but increase distress for the listener.[52] Recognize that supporting another person is a worthwhile but potentially taxing venture.

MindTap° PRACTICE...
Your skill at empathic listening by completing the Concepts in Play activity online.

HOW TO HELP ...
AND NOT HELP

Susan Silk is a clinical psychologist. Barry Goldman is an arbitrator and mediator and the author of The Science of Settlement: Ideas for Negotiators.

When Susan had breast cancer, we heard a lot of lame remarks, but our favorite came from one of Susan's colleagues. She wanted, she needed, to visit Susan after the surgery, but Susan didn't feel like having visitors, and she said so. Her colleague's response? "This isn't just about you."

"It's not?" Susan wondered. "My breast cancer is not about me? It's about you?"

Susan has since developed a simple technique to help people avoid this mistake. It works for all kinds of crises: medical, legal, financial, romantic, even existential. She calls it the Ring Theory.

Draw a circle. This is the center ring. In it, put the name of the person at the center of the current trauma. Now draw a larger circle around the first one. In that ring, put the name of the person next closest to the trauma. Repeat the process as many times as you need to. In each larger ring, put the next closest people. Parents and children before more distant relatives. Intimate friends in smaller rings, less intimate friends in larger ones.

Here are the rules. The person in the center ring can say anything she wants to anyone, anywhere.

She can kvetch and complain and whine and moan and curse the heavens and say, "Life is unfair" and "Why me?" That's the one payoff for being in the center ring.

Everyone else can say those things too, but only to people in larger rings.

When you are talking to a person in a ring smaller than yours, someone closer to the center of the crisis, the goal is to help. Listening is often more helpful than talking. But if you're going to open your mouth, ask yourself if what you are about to say is likely to provide comfort and support. If it isn't, don't say it.

Don't, for example, give advice. People who are suffering from trauma don't need advice. They need comfort and support. So say "I'm sorry" or "This must really be

hard for you" or "Can I bring you a pot roast?" Don't say "You should hear what happened to me" or "Here's what I would do if I were you." And don't say "This is really bringing me down."

If you want to scream or cry or complain, if you want to tell someone how shocked you are or how icky you feel or whine about how it reminds you of all the terrible things that have happened to you lately, that's fine. It's a perfectly normal response. Just do it to someone in a bigger ring.

Comfort IN, dump OUT.

Remember, you can say whatever you want if you just wait until you're talking to someone in a larger ring than yours.

And don't worry. You'll get your turn in the center ring. You can count on that.

MindTap ENHANCE ... your understanding by answering the following questions, either here or online.

1. Offer an example of a time when you or someone you know violated the principle of "Comfort IN, dump OUT." What were the results?

2. Why do you think people find it difficult to follow this principle?

3. Describe a situation where you could use the principle of "Comfort IN, dump OUT."

Analyzing

When **analyzing**, the listener offers an interpretation of a speaker's message. Analyses like these are probably familiar to you:

"I think what's really bothering you is …"

"She's doing it because …"

"I don't think you really meant that."

"Maybe the problem started when he …"

Interpretations are often effective ways to help people with problems to consider alternative meanings—meanings they would have never thought of without your help. Sometimes an analysis will make a confusing problem suddenly clear, either suggesting a solution or at least providing an understanding of what is occurring.

In other cases, an analysis can create more problems than it solves. There are two potential problems with analyzing. First, your interpretation may not be correct, in which case the speaker may become even more confused by accepting it. Second, even if your analysis is correct, telling it to the problem holder might not be useful. There's a chance that it will arouse defensiveness (because analysis implies superiority). Even if it doesn't, the person may not be able to understand your view of the problem without working it out personally.

How can you know when it's helpful to offer an analysis? There are several guidelines to follow:

- *Offer your interpretation as tentative rather than as absolute fact.* There's a big difference between saying "Maybe the reason is …" or "The way it looks to me …" and insisting "This is the truth."

- *You ought to be sure that the other person will be receptive to your analysis.* Even if you're completely accurate, your thoughts won't help if the problem holder isn't ready to consider them.

- *Be sure that your motive for offering an analysis is truly to help the other person.* It can be tempting to offer an analysis to show how brilliant you are or even to make the other person feel bad for not having thought of the right answer in the first place. Needless to say, an analysis offered under such conditions isn't helpful.

Advising

When we are approached with another's problem, a common tendency is to respond with **advising**: to help by offering a solution.[53] Advice can sometimes be helpful, as long as it's given in a respectful, caring way.[54]

Despite its apparent value, advice has its limits. Research has shown that it is actually *unhelpful* at least as often as it's helpful.[55]

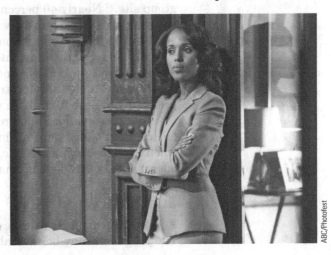

▼ If you're looking for a shoulder to cry on when you're in trouble, *Scandal's* Olivia Pope (Kerry Washington) is probably the wrong person. Pope's strength is quickly sizing up a problem and then giving directive solutions. She's far more likely to say "Here's what you need to do" than "I'm sorry to hear that." Are there times when you want advice more than empathy? Is it possible to give some of both?

ABC/Photofest

Studies on advice giving offer the following important considerations when trying to help others:[56]

- *Is the advice needed?* If the person has already taken a course of action, giving advice after the fact ("I can't believe you got back together with him") is rarely appreciated.

- *Is the advice wanted?* People generally don't value unsolicited advice. It's usually best to ask if the speaker is interested in hearing your counsel. Remember that sometimes people just want a listening ear, not solutions to their problems.

- *Is the advice given in the right sequence?* Advice is more likely to be received after the listener first seeks to understand the speaker and the situation. For instance, teachers who ask questions in parent-teacher conversations before launching into problem-solving are perceived as more effective communicators.[57] It helps to know the facts prior to offering advice.

- *Is the advice coming from an expert?* If you want to offer advice about anything from car purchasing to relationship managing, it's important to have experience and success in those matters. If you *don't* have expertise, it's a good idea to offer the speaker supportive responses, then encourage that person to seek out expert counsel.

- *Is the advisor a close and trusted person?* Although sometimes we seek out advice from people we don't know well (perhaps because they have expertise), in most cases we value advice given within the context of a close and ongoing interpersonal relationship.

- *Is the advice offered in a sensitive, face-saving manner?* No one likes to feel bossed or belittled, even if the advice is good. Remember that messages have both content and relational dimensions, and sometimes the unstated relational messages when giving advice ("I'm smarter than you"; "You're not bright enough to figure this out yourself") will keep people from hearing counsel.[58]

To see these recommendations in practice, we can look at how one study categorized and analyzed advice exchanges in an online breast cancer support group site.[59] Nearly 40 percent of the posted messages involved advice seeking or giving, so it's clearly a site where people look for and extend counsel. However, very few posters asked the community to tell them what they "should do." They typically requested "comments" rather than "advice." Recommendations were often couched within personal narratives, using a "here's what worked for me" format. Advice seekers tried to find people who were "in the same boat," preferring to hear from those whose situations matched their own.

These observations reinforce some important principles about communicating advice. People are more willing to listen to advice that's requested, especially when it comes from a credible, empathic source. When giving advice, it's best to offer it as open-handed information rather than as heavy-handed prescriptions.

Judging

A **judging** response evaluates the sender's thoughts or behaviors in some way. The judgment may be favorable—"That's a good idea" or "You're on the right

PAUSE *and* REFLECT

When Advising Does and Doesn't Work

MindTap® REFLECT ... on your advising skills by answering the following questions, either here or online.

To see why advising can be tricky business, follow these steps:

1. Recall an instance when someone gave you advice that proved helpful. Review the guidelines for offering advice in this section and see if you recognize any that your advice giver followed.

2. Now recall an instance when someone gave you advice that *wasn't* helpful. Again, review the guidelines. Did that person violate any of them? Which ones?

3. Based on your insights here, describe how you can advise (or not advise) others in a way that is truly helpful.

track now"—or unfavorable—"An attitude like that won't get you anywhere." But in either case, it implies that the person doing the judging is in some way qualified to pass judgment on the speaker's thoughts or actions.

Sometimes negative judgments are purely critical. How many times have you heard such responses as "Well, you asked for it!" or "I *told* you so!" or "You're just feeling sorry for yourself"? Although responses like these can sometimes serve as a verbal slap that brings problem holders to their senses, they usually make matters worse.

In other cases, negative judgments are less critical. These involve what we usually call *constructive criticism*, which is intended to help the problem holder improve in the future. This is the sort of response given by friends about everything from the choice of clothing to jobs to friends. Another common setting for constructive criticism occurs in school, where instructors evaluate students' work to help them master concepts and skills. But whether it's justified or not, even constructive criticism runs the risk of arousing defensiveness because it may threaten the self-concept of the person at whom it is directed (we'll discuss this further in Chapter 11).

Judgments have the best chance of being received when two conditions exist:

1. The person with the problem has requested an evaluation from you. Occasionally an unsolicited evaluation may bring someone to his or her senses, but more often an unsolicited evaluation will trigger a defensive response.
2. The intent of your judgment has genuinely constructive and not designed as a put-down. If you are tempted to use judgments as a weapon, don't fool yourself into thinking that you are being helpful. Often the statement "I'm telling you this for your own good ..." simply isn't true.

Now that you're aware of all the possible listening responses, try the following Pause and Reflect exercise in this section to see how you might use them in everyday situations.

PAUSE *and* REFLECT

What Would You Say?

MindTap® REFLECT ... on how you would respond by answering the following questions, either here or online.

1. In each of the following situations, describe what you would say in response to the problem being shared and identify the response type(s) used.

   a. My family doesn't understand me. Everything I like seems to go against their values, and they just won't accept my feelings as being right for me. It's not that they don't love me—they do. But they don't accept me.

   b. I've been pretty discouraged lately. I just can't get a good relationship going with any guys. I've got plenty of male friends, but that's always as far as it goes. I'm tired of being just a pal ... I want to be more than that.

   c. *(Child to parents)* I hate you! You always go out and leave me with some stupid sitter. Why don't you like me?

   d. I don't know what I want to do with my life. I'm tired of school, but there aren't any good jobs around. I could just drop out for a while, but that doesn't really sound very good, either.

   e. Things really seem to be kind of lousy in my marriage lately. It's not that we fight much, but all the excitement seems to be gone. We're in a rut, and it keeps getting worse. ...

   f. I keep getting the idea that my boss is angry at me. It seems as if lately he hasn't been joking around very much, and he hasn't said anything at all about my work for about three weeks now. I wonder what I should do.

2. After you've written your response to each of these messages, imagine the probable outcome of the conversation that would have followed. If you've tried this exercise in class, you might have two group members role-play each response. Based on your idea of how the conversation might have gone, decide which responses were likely to be productive and which were unproductive, identify which response skills were likely to be productive and which were unproductive, and reflect on what you've learned from this exercise.

Choosing the Best Response

By now you can see that there are many ways to respond as a listener. Research shows that, in the right circumstances, *all* response styles can help others accept their situation, feel better, and have a sense of control over their problems.[60] But there is enormous variability in which style will work with a given person.[61] This fact explains why communicators who use a wide variety of response styles are usually more effective than those who use just one or two styles.[62] However, there are other factors to consider when choosing how to respond to a speaker.

Creatista/Shutterstock.com

Gender   Research shows that men and women differ in the ways they listen and respond to others.[63] Women are more likely than men to give supportive responses when presented with another person's problem,[64] are more skillful at composing such messages,[65] and are more likely to seek out such responses from listeners.[66] By contrast, men are less skillful at providing emotional support to those who are distressed,[67] and they're more likely to respond to others' problems by offering advice or by diverting the topic. In a study of helping styles in sororities and fraternities, researchers found that sorority women frequently respond with emotional support when asked to help; also, they rated their sisters as being better at listening nonjudgmentally and on comforting and showing concern for them. Fraternity men, on the other hand, fit the stereotypical pattern of offering help by challenging their brothers to evaluate their attitudes and values.[68]

The temptation when hearing these facts is to conclude that in times of distress, women want support and men want advice—but research doesn't bear that out. Numerous studies show that both men and women prefer and want supportive, endorsing messages in difficult situations.[69] The fact that women are more adept at creating and delivering such messages explains why both males and females tend to seek out women listeners when they want emotional support. When it comes to gender, it's important to remember that while men and women sometimes use different response styles, they all need a listening ear.

The Situation   Sometimes people need your advice. At other times, people need encouragement and support, and, in still other cases, your analysis or judgment will be most helpful. And, as you have seen, sometimes your probes and paraphrasing can help people find their own answers. In other words, a competent communicator needs to analyze the situation and develop an appropriate response.[70] As a rule of thumb, it's often wise to begin with responses that seek understanding and offer a minimum of direction, such as prompting, questioning, paraphrasing, and supporting. Once you've gathered the facts and demonstrated your interest and concern, it's likely that the speaker will be more receptive to (and perhaps even ask for) your analyzing, advising, and evaluating responses.[71]

The Other Person Besides considering the situation, you should also consider the other person when deciding which style to use. Some people are able to consider advice thoughtfully, whereas others use advice to avoid making their own decisions. Many communicators are extremely defensive and aren't capable of receiving analysis or judgments without lashing out. Still others aren't equipped to think through problems clearly enough to profit from paraphrasing and probing. One study found that highly rational people tend to respond more positively to advice than do more emotional people.[72]

Sophisticated listeners choose a style that fits the person. One way to determine the most appropriate response is to ask the speaker what she or he wants from you. A simple question such as "Are you looking for my advice, or do you just want a listening ear right now?" can help you give others the kinds of responses they're looking for.

Your Personal Style Finally, consider yourself when deciding how to respond. Most of us reflexively use one or two response styles. You may be best at listening quietly, offering a prompt from time to time. Or perhaps you are especially insightful and can offer a truly useful analysis of the problem.

ETHICAL *Challenge*

Unconditional Positive Regard

Carl Rogers was the best-known advocate of paraphrasing as a helping tool. As a psychotherapist, Rogers focused on how professionals can help others, but he and his followers were convinced that the same approach can work in all interpersonal relationships.

Rogers used several terms to describe his approach. Sometimes he labeled it *nondirective*, sometimes *client-centered*, and at other times *person-centered*.[a] All of these terms reflect his belief that the best way to help another is to offer a supportive climate in which the people seeking help can find their own answers. Rogers believed that advising, judging, analyzing, and questioning are not the best ways to help others solve their problems. Instead, Rogers and his followers were convinced that people are basically good and that they can improve without receiving any guidance from others, after they accept and respect themselves.

An essential ingredient for person-centered helping is what Rogers called *unconditional positive regard*. This attitude requires the helper to treat the speaker's ideas respectfully and nonjudgmentally. Unconditional positive regard means accepting others for who they are, even when you don't approve of their posture toward life. Treating a help seeker with unconditional positive regard doesn't oblige you to agree with everything the help seeker thinks, feels, or does, but it does oblige you to suspend judgment about the rightness or wrongness of the help seeker's thoughts and actions.

A person-centered approach to helping places heavy demands on the listener. At the skill level, it demands an ability to reflect the speaker's thoughts and feelings perceptively and accurately. Even more difficult, though, is the challenge of listening and responding without passing judgment on the speaker's ideas or behavior.[b]

Unconditional positive regard is especially hard when we are faced with the challenge of listening and responding to someone whose beliefs, attitudes, and values differ profoundly from our own. This approach requires the helper to follow the familiar prescription of loving the sinner while hating the sin.

Of course, it's also possible to rely on a response style that is unhelpful. You may be overly judgmental or too eager to advise, even when your suggestions aren't invited or productive. As you think about how to respond to another's messages, consider both your strengths and weaknesses and adapt accordingly.

SUMMARY

Listening is the most common—and perhaps the most overlooked—form of communication. There is a difference between hearing and listening, and there is also a difference between mindless and mindful listening. Listening, defined as the process of making sense of others' messages, consists of five elements: hearing, attending, understanding, responding, and remembering.

Several responding styles masquerade as listening but actually are only poor imitations of the real thing. We listen poorly for a variety of reasons. Some reasons have to do with the tremendous number of messages that bombard us daily and with the personal preoccupations, noise, and rapid thoughts that distract us from focusing on the information we are exposed to. Another set of reasons has to do with the considerable effort involved in listening carefully and the mistaken belief that there are more rewards in speaking than in listening. A few listeners fail to receive messages because of physical hearing defects; others listen poorly because of lack of training. Some keys to better listening are to talk less, reduce distractions, avoid making premature judgments, and seek the speaker's key ideas.

Listening responses are the primary way we evaluate whether and how others are paying attention to us. Some listening responses put a premium on gathering information and providing support; these include prompting, questioning, paraphrasing, and supporting. Other listening responses focus more on providing direction and evaluation; these include analyzing, advising, and judging. The most effective communicators use a variety of these styles, taking into consideration factors such as gender, the situation at hand, the person with the problem, and their own personal style.

KEY TERMS

advising
ambushing
analyzing
attending
counterfeit questions
defensive listening
hearing
insensitive listening
insulated listening
judging
listening
listening fidelity
mindful listening

mindless listening
paraphrasing
prompting
pseudolistening
questioning
remembering
responding
selective listening
sincere questions
stage-hogging
supporting
understanding

11

IMPROVING COMMUNICATION CLIMATES

AFTER STUDYING THE TOPICS IN THIS CHAPTER,
YOU SHOULD BE ABLE TO:

1. Identify confirming, disagreeing, and disconfirming messages and patterns in your own important relationships and describe their consequences.

2. Describe how the messages you identified in the previous objective either threaten or honor the self (face) of the communicators involved.

3. Use Gibb's categories and the assertive message format to create messages that are likely to build supportive rather than defensive communication climates.

4. Create appropriate nondefensive responses to real or hypothetical criticisms.

*P*ersonal relationships are a lot like the weather. Some are fair and warm, whereas others are stormy and cold; some are polluted and others healthy. Some relationships have stable climates, whereas others change dramatically—calm one moment and turbulent the next. You can't measure the interpersonal climate by looking at a thermometer or glancing at the sky, but it's there nonetheless. Every relationship has a feeling, a pervasive mood that colors the interactions of the participants. What meteorological terms would you use to describe the prevailing communication climate in your most important relationships? How do the same events and activities feel different when the climate is better? Worse?

Although we can't change the external weather, we *can* change an interpersonal climate. This chapter will explain the forces that make some relationships pleasant and others unpleasant. You will learn what kinds of behavior contribute to defensiveness and hostility and what kinds lead to more positive feelings. After reading this chapter, you will have a better idea of the climate in each of your important relationships and—even more important—how to improve it.

COMMUNICATION CLIMATE AND CONFIRMING MESSAGES

The term **communication climate** refers to the emotional tone of a relationship. A climate doesn't involve specific activities as much as the way people feel about and treat each other as they carry out those activities. Consider two interpersonal communication classes, for example. Both meet for the same length of time and follow the same syllabus. It's easy to imagine how one of these classes might be a friendly, comfortable place to learn, whereas the other could be cold and tense—even hostile.

The same principle holds in close relationships. A large body of research confirms what intuition suggests: Couples who create and maintain emotionally healthy, positive climates have happy, enduring relationships.[1] By contrast, couples who are unsupportive—whether straight or gay, rich or poor, parents or childless—are likely to break up or endure joyless lives together.[2] The communication climate that parents create for their children affects the way they interact.[3] Children who lack confirmation suffer a broad range of emotional and behavioral problems, whereas those who feel confirmed have more open communication with their parents, higher self-esteem, and lower levels of stress.[4] The satisfaction that siblings feel with one another drops sharply as aggressive, disconfirming messages increase.[5]

A healthy communication climate is just as important on the job as it is in personal relationships. Positive communication climates lead to increased job satisfaction.[6] Two factors are consistently connected to supportive workplace environments.[7] The first is praise and encouragement: Employees feel valued when their work is recognized. Acknowledgment doesn't require promotions, raises, or awards, although those are always welcome. As researcher Daniel Goleman notes, "Small exchanges—a compliment on work well done, a word of support after a setback—add up to how we feel on the job."[8] The second climate-boosting practice is open communication. Employees appreciate managers and coworkers with open-door policies, allowing them opportunities to get and give feedback, make suggestions, and voice concerns.

Like their meteorological counterparts, communication climates are shared by everyone involved. It's rare to find one person describing a relationship as open and positive while another describes it as cold and hostile. Also, just like the weather, communication climates can change. A relationship can be overcast at one time and sunny at another. Carrying the analogy to its conclusion, we need to acknowledge that communication climate forecasting is not a perfect science. Unlike the weather, however, people can change the communication climates in their relationships.

∧ Despite some quirky characters and eccentric personalities, the office climate for the employees of *Parks and Recreation* is generally sunny and warm. The leadership of Leslie Knope (Amy Poehler) goes a long way toward creating their positive workplace environment. What has the communication climate been like at places where you've worked? What role did supervisors have in setting and maintaining that climate?

Levels of Message Confirmation

What makes a communication climate positive or negative? In large part, the answer is surprisingly simple. The climate of a relationship is shaped by the degree to which the people believe themselves to be *valued* by one another.

Social scientists use the term **confirming communication** to describe messages that convey valuing and **disconfirming communication** to describe those that show a lack of regard. In one form or another, confirming messages say "You exist," "You matter," "You're important." By contrast, disconfirming communication signals a lack of value. In one form or another, disconfirming messages say "I don't care about you," "I don't like you," "You're not important to me."

Like beauty, the decision about whether a message is confirming or disconfirming is determined by the beholder.[9] Consider, for example, times when you took a comment that might have sounded unsupportive to an outsider ("You turkey!") as a sign of affection within the context of your personal relationship. Likewise, a comment that the sender might have meant to be helpful ("I'm telling you this for your own good ...") could easily be regarded as a disconfirming attack.

What makes some messages more confirming than others? Table 11.1 outlines the levels of message confirmation that are described.

Disconfirming Messages Disconfirming communication shows a lack of value for the other person, either by disregarding or ignoring some important part of that person's message.[10] Communication researchers have identified seven types of disconfirming messages.[11]

TABLE 11.1 Levels of Message Confirmation and Disconfirmation

DISCONFIRMING	DISAGREEING		CONFIRMING
Impervious	Aggressiveness		
Interrupting	Complaining		
Irrelevant	Argumentativeness		
Tangential		Recognition	
Impersonal		Acknowledgment	
Ambiguous			Endorsement
Incongruous			
Least Valuing			**Most Valuing**

Impervious Responses An **impervious response** doesn't acknowledge the other person's message. Whether it's accidental or intentional, few things are more disconcerting than getting no reaction from the person with whom you're attempting to communicate.

As you read in the opening of Chapter 1, being ignored can be more disconfirming than being dismissed or attacked. In the working world, research shows that employees sometimes nudge unwanted coworkers to quit their jobs by avoiding interaction with them, creating a chilling communication climate.[12] In marriage, ignoring a partner (sometimes called *stonewalling*) has been identified as a strong predictor of divorce.[13] On a less-deliberate level, people who tune out others while texting may communicate imperviousness.

Interrupting Beginning to speak before the other person has finished talking can show a lack of concern about what the other person has to say. The occasional **interrupting response** is not likely to be taken as a disconfirmation, but repeatedly interrupting a speaker can be both discouraging and irritating.

Irrelevant Responses A comment unrelated to what the other person has just said is an **irrelevant response**.

A: What a day! I thought it would never end. First the car overheated, and I had to call a tow truck, and then the computer broke down at work.

B: Listen, we have to talk about a present for Ann's birthday. The party is on Saturday, and I have only tomorrow to shop for it.

A: I'm really beat. Could we talk about it in a few minutes? I've never seen a day like this one.

B: I just can't figure out what would suit Ann. She's got everything. …

Tangential Responses Conversational "takeaways" are called **tangential responses**. Instead of ignoring the speaker's remarks completely, the other party uses them as a starting point for a shift to a different topic.

A: I'd like to know for sure whether you want to go skiing during vacation. If we don't decide whether to go soon, it'll be impossible to get reservations anywhere.

B: Yeah, and if I don't pass my botany class, I won't be in the mood to go anywhere. Could you give me some help with this homework?

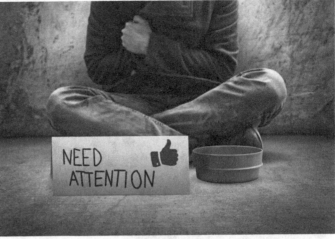

Impersonal Responses **Impersonal responses** are loaded with clichés and other statements that never truly respond to the speaker.

A: I've been having some personal problems lately, and I'd like to take off work early a couple of afternoons to clear them up.

B: Ah, yes. We all have personal problems. It seems to be a sign of the times.

Ambiguous Responses **Ambiguous responses** contain messages with more than one meaning, leaving the other party unsure of the responder's position.

A: I'd like to get together with you soon. How about Tuesday?
B: Uh, maybe so.
A: Well, how about it? Can we talk Tuesday?
B: Oh, probably. See you later.

Incongruous Responses An **incongruous response** contains two messages that seem to deny or contradict each other. Often at least one of these messages is nonverbal.

A: Darling, I love you.
B: I love you, too. (*said in a monotone while watching TV*)

Disagreeing Messages Between disconfirming and confirming communication lie disagreeing messages. As their name implies, **disagreeing messages** say "You're wrong" in one way or another. As you'll read here, some disagreements are quite hostile. But others aren't so disconfirming as they might first seem. Because there are better and worse ways to disagree with others, disagreeing messages need to be put on a negative-to-positive scale. We will do just that in this section as we discuss three types of disagreement: aggressiveness, complaining, and argumentativeness.

Aggressiveness The most destructive way to disagree with another person is through **aggressiveness**. Researchers define verbal aggressiveness as the tendency to attack the self-concepts of other people in order to inflict psychological pain.[14] Unlike argumentativeness (described later), aggressiveness demeans the worth of others. Name-calling, put-downs, sarcasm, taunting, yelling, badgering—all are methods of "winning" disagreements at others' expense.

One form of aggressiveness—bullying—has received a good deal of attention in the media and from scholars in recent years. The word "bully" often

⋀ Professional football tackle Jonathan Martin walked away from the Miami Dolphins team, saying he was bullied and harassed by teammates. The story brought new light to the notion that aggressive taunting and name-calling causes pain in adult relationships, not just among children. Have you encountered bullying in the workplace?

conjures up images of a tough kid on the school playground, but bullying can occur in a variety of contexts. For instance, studies show that it can take place in families, with sibling bullying having long-lasting psychological effects.[15] And as the photo in this section shows, bullying can happen among adults in the workplace.

Aggressiveness isn't limited to face-to-face encounters. Cyberbullying is disturbingly common: About 15 percent of students report abusing someone else online, and twice as many report having been victims.[16] The consequences of cyberbullying can be devastating. Online abuse leaves victims feeling angry, frustrated, sad, frightened, and embarrassed. Targets often respond with apathy and cheating in school, substance abuse, violence, and self-destructive behaviors—and suicide in the most severe cases. And cyberbullying isn't limited to one's school years. Fully 73 percent of adult Internet users have seen someone be harassed online and 40 percent have personally experienced it.[17] See Chapter 2 for more on cyberbullying.

It's no surprise that aggressiveness has such serious consequences. Chapter 12 describes how win–win approaches to conflict are healthier and more productive than the win–lose tactics of aggression.

Complaining When communicators aren't prepared to argue but still want to register dissatisfaction, they often complain. As is true of all disagreeing messages, some ways of **complaining** are better than others. Satisfied couples tend to offer behavioral complaints ("You always throw your socks on the floor"), whereas unsatisfied couples make more complaints aimed at personal characteristics ("You're a slob").[18] Personal complaints are more likely to result in an escalated conflict episode.[19] The reason should be obvious: Complaints about personal characteristics attack a more fundamental part of the presenting self. Talking about socks deals with a habit that can be changed; calling someone a slob is a character assault that is unlikely to be forgotten when the conflict is over. Marriage researcher John Gottman has found that complaining isn't necessarily a sign of a troubled relationship. In fact, it's usually healthy for spouses to get their concerns out in the open as long as the complaint is a behavioral description rather than a personal criticism.[20]

Argumentativeness Normally, when we call a person *argumentative*, we're making an unfavorable evaluation. However, the ability to create and deliver a sound argument is something we admire in lawyers, talk-show participants, letters to the editor, and political debates. Taking a positive approach to the term, communication researchers define **argumentativeness** as presenting and defending positions on issues while attacking positions taken by others.[21] Rather than being a negative trait, argumentativeness is associated with several positive attributes such as enhanced self-concept, communicative competence, and positive climate in the workplace.

The key for maintaining a positive climate while arguing a point is the *way* you present your ideas. It is crucial to attack issues, not people. In addition, a sound argument is better received when it's delivered in an affirming manner.[22] The supportive kinds of messages outlined later in this chapter show how it is possible to argue in a respectful, constructive way.

Confirming Messages   Research shows that three increasingly positive types of messages have the best chance of being confirming: recognition, acknowledgment, and endorsement.[23]

Recognition The most fundamental act of confirmation is to recognize the other person. Recognition seems easy and obvious, and yet there are many times when we don't respond to others on this basic level. Failure to return an email or phone message are common examples. So is a sales clerk who fails to signal awareness that you're waiting for service. Of course, this lack of recognition may simply be an oversight. Nonetheless, if the other person *perceives* you as avoiding contact, then the message has the effect of being disconfirming.

Acknowledgment Acknowledging the ideas and feelings of others is a stronger form of confirmation. Listening is probably the most common form of acknowledgment. Of course, counterfeit listening—ambushing, stage hogging, pseudolistening, and so on—has the opposite effect of acknowledgment. More active acknowledgment includes asking questions, paraphrasing, and reflecting. It is not surprising that employees highly rate managers who solicit their opinions—even when the managers don't accept every opinion.[24] As you read in Chapter 8, reflecting the speaker's thoughts and feelings can be a powerful way to offer support when others have problems.

Endorsement Whereas acknowledgment means that you are interested in another's ideas, endorsement means that you agree with them or otherwise find them important. It's easy to see why endorsement is the strongest type of confirming message: It communicates the highest form of valuing. The most obvious form of endorsement is agreeing. Fortunately, it isn't necessary to agree completely with another person in order to endorse her or his message. You can probably find something in the message that you endorse. "I can see why you were so angry," you might reply to a friend, even if you don't approve of his outburst. Of course, outright praise is a strong form of endorsement and one that you can use surprisingly often after you look for opportunities to compliment others.

How Communication Climates Develop

As soon as two people start to communicate, a relational climate begins to develop. If their messages are confirming, then the climate is likely to be a positive one. If their messages are disconfirming, then the relationship is likely to be hostile, cold, or defensive.

Verbal messages certainly contribute to the climate of a relationship, but many climate-shaping messages are nonverbal.[25] The very act of approaching others is confirming—and avoiding them can be disconfirming. Smiles or frowns, the presence or absence of eye contact, tone of voice, the use of personal space—all these and other cues send messages about how the parties feel toward one another.

AN UNLIKELY FRIENDSHIP

*I*am coming out in a new way, as a friend of Chick-fil-A's president and COO, Dan Cathy, and I am nervous about it.

For many this news of friendship might be shocking. I am an out, 40-year-old gay man and a lifelong activist for equality. For nearly a decade, my organization, Campus Pride, has been protesting Chick-fil-A. I had researched Chick-fil-A's nearly $5 million in funding to anti-LGBT groups. And the whole nation was aware that Dan was "guilty as charged" in his support of a "biblical definition" of marriage. What more was there to know?

In the heat of the controversy, I got a surprise call from Dan Cathy. I took the call with great caution. He was going to tear me apart, right? Give me a piece of his mind? Turn his lawyers on me?

The first call lasted over an hour. His questions and a series of deeper conversations ultimately led to a number of in-person meetings. It is not often that people with deeply held and completely opposing viewpoints actually risk sitting down and listening to one another.

Dan and I shared respectful, enduring communication and built trust. Even when I continued to question his public actions and the funding decisions, Dan embraced

the opportunity to have dialogue and hear my perspective. He and I were committed to a better understanding of one another. We see this failure to listen and learn in our government, in our communities and in our own families. Dan Cathy and I would, together, try to do better than each of us had experienced before.

Throughout the conversations Dan expressed a sincere interest in my life. He wanted to know about where I grew up, my faith, my family, even my husband. In return, I learned about his wife and kids and gained an appreciation for his commitment to being "a follower of Christ" more than a "Christian." Dan expressed regret and genuine

sadness when he heard of people being treated unkindly in the name of Chick-fil-A—but he offered no apologies for his genuine beliefs about marriage.

And in that we had great commonality: We were each entirely ourselves. We both wanted to be respected and for others to understand our views. We were different but in dialogue. That was progress.

In the end, it is not about eating a certain chicken sandwich. It is about sitting down at a table together and sharing our views as human beings, engaged in real, respectful, civil dialogue. Dan would probably call this act the biblical definition of hospitality. I would call it human decency. So long as we are all at the same table and talking, does it matter what we call it or what we eat?

Shane L. Windmeyer

Andrew Baker/Getty Images

After a climate is formed, it can take on a life of its own and grow in a self-perpetuating **spiral**: a reciprocating communication pattern in which each person's message reinforces the other's.[26] In positive spirals, one partner's confirming message leads to a similar message from the other person. This positive reaction leads the first person to be even more confirming. Negative spirals are just as powerful, although they leave the partners feeling worse about themselves and each other.

Research shows how spirals operate in relationships to reinforce the principle that "what goes around comes around." In one study of married couples, each spouse's response in conflict situations was similar to the other's statement.[27] Conciliatory statements (e.g., supporting, accepting responsibilities, agreeing) were likely to be followed by conciliatory responses. Confrontational acts (such as criticism, hostile questions, and fault finding) were likely to trigger equally confrontational responses. The same pattern held for other kinds of messages: Avoidance begets avoidance, analysis begets analysis, and so on. Table 11.2 illustrates reciprocal communication patterns that have the potential to create positive and negative spirals.

Escalatory conflict spirals are the most visible way that disconfirming messages reinforce one another.[28] One attack leads to another until a skirmish escalates into a full-fledged battle:

A: (*Mildly irritated*) Where were you? I thought we agreed to meet here a half-hour ago.

B: (*Defensively*) I'm sorry. I got hung up at the library. I don't have as much free time as you do, you know.

A: I wasn't blaming you, so don't get so touchy. I do resent what you just said, though. I'm plenty busy. And I've got lots of better things to do than wait around for you!

B: Who's getting touchy? I just made a simple comment. You've sure been defensive lately. What's the matter with you?

Although they are less obvious, **de-escalatory conflict spirals** can also be destructive.[29] Rather than fighting, the parties slowly lessen their dependence on each other, withdraw, and become less invested in the relationship. The good news is that spirals can also be positive. A word of praise can lead to a *returned compliment* that can lead to an act of kindness, which can result in an improved relational climate.

Spirals—whether positive or negative—rarely go on indefinitely. Most relationships pass through cycles of progression and regression. If the spiral is negative, partners may find the exchange growing so unpleasant that they switch from negative to positive messages without discussing the matter. In

Game called on account of infinity.

TABLE 11.2 Positive and Negative Reciprocal Communication Patterns

NEGATIVE RECIPROCAL PATTERN

Pattern	Example
Complaint–countercomplaint	A: I wish you weren't so self-centered. B: Well, I wish you weren't so critical.
Disagreement–disagreement	A: Why are you so hard on Marta? She's a great boss. B: Are you kidding? She's the biggest phony I've ever seen. A: You wouldn't know a good boss if you saw one. B: Neither would you.
Mutual indifference	A: I don't care if you want to stay. I'm exhausted, and I'm getting out of here. B: Go ahead if you want, but find your own way home.
Arguments involving punctuation	A: How can I talk when you won't listen? B: How can I listen when you won't talk?

POSITIVE RECIPROCAL PATTERNS

Pattern	Example
Validation of other's perspective	A: This assignment is really confusing. Nobody can figure out what we're supposed to do. B: I can understand how it might be unclear. Let me try to explain …
Recognizing similarities	A: I can't believe you want to take an expensive vacation! We should be saving money, not spending more! B: I agree we should be saving. But I think we can take this trip and still save some money. Let me show you what I've figured out …
Supportiveness	A: I'm going crazy with this job. It was supposed to be temporary. I have to do something different, and soon. B: I can see how much you hate it. Let's figure out how we can get the project finished soon, so you can get back to your regular work.

Adapted from *Competence and Interpersonal Conflict*, by W. Cupach and D. Canary. Reproduced by permission of William Cupach and Daniel Canary.

other cases, they may engage in *metacommunication*. "Hold on," one might say. "This is getting us nowhere." This ability to rebound from negative spirals and turn them in a positive direction is a hallmark of successful relationships.[30] However, if the partners pass the "point of no return" and continue spiraling downward, their relationship may end.

Positive spirals also have their limit. Even the best relationships go through periods of conflict and withdrawal, although a combination of time and communication skills can eventually bring the partners back into greater harmony.

PAUSE *and* REFLECT

Evaluating Communication Climates

MindTap® REFLECT... on communication climates by answering the following questions, either here or online.

You can probably recognize the communication climate in each of your relationships without much analysis. But taking the following steps will help explain why these climates exist. Taking these steps may also suggest ways in which to improve negative climates:

1. Identify the communication climate of an important interpersonal relationship.

2. List the confirming and/or disconfirming communications that created and now maintain this climate. Be sure to list both verbal and nonverbal messages.

3. Describe what you can do either to maintain and enhance the existing climate (if primarily positive) or to improve it (if primarily negative). Again, list both verbal and nonverbal messages.

DEFENSIVENESS: CAUSES AND REMEDIES

The word *defensiveness* suggests guarding oneself from attack, but what kind of attack? Surely, few if any of the times you become defensive involve a physical threat. If you're not threatened by bodily injury, then *what* are you guarding against? To answer this question, we need to talk more about the notions of the *presenting self* and *face* introduced in Chapter 3. Next, we'll look at ways to reduce defensiveness in others.

Face-Threatening Acts

Recall that a person's face consists of the physical traits, personality characteristics, attitudes, aptitudes, and all the other parts of the image that he or she wants to present to the world. Actually, it is a mistake to talk about a single face; we try to project different faces to different people. You might, for instance, try to impress a potential employer with your seriousness but want your friends to see you as a joker.

When others are willing to accept and acknowledge important parts of our presenting image, there is no need to feel defensive. On the other hand, when others confront us with **face-threatening acts**—messages that seem to challenge the image we want to project—we are likely to resist their messages.[31] Defensiveness, then, is the process of protecting our presenting

Photodisc/Getty Images

self, our face. While responding defensively to a face-threatening attack may seem logical, over time defensiveness erodes relationship stability.[32]

You can understand how defensiveness operates by imagining what might happen if an important part of your presenting self were attacked. Suppose, for instance, that your boss criticized you for making a stupid mistake. Or consider how you would feel if a friend called you self-centered or your sweetheart called you lazy. You would probably feel threatened if these attacks were unjustified. But notice that you might very well react defensively even if you knew deep inside that the attacks were justified. For instance, you have probably responded defensively at times when you *did* make a mistake, acted selfishly, or cut corners on your work. In fact, we often feel most defensive when criticism is right on target.[33] The drive to defend a presenting image—even when it is false—leads some people to act in destructive ways such as being sarcastic or verbally abusive.[34]

So far, we have talked about defensiveness as if it is the responsibility of only the person who feels threatened. If this were the case, then the prescription would be simple: Grow a thick skin, admit your flaws, and stop trying to manage impressions. This prescription isn't just unrealistic; it also ignores the role played by those who send face-threatening messages. In fact, competent communicators protect others' face needs as well as their own.[35] For instance, skilled instructors try to support their students' presenting faces, especially when offering constructive criticism. This facework leads to less-defensive responses from their students.[36] Likewise, effective supervisors use face-saving statements such as "You're on the right track, and your work has potential" to buffer corrections.[37] We'll talk more about the importance of sending face-saving messages later in this chapter.

Preventing Defensiveness in Others

The influential work of researcher Jack Gibb offers some useful tools for reducing defensiveness.[38] After observing groups for several years, Gibb was able to isolate six types of defense-arousing communication and six contrasting behaviors that lessen the level of threat and defensiveness by conveying face-honoring relational messages of respect. The **Gibb categories** are listed in Table 11.3 and summarized here.

Evaluation versus Description   The first type of defense-arousing behavior that Gibb noted is **evaluation**. Most people become irritated at judgmental statements, which they are likely to interpret as indicating a lack of regard. One form of evaluation is "you" language, which is described in Chapter 6.

Unlike evaluative "you" language, **description** focuses on the *speaker's* thoughts and feelings instead of judging the other person. Descriptive

TABLE 11.3 The Gibb Categories of Defensive and Supportive Behaviors

DEFENSIVE BEHAVIORS	SUPPORTIVE BEHAVIORS
1. Evaluation	1. Description
2. Control	2. Problem Orientation
3. Strategy	3. Spontaneity
4. Neutrality	4. Empathy
5. Superiority	5. Equality
6. Certainty	6. Provisionalism

Source: Jack Gibb

messages often are expressed in "I" language, which tends to provoke less defensiveness than "you" language.[39] Contrast the following evaluative "you" claims with their descriptive "I" counterparts:

Evaluation: "You don't know what you're talking about!"
Description: "I don't understand how you came up with that idea."

Evaluation: "This place is a mess!"
Description: "When you don't clean up, I have to either do it or live with your mess. That's why I'm mad!"

Evaluation: "Those jokes are disgusting!"
Description: "When you tell those off-color jokes, I get really embarrassed."

Note how each of the descriptive statements focuses on the speaker's thoughts and feelings without judging the other person. Despite its value, descriptive language isn't the only element necessary for success. Its effectiveness depends in part on when, where, and how the language is used. You can imagine how each of the preceding descriptive statements would go over if said in front of a room full of bystanders or in a whining tone of voice. Even the best timing and delivery of a descriptive message won't guarantee success. Some people will react defensively to anything you say or do. Nonetheless, it's easy to see that describing how the other person's behavior affects you is likely to produce better results than judgmentally attacking the other person.

Control versus Problem Orientation A second defense-provoking message involves some attempt to control another. **Controlling communication** occurs when a sender seems to be imposing a solution on the receiver with little regard for the receiver's needs or interests. The object of control can involve almost anything: where to eat dinner, what TV program to watch, whether to remain in a relationship, or how to spend a large sum of money. Whatever the situation, people who act in controlling ways create a defensive climate. Whether it is done through words, gestures, tone of voice, or some other channel, the controller generates hostility wherever he or she goes. The unspoken message that such behavior communicates is "I know what's best for you, and if you do as I say, we'll get along."

By contrast, communicators with a **problem orientation** focus on finding a solution that satisfies both their needs and those of the others involved. The goal here isn't to win at the expense of your partner, but rather to work out some arrangement in which everybody feels like a winner. Problem orientation is often typified by "we" language (see Chapter 6), which suggests the speaker is making decisions *with* rather than *for* other people.[40] University chairpersons found to be most effective by members of their departments were best characterized as using few control communications and adopting a problem orientation.[41] Chapter 12 has a great deal to say about win–win problem-solving as a way to find problem-oriented solutions.

Here are some examples of how some controlling and problem-orientation messages might sound.

Controlling:	"You need to stick around for the next two hours."
Problem orientation:	"I'm expecting an important package to arrive soon. Can you cover the office while I go on a sales call?"
Controlling:	"There's only one way to handle this problem ..."
Problem orientation:	"Looks like we have a problem. Let's work out a solution we can both live with."

Strategy versus Spontaneity   Gibb uses the word *strategy* to characterize defense-arousing messages in which speakers hide their ulterior motives. The words *dishonesty* and *manipulation* capture the essence of strategy. Even if the motives of strategic communication are honorable, the victim of such deception who discovers the attempt to deceive is likely to feel offended at being played for a naïve sucker.

Spontaneity is the behavior that contrasts with strategy. Spontaneity simply means being honest with others rather than manipulating them. What it doesn't mean is blurting out what you're thinking as soon as an idea comes to you. As we discussed in Chapter 3, there are appropriate (and inappropriate) times for self-disclosure. You would undoubtedly threaten others' presenting selves if you were "spontaneous" about every opinion that crossed your mind. Gibb's notion of spontaneity involves setting aside hidden agendas that others both sense and resist. These examples illustrate the difference.

Strategy:	"What are you doing Friday after work?"
Spontaneity:	"I have a piano I need to move Friday after work. Can you give me a hand?"
Strategy:	"Jermaine and Brianna go out to dinner every week."
Spontaneity:	"I'd like to go out to dinner more often."

Spontaneity doesn't mean indiscriminately saying whatever you're thinking and feeling. That's called *blurting*—and research shows that it's detrimental to interpersonal relationships.[42] Blurters tend to be high in verbal aggressiveness and neuroticism; they rate low in empathy and perspective-taking. They are also relatively unconcerned about the harm their comments might do to others and to their relationships.

Paradoxically, spontaneity can be a strategy, too. Sometimes you'll see people using honesty in a calculating way, being just frank enough to win someone's trust or sympathy. This "leveling" is probably the most defense-arousing strategy of all, because once you have learned someone is using frankness as a manipulation, you are less likely to trust that person in the future.

Neutrality versus Empathy Gibb uses the term **neutrality** to describe a fourth behavior that arouses defensiveness. Probably a better descriptive word would be *indifference*. A neutral attitude is disconfirming because it communicates a lack of concern and implies that the welfare of the other person isn't very important to you. This perceived indifference is likely to promote defensiveness, because people do not like to think of themselves as worthless, and they'll protect a self-concept that regards them as worthwhile.

Notice the following differences between neutral and empathic statements.

Neutral:	"That's what happens when you don't plan properly."
Empathic:	"Ouch—looks like this didn't turn out the way you expected."
Neutral:	"Sometimes things just don't work out. That's the way it goes."
Empathic:	"I know you put a lot of time and effort into this project."

The negative effects of neutrality become apparent when you consider the hostility that most people have for the large, impersonal organizations with which they have to deal: "They think of me as a number instead of a person"; "I felt as if I were being handled by computers and not human beings." These two common statements reflect reactions to being handled in an indifferent way. Gibb found that empathy helps rid communication of the quality of indifference. **Empathy** means accepting another's feelings and putting yourself in another's place. This doesn't mean that you need to agree with that person. By simply letting that person know of your care and respect, you'll be acting in a supportive way.

Superiority versus Equality A fifth behavior that arouses defensiveness is **superiority**. Any message that suggests "I'm better than you" is likely to arouse feelings of defensiveness in the recipients. A body of research confirms that patronizing messages irritate recipients ranging from young students to senior citizens, at least in Western cultures.[43] Some superiority comes from the content of messages. In other cases, the *way* we deliver messages suggests a one-up approach. Consider, for example, how using simplified grammar and vocabulary, talking loudly and slowly, not listening, and varying speaking pitch convey a patronizing attitude.

Andersen Ross/Blend Images/Jupiter Images

Here are two examples of the difference between superiority and equality.

Superior:	"You don't know what you're talking about."
Equal:	"I see it a different way."
Superior:	"No, that's not the right way to do it!"
Equal:	"If you want, I can show you a way that has worked for me."

On the JOB

Intellectual Humility at Google

Google has been notorious for job interview brainteasers like "How many times a day do a clock's hands overlap?" More recently the company has declared oddball questions useless in hiring. According to Laszlo Bock, that company's head of people operations, pedigrees from elite colleges and even high GPAs are also poor at predicting job performance.[a]

Bock explained that Google now looks for "the ability to step back and embrace other people's ideas when they're better."[b] This "intellectual humility," as Bock calls it, is fundamental to learning. It's expressed as an ability to process information on the fly and to absorb the lessons of failure. Google interviewers screen for it by asking how applicants handled tough situations.

Being intellectually humble does not mean being wishy-washy. As Bock describes it, employees who possess this quality will "fight like hell" for their position. But if a new fact is introduced, they are unafraid to say, "That changes things. You are right."

How could embracing another point of view make you more successful? What difference would it make to work in an organization that values provisionalism compared to one characterized by certainty?

There are certainly times when we communicate with others who possess talents or knowledge lesser than ours, but even then it isn't necessary to communicate an attitude of superiority. Gibb found ample evidence that many people who have superior skills and talents are capable of projecting feelings of **equality** rather than superiority. Such people convey the attitude that, although they may have greater talent in certain areas, they see others as having just as much worth as human beings.

"I understand completely. I like good movies, and you like bad movies."

Certainty versus Provisionalism Have you ever run into people who are positive they're right, who know that theirs is the only or proper way of doing something, who insist that they have all the facts and need no additional information? If you have, then you've met individuals who project the defense-arousing behavior that Gibb calls **certainty**. Communicators who regard their own opinions with certainty while disregarding the ideas of others demonstrate a lack of regard and respect. It's likely that the receiver will take the certainty as a personal affront and react defensively.

In contrast to certainty is **provisionalism**, in which people may have strong opinions but are willing to acknowledge that they don't have a corner on the truth and will change their stance if another position seems more reasonable. Consider these examples that contrast certain and provisional approaches.

Certain:	"That will never work!"
Provisional:	"I think you'll run into problems with that approach."
Certain:	"You don't know what you're talking about!"
Provisional:	"I've never heard anything like that before. Where did you hear it?"

As these examples suggest, provisionalism often surfaces in word choices. While dogmatic communicators use words like *can't, never, always, must,* and *have to*, more provisional speakers say *perhaps, maybe, possibly, might,* and *could*. It's not that provisional people are spineless; they simply recognize what research confirms: People respond better to open-minded messages.[44]

There is no guarantee that using Gibb's supportive, confirming approach to communication will build a positive climate. First, Gibb's emphasis on being direct is better suited for a low-context culture such as the United States, which values self-assertion, than for high-context cultures. Even in a culture that values directness, your appeals may not always be well received. But the chances for a constructive relationship will be greatest when communication consists of the supportive approach described here. Besides boosting the odds of getting a positive response from others, supportive communication can leave you feeling better in a variety of ways: more in control of your relationships, more comfortable, and more positive toward others.

Looking at DIVERSITY

Courtesy of Russel Proctor

Abdel Jalil Elayyadi: Promoting Understanding

I grew up in Morocco and moved to the United States when I was 19. I love the U.S. and have many wonderful friends here—but communicating with strangers is often tense because I'm an Arab Muslim. Many Americans equate Arabs and Muslims with terrorism, and that creates a defensive communication climate.

I feel as if I'm easily stereotyped and misunderstood by people who prejudge me because of my religion and nationality. When I encounter people who think that all Muslims are terrorists who hate Americans, I try to do three things to change the defensive climate.

First, I quickly explain that Muslims are peace-loving people who abhor the taking of innocent life. I want them to know that I completely agree with their disdain for the terrorists. That builds a bridge of trust that allows us to keep talking.

Second, I try to use examples to help them understand how terrorists don't represent most Muslims

or Arabs. I ask them how they would feel if Arabs judged Americans by the acts of Oklahoma City bomber Timothy McVeigh, or Christians by the acts of the Ku Klux Klan. This usually helps them view Muslims in a different and more accurate light.

Finally, the more we talk, the more we focus on things we have in common and beliefs we share. The goal is to discover that we are not enemies simply because we have different religions or nationalities—and in fact, there is no reason we can't be friends.

What do these conversations accomplish? In some cases, not a lot—because there are a few people who prefer to keep their prejudices rather than change them. But in other cases, I think I've made a difference, however small, in promoting peace and understanding in the world.

"Promoting Understanding" by Abdel Jalil Elayyadi. Used with permission of author.

SAVING FACE

Gibb's categories of supportive communication offer useful guidelines for reducing defensiveness. You will learn some specific ways to use these approaches when you need to deliver challenging messages.

The Assertive Message Format

As you've already seen, an essential ingredient in building a supportive climate is to avoid attacking others—to preserve their face. At the same time, you need to share your legitimate concerns when problems arise in a relationship.

The following will describe a method for speaking your mind in a clear, direct, yet nonthreatening assertive way that expresses your needs, thoughts, and feelings clearly and directly without judging or dictating to others. This **assertive message format** builds on the perception-checking skill you learned in Chapter 4 and the "I" language approach you learned in Chapter 6. This new skill works for a variety of messages: your hopes, problems, complaints, and appreciations.[45] We'll examine each part one by one and then discuss how to combine them in your everyday communication.

Behavior   As you read in Chapter 6, a behavioral description describes the raw material to which you react. A behavioral description should be *objective*, describing an event without interpreting it. Two examples of behavioral descriptions might look like this:

Example 1

"One week ago John promised me that he would ask my permission before smoking in the same room with me. Just a moment ago he lit up a cigarette without asking for my OK."

Example 2

"Chris has acted differently over the last week. I can't remember her laughing once since the holiday weekend. She hasn't dropped by my place like she usually does, hasn't suggested we play tennis, and hasn't returned my phone calls."

Notice that both statements describe only facts. The observer hasn't attached any meaning.

Interpretation   An **interpretation statement** describes the meaning you've attached to the other person's behavior. The important thing to realize about interpretations is that they are *subjective*. As you learned via the skill of perception checking (see Chapter 4), we can attach more than one interpretation to any behavior. For example, look at these two different interpretations of each of the preceding descriptions:

Example 1

Interpretation A: "John must have forgotten about our agreement that he wouldn't smoke without asking me first. I'm sure he's too considerate to go back on his word on something he knows I feel strongly about."

Interpretation B: "John is a rude, inconsiderate person. After promising not to smoke around me without asking, he's just deliberately done so. This shows that he cares only about himself. In fact, I bet he's deliberately doing this to drive me crazy!"

Example 2

Interpretation A: "Something must be bothering Chris. It's probably her family. She'll probably just feel worse if I keep pestering her."

Interpretation B: "Chris is probably mad at me. It's probably because I kidded her about losing so often at tennis. I'd better leave her alone until she cools off."

After you become aware of the difference between observable behavior and interpretation, some of the reasons for communication difficulties become clear. Many problems occur when a sender fails to describe the behavior on which an interpretation is based. For instance, imagine the difference between hearing a friend say

"You are a tightwad!" (*No behavioral description*)

versus explaining

"When you never offer to pay me back for the coffee and snacks I often buy you, I think you're a tightwad." (*Behavior plus interpretation*)

Feeling   Reporting behavior and sharing your interpretations are important, but **feeling statements** add a new dimension to a message. For example, consider the difference between saying

"When you laugh at me *(behavior)*, I think you find my comments foolish *(interpretation)*, and *I feel embarrassed.*"

And

"When you laugh at me, I think you find my comments foolish, and *I feel angry.*"

SKILL *Builder*

Behaviors and Interpretations

MindTap PRACTICE ... your skill at interpreting behaviors by answering the following questions online.

1. Think of two situations when you recently made interpretations about other people in your life. For each interpretation, describe the behavior on which you based your interpretations.

2. Next, consider some alternate interpretations of the behavior that might be as plausible as your original one.

3. After considering the alternate interpretations, decide

   a. which one was most reasonable and

   b. how you might share that interpretation (along with the behavior) with the other person involved in a tentative, provisional way.

SKILL *Builder*

Name the Feeling

MindTap® **PRACTICE ...** your skill at identifying feelings by answering the following questions online.

Add a feeling that you would be likely to have to each of the following messages:

1. I felt ___ when I found out you didn't invite me on the camping trip. You said you thought I wouldn't want to go, but I have a hard time accepting that.

2. I felt ___ when you offered to help me move. I know how busy you are.

3. When you tell me you still want to be a friend but you want to "lighten up a little," I get the idea you're tired of me, and I feel ___.

4. You told me you wanted my honest opinion about your paintings, and then when I tell you what I think, you say I don't understand them. I'm ___.

How would the impact of each message be different if it didn't include a feeling statement?

It's important to recognize that some statements *seem* as if they're expressing feelings but are actually interpretations or statements of intention. For instance, it's not accurate to say "I feel like leaving" (really an intention) or "I feel you're wrong" (an interpretation). Statements like these obscure the true expression of feelings.

Consequence   A **consequence statement** explains what happens as a result of the situation you've described so far. There are three types of consequences:

- What happens to you, the speaker

  "When you didn't tell me that the landlord came by to ask about last month's rent *(behavior)*, I didn't know that my check had bounced *(consequences)*. It seems to me that you don't care about my credit record or appreciate what it takes for me to handle our rent for the apartment *(interpretation)*, and that's why I'm so mad *(feeling)*."

- What happens to the person you're addressing

  "When you have four or five drinks at a party after I've warned you to slow down *(behavior)*, you start to act strange: You make crude jokes that offend everybody, and on the way home you drive poorly *(consequences)*. For instance, last night you almost hit a telephone pole while you were backing out of the driveway *(more behavior)*. I don't think you realize how differently you act *(interpretation)*, and I'm worried *(feeling)* about what will happen if you don't drink less."

- What happens to others

  "You probably don't know because you couldn't hear her cry *(interpretation)*, but when you rehearse your lines for the play without closing the doors *(behavior)*, the baby can't sleep *(consequence)*. I'm especially concerned *(feeling)* about her because she's had a cold lately."

Consequence statements are valuable for two reasons. First, they help you understand more clearly why you are bothered or pleased by another's behavior. Just as important, telling others about the consequences of their actions can clarify for them the results of their behavior. As with interpretations, we often think that others should be aware of consequences without being told, but the fact is that they often aren't. By explicitly stating consequences, you can be sure that you or your message leaves nothing to the listener's imagination.

Intention   **Intention statements** are the final element of the assertive message format. They can communicate three kinds of messages:

- Where you stand on an issue

  "When you call us 'girls' after I've told you we want to be called 'women' *(behavior)*, I get the idea you don't appreciate how important the difference is to us *(interpretation)* and how demeaning it feels *(feeling)*. Now I'm in an awkward spot: Either I have to keep bringing the subject up or else drop it and feel bad *(consequence)*. I want you to know how much this bothers me *(intention)*."

- Requests of others

  "When I didn't hear from you last night *(behavior)*, I thought you were mad at me *(interpretation)*. I've been thinking about it ever since *(consequence)*, and I'm still worried *(feeling)*. I'd like to know whether you are angry *(intention)*."

- Descriptions of how you plan to act in the future

  "I've asked you to repay the twenty-five dollars I lent you three times now *(behavior)*. I'm getting the idea that you've been avoiding me *(interpretation)*, and I'm pretty angry about it *(feeling)*. I want you to know that unless we clear this up now, you shouldn't expect me ever to lend you anything again *(intention)*."

As in the preceding cases, we are often motivated by one single intention. Sometimes, however, we act from a combination of intentions, which may even be in conflict with each other. When this happens, our conflicting intentions often make it difficult for us to reach decisions:

"I want to be truthful with you, but I don't want to violate my friend's privacy."

"I want to continue to enjoy your friendship and company, but I don't want to get too attached right now."

"I want to have time to study and get good grades, but I also want to have a job with some money coming in."

Using the Assertive Message Format   Before you try to deliver messages by using the clear message format, there are a few points to remember.

1. **The elements may be delivered in mixed order.** As the previous examples show, it's sometimes best to begin by stating your feelings. At other times you can start by sharing your intentions or interpretations or by describing consequences.

In REAL LIFE

The Assertive Message Format

While the elements of the assertive message format don't vary, the way they sound will depend on the situation and your personal style. Here are a few examples to show how this approach can operate in real life.

You can appreciate the value of the assertive approach by imagining how different the likely outcome would be if each message had been delivered in a blaming, aggressive way ... or not at all.

To a Neighbor

I had an awful scare just now *(feeling)*. I was backing out of the driveway, and Angela *(neighbor's toddler)* wandered right behind my car *(behavior)*. Thank God I saw her, but she is so small, and it would have been easy to miss her. I can't bear to think what might have happened if I hadn't seen her *(consequences for others)*. I know how hard it is to keep an eye on little kids *(interpretation)*, but I really hope you can keep her inside unless you're watching her *(intention)*.

To a Friend

I just checked my Facebook account and saw that you tagged me in your photos from the party last weekend *(behavior)*. I told you before that I'm trying to get a good job, and I'm afraid those kinds of pictures could blow my chance *(consequence for you)*. I know you like to post lots of pictures, and you probably think I'm overreacting *(interpretations)*. Anyway,

this is a big deal for me. So I need you to remember not to post any pictures that you think would embarrass me. If you aren't sure about a photo, just ask me *(intention)*.

To a Boss

I've got a favor to ask *(intention)*. Last month I told you I wanted to work extra hours, and I know you're doing me a favor by giving me more shifts *(interpretation)*. But it would really help if you could give me a couple of days' advance notice instead of telling me the night before you want me to work *(clarifies intention)*. That way I can say "yes" to the extra shifts *(consequence for boss)*. It would also cause a lot less stress for me *(feeling)*.

To an Auto Mechanic

I need to tell you that I'm pretty unhappy *(feeling)*. When I dropped the car off yesterday, you told me it would definitely be ready today by noon. Now it's 12:30 and it isn't done *(behavior)*. I'm going to be late for an important meeting *(consequence for you)*. I know you aim to please *(interpretation)*, but you have to understand that I can't bring my car to you unless I can count on it being ready when you promise *(consequence for others)*.

MindTap® APPLY ... the Assertive Message Format to a situation in your life online.

2. **Word the message to suit your personal style**. Instead of saying, "I interpret your behavior to mean ..." you might choose to say "I think ..." or "It seems to me ..." or perhaps "I get the idea. ..."
    In the same way, you can express your intentions by saying, "I hope you'll understand (or do) ..." or perhaps, "I wish you would. ..." The words that you choose should sound authentic in order to reinforce the genuineness of your statement.

3. **When appropriate, combine two elements in a single phrase**. The statement "... and ever since then I've been wanting to talk to you" expresses both a consequence and an intention. In the same way, saying "... and after you said that, I felt confused" expresses a consequence and

SKILL *Builder*

Putting Your Message Together

1. Join with two other class members. Each person in turn should share a message that he or she might want to send to another person, being sure to include behavior, interpretation, feeling, consequence, and intention statements in the message.

2. The others in the group should help the speaker by offering feedback about how the message could be made clearer if there is any question about the meaning.

3. After the speaker has composed a satisfactory message, he or she should practice actually delivering it by having another group member play the role of the intended receiver. Continue this practice until the speaker is confident that he or she can deliver the message effectively.

4. Repeat this process until each group member has had a chance to practice delivering a message.

a feeling. Whether you combine elements or state them separately, the important point is to be sure that each one is present in your statement.

4. **Take your time delivering the message**. It isn't always possible to deliver messages such as the ones here all at one time, wrapped up in neat paragraphs. It will often be necessary to repeat or restate one part before the other person understands what you're saying. As you've already read, there are many types of psychological and physical noise that make it difficult for us to understand each other. In communication, as in many other activities, patience and persistence are essential.

Now try your hand at combining all these elements in the Skill Builder "Putting Your Message Together."

Responding Nondefensively to Criticism

The world would be a happier place if everyone communicated supportively and assertively. But how can you respond nondefensively when others send aggressive messages that don't match the prescriptions outlined in this chapter? Despite your best intentions, it's difficult to be reasonable when you're being attacked. Being attacked is hard enough when the criticism is clearly unfair, but it's often even harder when the criticism is on target. Despite the accuracy of your critic, the tendency is either to counterattack aggressively with a barrage of verbal aggression or to withdraw nonassertively.

Because neither of these counterattacks is likely to resolve a dispute, we need alternative ways of behaving. There are two such ways. Despite their apparent simplicity, they have proven to be among the most valuable skills many communicators have learned.[46]

Otto Greule Jr/Getty Images Sport/Getty Images

Seek More Information

The response of seeking more information makes good sense when you realize that it's foolish to respond to a critical attack until you understand what the other person has said. Even attacks that on first consideration appear to be totally unjustified or foolish often prove to contain at least a grain of truth and sometimes much more.

Many readers object to the idea of asking for details when they are criticized. Their resistance stems from confusing the act of *listening open-mindedly* to a speaker's comments with *accepting* the comments. After you realize that you can listen to, understand, and even acknowledge the most hostile comments without necessarily accepting them, it becomes much easier to hear another person out. If you disagree with a person's criticism, you will be in a much better position to explain yourself after you understand the criticism. On the other hand, after carefully listening to the person's criticism, you might just see that it is valid, in which case you have learned some valuable information about yourself. In either case, you have everything to gain and nothing to lose by paying attention to the critic.

Of course, after one has spent years instinctively resisting criticism, learning to listen to the other person will take some practice. To make matters clearer, here are several ways in which you can seek additional information from your critics.

Ask for Specifics Often the vague attack of a critic is virtually useless even if you sincerely want to change. Abstract attacks such as "You're being unfair" or "You never help out" can be difficult to understand. In such cases it is a good idea to request more specific information from the sender. "What do I *do* that's unfair?" is an important question to ask before you can judge whether the attack is correct. "When haven't I helped out?" you might ask before agreeing with or disagreeing with the attack.

If you have already asked for specifics and are still accused of reacting defensively, the problem may be in the *way* you ask. Your tone of voice and facial expression, posture, and other nonverbal clues can give the same words radically different connotations. For example, think of how you could use the words "Exactly what are you talking about?" to communicate either a genuine desire to know or your belief that the speaker is crazy. It's important to request specific information only when you genuinely want to learn more from the speaker because asking under any other circumstances will only make matters worse.

Guess about Specifics On some occasions even your sincere and well-phrased requests for specific information won't meet with success. Sometimes your critics won't be able to define precisely the behavior they find offensive. At these times, you'll hear such comments as "I can't tell you exactly what's wrong with your sense of humor—all I can say is that I don't like it." At other times, your critics may know the exact behaviors they don't like, but for some reason seem to get a perverse satisfaction out of making you struggle to figure it out. At times like this, you hear such comments as, "Well, if you don't know what you did to hurt my feelings, I'm certainly not going to tell you!"

Needless to say, failing to learn the specifics of another's criticism when you genuinely want to know can be frustrating. In instances like these, you can often learn more clearly what is bothering your critic by *guessing* at the specifics of a criticism. In a sense you become both detective and suspect, the goal being to figure out exactly what "crime" you have committed. Like the technique of asking for specifics, guessing must be done with goodwill if it's to produce satisfying results. You need to convey to the critic that for both your sakes you're truly interested in finding out what is the matter. After you have communicated this intention, the emotional climate generally becomes more comfortable because, in effect, both you and the critic are seeking the same goal.

Here are some typical questions you might hear from someone guessing about the specifics of another's criticism:

"When will he be able to sit up and take criticism?"

"So you object to the language I used in writing the paper. Was my language too formal?"

"Okay, I understand that you think the outfit looks funny. What's so bad? Is it the color? Does it have something to do with the fit? The fabric?"

"When you say that I'm not doing my share around the house, do you mean that I haven't been helping enough with the cleaning?"

Paraphrase the Speaker's Ideas Another strategy is to draw out confused or reluctant speakers by paraphrasing their thoughts and feelings and using the active listening skills described in Chapter 8. Paraphrasing is especially good in helping others solve their problems. Because people generally criticize you because your behavior creates some problem for them, the strategy is especially appropriate at such times.

One advantage of paraphrasing is that you don't have to guess about the specifics of your behavior that might be offensive. By clarifying or amplifying what you understand critics to be saying, you'll learn more about their objections. A brief dialogue between a disgruntled customer and an especially talented store manager using paraphrasing might sound like the following.

Customer:	The way you people run this store is disgusting! I just want to tell you that I'll never shop here again.
Manager:	(*Reflecting the customer's feeling*) It seems that you're quite upset. Can you tell me your problem?
Customer:	It isn't *my* problem; it's the problem your salespeople have. They seem to think it's a great inconvenience to help a customer find anything around here.
Manager:	So you didn't get enough help locating the items you were looking for, is that it?
Customer:	Help? I spent twenty minutes looking around in here before I even talked to a clerk. All I can say is that it's a hell of a way to run a store.
Manager:	So what you're saying is that the clerks seemed to be ignoring the customers?

Customer:	No. They were all busy with other people. It just seems to me that you ought to have enough help around to handle the crowds that come in at this hour.
Manager:	I understand now. What frustrated you most was the fact that we didn't have enough staff to serve you promptly.
Customer:	That's right. I have no complaint with the service I get after I'm waited on, and I've always thought you had a good selection here. It's just that I'm too busy to wait so long for help.
Manager:	Well, I'm glad you brought this to my attention. We certainly don't want loyal customers going away mad. I'll try to see that it doesn't happen again.

This conversation illustrates two advantages of paraphrasing. First, the critic often reduces the intensity of the attack after he or she realizes that the complaint is being heard. As soon as the manager genuinely demonstrated interest in the customer's plight, the customer began to feel better and was able to leave the store relatively calm. Of course, this sort of reflective listening won't always mollify your critic, but even when it doesn't, there's still another benefit that makes the strategy worthwhile. In the sample conversation, for instance, the manager learned some valuable information by taking time to understand the customer. The manager discovered that there were certain times when the number of employees was insufficient to help the crowd of shoppers and also that the delays at these times seriously annoyed at least some shoppers, thus threatening a loss in business. This knowledge is certainly important, and by reacting defensively to the customer's complaint, the manager would not have learned from it.

Ask What the Critic Wants Sometimes your critic's demand will be obvious:

"Turn down that music!"

"I wish you'd remember to tell me about phone messages."

"Would you clean up your dirty dishes now?"

At other times, however, you'll need to do some investigating to find out what the critic wants from you:

Abel:	I can't believe you invited all those people over without asking me first!
Brenda:	Are you saying you want me to cancel the party?
Abel:	No, I just wish you'd ask me before you make plans.
Chen:	You're so critical! It sounds like you don't like anything about this paper.
Deven:	But you asked for my opinion. What do you expect me to do when you ask?
Chen:	I want to know what's wrong, but I don't just want to hear criticisms. If you think there's anything good about my work, I wish you'd tell me that, too.

This last example illustrates the importance of accompanying your questions with the right nonverbal behavior. It's easy to imagine two ways in which Deven could have nonverbally supported her response, "What do you expect me to do when you ask?" One would show a genuine desire to clarify what Chen wanted, whereas the other would have been clearly hostile and defensive. As with all the styles in this section, your responses to criticism have to be sincere to work.

Ask about the Consequences of Your Behavior As a rule, people criticize your behavior only when some need of theirs is not being met. One way to respond to this kind of criticism is to find out exactly what troublesome consequences your behavior has for them. You'll often find that behaviors that seem perfectly legitimate to you cause some difficulty for your critic. After you have understood this, criticisms that previously sounded foolish take on a new meaning.

Neighbor A: You say that I ought to have my cat neutered. Why is that important to you?

Neighbor B: Because at night he picks fights with my cat, and I'm tired of paying the vet's bills.

Worker A: Why do you care whether I'm late to work?

Worker B: Because when the boss asks, I feel obligated to make up some story so you won't get in trouble, and I don't like to lie.

Husband: Why does it bother you when I lose money at poker? You know I never gamble more than I can afford.

Wife: It's not the cash itself. It's that when you lose, you're in a grumpy mood for two or three days, and that's no fun for me.

Ask What Else Is Wrong It might seem crazy to invite more criticism, but sometimes asking about other complaints can uncover the real problem:

Raul: Are you mad at me?

Tina: No. Why are you asking?

Raul: Because the whole time we were at the picnic you hardly spent any time talking to me. In fact, it seemed like whenever I came over to where you were, you went off somewhere else.

Tina: Is anything else wrong?

Raul: Well, I've been wondering lately if you're tired of me.

This example shows that asking if anything else bothers your critic isn't just an exercise in masochism. If you can keep your defensiveness in check, probing further can lead the conversation to issues that are the source of the critic's real dissatisfaction.

Sometimes soliciting more information from a critic isn't enough. What do you do, for instance, when you fully understand the other person's criticism and still feel a defensive response on the tip of your tongue? You know that if you try to defend yourself, you'll wind up in an argument. On the other hand, you simply can't accept what the other person is saying about you. The solution to such a dilemma is outrageously simple and is discussed in the following section.

Agree with the Critic

But, you protest, how can you honestly agree with criticisms that you don't believe are true? The following will answer this question by showing that in virtually every situation you can honestly accept the other person's point of view while still maintaining your own position. To see how this can be so, you need to realize that there are two different types of agreement you can use in almost any situation.

Agree with the Facts This is the easiest type of agreement to understand, though not always to practice. Research suggests that it is also highly effective in restoring a damaged reputation with a critic.[47] You agree with your critic when the accusation is factually correct:

"You're right, I am angry."

"I suppose I *was* being defensive."

"Now that you mention it, I did get pretty sarcastic."

Agreeing with the facts seems sensible when you realize that certain facts are indisputable. If you agree to be somewhere at four o'clock and don't show up until five o'clock, you are tardy, no matter how good your explanation for tardiness. If you've broken a borrowed object, run out of gas, or failed to finish

ETHICAL *Challenge*

Nonviolence: A Legacy of Principled Effectiveness

Among the most familiar and challenging biblical injunctions is Christ's mandate, "If someone strikes you on one cheek, turn to him the other. ..."

The notion of meeting aggression with nonviolence is an ancient one. The Taoist doctrine of *wu-wei*, promulgated more than 2,400 years ago in China, advocates nonaction in the face of an attack. In ancient India, the principle of *ahimsa*—nonharming—was shared by Buddhists, Jains, and many Hindus. In the West, some Greek stoics advocated nonaction in the face of threats.

Pacifism has a moral foundation, but by the nineteenth century it was used as a potent strategy for achieving political goals. In the United States, abolitionist William Lloyd Garrison advocated the use of nonviolence to protest slavery. On both sides of the Atlantic, the suffragette movement used nonviolent resistance as a tool to secure rights for women. In

czarist Russia, Count Leo Tolstoy led a pacifist movement rejecting war and advocating civil disobedience as a tool for inhibiting violence.

In the twentieth century, nonviolence proved to be a powerful tool for political change. Mahatma Gandhi was demonstrably the most successful practitioner of this tool, first in South Africa and later in India, where his approach of *satyagraha* (truth-force) played a decisive role in the 1947 withdrawal of imperial Britain from India. In the 1950s and 1960s, Martin Luther King, Jr., and his followers used nonviolence to demonstrate against the evils of racial segregation, contributing to the passage of groundbreaking civil rights laws.

The effectiveness of nonviolence in achieving social change can also be effective in interpersonal situations. Nonconfrontational strategies provide communicators with an approach that is both principled and pragmatic.

SKILL *Builder*

Coping with Criticism

MindTap® PRACTICE ... coping with criticism by answering the following questions, either here or online.

Take turns practicing nondefensive responses with a partner:

1. Choose one of the following criticisms that feels "familiar" to you. Give your partner some examples of how they might direct this criticism at you as part of a larger story.

   a. You're so selfish sometimes. You think only of yourself.

   b. Don't be so touchy!

   c. You say you understand me, but you don't really.

   d. I wish you'd do your share around here.

   e. You're so critical!

2. As your partner criticizes you, answer with the appropriate response from this section. As you do so, try to adopt an attitude of genuinely wanting to understand the criticism and finding parts with which you can sincerely agree.

3. Ask your partner to evaluate your response. Does it follow the forms described in this section? Does it sound sincere?

4. Replay the same scene, trying to improve your response.

---

a job you started, there's no point in denying it. In the same way, if you're honest, you may have to agree with many interpretations of your behavior even when they're not flattering. You do get angry, act foolishly, fail to listen, and behave inconsiderately. After you rid yourself of the myth of perfection, it's much easier to acknowledge these truths.

If many criticisms aimed at you are accurate, why is it so difficult to accept them without being defensive? The answer to this question lies in a confusion between agreeing with the *facts* and accepting the *judgment* that so often accompanies them. Most critics don't merely describe the action that offends them; they also evaluate it, and it's this evaluation that we resist:

"It's silly to be angry."

"You have no reason for being defensive."

"You were wrong to be so sarcastic."

It's evaluations like these that we resent. By realizing that you can agree with—and even learn from—the descriptive part of many criticisms and still not accept the accompanying evaluations, you'll often have a response that is both honest and nondefensive.

Of course, to reduce defensiveness, your agreements with the facts must be honest ones admitted without malice. It's humiliating to accept descriptions that aren't accurate, and manipulatively pretending to accept these leads only to trouble. You can imagine how unproductive the conversation given earlier would have been if the store manager had spoken the same words in a

In REAL LIFE

Responding Nondefensively to Criticism

Defending yourself—even when you're right—isn't always the best approach. This dialogue shows the importance of using self-control and thinking before responding when you are being criticized. The employee realizes that arguing won't change her boss's mind, so she decides to reply as honestly as she can without becoming defensive.

© Jason Harris/Cengage Learning

Boss: How'd things go while I was out?

Employee: Pretty well, except for one thing. Mr. Macintosh—he said you knew him—came in and wanted to buy about $200 worth of stuff. He wanted me to charge him wholesale, and I asked him for his tax resale number, just like you told me. He said he didn't have it, so I told him he'd have to pay retail. He got pretty mad.

Boss: He's a good customer. I hope you gave him the discount.

Employee: *(Beginning to sound defensive)* Well, I didn't. You told me last week that the law said we had to charge full price and sales tax unless the customer had a resale number.

Boss: Oh, my gosh! Didn't Macintosh tell you he had a number?

Employee: *(Becoming more defensive)* He did, but he didn't have it with him. I didn't want to get you mad at me for breaking the law.

Boss: *(Barely concealing her exasperation)* Well, customers don't always have their resale numbers memorized. Macintosh has been coming here for years, and we just fill in his number on the records later.

Employee: *(Deciding to respond nondefensively instead of getting into an argument that she knows she can't win)* I can see why it looks like I gave Mr. Macintosh a hard time. You don't ask him for the number, and I insisted on having it. *(Agrees with the boss's perception)*

Boss: Yes! There's a lot of competition in this business, and we have to keep our customers happy—especially the good ones—or we'll lose them. Macintosh drives across town to do business with us. There are places right near him. If we jerk him around, he'll go there, and we'll lose a good customer.

Employee: That's true. *(Agrees with the fact that it is important to keep customers happy)* And I want to know how to treat customers right. But I'm confused about how to handle people who want a discount and

---

sarcastic tone. Agree with the facts only when you can do so sincerely. Though this won't always be possible, you'll be surprised at how often you can use this simple response.

Agree with the Critic's Perception Agreeing with your critics may be fine when you acknowledge that the criticisms are justified, but how can you agree when they seem to be completely unjustified? You've listened carefully and asked questions to make sure you understand the criticisms, but the more you listen, don't have resale numbers. What should I do? (*Asks what the boss wants*)

Boss: Well, you need to be a little flexible with good customers.

Employee: How should I do that? (*Asks for specifics*)

Boss: Well, it's OK to trust people who are regulars.

Employee: So I don't need to ask regular customers for their resale numbers. I should look them up later? (*Paraphrases to clarify boss's ambiguous directions to "trust" regular customers*)

Boss: That's right. You've got to use your head in business!

Employee: (*Ignores the indirect accusation about not "using her head," recognizing that there's no point in defending herself*) OK, so when regular customers come in, I won't even ask them for their resale numbers … right? (*Paraphrases again to be sure she has the message correct; the employee has no desire to get criticized again about this matter*)

Boss: No, go ahead and ask for the number. If they have it, we won't have to look it up later. But if they don't have the number, just say OK and give them the discount.

Employee: Got it. I only have one question: How can I know who the regular customers are? Should I take their word for it? (*Asks for specifics*)

Boss: Well, you'll get to know most of them after you've been here awhile. But it's OK to trust them until

then. If they say they're regulars, just take their word for it. You've got to trust people sometimes, you know!

Employee: (*Ignores the fact that the boss originally told her not to trust people but rather to insist on getting their number; decides instead to agree with the boss*) I can see how important it is to trust good customers.

Boss: Right.

Employee: Thanks for clearing up how to handle the resale numbers. Is there anything else I ought to know so things will run smoothly when you're not in the store? (*Asks if anything else is wrong*)

Boss: I don't think so. (*Patronizingly*) Don't get discouraged; you'll catch on. It took me twenty years to build this business. Stick with it, and some day you could be running a place like this.

Employee: (*Trying to agree with her boss without sounding sarcastic*) That would be great.

The employee's refusal to act defensively turned what might have been a scolding into a discussion about how to handle a business challenge in the future. The employee might not like the boss's patronizing attitude and contradictory directions, but her communication skill kept the communication climate positive—probably the best possible outcome for this situation.

MindTap APPLY … this situation to your life by answering questions online.

the more positive you are that the critics are totally out of line. Even in these cases there is a way of agreeing—this time not with the critics' conclusions but with their right to see things their way.

A: I don't believe that you've been all the places you were just describing. You're probably just making all this up to impress us.

B: Well, I can see how you might think that. I've known people who lie to get approval.

C: I want to let you know right from the start that I was against hiring you for the job. I think you got it because you're a woman.

D: I can understand why you'd believe that with all the antidiscrimination laws on the books. I hope that after I've been here for awhile, you'll change your mind.

E: I don't think you're being totally honest about your reason for wanting to stay home. You say it's because you have a headache, but I think you're avoiding Mary.

F: I can see why that would make sense to you because Mary and I got into an argument the last time we were together. All I can say is that I do have a headache.

One key to feeling comfortable with acknowledging accurate criticism is to understand that *agreeing* with a critic doesn't necessarily oblige you to *apologize*. Sometimes you aren't responsible for the behavior that your critic finds objectionable, in which case an explanation might be more appropriate than an apology:

> "I know I'm late. There was an accident downtown, and the streets are jammed." *(Spoken in an explanatory, nondefensive tone)*

In other cases, your behavior might be understandable, if not perfect. When this happens, you can acknowledge the validity of the criticism without apologizing:

> "You're right. I *did* lose my temper. I've had to remind you three or four times, and I guess I finally used up all my patience." *(Again, delivered as an explanation, not a defense or counterattack)*

In still other cases, you can acknowledge your critic's right to see things differently than you without backing off from your position.

> "I can understand why you think I'm overreacting. I know this doesn't seem as important to you as it does to me. I hope you can understand why I think this is such a big deal."

Apologizing is fine if you can do so sincerely, but you will be able to agree with critics more often if you understand that doing so doesn't require you to grovel.

Some critics don't seem to deserve the kinds of respectful responses outlined here. They seem more interested in attacking you than explaining themselves. Before you counterattack these hostile critics, ask yourself whether a defensive response will be worth the consequences.

SUMMARY

Every relationship has a communication climate. Positive climates are characterized by confirming messages, which make it clear that the parties value one another. Negative climates are usually disconfirming. In one way or another, messages in disconfirming relationships convey indifference or hostility. Disagreeing messages have some combination of confirmation and disconfirmation. Communication climates develop early in a relationship from both verbal and nonverbal messages. After they are created, reciprocal messages create either positive or negative spirals in which the frequency and intensity of either positive or negative messages are likely to grow.

Defensiveness hinders effective communication. Most defensiveness occurs when people try to protect key parts of a presenting self-image that they believe is under attack. Using the supportive behaviors defined by Jack Gibb when expressing potentially threatening messages can reduce the likelihood of triggering defensive reactions in others. In addition, we can share our thoughts and feelings with others in face-saving ways by using the assertive message format. A complete, clear message describes the behavior in question, at least one interpretation, the speaker's feelings, the consequences of the situation, and the speaker's intentions in making the statement.

When faced with criticism by others, it is possible to respond nondefensively by attempting to understand the criticism and by agreeing with either the facts or the critic's perception.

KEY TERMS

aggressiveness
ambiguous response
argumentativeness
assertive message format
certainty
communication climate
complaining
confirming communication
consequence statement
controlling communication
de-escalatory conflict spiral
defensiveness
description
disagreeing messages
disconfirming communication
empathy
equality
escalatory conflict spiral
evaluation

face-threatening act
feeling statement
Gibb categories
impersonal response
impervious response
incongruous response
intention statement
interpretation statement
interrupting response
irrelevant response
neutrality
problem orientation
provisionalism
spiral
spontaneity
strategy
superiority
tangential response

12

MANAGING INTERPERSONAL CONFLICTS

AFTER STUDYING THE TOPICS IN THIS CHAPTER, YOU SHOULD BE ABLE TO:

1. Identify the conflicts in your important relationships and how satisfied you are with the way they have been handled.

2. Describe your personal conflict styles, evaluate their effectiveness, and suggest alternatives as appropriate.

3. Identify the relational conflict styles, patterns of behavior, and conflict rituals that define a given relationship.

4. Demonstrate how you could use the win–win approach in a given conflict.

*F*or most people, conflict has about the same appeal as a trip to the dentist. A quick look at a thesaurus offers a clue about the distasteful nature of conflict. Synonyms for the term include *battle*, *brawl*, *clash*, *competition*, *discord*, *disharmony*, *duel*, *fight*, *strife*, *struggle*, *trouble*, and *violence*.

Even the metaphors we use to describe our conflicts show that we view conflict as something to be avoided.[1] We often talk about conflict as a kind of war: "He shot down my arguments." "Okay, fire away." "Don't try to defend yourself!" Other metaphors suggest that conflict is explosive: "Don't blow up!" "I needed to let off steam." "You've got a short fuse." Sometimes conflict seems like a kind of trial in which one party accuses another: "Come on, admit you're guilty." "Stop accusing me!" "Just listen to my case." Language suggesting that conflict is a mess is also common: "Let's not open this can of worms." "That's a sticky situation." "Don't make such a stink!" Even the metaphor of a game implies that one side has to defeat the other: "That was out of bounds." "You're not playing fair." "I give up; you win!"

Despite images like these, the truth is that conflict *can* be constructive. With the right set of communication skills, conflict can be less like a struggle and more like a kind of dance in which partners work together to create something that would be impossible without their cooperation. You may have to persuade the other person to become your partner rather than your adversary, and you may be clumsy at first, but with enough practice and goodwill, you can work together instead of at cross-purposes.

The attitude you bring to your conflicts can make a tremendous difference between success and failure. One study revealed that college students in close romantic relationships who believed that conflicts are destructive were most likely to neglect or quit the relationship and less likely to seek a solution than couples who had less-negative attitudes.[2] Of course, attitudes alone won't always guarantee satisfying solutions to conflicts—but the kinds of skills you will learn in this chapter can help well-intentioned partners handle their disagreements constructively.

THE NATURE OF CONFLICT

Before focusing on how to solve interpersonal problems constructively, we need to look briefly at the nature of conflict. What is it? Why is it an inevitable part of life? How can it be beneficial?

Conflict Defined

Before reading further, make a list of the interpersonal conflicts in your life. They probably involve many different people, revolve around very different subjects, and take many different forms. Some become loud, angry arguments. Others may be expressed in calm, rational discussions. Still others might simmer along most of the time with brief but bitter flare-ups.

Whatever form they may take, all interpersonal conflicts share certain characteristics. William Wilmot and Joyce Hocker provide a thorough definition when they define **conflict** as "an expressed struggle between at least two interdependent parties who perceive incompatible goals, scarce resources, and interference from the other party in achieving their goals."[3] A closer look at the key parts of this definition will help you recognize how conflict operates in your life.

Expressed Struggle A conflict can exist only when both parties are aware of a disagreement. For instance, you may be upset for months because a neighbor's loud stereo keeps you awake at night, but no conflict exists between the two of you until the neighbor learns of your problem. Of course, the expressed struggle doesn't have to be verbal. A dirty look, the silent treatment, and avoiding the other person are all ways of expressing yourself. One way or another, both parties must know that a problem exists before they're in conflict.

∧ In *The Hunger Games* trilogy, Katniss Everdeen (Jennifer Lawrence) faces conflicts with life-or-death consequences. Even when resources are scarce and goals seem incompatible, she learns that interdependence and collaboration are keys to survival. What lessons for managing interpersonal conflict can you learn from stories like these?

Perceived Incompatible Goals All conflicts look as if one party's gain would be another's loss. For instance, consider the neighbor whose stereo keeps you awake at night. Doesn't somebody have to lose? If the neighbor turns down the noise, she loses the enjoyment of hearing the music at full volume, but if the neighbor keeps the volume up, you're still awake and unhappy.

The goals in this situation really aren't completely incompatible; there are solutions that allow both parties to get what they want. For instance, you could achieve peace and quiet by closing your windows or getting the neighbor to close hers. You might use a pair of earplugs, or perhaps the neighbor could get a set of earphones, allowing the music to be played at full volume without bothering anyone. If any of these solutions prove workable, then the conflict disappears. Unfortunately, people often fail to see mutually satisfying solutions to their problems. As long as they *perceive* their goals to be mutually exclusive, a conflict exists.

Perceived Scarce Resources Conflicts also exist when people believe there isn't enough of something to go around. The most obvious example of a scarce resource is money—a cause of many conflicts. If a worker asks for a raise in pay and the boss would rather keep the money or use it to expand the business, then the two parties are in conflict.

Time is another scarce commodity. Many people struggle to meet the competing demands of school, work, family, and friends. "If there were only more hours in a day" is a common refrain, and making time for the people in your life—and for yourself—is a constant source of conflict.

Interdependence However antagonistic they might feel, the parties in conflict are usually dependent on each other. The welfare and satisfaction of one depend on the actions of another. If not, then even in the face of scarce resources and incompatible goals, there would be no need for conflict. Interdependence exists between conflicting nations, social groups, organizations, friends, and lovers. In each case, if the two parties didn't need each other to solve the problem, they would go their separate ways. One of the first steps toward resolving a conflict is to take the attitude that "we're all in this together."

Interference from the Other Party   No matter how much one person's position may differ from another's, a full-fledged conflict won't occur until the participants act in ways that prevent one another from reaching their goals. For example, you might let some friends know that you object to their driving after drinking alcohol, but the conflict won't escalate until you act in ways that prevent them from getting behind the wheel. Likewise, a parent–child dispute about what clothing and music are appropriate will blossom into a conflict when the parents try to impose their position on the child.

Conflict Is Natural

Every relationship of any depth at all has conflict.[4] No matter how close, how understanding, how compatible you and other people are, there will be times when your ideas or actions or needs or goals won't match. You like rap music, but your companion likes classical; you want to date other people, but your partner wants to keep the relationship exclusive; you think a paper that you've written is fine, but your instructor wants it changed; you like to sleep late on Sunday mornings, but your housemate likes to get up early and exercise loudly. There's no end to the number and kinds of disagreements possible.

College students who have kept diaries of their relationships report that they take part in about seven arguments per week. Most have argued with the other person before, often about the same topic.[5] In another survey, 81 percent of the respondents acknowledged that they had conflicts with friends.[6] Even the 19 percent who claimed that their friendships were conflict free used phrases such as "push and pull" and "little disagreements" to describe the tensions that inevitably occurred. Among families, conflict can be even more frequent. Researchers recorded dinner conversations for fifty-two families and found an average of 3.3 "conflict episodes" per meal.[7]

At first this might seem depressing. If problems are inevitable in even the best relationships, does this mean that you're doomed to relive the same arguments, the same hurt feelings, over and over? Fortunately, the answer to this question is a definite "no." Even though conflict is part of a meaningful relationship, you can change the way you deal with it.

Conflict Can Be Beneficial

Because it is impossible to avoid conflicts, the challenge is to handle them well when they do arise. Effective communication during conflicts can actually keep good relationships strong. People who use the constructive skills described in this chapter are more satisfied with their relationships[8] and with the outcomes of their conflicts.[9]

Perhaps the best evidence of how constructive conflict skills can benefit a relationship focuses on communication between husbands and wives. More than twenty years of research shows that couples in both happy and unhappy marriages have conflicts, but that they manage conflict in very different ways.[10] One nine-year study revealed that unhappy couples argue in ways that we have catalogued in this book as destructive.[11] They are more concerned with defending themselves than with being problem oriented; they fail to listen carefully to each other, have little or no empathy for their partners, use evaluative "you" language, and ignore each other's nonverbal relational messages.

Many satisfied couples think and communicate differently when they disagree. They view disagreements as healthy and recognize that conflicts need to be faced.[12] Although they may argue vigorously, they use skills such as perception checking to find out what the other person is thinking, and they let each other know that they understand the other side of the argument.[13] They are willing to admit their mistakes, which contributes not only to a harmonious relationship but also to solving the problem at hand.

We'll review communication skills that can make conflicts constructive and introduce still more skills that you can use to resolve the inevitable conflicts you face. Before doing so, however, we need to examine how individuals behave when faced with a dispute.

CONFLICT STYLES

Most people have default styles of handling conflict. (See Figure 12.1.) These habitual styles work sometimes, but they may not be effective in all situations. What styles do you typically use to deal with conflict? Find out by thinking about how two hypothetical characters—Paul and Lucia—manage a problem.

◄ FIGURE 12.1
Conflict Styles

Paul and Lucia have been running partners for more than a year. Three times every week, they spend an hour or more together working out. The two runners are equally matched, and they enjoy challenging one another to cover longer distances at a quicker pace. During their time on the road, the friends have grown quite close. Now they often talk about personal matters that they don't share with anyone else.

Recently, Lucia has started to invite some of her friends along on the runs. Paul likes Lucia's friends, but they aren't strong athletes, so the outings become a much less-satisfying workout. Also, Paul fears losing the special one-on-one time that he and Lucia have had. Paul shared his concerns with Lucia, but she dismissed them. "I don't see what the problem is," she replied. "We still get plenty of time on the road, and you said you like my friends." "But it isn't the same," replied Paul.

This situation has all the elements of a conflict: expressed struggle (their differences are in the open, and they still disagree), seemingly incompatible goals and interference (Lucia wants to run with her friends; Paul wants to run with just Lucia), apparently scarce resources (they only have so much time for running), and interdependence (they enjoy one another's company and run better together than separately).

Here are five ways Paul and Lucia could handle the matter. Each represents a particular approach to managing conflict:

- They could say "Let's just forget it" and stop running together.

- Paul could give in, sacrificing his desire for one-on-one conversations and challenging runs. Or Lucia could give in, sacrificing her other friendships to maintain her friendship with Paul.

- One or the other could issue an ultimatum: "Either we do it my way, or we stop running together."

- They could compromise, inviting friends along on some runs but excluding them on other days.

- Lucia and Paul could brainstorm ways they could run with her friends and still get their workouts and one-on-one time with each other.

These approaches represent the five styles depicted in Figure 12.1, each of which is described in the following paragraphs.

Avoiding (Lose–Lose)

Avoiding occurs when people nonassertively ignore or stay away from conflict. Avoidance can be physical (steering clear of a friend after having an argument) or conversational (changing the topic, joking, or denying that a problem exists). It can be tempting to avoid conflict, but research suggests that this approach has its costs: Partners of *self-silencers* report more frustration and discomfort when dealing with the avoiding partner than with those who face conflict more constructively.[14]

Avoidance reflects a pessimistic attitude about conflict under the belief that there is no good way to resolve the issue at hand. Some avoiders believe it's easier to put up with the status quo than to face the problem head-on and try to solve it. Other avoiders believe it's better to quit (on either the topic or the relationship) than to keep facing the same issues without hope of solution. In either case, avoiding often results in *lose–lose* outcomes in which no party gets what it wants.

In the case of Paul and Lucia, avoiding means that, rather than struggling with their disagreement, they just stop running together. Although it means they'll no longer be fighting, it also means they'll both lose a running partner and an important component of their friendship (and maybe their friendship altogether). This solution illustrates how avoiding can produce lose–lose results.

Phildate/BigStock

Although avoiding may keep the peace temporarily, it typically leads to unsatisfying relationships.[15] Chronic misunderstandings, resentments, and disappointments pile up and contaminate the emotional climate. For this reason, we can say that avoiders have a low concern both for their own needs and for the interests of the other person, who is also likely to suffer from unaddressed issues (see Figure 12.1).

Despite its obvious shortcomings, avoiding isn't always a bad idea.[16] You might choose to avoid certain topics or situations if the risk of speaking up is too great, such as triggering an embarrassing fight in public or even risking physical harm. You might also avoid a conflict if the relationship it involves isn't worth the effort. Even in close relationships, though, avoidance has its logic. If the issue is temporary or minor, then you might let it pass. These reasons help explain why the communication of many happily married couples is characterized by "selectively ignoring" the other person's minor flaws.[17] This doesn't mean that a key to successful relationships is avoiding *all* conflicts. Instead, it suggests that it's smart to save energy for the truly important ones.

Accommodating (Lose–Win)

Accommodating occurs when you allow others to have their way rather than asserting your own point of view. Figure 12.1 depicts accommodators as having low concern for themselves and high concern for others, which results in *lose–win*, "we'll do it your way" outcomes. In our hypothetical scenario, Paul could accommodate Lucia by letting her friends join in on their runs, even though it means less of a physical challenge and quality time with Lucia—or Lucia could accommodate Paul by running with just him.

The motivation of an accommodator plays a significant role in this style's effectiveness. If accommodation is a genuine act of kindness, generosity, or love, then chances are good that it will enhance the relationship. Most people appreciate those who "take one for the team," "treat others as they want to be treated," or "lose the battle to win the war." However, people are far less appreciative of those who habitually use this style to play the role of "martyr, bitter complainer, whiner, or saboteur."[18]

On the JOB

Picking Your Workplace Battles

Conflicts are a fact of life, even in the best job. Issues are bound to arise with your boss, coworkers, subordinates, and people outside the organization. Your career success and peace of mind will depend on when and how you deal with those conflicts—and when you choose to keep quiet.

Deciding when to speak up is the first step in managing conflicts successfully. Staying silent about important issues can damage your career and leave you feeling like a doormat. But asserting yourself too often or in the wrong way can earn you a reputation as a whiner or hothead.

Management consultants offer guidelines to help you choose when to speak up and when to let go of an issue.[a]

Consider a retreat when

- The issue isn't important to your organization or your ability to work.

- You can't offer a constructive approach to a solution.

- The issue is outside your area of responsibility.

- The others involved are much more powerful than you.

Before speaking up, be prepared to

1. Test support for your position informally with trusted colleagues.

2. Speak with the person who has the power to do something about the problem.

3. Describe the problem clearly and objectively.

4. Control your emotions during discussions.

5. Be prepared to deal with criticisms that may be directed back at you.

We should pause here to mention the important role that culture plays in perceptions of conflict styles. People from high-context, collectivist backgrounds (such as many Asian cultures) are likely to regard avoidance and accommodation as face-saving and noble ways to handle conflict.[19] In low-context, individualist cultures (such as the United States), avoidance and accommodation are often viewed less positively. For instance, think of the many unflattering terms that Americans use for people who give up or give in during conflicts ("pushover," "yes-man," "doormat," "spineless"). As you will read later in this chapter, collectivist cultures have virtuous words and phrases to describe these same traits. The point here is that all conflict styles have value in certain situations and that culture plays a significant role in determining how each style is valued.

Competing (Win–Lose)

The flip side of accommodating is **competing**. This *win–lose* approach to conflict involves high concern for self and low concern for others. As Figure 12.1 shows, competition seeks to resolve conflicts "my way." If Lucia and Paul each tried to force the other to concede, one of them might prevail, but at the other's expense.

People resort to competing when they perceive a situation as being an either–or one: Either I get what I want, or you get what you want. The most clear-cut examples of win–lose situations are certain games such as baseball or poker in which the rules require a winner and a loser. Some interpersonal issues seem to fit into this win–lose framework: two coworkers seeking a promotion to the same job, or a couple who disagree on how to spend their limited money.

There are cases when competing can enhance a relationship. One study revealed that some men and women in satisfying dating relationships use competition to enrich their interaction.[20] For example, some found satisfaction by competing in play (who's the better racquetball player?), in achievement (who gets the better job offer?), and in altruism (who's more romantic?). These satisfied couples developed a shared narrative (see Chapter 4) that defined competition as a measure of regard, quite different from conflict that signaled a lack of appreciation and respect. Of course, it's easy to see how these arrangements could backfire if one partner became a gloating winner or a sore loser. Feeling like you've been defeated can leave you wanting to get even, creating a downward competitive spiral that degrades to a *lose–lose* relationship.[21]

Power is the distinguishing characteristic in win–lose problem solving because it is necessary to defeat an opponent to get what one wants. The most obvious kind of power is physical. Some parents threaten their children with warnings such as "Stop misbehaving or I'll send you to your room." Adults who use physical power to deal with each other usually aren't so blunt, but the legal system is the implied threat: "Follow the rules or we'll lock you up."

Real or implied force isn't the only kind of power used in conflicts. People who rely on authority of many types engage in win–lose methods without ever threatening physical coercion. In most jobs, supervisors have the authority to assign working hours, job promotions, and desirable or undesirable tasks—and, of course, to fire an unsatisfactory employee. Teachers can use the power of grades to coerce students to act in desired ways. Even the usually admired democratic system of majority rule is a win–lose method of resolving conflicts. However fair it may seem, with this system one group is satisfied and the other is defeated.

The dark side of competition is that it often breeds aggression.[22] Sometimes aggression is obvious, but at other times it can be more subtle. To understand how, read on.

Direct Aggression **Direct aggression** occurs when a communicator expresses a criticism or demand that threatens the face of the person at whom it is directed. Communication researcher Dominic Infante identified several types of direct aggression: character attacks, competence attacks, physical appearance attacks, maledictions (wishing the other ill fortune), teasing, ridicule, threats, swearing, and nonverbal emblems.[23]

Direct aggression can severely affect the target. Recipients can feel embarrassed, inadequate, humiliated, hopeless, desperate, or depressed.[24] These results can lead to decreased effectiveness in personal relationships, on the job, and in families.[25] There is a significant connection between verbal aggression and physical aggression,[26] but even if the attacks never lead to blows, the psychological effects can be devastating. For example, siblings who were teased by a brother or sister report less satisfaction and trust than those whose relationships were relatively free of this sort of aggression,[27] and high school teams with aggressive coaches lose more games than those whose coaches are less aggressive.[28]

Passive Aggression   **Passive aggression** occurs when a communicator expresses hostility in an obscure or manipulative way. As the Ethical Challenge in this section explains, this behavior has been termed **crazymaking**. It occurs when people have feelings of resentment, anger, or rage that they are unable or unwilling to express directly. Instead of keeping these feelings to themselves, a crazymaker sends aggressive messages in subtle, indirect ways, thus maintaining the front of kindness. This amiable façade eventually crumbles, leaving the crazymaker's victim confused and angry at having been fooled. The targets of the crazymaker can either react with aggressive behavior of their own or retreat to nurse their hurt feelings. In either case, passive aggression seldom has anything but harmful effects on a relationship.[29] In our scenario, Lucia could take a passive-aggressive approach to Paul's desire to keep their workouts exclusive by showing up late to run just to annoy him. Paul could become passive aggressive by agreeing to include Lucia's friends, then pouring on the speed and leaving them behind.

Compromising (Partial Lose–Lose)

Compromising gives both people at least some of what they want, although both sacrifice part of their goals. People usually settle for a compromise when it seems that partial satisfaction is the best they can hope for. In the case of Paul and Lucia, they could strike a deal by alternating workouts with and without her friends. Unlike avoidance, where both parties lose because they don't address their problem, compromisers actually negotiate a solution that gives them some of what they want, but it also leaves everybody losing something.

Compromise may be better than losing everything, but there are times when this approach hardly seems ideal. One observer has asked why it is that if someone says, "I will compromise my values," we view the action unfavorably, yet we have favorable views of parties in a conflict who compromise to reach a solution.[30] Although compromises may be the best obtainable result in some conflicts, it's important to realize that both people in a conflict can often work together to find much better solutions. In such cases, *compromise* is a negative word.

Most of us are surrounded by the results of bad compromises. Consider a common example: the conflict between one person's desire to smoke cigarettes and another's need for clean air. The win–lose outcomes of this issue are obvious: Either the smoker abstains, or the nonsmoker gets polluted lungs—neither option is very satisfying. But a compromise in which the smoker gets to enjoy only a rare cigarette or must retreat outdoors and in which the nonsmoker still must inhale some fumes or feel like an ogre is hardly better. Both sides have lost a considerable amount of both comfort and goodwill. Of course, the costs involved in other compromises are even greater. For example, if a divorced couple compromises on child care by haggling over custody and then grudgingly agrees to split the time with their children, it's hard to say that anybody has won.

Some compromises do leave both parties satisfied. You and the seller might settle on a price for a used car that is between what the seller was asking and what you wanted to pay. Although neither of you got everything you wanted, the outcome would still leave both of you satisfied. Likewise, you and your companion might agree to see a film that is the second choice for both of you in order to spend an evening together. As long as everyone

ETHICAL *Challenge*

Dirty Fighting with Crazymakers

Psychologist George Bach uses the term *crazymakers* to describe passive-aggressive behavior. His term reflects the insidious nature of indirect aggression, which can confuse and anger a victim who may not even be aware of being victimized. Although a case can be made for using all of the other approaches to conflict described in this chapter, it is difficult to find a justification for passive-aggressive crazymaking.

The following categories represent a nonexhaustive list of crazymaking. They are presented here as a warning for potential victims, who might choose to use perception checking, "I" language, assertion, or other communication strategies to explore whether the user has a complaint that can be addressed in a more constructive manner.

The Avoider. Avoiders refuse to fight. When a conflict arises, they leave, fall asleep, pretend to be busy at work, or keep from facing the problem in some other way. Because avoiders won't fight back, this strategy can frustrate the person who wants to address an issue.

The Pseudoaccommodator. Pseudoaccommodators pretend to give in and then continue to act in the same way.

The Guiltmaker. Instead of expressing dissatisfaction directly, guiltmakers try to make others feel responsible for causing pain. A guiltmaker's favorite line is "It's okay; don't worry about me ..." accompanied by a big sigh.

The Mind Reader. Instead of allowing their partners to express feelings honestly, mind readers go into character analysis, explaining what the partner really means or what's wrong with the partner. By behaving this way, mind readers refuse to handle their own feelings and leave no room for their partners to express themselves.

The Trapper. Trappers play an especially dirty trick by setting up a desired behavior for their partners and then, when it's met, attacking the very behavior they requested. An example of this technique is for the trapper to say, "Let's be totally honest with each other" and then attack the partner's self-disclosure.

The Crisis Tickler. Crisis ticklers almost bring what's bothering them to the surface but never quite come out and express themselves. Instead of admitting concern about the finances, they innocently ask, "Gee, how much did that cost?," dropping a rather obvious hint but never really dealing with the crisis.

The Gunnysacker. These people don't share complaints as they arise. Instead, they put their resentments into a psychological gunnysack, which bulges after awhile with both large and small gripes. Then, when the sack is about to burst, the gunnysacker pours out all the pent-up aggressions on the overwhelmed and unsuspecting victim.

The Trivial Tyrannizer. Instead of honestly sharing their resentments, trivial tyrannizers do things they know will get their partners' goat—leaving dirty dishes in the sink, clipping fingernails in bed, belching out loud, turning up the television too loud, and so on.

The Beltliner. Everyone has a psychological "beltline," and below it are subjects too sensitive to be approached without damaging the relationship. Beltlines may have to do with physical characteristics, intelligence, past behavior, or deeply ingrained personality traits that a person is trying to overcome. In an attempt to "get even" or hurt their partners, beltliners will use intimate knowledge to hit below the belt, knowing it will hurt.

The Joker. Because they are afraid to face conflicts squarely, jokers kid around when their partners want to be serious, thus blocking the expression of important feelings.

The Withholder. Instead of expressing their anger honestly and directly, withholders punish their partners by keeping back something—courtesy, affection, good cooking, humor, sex. As you can imagine, this is likely to build up even greater resentments in the relationship.

The Benedict Arnold. These characters get back at their partners by sabotage, by failing to defend them from attackers, and even by encouraging ridicule or disregard from outside the relationship.

SOFTWARE TACKLES ROOMMATE CONFLICTS

Roompact, a Chicago start-up, hopes that its digital tools will tackle college-roommate conflicts. The company has developed an online, customizable roommate agreement for incoming students, according to Matt Unger, chief executive. Using the site, roommates can agree on parameters for room cleanliness, when the lights go out, expectations for inviting guests, and other issues.

The Roompact system also sends each student a weekly or bi-weekly text message asking for a roommate-relationship rating—what the company calls "micro-surveys." Students may also respond to the text message with more detailed complaints, which would trigger suggestions by Roompact.

Shawn McQuillan, associate director of residential life at University of Hartford, thinks Roompact's notification system will benefit the university in dealing with disagreements between students who do not seek out help from staff members.

"[Students] either ignore the problem, think it will go away or live with it. Often when they do this, they let it build up until it has a negative impact on their overall experience and student success," he says. "Our hope is with the micro-surveys we can take an even more proactive approach to resolving roommate disputes, especially among those students who struggle with coming to a staff member for help."

McQuillan also believes Roompact's online system will appeal to Millennials. "In this day and age, our students are beyond a doubt tech savvy," he says. "They want to have more resources available to them electronically and in many cases are more likely to complete something that is online and that can be accessed by a click of a button."

Karen Erlandson, professor of communication studies at Albion College, developed Roompact's student-diagnostic survey. "The diagnostic improves communication," she says. "Roompact's system helps students identify areas of conflict that are specific to them and urges them to include these potential 'hot spots' in their roommate contract."

"One component of the Roompact system is to provide students with methods to constructively confront and solve conflict when it first occurs," Erlandson says. "When potential problems are detected by Roompact, students are provided a set of guidelines for initiating and engaging in productive, rational conflict."

Echoing Erlandson, Unger says that Roompact is not meant to encourage students to replace real dialogue with a technology-based solution. "We try to use technology to help students to learn how to interact face-to-face and interact with people who are not like them," he says.

Jonathan Swartz

MindTap' **Enhance ...** your understanding by answering the following questions, either here or online.

1. Identify pros and cons of the approach described in this reading. In what ways do you think this technology could help or hurt conflict management between roommates?

2. Describe the conflict management principles you could adopt from this program, even if you didn't use the software.

is satisfied with an outcome, compromise can be an effective way to resolve conflicts. When compromises are satisfying and successful, it might be more accurate to categorize them as the final style we'll discuss: collaborating.

Collaborating (Win–Win)

Collaborating seeks *win–win* solutions to conflict. Collaborators show a high degree of concern for both themselves and others. Rather than trying to solve problems "my way" or "your way," their focus is on "our way." In the best case, collaborating can lead to a win–win outcome: Everybody gets what they want.

If Lucia and Paul were to collaborate, they might determine that the best way for both of them to get what they want is to continue their one-on-one workouts but invite Lucia's friends to join in for a few miles at the end of each run. They might schedule other, less-challenging workouts that include the friends. Or they might find other ways to get together with Lucia's friends that are fun for both of them.

The goal of collaboration is to find a solution that satisfies the needs of everyone involved. Not only do the partners avoid trying to win at the other's expense, but they also believe that by working together it is possible to find a solution that goes beyond a mere compromise and allows all parties to reach their goals. Consider a few examples.

- A newly married husband and wife find themselves arguing frequently over their budget. The husband enjoys buying impractical and enjoyable items for himself and for the house, whereas the wife fears that such purchases will ruin their carefully constructed budget. Their solution is to set aside a small amount of money each month for "fun purchases." The amount is small enough to be affordable yet gives the husband a chance to escape from their spartan lifestyle. The wife is satisfied with the arrangement because the luxury money is now a budget category by itself, which gets rid of the out-of-control feeling that comes when her husband makes unexpected purchases. The plan works so well that the couple continues to use it even after their income rises, increasing the amount devoted to luxuries.

- Marta, a store manager, hates the task of rescheduling employee work shifts to accommodate their social and family needs. She and her staff develop an arrangement in which employees arrange schedule-swaps on their own and notify her in writing after they are made.

- Wendy and Kathy are roommates who have different study habits. Wendy likes to do her work in the evenings, which leaves her days free for other things, but Kathy feels that nighttime is party time. The solution they worked out is that Monday through Wednesday evenings Wendy studies at her boyfriend's place while Kathy does anything she wants; Thursday through Sunday, Kathy agrees to keep things quiet around the house.

The point here isn't that these solutions are the correct ones for everybody with similar problems. The win–win method doesn't work that way. Different people might have found other solutions that suit them better. Collaboration gives you a way of creatively finding just the right answer for your unique problem—and that answer might be one that neither party thought of or expected before collaborating. By generating win–win solutions, you can create a way of resolving your conflicts that everyone can live with comfortably. Later in this chapter, you'll learn a specific process for arriving at collaborative solutions to problems.

Which Style to Use?

Collaborating might seem like the ideal approach to solving problems, but it's an oversimplification to imagine that there is a single "best" way.[31] Generally speaking, win–win approaches are preferable to win–lose and lose–lose solutions. But we've already seen that there are times when avoiding, accommodating, competing, and compromising are appropriate. Table 12.1 lists some of the issues to consider when deciding which style to use when facing a conflict. As you decide which approach to use, consider the following factors.

1. **The relationship.** When someone else clearly has more power than you, accommodating may be the best approach. If the boss tells you to fill that order "Now!," it may be smart to do so without comment. A more assertive response ("I'm still tied up with the job you gave me yesterday") might be reasonable, but it could also cost you your job.

TABLE 12.1 Factors to Consider When Choosing the Most Appropriate Conflict Style

AVOIDING (LOSE–LOSE)	ACCOMMODATING (LOSE–WIN)	COMPETING (WIN–LOSE)	COMPROMISING (PARTIAL LOSE–LOSE)	COLLABORATING (WIN–WIN)
When the issue is of little importance	When you discover you are wrong	When there is not enough time to seek a win–win outcome	To achieve quick, temporary solutions to complex problems	When the issue is too important for a compromise
When the costs of confrontation outweigh the benefits	When the issue is more important to the other person than it is to you	When the issue is not important enough to negotiate at length	When opponents are strongly committed to mutually exclusive goals	When a long-term relationship between you and the other person is important
To cool down and gain perspective	When the long-term cost of winning isn't worth the short-term gain	When the other person is not willing to cooperate	When the issues are moderately important but not enough for a stalemate	To merge insights with someone who has a different perspective on the problem
	To build up credits for later conflicts	When you are convinced that your position is right and necessary	As a backup mode when collaboration doesn't work	To develop a relationship by showing commitment to the concerns of both parties
	To let others learn by making their own mistakes	To protect yourself against a person who takes advantage of noncompetitive people	To come up with creative and unique solutions to problems	

2. **The situation**. Different situations call for different conflict styles. After haggling over the price of a car for hours, it might be best to compromise by simply splitting the difference. In other cases, though, it may be a matter of principle for you to "stick to your guns" and attempt to get what you believe is right.

3. **The other person.** Win–win is a fine ideal, but sometimes the other person isn't willing or able to collaborate. You probably know communicators who are so competitive that they put winning on even minor issues ahead of the well-being of your relationship. In such cases, your efforts to collaborate may have a low chance of success.

4. **Your goals.** Sometimes your overriding concern may be to calm down an enraged or upset person. Accommodating an outburst from your crotchety and sick neighbor, for example, is probably better than standing up for yourself and triggering a stroke. In still other cases, your moral principles might compel an aggressive statement even though it might not get you what you originally sought: "I've had enough of your racist jokes. I've tried to explain why they're so offensive, but you obviously haven't listened. I'm leaving!"

MindTap PRACTICE... your understanding of conflict styles by completing the Concepts in Play activity online.

CONFLICT IN RELATIONAL SYSTEMS

So far we have focused on individual conflict styles. Even though the style you choose in a conflict is important, your style isn't the only factor that will determine how a conflict unfolds. In reality, conflict is relational: Its character usually is determined by the way the parties interact with each other.[32] You might, for example, be determined to handle a conflict with your neighbor assertively only to be driven to aggression by his uncooperative nature—or even to avoidance by his physical threats. Likewise, you might plan to hint to a professor that you are bothered by her apparent indifference but wind up discussing the matter in an open, assertive way in reaction to her constructive response.

Examples like these suggest that conflict doesn't depend on just individual choice. Rather, it depends on how the partners interact. When two or more people are in a long-term relationship, they develop their own **relational conflict style**—a pattern of managing disagreements. The mutual influence that parties have on each other is so powerful that it can overcome the disposition to handle conflicts in the manner that comes most easily to one or the other.[33] As we will soon see, some relational conflict styles are constructive, whereas others can make life miserable and threaten relationships.

Complementary, Symmetrical, and Parallel Styles

Partners in interpersonal relationships—and impersonal ones, too—can use one of three styles to manage their conflicts. In relationships with **a complementary conflict style**, the partners use different but mutually reinforcing behaviors. In a **symmetrical conflict style**, both partners use the same behaviors. In a **parallel conflict style**, both partners shift between complementary and symmetrical patterns from one issue to another. Table 12.2 illustrates how the same conflict can unfold in very different ways, depending on whether the partners' communication is symmetrical or complementary. A parallel style would alternate between these two patterns, depending on the situation.

Research shows that a complementary *fight–flight* style is common in many unhappy marriages. One partner—most commonly the wife—addresses the conflict directly, whereas the other—usually the husband—withdraws.[34] It's easy to see how this pattern can lead to a cycle of increasing hostility and isolation because each partner punctuates the conflict differently, blaming the other for making matters worse. "I withdraw because she's so critical," a husband might say. The wife wouldn't organize the sequence in the same way, however. "I criticize because he withdraws" would be her perception.

Complementary styles aren't the only ones that can lead to problems. Some distressed marriages suffer from destructively symmetrical communication. If both partners treat each other with matching hostility, one threat or insult leads to another in an escalatory spiral. If the partners both withdraw from each other instead of facing their problems, a de-escalatory spiral results in which the satisfaction and vitality ebb from the relationship, leaving it a shell of its former self.

As Table 12.2 shows, complementary and symmetrical behaviors can produce both "good" and "bad" results. If the complementary behaviors are positive, then a positive spiral results and the conflict stands a good chance of being resolved. This is the case in Example 2 in Table 12.2, where the boss is open to hearing the employee's concerns, listening willingly as the employee talks. Here, a complementary talk–listen pattern works well.

TABLE 12.2 Complementary and Symmetrical Conflict Styles

SITUATION	COMPLEMENTARY STYLES	SYMMETRICAL STYLES
Example 1: Wife is upset because husband is spending little time at home.	Wife complains. Husband withdraws, spending even less time at home. *(Destructive)*	Wife complains. Husband responds angrily and defensively. *(Destructive)*
Example 2: Female employee is offended when a male boss calls her "sweetie."	Employee objects to boss, explaining her reasons for being offended. Boss apologizes for his unintentional insult. *(Constructive)*	Employee maliciously "jokes" about boss at company party. *(Destructive)*
Example 3: Parents are uncomfortable with teenager's new friends.	Parents express concerns. Teen dismisses them, saying "There's nothing to worry about." *(Destructive)*	Teen expresses discomfort with parents' protectiveness. Parents and teen negotiate a mutually agreeable solution. *(Constructive)*

PAUSE *and* REFLECT

Understanding Conflict Styles

MindTap® REFLECT ... on conflict styles by answering the following questions, either here or online.

You can gain a clearer idea of how conflict styles differ by completing the following exercise.

1. Join a partner and choose one of the following conflicts to work on. If you prefer, you may substitute a conflict of your own.

   a. Roommates disagree about the noise level in their apartment.

   b. Parents want their college sophomore son or daughter to stay home for the winter vacation. The son or daughter wants to travel with friends.

   c. One person in a couple wants to spend free time socializing with friends. The other wants to stay at home together.

2. Role play the conflict four times, reflecting each of the following styles:

   a. Complementary (constructive)

   b. Complementary (destructive)

   c. Symmetrical (constructive)

   d. Symmetrical (destructive)

3. After experiencing each style with your partner, reflect on which of the conflict styles characterizes the way conflict is managed in one of your interpersonal relationships. Are you satisfied with this approach? If not, describe what style would be more appropriate.

Symmetrical styles can also be beneficial. The clearest example of constructive symmetry occurs when both parties communicate assertively, listening to each other's concerns and working together to resolve them. The potential for this sort of solution occurs in Example 3, in the parent–teenager conflict. With enough mutual respect and careful listening, both the parents and their teenager can understand one another's concerns and very possibly find a way to give both parties what they want.

Destructive Conflict Patterns: The Four Horsemen

Some conflict styles are so destructive that they are almost guaranteed to wreak havoc on relationships. These toxic forms of communication include what John Gottman calls "The Four Horsemen of the Apocalypse."[35]

Gottman has gathered decades of data about newlywed couples and their communication patterns. By observing their interactions, he has been able to predict with more than 90 percent accuracy whether the newlyweds will end up divorcing. Here are the four destructive signs he looks for:

1. **Criticism**. These are attacks on a person's character. As you read in Chapters 6 and 11, there's a significant difference between legitimate complaints about behavior phrased in descriptive "I" language ("I wish you had been on time—we're going to be late to the movie") and critical character assaults stated as evaluative "you" messages ("You're so thoughtless—you never think of anyone but yourself").

2. **Defensiveness**. As Chapter 11 explained, defensiveness is a reaction that aims to protect one's presenting self by denying responsibility ("You're crazy—I never do that") and counterattacking ("You're worse about that than I am"). Although some self-protection is understandable, problems arise when a person refuses to listen to or even acknowledge another's concerns.

3. **Contempt**. A contemptuous comment belittles and demeans. It can take the form of name-calling putdowns ("You're a real jerk") or sarcastic barbs ("Oh, *that* was brilliant"). Contempt can also be communicated nonverbally through dramatic eye rolls or disgusted sighs. (Try doing both of those at the same time and imagine how dismissive they can be.)

4. **Stonewalling**. Stonewalling occurs when one person in a relationship withdraws from the interaction, shutting down dialogue—and any chance of resolving the problem in a mutually satisfactory way. It sends a disconfirming "You don't matter" message to the other person.

Here's a brief exchange illustrating how the "four horsemen" can lead to a destructive spiral of aggression:

"You overdrew our account again—can't you do *anything* right?" *(Criticism)*

"Hey, don't blame me—you're the one who spends most of the money." *(Defensiveness)*

"At least I have better math skills than a first grader. Way to go, Einstein." *(Contempt)*

"Whatever." *(said while walking out of the room) (Stonewalling)*

It's easy to see how this kind of communication can be destructive in any relationship, not just a marriage. It's also easy to see how these kinds of comments can feed off each other and develop into destructive conflict rituals, as we'll discuss now.

Conflict Rituals

When people have been in a relationship for some time, their communication often develops into **conflict rituals**—usually unacknowledged but very real patterns of interlocking behavior.[36] Consider the following common rituals.

- A young child interrupts her parents, demanding to be included in their conversation. At first the parents tell the child to wait, but she whines and cries until the parents find it easier to listen than to ignore the fussing.

- A couple fights. One partner leaves. The other accepts the blame for the problem and begs forgiveness. The first partner returns, and a happy reunion takes place. Soon they fight again.

- A boss flies into rage when the pressure builds at work. Recognizing this, the employees avoid him as much as possible. When the crisis is over, the boss compensates for his outbursts by being especially receptive to employee requests.

- Roommates have a blowout over housekeeping responsibilities. One roommate gives the other the "silent treatment" for several days, then begins picking up around the house without admitting being wrong.

There's nothing inherently wrong with the interaction in many rituals, especially when everybody involved accepts them as ways of managing conflict.[37] Consider the preceding examples. In the first, the little girl's whining may be the only way she can get the parents' attention. In the second, both partners might use the fighting as a way to blow off steam, and both might find that the joy of a reunion is worth the grief of the separation. In the third, the ritual might work well for the boss (as a way of releasing pressure) and for employees (as a way of getting their requests met). And in the fourth, at least the house gets cleaned—eventually.

Rituals can cause problems, though, when they become the *only* way relational partners handle their conflicts. As you learned in Chapter 1, competent communicators have a large repertoire of behaviors, and they are able to choose the most effective response for a given situation. Relying on one ritual pattern to handle all conflicts is no more effective than using a screwdriver to handle every home repair or putting the same seasoning on every dish you cook. Conflict rituals may be familiar and comfortable, but they aren't always the best way to resolve the various conflicts that are part of any relationship.

"I'm not yelling *at* you, I'm yelling *with* you."

PAUSE *and* REFLECT

Your Conflict Rituals

MindTap® REFLECT ... on your conflict rituals by answering the following questions, either here or online.

Describe two conflict rituals in one of your important relationships. One of your examples should consist of a positive ritual and the other of a negative ritual. For each example, explain:

1. a subject that is likely to trigger the conflict (such as money, leisure time, affection)

2. the behavior of one partner that initiates the ritual

3. the series of responses by both partners that follows the initiating event

4. how the ritual ends

Based on your description, explain an alternative to the unsatisfying ritual, and describe how you might be able to manage the conflict in a more satisfying way.

VARIABLES IN CONFLICT STYLES

By now you can see that every relational system is unique. The communication patterns in one family, business, or classroom are likely to be very different from those in any other. But along with the differences that arise in individual relationships, two powerful variables affect the way people manage conflict: gender and culture. We will now look at each variable and see how it affects how conflict is managed.

Gender

Men and women often approach conflicts differently. Even in childhood, males are more likely to be aggressive, demanding, and competitive, whereas females are more likely to be cooperative. Studies of children from preschool to early adolescence have shown that boys try to get their way by ordering one another around: "Lie down." "Get off my steps." "Gimme your arm." By contrast, girls are more likely to make proposals for action, beginning with the verb *let's*: "Let's go find some." "Let's ask her, 'Do you have any bottles?'" "Let's move these out first."[38] Whereas boys tell each other what role to take in pretend play ("Come on, be a doctor"), girls more commonly ask each other what role they want ("Will you be the patient for a few minutes?") or make a joint proposal ("We can both be doctors"). Furthermore, boys often make demands without offering an explanation ("Look, man. I want the wire cutters right now"). By contrast, girls often give reasons for their suggestions ("We gotta clean 'em first ... 'cause they got germs").[39]

Adolescent girls use aggression in conflicts, but their methods are usually more indirect than those of boys. Whereas teenage boys often engage in verbal showdowns and may even engage in physical fights, teenage girls typically use gossip, backbiting, and social exclusion.[40] This is not to suggest that girls' aggression is any less destructive than boys'. The film *Mean Girls* (based on the book *Queen Bees and Wannabes*[41]) offers a vivid depiction of just how injurious these indirect assaults can be on the self-concepts and relationships of young women.

Gender differences in dealing with conflict often persist into adulthood. One survey of college students revealed that men and women viewed conflicts in contrasting ways.[42] Regardless of their cultural background, female students described men as being concerned with power and more interested in content than relational issues. Phrases used to describe male conflict styles included: "The most important thing to males in conflict is their egos." "Men don't worry about feelings." "Men are more direct." By contrast, women were described as being more concerned with maintaining the relationship during a

Bill Sykes Images/The Image Bank/Getty Images

conflict. Phrases used to describe female conflict styles included: "Women are better listeners." "Women try to solve problems without controlling the other person." "Females are more concerned with others' feelings."

These sorts of differences don't mean that men are incapable of forming good relationships. Instead, their notions of what makes a good relationship are different. For some men, friendship and aggression aren't mutually exclusive. In fact, many strong male relationships are built around competition (e.g., at work or in athletics). Women can be competitive, too, but they also are more likely to use logical reasoning and bargaining than aggression.[43] And when it comes to avoidance, women tend to view withdrawal from conflict as more injurious to a relationship than do men (which is why women are more likely to say, "We *have* to talk about this").[44]

A look at the entire body of research on gender and conflict suggests that the differences in how the two sexes handle conflict are relatively small and sometimes different from the stereotypical picture of aggressive men and passive women.[45] It would appear that people may *think* there are greater differences in male and female ways of handling conflicts than there actually are.[46] People who assume that men are aggressive and women are accommodating may notice behavior that fits these stereotypes ("See how much he bosses her around. A typical man!"). On the other hand, behavior that doesn't fit these stereotypes (accommodating men, pushy women) goes unnoticed.

While men and women do have characteristically different conflict styles, the reasons may have little to do with gender. The situation at hand has a greater influence on shaping the way a person handles conflict.[47] For example, both men and women are more likely to respond aggressively when attacked by the other person. (Recall the discussion of defensive spirals in Chapter 11.) In fact, researchers exploring how married couples handle disagreements found that the importance of gender in determining conflict style is "dwarfed" by the behavior of the other person.[48]

What, then, can we conclude about the influence of gender on conflict? Research has demonstrated that there are, indeed, some small but measurable differences in the two sexes. But, although men and women may have characteristically different conflict styles, the individual style of each communicator—regardless of gender—and the nature of the relationship are more important than gender in shaping the way he or she handles conflict.

Culture

The way in which people manage conflict varies tremendously depending on their cultural background. The straight-talking, assertive approach that characterizes many North Americans is not the universal norm.[49]

Perhaps the most important cultural factor in shaping attitudes toward conflict is an orientation toward individualism or collectivism.[50] In individualistic cultures like the United States, the goals, rights, and needs of each person are considered important, and most people would agree that it is an individual's right to stand up for him- or herself. By contrast, collectivist cultures (more common in Latin America and Asia) consider the concerns of the group to be more important than those of any individual. In these cultures, the kind of assertive behavior

ABC/Photofest

∧ Culture plays a role in conflict management on the TV show *Blackish*. Andre "Dre" (Anthony Anderson) and Rainbow "Bow" (Tracee Ellis Ross) Johnson are professionals living in an upper-middle-class environment that is different from their upbringings. They and their children struggle to accommodate their cultural heritage with their unique aspirations and personalities. How do culture and social class affect your personal and professional relationships? Are these factors sometimes a source of conflict—and if so, how do you manage them?

that might seem perfectly appropriate to a North American would be regarded as rude and insensitive.

Another factor that affects conflict is the difference between high- and low-context cultural styles.[51] Recall from our discussion in Chapter 6 that low-context cultures like the United States place a premium on being direct and literal. By contrast, high-context cultures like Japan value self-restraint and avoiding confrontation. For this reason, what seems like "beating around the bush" to an American would seem polite to an Asian. In Japan, for example, even a simple request like "Close the door" would be too straightforward.[52] A more indirect statement such as "It is somewhat cold today" would be more appropriate. Perhaps more important, Japanese are reluctant to say "No" to a request. A more likely answer would be "Let me think about it for a while," which anyone familiar with Japanese culture would recognize as a refusal.

When indirect communication is a cultural norm, it is unreasonable to expect more straightforward approaches to succeed. When people from different cultures face a conflict, their habitual communication patterns may not mesh smoothly. The challenge faced by an American husband and his Taiwanese wife illustrates this sort of problem. The husband would try to confront his wife verbally and directly (as is typical in the United States), leading her to either become defensive or withdraw completely from the discussion. She, on the other hand, would attempt to indicate her displeasure by changes in mood and eye contact (typical of Chinese culture) that were either not noticed or were uninterpretable by her husband. Thus, neither "his way" nor "her way" was working, and they could not see any realistic way to "compromise."[53]

It isn't necessary to look only at Asia to encounter cultural differences in conflict. Americans visiting Greece, for example, often think they are witnessing an argument when they are overhearing a friendly conversation.[54] A comparative study of American and Italian nursery-school children showed that one of the Italian childrens' favorite pastimes was a kind of heated debating that Italians call *discussione* but that Americans would call *arguing*. Likewise, research has shown that the conversations of working-class Jewish people of eastern European origin used arguments as a means of being sociable.

Even within the United States, the ethnic background of communicators plays a role in their ideas about conflict. When members of a group of Mexican American and Anglo American college students were asked about their views regarding conflict, some important differences emerged.[55] For example, Anglo Americans seemed more willing to accept conflict as a natural part of relationships, whereas Mexican Americans were more concerned about the short- and long-term dangers of conflict. It's not surprising that people from collectivist, high-context cultures emphasizing harmony tend to handle conflicts in less-direct ways. With differences like these, it's easy to imagine how two friends, lovers, or fellow workers from different cultural backgrounds might have trouble finding a conflict style that is comfortable for them both.

Despite these differences, it's important to realize that culture isn't the only factor that influences the way people approach conflict or how they

Looking at DIVERSITY

Mandel Ngan/Getty Images

James Comey: Searching for Accord in Troubled Times

Even as some African Americans achieved the highest positions of respect and accomplishment, others died at the hands of white police officers in a series of high profile cases that outraged many citizens. At this difficult time, FBI director James Comey delivered a speech that is excerpted here. His remarks emphasize the importance of reaching across the divide of race and personal experience to regard one another as individuals. Note how he asks parties to move past win–lose conflict approaches and seek more collaborative solutions.

We are at a crossroads. As a society, we can choose to live our everyday lives, raising our families and going to work, hoping that someone, somewhere, will do something to ease the tension—to smooth over the conflict. We can roll up our car windows, turn up the radio, and drive around these problems, or we can choose to have an open and honest discussion about what our relationship is today—what it should be, what it could be, and what it needs to be—if we took more time to better understand one another.

Let me start by sharing some of my own hard truths:

First, all of us in law enforcement must be honest enough to acknowledge that much of our history is not pretty. At many points in American history, law enforcement enforced the status quo, a status quo that was often brutally unfair to disfavored groups. I am descended from Irish immigrants. A century ago, the Irish knew well how American society—and law enforcement—viewed them: as drunks, ruffians, and criminals. The Irish had tough times, but little compares to the experience on our soil of black Americans. That experience should be part of every American's consciousness, and law enforcement's role in that experience—including in recent times—must be remembered. It is our cultural inheritance.

A second hard truth: Much research points to the widespread existence of unconscious bias. Many people in our white-majority culture have unconscious racial biases and react differently to a white face than a black face. In fact, we all, white and black, carry various biases around with us. I am reminded of the song from the Broadway hit, *Avenue Q:* "Everyone's a Little Bit Racist." But if we can't help our latent biases, we can help our behavior in response to those instinctive reactions. Although the research may be unsettling, it is what we do next that matters most.

I believe law enforcement overwhelmingly attracts people who want to do good for a living—people who risk their lives because they want to help other people. They don't sign up to be cops in New York or Chicago or L.A. to help white people or black people or Hispanic people or Asian people. They sign up because they want to help all people. And they do some of the hardest, most dangerous policing to protect people of color.

But that leads me to my third hard truth: something happens to people in law enforcement. Many of us develop different flavors of cynicism that we work hard to resist because they can be lazy mental shortcuts. For example, criminal suspects routinely lie about their guilt, and nearly everybody we charge is guilty. That makes it easy for some folks in law enforcement to assume that everybody is lying and that no suspect, regardless of their race, could be innocent. Easy, but wrong.

Let me be transparent about my affection for cops. When you dial 911, whether you are white or black, the cops come, and they come quickly, and they come quickly whether they are white or black. That's what cops do.

Those of us in law enforcement must redouble our efforts to resist bias and prejudice. We must better understand the people we serve and protect—by trying to know, deep in our gut, what it feels like to be a law-abiding young black man walking on the street and encountering law enforcement. We must understand how that young man may see us. We must resist the lazy shortcuts of cynicism and approach him with respect and decency.

But the "seeing" needs to flow in both directions. Citizens also need to really see the men and women of law enforcement. They need to see the risks and dangers law enforcement officers encounter on a typical late-night shift. They need to understand the difficult and frightening work they do to keep us safe. They need to give them the space and respect to do their work, well and properly. If they take the time to do that, what they will see are officers who are human, who are overwhelmingly doing the right thing for the right reasons, and who are too often operating in communities—and facing challenges—most of us choose to drive around.

In the words of Dr. King, "We must learn to live together as brothers or we will all perish together as fools." Relationships are hard. Relationships require work. So let's begin that work.

behave when they disagree. Some research suggests that our approach to conflict may be part of our biological makeup.[56] Furthermore, scholarship suggests that a person's self-concept is more powerful than his or her culture in determining conflict style.[57] For example, an assertive person raised in an environment that downplays conflict is still likely to be more aggressive than an unassertive person who grew up in a culture where conflicts are common. You might handle conflicts calmly in a job where rationality and civility are the norm but shriek like a banshee at home if that's the way you and a relational partner handle conflicts. Finally, the way each of us deals with conflict is a matter of personal choice. We can choose to follow unproductive patterns or we can choose more constructive approaches.

CONSTRUCTIVE CONFLICT SKILLS

The collaborative, win–win conflict style described earlier in this chapter has many advantages over win–lose and lose–lose approaches. Why, then, is it so rarely used? There are three reasons. The first is lack of awareness. Some people are so used to competition that they mistakenly think that winning requires them to defeat their "opponent."

Even when they know better, there is another factor that prevents many people from seeking win–win solutions. Conflicts are often emotional affairs in which people react combatively without stopping to think of better alternatives. Because this kind of emotional reflex prevents constructive solutions, it's often necessary to stop yourself from speaking out aggressively during a conflict and starting an escalating spiral of defensiveness. The time-honored advice of "stopping and counting to ten" applies here. After you've thought about the matter a bit, you'll be able to *act* constructively instead of *reacting* in a way that's likely to produce a lose–lose outcome.

A third reason win–win solutions are rare is that they require the other person's cooperation. It's difficult to negotiate constructively with someone who insists on trying to defeat you. In this case, use your best persuasive skills to explain that by working together you can find a solution that satisfies both of you.

Collaborative Problem Solving

Despite these challenges, it is definitely possible to become better at resolving conflicts. We will outline a method to increase your chances of being able to handle your conflicts in a collaborative, win–win manner. In a longitudinal study following one hundred couples who had conflict skills training, researchers found that the method works for couples willing to focus on improving their relationships.[58] As you read the following steps, try to imagine yourself applying them to a problem that's bothering you now.

Identify Your Problem and Unmet Needs   Before you speak out, it's important to realize that the problem that is causing conflict is yours. Whether you want to return an unsatisfactory piece of merchandise, complain to noisy neighbors because your sleep is being disturbed by their barking dog, or request a change in working conditions from your employer, the problem is yours. Why? Because in each case you are the person who "owns" the problem— the one who is dissatisfied. You are the one who has paid for the unsatisfactory merchandise; the merchant who sold it to you has the use of your good money. You are the one who is losing sleep as a result of your neighbors' dog; they are content to go on as before. You are the one who is unhappy with your working conditions, not your employer.

Realizing that the problem is yours will make a big difference when the time comes to approach the other party. Instead of feeling and acting in an evaluative way, you'll be more likely to state your problem in a descriptive way, which will not only be more accurate but also reduce the chance of a defensive reaction.

After you realize that the problem is yours, the next step is to identify the unmet needs that make you dissatisfied. For instance, in the barking dog example, your need may be to get some sleep or to study without interruptions. In the case of a friend who teases you in public, your need would probably be to avoid embarrassment.

Sometimes the task of identifying your needs isn't as simple as it first seems. Behind the apparent content of an issue is often a relational need. Consider this example: A friend hasn't returned some money you lent long ago. Your apparent need in this situation might be to get the money back. But a little thought will probably show that this isn't the only, or even the main, thing you want. Even if you were rolling in money, you'd probably want the loan repaid because of a more important need: *to avoid feeling victimized by your friend's taking advantage of you.*

As you'll soon see, the ability to identify your real needs plays a key role in solving interpersonal problems. For now, the point to remember is that before you voice your problem to your partner, you ought to be clear about which of your needs aren't being met.

Make a Date   Destructive fights often start because the initiator confronts a partner who isn't ready. There are many times when a person isn't in the right frame of mind to face a conflict, perhaps owing to fatigue, being in too much of a hurry to take the necessary time, being upset over another problem, or not feeling well. At times like these, it's unfair to "jump" a person without notice and expect to get full attention for your problem. If you do persist, you'll probably have an ugly fight on your hands.

SIPRESS

"Is this a good time to have a big fight?"

After you have a clear idea of the problem, approach your partner with a request to try to solve it. For example, "Something's been bothering me. Can we talk about it?" If the answer is "Yes," then you're ready to go further. If it isn't the right time to confront your partner, then find a time that's agreeable to both of you.

Describe Your Problem and Needs   Your partner can't possibly meet your needs without knowing why you're upset and what you want. Therefore, it's up to you to describe your problem as specifically as possible. The best way to deliver a complete, accurate message is to use the assertive message format discussed in Chapter 11. Notice how well this approach works in the following examples:

Example 1

"I have a problem. It's about your leaving dirty clothes around the house after I've told you how much it bothers me *(behavior)*. It's a problem because I have to run around like crazy and pick things up whenever guests come, which is no fun at all *(consequence)*. I'm starting to think that either you're not paying attention to my requests or you're trying to drive me crazy *(thoughts)*, and either way, I'm getting more and more resentful *(feeling)*. I'd like to find some way to have a neat place without my having to be a maid or a nag."

Example 2

"I have a problem. When you drop by without calling ahead, and I'm studying *(behavior)*, I don't know whether to visit or ask you to leave *(thought)*. Either way, I get uncomfortable *(feeling)*, and it seems like whatever I do, I lose: Either I have to put you off or get behind in my work *(consequences)*. I'd like to find a way to get my studying done and still socialize with you *(intention)*."

Example 3

"Something is bothering me. When you tell me you love me and yet spend almost all your free time with your other friends *(behavior)*, I wonder whether you mean it *(thought)*. I get insecure *(feeling)*, and then I start acting moody *(consequence)*. I need some way of finding out for sure how you feel about me *(intention)*."

After stating your problem and describing what you need, it's important to make sure that your partner has understood what you've said. As you can remember from the discussion of listening in Chapter 8, there's a good chance—especially in a stressful conflict—that your words will be misinterpreted.

It's usually unrealistic to insist that your partner paraphrase your statement, and fortunately there are more tactful and subtle ways to make sure that you've been understood. For instance, you might try saying, "I'm not sure I expressed myself very well just now—maybe you should tell me what you heard me say so I can be sure I got it right." In any case, be absolutely sure that your partner understands your whole message before going any further. Legitimate agreements are tough enough without getting upset about a conflict that doesn't even exist.

Consider Your Partner's Point of View   After you have made your position clear, it's time to find out what your partner needs to feel satisfied about this issue. There are two reasons why it's important to discover your partner's needs. First, it's fair: Your partner has just as much right as you to feel satisfied, and if you expect help in meeting your needs, then it's reasonable that you behave in the same way. But in addition to fairness, there's another practical reason for concerning yourself with what your partner wants. Just as an unhappy partner will make it hard for you to become satisfied, a happy partner will be more likely to cooperate in letting you reach your goals. Thus, it's in your own self-interest to discover and meet your partner's needs.

You can learn about your partner's needs simply by asking about them: "Now I've told you what I want and why. Tell me what you need to feel okay about this." After your partner begins to talk, your job is to use the listening skills discussed earlier in this book to make sure that you understand.

Negotiate a Solution   Now that you and your partner understand each other's needs, the goal becomes finding a way to meet them. This is done by developing as many potential solutions as possible and then evaluating them to decide which one best meets everyone's needs. Probably the best description of the win–win approach was written by Thomas Gordon in his book *Parent Effectiveness Training*.[59] The following steps are a modification of this approach.

1. Identify and define the conflict. We've previously discussed identifying and defining the conflict. These consist of discovering each person's problem and needs and then setting the stage for meeting all of them.
2. Generate a number of possible solutions. In this step, the partners work together to think of as many means as possible to reach their stated ends. The key concept here is quantity: It's important to generate as many ideas as you can think of without worrying about which ones are good or bad. Write down every thought that comes up, no matter how unworkable. Sometimes a far-fetched idea will lead to a more workable one.

3. Evaluate the alternative solutions. This is the time to talk about which solutions will work and which ones won't. It's important for all parties to be honest about their willingness to accept an idea. If a solution is going to work, everyone involved has to support it.

4. Decide on the best solution. Now that you've looked at all the alternatives, pick the one that looks best to everyone. It's important to be sure that everybody understands the solution and is willing to try it out. Remember that your decision doesn't have to be final, but it should look potentially successful.

Follow Up the Solution You can't be sure that the solution will work until you try it. After you've tested it for a while, it's a good idea to set aside some time to talk over its progress. You may find that you need to make some changes or even rethink the whole problem. The idea is to keep on top of the problem, and to keep using creativity to solve it.

You can expect and prepare for a certain amount of resistance from the other person. When a step doesn't meet with success, simply move back and repeat the preceding ones as necessary.

Win–win solutions aren't always possible. There will be times when even the best-intentioned people simply won't be able to find a way of meeting all their needs. In times like these, the process of negotiation has to include some compromises, but even then the preceding steps haven't been wasted. The genuine desire to learn what the other person wants and to try to satisfy those wants will build a climate of goodwill that can help you find the best solution to the present problem and also improve your relationship in the future.

Constructive Conflict: Questions and Answers

After learning about win–win negotiating, people often express doubts about how well it can work. "It sounds like a good idea," they say, "but…." Four questions arise more than any others, and they deserve answers.

Isn't the Win–Win Approach Too Good to Be True? Research shows that seeking mutual benefit is not just a good idea—it actually works. In fact, the win–win approach produces better results than a win–lose approach. In a series of experiments, researchers presented subjects with a bargaining situation called "the prisoner's dilemma," in which they could choose either to cooperate or betray a confederate.[60] There are three types of outcomes in the prisoner's dilemma: One partner can win big by betraying a confederate, both can win by cooperating, or both can lose by betraying each other. Although cynics might assume that the most effective strategy is to betray a partner (a win–lose approach), researchers found that cooperation is actually the best hard-nosed strategy. Players who demonstrated their willingness to support the other person and not hold grudges did better than those using a more competitive approach.

Isn't the Win–Win Approach Too Elaborate?   The win–win approach is detailed and highly structured. In everyday life, you may rarely use every step. Sometimes the problem at hand won't justify the effort, and at other times you and your partner might not need to be so deliberate to take care of the problem. Nonetheless, while learning to use the approach, try to follow all of the steps carefully. After you have become familiar with and skillful at using them all, you will be able to use whichever ones prove necessary in a given situation. For important issues, you are likely to find that every step of the win–win approach is important. If this process seems time consuming, just consider the time and energy that will likely be required if you don't resolve the issue at hand.

Isn't Win–Win Negotiating Too Rational?   Frustrated readers often complain that the win–win approach is so sensible that only a saint could use it successfully. "Sometimes I'm so angry that I don't care about being supportive or empathetic or anything else," they say. "I just want to blow my top!"

At times like this, you might need to temporarily remove yourself from the situation so you don't say or do something you'll later regret. You might feel better confiding in a third party. Or you might blow off steam with physical exercise. There are even cases when an understanding partner might allow you to have what has been called a "Vesuvius"—an uncontrolled, spontaneous explosion. Before you blow your top, though, be sure that your partner understands what you're doing and realizes that whatever you say doesn't call for a response. Your partner should let you rant and rave for as long as you want without getting defensive or "tying in." Then when your eruption subsides, you can take steps to work through whatever still troubles you.

Is It Possible to Change Others?   Readers often agree that win–win problem solving would be terrific—if everyone had read *Looking Out Looking In* and understood the method. "How can I get the other person to cooperate?" the question goes. Though you won't always be able to gain your partner's cooperation, a good job of selling can do the trick most of the time. The key lies in showing that it's in your partner's self-interest to work together with you: "Look, if we can't settle this, we'll both feel miserable. But if we can find an answer, think how much better off we'll be." Notice that this sort of explanation projects both the favorable consequences of cooperating and the unfavorable consequences of competing.

You can also boost the odds of getting your partner's cooperation by modeling the communication skills described in this book. You've read that defense-arousing behavior is reciprocal, but so is supportive communication. If you can listen sincerely, avoid evaluative attacks, and empathize with your partner's concerns, for example, there's a good chance that you'll get the same kind of behavior in return. And even if your cooperative attitude doesn't succeed, you'll gain self-respect from knowing that at least you behaved honorably and constructively.

In REAL LIFE

Win–Win Problem Solving

It is 7:15 A.M. on a typical school day. Chris enters the kitchen and finds the sink full of dirty dishes. It was her roommate Terry's turn to do them. She sighs in disgust and begins to clean up, slamming pots and pans.

© Jason Harris/Cengage Learning

Terry: Can't you be a little more quiet? I don't have a class till 10:00, and I want to catch up on sleep.

Chris: *(Expressing her aggression indirectly in a sarcastic tone of voice)* Sorry to bother you. I was cleaning up last night's dinner dishes.

Terry: *(Misses the message)* Well, I wish you'd do it a little more quietly. I was up late studying last night, and I'm beat.

Chris: *(Decides to communicate her irritation more directly, if aggressively)* Well, if you'd done the dishes last night, I wouldn't have had to wash them now.

Terry: *(Finally realizes that Chris is mad at her, responds defensively)* I was going to do them when I got up. I've got two midterms this week, and I was studying until midnight last night. What's more important—grades or a spotless kitchen?

Chris: *(Perpetuating the growing defensive spiral)* I've got classes, too, you know. But that doesn't mean we have to live like pigs!

Terry: *(Angrily)* Forget it. If it's such a big deal, I'll never leave another dirty dish!

Chris and Terry avoid each other as they get ready for school. During the day, Chris realizes that attacking Terry will only make matters worse. She decides on a more constructive approach that evening.

Chris: That wasn't much fun this morning. Want to talk about it?

Terry: I suppose so. But I'm going out to study with Kim and Alisa in a few minutes.

Chris: *(Realizing that it's important to talk at a good time)* If you have to leave soon, let's not get into it now. How about talking when you get back?

Terry: Okay, if I'm not too tired.

Chris: Or we could talk tomorrow before class.

Terry: Okay.

Later that evening Terry and Chris continue their conversation.

Chris: *(Defines the issue as her problem by using the assertive message format)* I hated to start the day with a fight. But I also hate having to do the dishes when it's not my turn *(behavior)*. It doesn't seem fair for me to do my job and yours *(interpretation)*, and that's why I got so mad *(feeling)* and nagged at you *(consequence)*.

Terry: But I was studying! You know how much I have to do. It's not like I was partying.

Chris: *(Avoids attacking Terry by sincerely agreeing with the facts and explaining further why she was upset)* I know. It wasn't just doing the dishes that got me upset. It seems like there have been a lot of times when I've done your jobs and mine, too.

Terry: *(Defensively)* Like when?

Chris: *(Gives specific descriptions of Terry's behavior)* Well, this was the third time this week that I've done the dishes when it's your turn, and I can think of a couple of times lately when I've had to clean up your stuff before people came over.

Terry: I don't see why it's such a big deal. If you just leave the stuff there, I'll clean it up.

Chris: *(Still trying to explain herself, she continues to use "I" language)* I know you would. I guess it's harder for me to put up with a messy place than it is for you.

Terry: Yeah. If you'd just relax, living together would be a lot easier!

Chris: *(Resenting Terry's judgmental accusation that the problem is all hers)* Hey, wait a second! Don't blame the whole thing on me. It's just that we have different standards. It looks to you like I'm too hung up on keeping the place clean …

Terry: Right.

Chris: ... and if we do it your way, then I'd be giving up. I'd have to either live with the place messier than I like it or clean everything up myself. Then I'd get mad at you, and things would be pretty tense around here. *(Describes the unpleasant consequences of not solving the problem in a mutually satisfactory way)*

Terry: I suppose so.

Chris: We need to figure out how to take care of the apartment in a way that we can both live with. *(Describes the broad outline of a win–win solution)*

Terry: Yeah.

Chris: So what could we do?

Terry: *(Sounding resigned)* Look, from now on I'll just do the dishes right away. It isn't worth arguing about.

Chris: Sure it is. If you're sore, the apartment may be clean, but it won't be worth it.

Terry: *(Skeptically)* Okay, what do you suggest?

Chris: Well, I'm not sure. You don't want the pressure of having to clean up right away, and I don't want to have to do my jobs and yours, too. Right?

Terry: Yeah. *(Still sounding skeptical)* So what are we going to do—hire a housekeeper to clean up?

Chris: *(Refusing to let Terry sidetrack the discussion)* That would be great if we could afford it. How about using paper plates? That would make cleaning up from meals easier.

Terry: Yeah, but there would still be pots and pans.

Chris: Well, it's not a perfect fix, but it might help a little. *(Goes on to suggest other ideas)* How about cooking meals that don't take a lot of work to clean up—maybe more salads and less fried stuff that sticks to pans? That would be a better diet, too.

Terry: Yeah. I do hate to scrub crusty frying pans. But that doesn't do anything about your wanting the living room picked up all the time, and I bet I still wouldn't keep the kitchen as clean as you like it. Keeping the place super clean just isn't as big a deal to me as it is for you.

Chris: That's true, and I don't want to have to nag you! *(Clarifies the end she's seeking)* You know, it's not

really cleaning up that bothers me. It's doing more than my share of work. I wonder if there's a way I could be responsible for keeping the kitchen clean and picking up if you could do something else to keep the workload even.

Terry: Are you serious? I'd love to get out of doing the dishes! You mean you'd do them ... and keep the place picked up ... if I did something else?

Chris: As long as the work was equal and you really did your jobs without me having to remind you.

Terry: What kind of work would you want me to do?

Chris: How about cleaning up the bathroom?

Terry: Forget it. That's worse than doing the dishes.

Chris: Okay. How about cooking?

Terry: That might work, but then we'd have to eat together all the time. It's nice to do our own cooking when we want to. It's more flexible that way.

Chris: Okay. But what about shopping? I hate the time it takes, and you don't mind it that much, do you?

Terry: You mean shop for groceries? You'd trade that for cleaning the kitchen?

Chris: Sure. And picking up the living room. It takes an hour each time we shop, and we make two trips every week. Doing the dishes would be much quicker.

Terry: All right!

The plan didn't work perfectly. At first Terry put off shopping until all the food was gone, and Chris took advantage by asking Terry to run other errands during her shopping trips. But their new arrangement proved much more successful than the old arrangement. The apartment was cleaner and the workload more even, which satisfied Chris. Terry was less frequently the object of Chris's nagging, and she had no kitchen chores, which made her happier. Just as important, the relationship between Chris and Terry was more comfortable—thanks to win–win problem solving.

MindTap® **APPLY ...** this situation to your life by answering questions online.

SUMMARY

Conflict is a fact of life in every interpersonal relationship. The way in which conflicts are handled plays a major role in the quality of a relationship. When managed constructively, conflicts can lead to stronger and more satisfying interaction; but when they are handled poorly, relationships will suffer.

Communicators can respond to conflicts in a variety of ways: avoiding, accommodating, competing, compromising, or collaborating. Each approach can be justified in certain circumstances. The way a conflict is handled is not always the choice of a single person: The parties influence each other as they develop a relational conflict style. This style may be complementary, symmetrical, or parallel, and it can involve constructive or destructive rituals. The "four horsemen" of criticism, defensiveness, contempt, and stonewalling are counterproductive ways to communicate during conflict.

Besides being shaped by the relationship, a conflict style is also shaped by a person's gender and cultural background. In most circumstances a collaborative, win–win outcome is the ideal, and it can be achieved by following the constructive conflict skills discussed.

KEY TERMS

accommodating

avoiding

collaborating

competing

complementary conflict style

compromising

conflict

conflict ritual

crazymaking

direct aggression

parallel conflict style

passive aggression

relational conflict style

symmetrical conflict style

GLOSSARY

abstract language Language that is vague and general rather than concrete and specific. *See also* behavioral language.

abstraction ladder A range of more to less abstract terms describing an event or object.

accenting Nonverbal behaviors that emphasize part of a verbal message.

accommodating A lose–win conflict style in which the communicator submits to a situation rather than attempts to have his or her needs met.

adaptors Unconscious bodily movements in response to the environment.

advising A listening response in which the receiver offers suggestions about how the speaker should deal with a problem.

affinity The degree to which persons like or appreciate one another.

aggressiveness Verbal attacks that demean another's self-concept and inflict psychological pain.

ambiguous response A disconfirming response with more than one meaning, leaving the other party unsure of the responder's position.

ambushing A style in which the receiver listens carefully in order to gather information to use in an attack on the speaker.

analyzing A listening response in which the receiver offers an interpretation of a speaker's message.

androgynous Possessing both masculine and feminine traits.

argumentativeness Presenting and defending positions on issues while attacking positions taken by others.

assertive message format A direct expression of the sender's needs and thoughts delivered in a way that does not attack the receiver's dignity. A complete assertive message describes behavior, interpretation, feeling, consequence, and intention.

asynchronous communication Communication that occurs when there is a time gap between when the message is sent and when it is received. *See also* synchronous communication.

attending The process of filtering out some messages and focusing on others.

attribution The process of attaching meaning to behavior. *See also* interpretation statement.

avoiding (conflict style) A lose–lose conflict style in which the parties ignore the problem at hand.

avoiding (relational stage) A stage of relational deterioration immediately before terminating in which the parties minimize contact with one another.

behavioral description An account that refers only to observable phenomena.

behavioral language Language that describes observable behavior. *See also* abstract language.

benevolent lie A lie defined by the teller as not malicious, or even helpful, to the person to whom it is told.

body orientation A type of nonverbal communication characterized by the degree to which we face forward or away from someone.

bonding A stage of relational development in which the parties make symbolic public gestures to show that their relationship exists.

breadth A dimension of self-disclosure involving the range of subjects being discussed.

"but" statement A statement in which the word *but* cancels out the expression preceding it.

certainty An attitude behind messages that dogmatically implies that the speaker's position is correct and that the other person's ideas are not worth considering. Likely to generate a defensive response.

channel The medium through which a message passes from sender to receiver.

chronemics The study of how humans use and structure time.

circumscribing A stage of relational deterioration in which partners begin to reduce the scope of their contact and commitment to one another.

clichés Ritualized, stock statements delivered in response to a social situation.

co-culture A culture that exists within the larger culture of a country or society, such as subgroups defined by age, race or ethnicity, occupation, sexual orientation, physical disability, religion, avocation, and so on.

cognitive complexity The ability to construct a variety of frameworks for viewing an issue.

cognitive conservatism The tendency to seek and attend to information that conforms to an existing self-concept.

collaborating A conflict management style that seeks win–win solutions.

communication climate The emotional tone of a relationship between two or more individuals.

communication competence The ability to accomplish one's personal goals in a manner that maintains a relationship on terms that are acceptable to all parties.

competing A win–lose approach to conflicts that seeks to resolve them in one's own way.

complaining A disagreeing message that directly or indirectly communicates dissatisfaction with another person.

complementary conflict style A relational conflict style in which partners use different but mutually reinforcing behaviors.

complementing Nonverbal behavior that reinforces a verbal message.

compromising An approach to conflict resolution in which both parties attain at least part of what they wanted through self-sacrifice.

confirming communication A message that expresses caring or respect for another person.

conflict An expressed struggle between at least two interdependent parties who perceive incompatible goals, scarce resources, and interference from the other party in achieving their goals.

conflict ritual An unacknowledged repeating pattern of interlocking behavior used by participants in a conflict.

conformity orientation The degree to which a family enforces a uniformity of attitudes, values, and beliefs.

connection-autonomy dialectic The tension between the need for integration and the need for independence in a relationship.

consequence statement An explanation of the results that follow from either the behavior of the person to whom the message is addressed or the speaker's interpretation of the addressee's behavior. Consequence statements can describe what happens to the speaker, the addressee, or others.

content dimension The part of a message that communicates information about the subject being discussed. *See also* relational dimension.

contradicting Nonverbal behavior that is inconsistent with a verbal message.

control The social need to influence others.

controlling communication Messages in which the sender tries to impose some sort of outcome on the receiver, usually resulting in a defensive reaction.

convergence The process of adapting one's speech style to match that of others with whom the communicator wants to identify. *See also* divergence.

conversation orientation The degree of openness a family has in discussing a range of topics.

counterfeit questions Questions that disguise the speaker's true motives, which do not include a genuine desire to understand the other person. *See also* sincere questions.

crazymaking An indirect expression of aggression delivered in a way that allows the sender to maintain a façade of kindness. *Also called* passive aggression.

cyberbullying The aggressive harassment of others online.

cyberstalking Obsessive surveillance and pursuit of others online.

debilitative emotions Emotions that prevent a person from functioning effectively.

decode The process in which a receiver attaches meaning to a message.

de-escalatory conflict spiral A communication pattern in which the parties slowly lessen their dependence on one another, withdraw, and become less invested in the relationship. *See also* spiral.

defensive listening A response style in which the receiver perceives a speaker's comments as an attack.

defensiveness The attempt to protect a presenting image that a person believes is being attacked.

depth A dimension of self-disclosure involving a shift from relatively nonrevealing messages to more personal ones.

description Gibb's term for language that describes a complaint in behavioral terms rather than being judgmental, thereby creating a supportive communication climate. *See also* evaluation, "I" language.

dialectical tensions Inherent conflicts that arise when two opposing or incompatible forces exist simultaneously.

differentiating A relational stage in which the parties reestablish their individual identities after having bonded together.

direct aggression A criticism or demand that threatens the face of the person at whom it is directed.

disagreeing messages Messages that communicate to the other person, "You are wrong." Includes aggressiveness, complaining, and argumentativeness.

disconfirming communication A message that expresses a lack of caring or respect for another person.

disinhibition The tendency to transmit messages without considering their consequences; occurs more frequently in mediated communication.

divergence Language mannerisms that emphasize a communicator's differences from others. *See also* convergence.

dyad Two individuals communicating. The interaction may or may not be interpersonal in nature.

emblems Deliberate nonverbal behaviors with precise meanings that are known to virtually all members of a cultural group.

emotion labor Managing and even suppressing emotions when doing so is both appropriate and necessary.

emotional contagion The process by which emotions are transferred from one person to another.

emotional intelligence The ability to understand and manage one's own emotions and be sensitive to others' feelings.

emotive language Language that conveys the sender's attitude rather than simply offers an objective description.

empathy The ability to project oneself into another person's point of view so as to experience the other's thoughts and feelings. *See also* sympathy.

encode The process of putting thoughts into symbols, most commonly words.

environment The field of experiences that leads a person to make sense of another's behavior. Environments consist of physical characteristics, personal experiences, relational history, and cultural background.

equality A type of supportive communication described by Gibb that suggests that the sender regards the receiver as worthy of respect.

equivocal language Ambiguous language that has two or more equally plausible meanings.

escalatory conflict spiral A communication pattern in which one attack leads to another until the initial skirmish escalates into a full-fledged battle. *See also* spiral.

ethnocentrism The attitude that one's own culture is superior to others.

evaluation Gibb's term for judgmental assessments of another person's behavior, thereby increasing the odds of creating a defensive communication climate. *See also* description, "I" language.

experimenting An early stage in relational development consisting of a search for common ground. If the experimentation is successful, then the relationship will progress to intensifying. If not, it may go no further.

face The socially approved identity that a communicator tries to present. *See also* identity management.

face-threatening act Behavior by another that is perceived as attacking an individual's presenting image, or face.

facilitative emotions Emotions that contribute to effective functioning.

fallacy of approval The irrational belief that it is vital to win the approval of virtually every person a communicator deals with.

fallacy of catastrophic expectations The irrational belief that the worst possible outcome will probably occur.

fallacy of causation The irrational belief that emotions are caused by others and not by the person who has them.

fallacy of helplessness The irrational belief that satisfaction in life is determined by forces beyond one's control.

fallacy of overgeneralization Irrational beliefs in which (1) conclusions (usually negative) are based on limited evidence, or (2) communicators exaggerate their shortcomings.

fallacy of perfection The irrational belief that a worthwhile communicator should be able to handle every situation with complete confidence and skill.

fallacy of shoulds The irrational belief that people should behave in the most desirable way.

family communication pattern A mode of family interaction that involves a blending of conversation and conformity orientations. These include consensual, pluralistic, protective, and laissez-faire patterns.

family system A group of interdependent individuals who interact and adapt together as a whole.

feeling statement An expression of the sender's emotions that results from interpretation of sense data.

friends with benefits (FWB) A popular term for nonromantic heterosexual friendships that include sexual activity.

gender role Socially approved ways that men and women are expected to behave.

gestures Motions of the body, usually hands or arms, that have communicative value.

Gibb categories Six sets of contrasting styles of verbal and nonverbal behavior. Each set describes a communication style that is likely to arouse defensiveness and a contrasting style that is likely to prevent or reduce it. Developed by Jack Gibb.

halo effect The power of a first impression to influence subsequent perceptions.

haptics The study of touching.

hearing The physiological dimension of listening.

high-context cultures Cultures that avoid direct use of language, relying instead on the context of a message to convey meaning.

hyperpersonal communication An accelerated discussion of personal topics and relational development beyond what normally happens in face-to-face interactions.

"I" language A statement that clearly identifies the speaker as the source of a message. *See also* "you" language, description.

illustrators Nonverbal behaviors that accompany and support verbal messages.

immediacy The degree of interest and attention that we feel toward and communicate to others.

impersonal communication Behavior that treats others as objects rather than individuals. *See also* interpersonal communication.

impersonal response A disconfirming response that is superficial or trite.

impervious response A disconfirming response that ignores another person's attempt to communicate.

impression management The communication strategies people use to influence how others view them. *See also* face.

incongruous response A disconfirming response in which two messages, one of which is usually nonverbal, contradict each other.

initiating The first stage in relational development in which the parties express interest in one another.

insensitive listening Failure to recognize the thoughts or feelings that are not directly expressed by a speaker.

instrumental goals Goals aimed at getting others to behave in desired ways.

insulated listening A style in which the receiver ignores undesirable information.

integrating A stage of relational development in which the parties begin to take on a single identity.

intensifying A stage of relational development that precedes integrating in which the parties move toward integration by increasing the amount of contact and the breadth and depth of self-disclosure.

intention statement A description of where the speaker stands on an issue, what he or she wants, or how he or she plans to act in the future.

interpersonal communication A continuous, transactional process involving participants who occupy different but overlapping environments and create meaning and relationships through the exchange of messages, many of which are affected by external, physiological, and psychological noise.

interpretation The process of attaching meaning to sense data.

interpretation statement A statement that describes the speaker's interpretation of the meaning of another person's behavior. *See also* attribution.

interrupting response A disconfirming response in which one communicator interrupts another.

intimacy A state of closeness arising from physical, intellectual, or emotional contact or sometimes from shared activities.

intimate distance One of Hall's four distance zones, ranging from skin contact to 18 inches.

irrelevant response A disconfirming response in which one communicator's comments bear no relationship to the previous speaker's ideas.

"it" statements Statements that replace the personal pronoun "I" with the less immediate word "it," often reducing the speaker's acceptance of responsibility for the statement.

Johari Window A model that describes the relationship between self-disclosure and self-awareness.

judging A listening response in which the receiver evaluates the sender's message either favorably or unfavorably.

kinesics The study of body position and motion.

leakage Nonverbal behaviors that reveal information a communicator does not disclose verbally.

leanness Messages (usually electronic) that are stark from a lack of nonverbal information; opposite of richness.

linear communication model A characterization of communication as a one-way event in which a message flows from sender to receiver.

linguistic relativism The notion that the worldview of a culture is shaped and reflected by the language its members speak. *See also* Sapir-Whorf hypothesis.

listening Process that consists of hearing, attending, understanding, responding, and remembering others' messages.

listening fidelity The degree of congruence between what a listener understands and what the message sender was attempting to communicate.

love languages Modes of communicating affection in romantic relationships. These include words of affirmation, quality time, gifts, acts of service, and physical touch.

low-context cultures Cultures that use language primarily to express thoughts, feelings, and ideas as directly as possible.

manipulators A type of nonverbal adaptors involving self-touching behaviors.

mediated communication Communication between individuals that is conducted via electronic channels.

message Information sent from a sender to a receiver.

metacommunication Messages (usually relational) that refer to other messages; communication about communication.

microexpression A brief facial expression.

mindful listening Giving careful and thoughtful attention and responses to the messages we receive.

mindless listening Reacting to others' messages automatically and routinely without much mental investment.

mixed message Situation in which a person's words are incongruent with his or her nonverbal behavior.

monochronic Behavior emphasizing punctuality, schedules, and completing one task at a time.

narrative The stories used to describe one's personal world.

negotiation The sense making that occurs between and among people as they influence one another's perceptions

and try to achieve a shared perspective. Fourth stage in the perception process.

neutrality A defense-arousing behavior described by Gibb in which the sender expresses indifference toward a receiver.

noise External, physiological, and psychological distractions that interfere with the accurate transmission and reception of a message.

nonverbal communication Messages expressed by other than linguistic means.

online surveillance Monitoring the activities of unknowing targets through social media.

openness-privacy dialectic The tension between the need for disclosure and the need for secrecy in a relationship.

organization The second stage in the perception process in which selected information is arranged in some meaningful way.

paralanguage Nonlinguistic means of vocal expression: rate, pitch, tone, and so on.

parallel conflict style A relational conflict style in which the approach of the partners varies from one situation to another.

paraphrasing Restating a speaker's thoughts or feelings in the listener's own words.

passive aggression An indirect expression of aggression delivered in a way that allows the sender to maintain a façade of kindness. *Also called* crazymaking.

perceived self The person we believe ourselves to be in moments of candor. It may be identical to or different from the presenting and ideal self.

perception checking A three-part method for verifying the accuracy of interpretations, including a description of the sense data, two possible interpretations, and a request for confirmation of the interpretations.

personal distance One of Hall's four distance zones, ranging from 18 inches to 4 feet.

personality A relatively consistent set of traits exhibited by a person across a variety of situations.

pillow method A method for understanding an issue from several perspectives rather than with an egocentric "I'm right and you're wrong" attitude.

politeness Communicating in ways that save face for both senders and receivers.

polychronic An approach to the use of time that emphasizes flexibility and pursuing multiple tasks.

posture The way in which individuals carry themselves—erect, slumping, and so on.

powerless speech mannerisms Ways of speaking that may reduce perceptions of a communicator's power.

pragmatic rules Linguistic rules that help communicators understand how messages may be used and interpreted in a given context.

predictability-novelty dialectic The tension between the need for stability and the need for change in a relationship.

presenting self The image a person presents to others. It may be identical to or different from the perceived and ideal self.

privacy management The choices people make to reveal or conceal information about themselves.

problem orientation A supportive style of communication described by Gibb in which the communicators focus on working together to solve their problems instead of trying to impose their own solutions on one another.

prompting Using silences and brief statements of encouragement to draw out a speaker.

provisionalism A supportive style of communication described by Gibb in which the sender expresses a willingness to consider the other person's position.

proxemics The study of how people use interpersonal space and distance.

pseudolistening An imitation of true listening in which the receiver's mind is elsewhere.

public distance One of Hall's four distance zones, extending outward from 12 feet.

punctuation The process of determining the causal order of events.

questioning A listening response in which the receiver seeks additional information from the sender.

reappraisal Rethinking the meaning of emotionally charged events in ways that alter their emotional impact.

receiver One who notices and attends to a message.

reference groups Groups against which we compare ourselves, thereby influencing our self-concept and self-esteem.

reflected appraisal The theory that a person's self-concept mirrors the way the person believes others regard him or her.

regulating One function of nonverbal communication in which nonverbal cues control the flow of verbal communication among individuals.

relational commitment A promise—sometimes implied and sometimes explicit—to remain in a relationship and to make that relationship successful.

relational conflict style A pattern of managing disagreements that repeats itself over time in a relationship.

relational dimension The part of a message that expresses the social relationship between two or more individuals. *See also* content dimension.

relational maintenance Communication aimed at keeping relationships operating smoothly and satisfactorily.

relational transgression One partner's violation of the explicit or implicit terms of the relationship, letting the other one down in some important way.

relational turning point Transformative event that alters a relationship in a fundamental way.

relative words Words that gain their meaning by comparison.

remembering Ability to recall information.

repeating Nonverbal behaviors that duplicate the content of a verbal message.

respect The social need to be held in esteem by others.

responding Giving observable feedback to the speaker.

richness An abundance of nonverbal cues that add clarity to a verbal message; opposite of leanness.

role A set of expectations about how to communicate.

rumination Dwelling persistently on negative thoughts that, in turn, intensifies negative feelings.

Sapir-Whorf hypothesis Theory of linguistic relativity in which language shapes a culture's perceived reality. *See also* linguistic relativism.

selection The first stage in the perception process in which some data are chosen to attend to and others to ignore.

selective listening A listening style in which the receiver responds only to messages that interest him or her.

self-concept The relatively stable set of perceptions each individual holds of himself or herself.

self-disclosure The process of deliberately revealing information about oneself that is significant and that would not normally be known by others.

self-esteem The part of the self-concept that involves an individual's evaluations of his or her self-worth.

self-fulfilling prophecy An expectation of an event, followed by behaviors based on that expectation, that makes the outcome more likely to occur than would have been the case otherwise.

self-monitoring The process of attending to one's behavior and using these observations to shape the way one behaves.

self-serving bias The tendency to interpret and explain information in a way that casts the perceiver in the most favorable manner.

self-talk The nonvocal process of thinking; sometimes referred to as *intrapersonal communication.*

semantic rules Rules that govern the meaning of language as opposed to its structure. *See also* syntactic rules.

sender The creator of a message.

significant others People whose opinion is important enough to affect one's self-concept strongly.

sincere questions Attempts to elicit information that enable the asker to understand the other person. *See also* counterfeit questions.

social comparison Evaluation of oneself in terms of or by comparison to others.

social distance One of Hall's distance zones, ranging from 4 to 12 feet.

social media Forms of electronic communication through which users create online communities.

social penetration A model that describes relationships in terms of their breadth and depth.

social support Assistance for others provided through emotional, informational, or instrumental resources.

spiral A reciprocal communication pattern in which each person's message reinforces the other's. *See also* de-escalatory conflict spiral, escalatory conflict spiral.

spontaneity A supportive communication behavior described by Gibb in which the sender expresses a message without any attempt to manipulate the receiver.

stage-hogging A listening style in which the receiver is more concerned with making his or her own point than in understanding the speaker.

stagnating A stage of relational deterioration characterized by declining enthusiasm and by standardized forms of behavior.

static evaluation The tendency to view people or relationships as unchanging.

stereotyping Categorizing individuals according to a set of characteristics assumed to belong to all members of a group.

strategy A defense-arousing style of communication described by Gibb in which the sender tries to manipulate or deceive a receiver.

substituting Nonverbal behavior that takes the place of a verbal message.

superiority A defense-arousing style of communication described by Gibb in which the sender states or implies that the receiver is not worthy of respect.

supporting A listening response that demonstrates solidarity with a speaker's situation.

symmetrical conflict style A relational conflict style in which both partners use the same tactics.

sympathy Compassion for another's situation. *See also* empathy.

synchronous communication Communication that occurs in real time. *See also* asynchronous communication.

syntactic rules Rules that govern the ways symbols can be arranged, as opposed to the meanings of those symbols. *See also* semantic rules.

tangential response A disconfirming response that uses the speaker's remark as a starting point for a shift to a new topic.

terminating The concluding stage of relational deterioration, characterized by the acknowledgment of one or both parties that the relationship is over.

territory A stationary area claimed by an individual.

transactional communication model A characterization of communication as the simultaneous sending and receiving of messages in an ongoing, irreversible process.

understanding Occurs when sense is made of a message.

"we" language Statement that implies that the issue is the concern and responsibility of both the speaker and receiver of a message. *See also* "I" language, "you" language.

"you" language A statement that expresses or implies a judgment of the other person. *See also* "I" language.

NAME INDEX

SUBJECT INDEX

Note: page references followed by *f* indicate figures; those followed by *t* indicate tables.